Forty Camel Girl

Letters from Turkey

E. Grace Beyler

FORTY CAMEL GIRL
Letters from Turkey
E. Grace Beyler

Published by Özler Aykan Tanıtım ve İletişim Hizmetleri
Valikonagi Caddesi Sakayik Sokak Ihlamur Palas Apt. 40/3
34365, Tesvikiye, Istanbul, Turkey.
www.ozleraykan.com - www.ozleraykanbooks.com
info@ozleraykan.com - info@ozleraykanbooks.com

Catalogue records for this book are available from the Turkish National Library, Library of Turkish History Foundation, Turkish National Atatürk Library, Library of Istanbul University, Library of Ankara University, British Library, Library of Congress.

Forty Camel Girl
Letters from Turkey
E. Grace Beyler

www.fortycamelgirl.com
egracebeyler@hotmail.co.uk

ISBN 978-9944-5180-1-7

Editor: Özler Aykan
ozleraykan@hotmail.com

Cover design: Tim Wilson
www.brezein.co.uk
breze@madasafish.com

Designed by: Serhat Okan
serhatokan@gmail.com

Printed in Turkey
First Printing, May 2007
Ajans Plaza

Original First Edition

For Phyllis and Bill
who believed in this book - and in me

CONTENTS

FOREWORD

For several years now, we Turks have been engaged in an internal dialogue regarding our recent past. The past tells us where we come from, who we are; it also informs the choices we make for the future.

Into this mix comes Grace Beyler's letters. Written between 1969 - 1971, Grace records the events of a troubled period that has shaped our country ever since. Although primarily concerned with her own struggles and those of her Turkish fiancé's family, Grace's letters also reflect a time when our young republic was undergoing profound changes, politically, socially and economically. The book, in its way, becomes a metaphor for contemporary Turkey.

While recounting her own heart-warming story, Grace draws a picture of life before television, mobile phones, global brands and mass tourism. Using many different strands, she weaves a tapestry filled with adventure, pathos, humour and romance. Despite the difficulties around her, Grace sees through the superficial to the heart of the Turkish people, their warmth and friendship, their support and acceptance. Whatever her criticisms, we ultimately feel that she is cheering us on as we search for our place in the modern world.

Regardless of the topic under examination, Grace remains open in her outlook, objective in her assessment, and eager in her desire to learn and understand. She always seeks the truth and, in the process, examines our shortcomings while acknowledging our strengths. Written in a style that is both sure and light, the reader is engaged from the outset and is drawn immediately into Grace's world, one where laughter and tears exist side-by-side.

This is social history written from a very personal point of view, but one which enables us to see ourselves as others see us. We are grateful to Grace Beyler for her wonderful letters and thankful that she has chosen to share them with us.

Mehmet Dülger

Chairman of the Foreign Affairs Committee
of the Turkish Grand Assembly

Deputy of Antalya

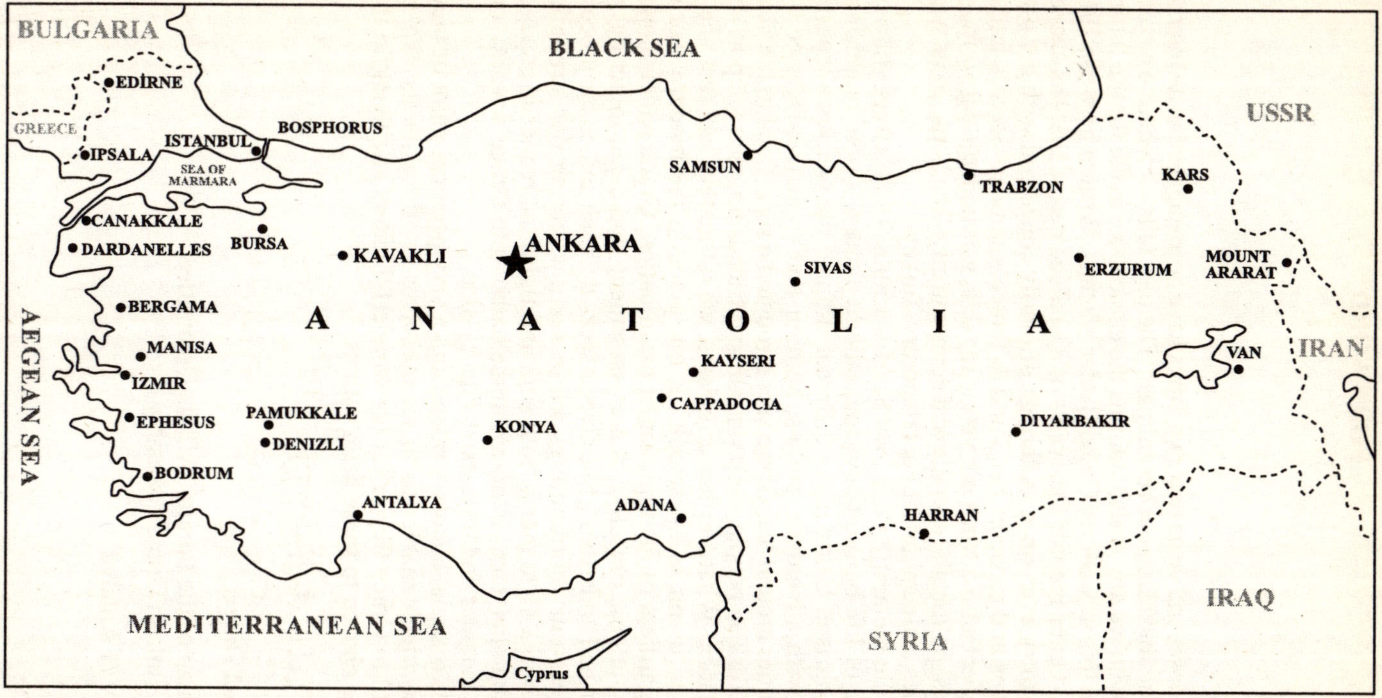

REPUBLIC OF TURKEY - 1970

GUIDE TO PRONUNCIATION

Until 1928 the Turkish language was written in a form of Arabic script known as Ottoman Turkish. Mustafa Kemal Atatürk, the founder of the Republic of Turkey, took the enlightened decision to change to the Latin alphabet, giving linguists the chance to regularize the language. Modern Turkish is logical in both spelling and pronunciation. It is phonetic; if you can read it, you can say it.

Vowels are consistently pronounced:
a as in *palm*
e as in *pet*
i as in *pit*
o as in *poet*
u as in *put*

There are three additional vowels not found in English but which are comparable to counterparts in German and French:

ı as in *this*
ö as the "oy" of *employ*
ü as the "ui" of *suit*

Consonants are pronounced as in English with the following exceptions:

c as the "j" in *just*
ç as the "ch" in *chair*
g as in *good* (always hard)
ğ is silent and lengthens the preceding vowel
ş as the "sh" in *short*

AUTHOR'S NOTES

Background

In the 1960s, using the telephone for long-distance calls was regarded as something of a luxury, reserved for special occasions. When I left home to go to college, my mother asked me to keep in touch by writing a letter once a week. This became the habit of a lifetime. Over the course of the next 40 years, I wrote more than 2000 letters to my family: my parents, Phyllis and Bill, and in the early days when they were still at home, my younger brothers, Bill and Peter. My parents kept almost all my letters (shoeboxes full), but it is those from my time in Turkey (October 1969 – September 1971) that form the basis of this story.

Word usage

Moslem/Muslim: In the 1960s and 70s, "Moslem" was in common usage. However, in the 1980s, "Muslim" began to come into circulation. As this is now the accepted spelling in English, I have replaced the old form as originally written in the letters.

Anne/Ana: The Turkish word for mother is "anne", but as this is also an English girl's name, I have adapted the spelling to avoid confusion.

PROLOGUE

When the black cab dropped me in leafy Notting Hill on a bright September day in 1968, I had no idea that my life was about to change forever. I merely saw some jerry cans and a length of rope near a loaded mini-van and thought I must be in the right place. Looking about for signs of life, I made my way to the front door and rang the bell. A young man opened up and gave me a cheeky grin as I hesitantly asked,

"Is this the right address for the trip to Turkey?"

"Hi. I'm Hakan. Come in. We all waiting for you," was his welcoming reply rendered in an unidentifiable foreign accent. Hakan motioned me to follow him through the house. "I like your red dress," he commented.

"Did I ask your opinion?" I thought, but said nothing. He bounded ahead of me with all the assurance of a newly elected politician. Though slim and good-looking, he was dressed like a tramp. A homemade sweater, knitted from bits of leftover wool, was full of dog hairs, and I could see mismatched socks showing at the back of his Swedish clogs. The noisy chatter of many voices emanated from the rear and echoed along the corridor as we approached the kitchen. It seemed that most of the other travellers had already assembled and were enjoying a toast to the coming journey. Introductions were made, and it was then I learned that Hakan was a Turk. This was something I would not have guessed as he had fair skin and dark brown hair that fell in a shock over his forehead. I was surprised that he didn't have black hair or a moustache. I thought all Turks had moustaches - and wore curly-toed slippers. I didn't know anything about Turks. I knew even less about Turkey.

As he laughed and joked with everyone, it was clear that Hakan was comfortable speaking his own brand of rough-and-ready English. His dark almond-shaped eyes flashed with mischief and hinted at ancestors from the eastern steppes. He exuded easy warmth that drew people to him, and he enjoyed being the centre of attention. At this point, I was getting my bearings and wanted to size up the company before plunging in, so I sipped a drink and watched the proceedings from a quiet corner.

Hakan was keeping his eye on me. He'd make comments and then look in my direction to see if I had noticed. Eventually, he made his way over and I asked about the dog.

"What dog?"

"The one whose hair is all over your sweater."

"Oh, that," he chuckled. "This is not dog hair. It's mohair. I'm sewing sheepskins in the basement."

He began to tell me about WML (Worldwide Merchandise Ltd), the import and manufacturing business which he ran with a Kiwi called Ken. This seemed to consist of bringing sheepskins from Turkey and making them up into coats and jackets for sale in Carnaby Street and the Kings Road. Hakan was friendly, open and extremely flirtatious. While teasing me about my floral suitcase and my American accent, he asked me numerous questions and wanted to hear what had brought me to London. In a short time, we managed to exchange a remarkable amount of information. I didn't know what to make of him as I found him by turns to be impressive and delightful, presumptuous and exasperating. Despite myself, I was disappointed to learn that Hakan would not be joining us on the imminent expedition.

As far as I was concerned, this trip would be my last adventure before returning to America. I came from a close-knit family and had grown up in a small town in western Pennsylvania where I lived with my parents, Phyllis and Bill, and my two younger brothers, Bill and Peter. After high school, I moved across the state to get my BA and then to teach primary school. A year in that role convinced me that I had chosen the wrong career, so I switched from a suburban classroom to the personnel department of a large insurance company in Philadelphia. My position there had been full of exciting projects and glamorous travel, but as this work ended, I found myself, age 24, office bound and suffering from terminal dissatisfaction. When an opportunity arose to spend July and August in London, I leapt at the chance, put the contents of my city-centre apartment into storage and quit my job. I would do what I had always longed to do: travel abroad. While the rest of the world watched the first man land on the moon and then enjoyed the "summer of love", I spent several self-indulgent weeks greedily exploring one of the world's great cities.

The time turned out not to be enough. Despite having made several excursions around the country and further afield to the continent, these experiences served only to whet my appetite. However, as my funds were running out, I realized that I would have to find a permanent job or return home. I dreaded the latter; quite simply, I was not ready to go back. Although I had applied for various posts, I was not confident of success. Jobs at that time were scarce, and no one was eager to hire a foreign professional who would need all kinds of paperwork to be legally employed. But instead of sitting around, waiting for rejections, I had decided to take this final trip to the very edge of Europe and then, see what turned up at the end of the month.

And so, on that autumn day, twelve of us left London to camp our way to Istanbul, taking a week to get there and a week to return, with a week in the city itself. Although I had gone expecting to be intrigued, I was unprepared for the seduction that followed. Charmed by both the city and its people, the trip did nothing to prepare me to return to the USA.

Hakan was a friend of Steve, our driver and tour organizer. Since he lived with Steve and his family, he was there to greet us when we got back. I was ecstatic to find that I had been offered a job after all and would be able to stay on indefinitely. Hakan had apparently been keeping himself informed about my situation and was quick off the mark to ask me out. As I got to know him, I discovered that he was ambitious and hard working, someone who thrived on challenges and competition. His effortless confidence was bolstered by utter self-belief. He was naturally exuberant and upbeat, and I knew that an evening with him would centre on pub gatherings, parties and friends. He knew an endless variety of people, all of whom were subject to his fearless conversations and joking chitchat, which could be wildly provocative but never cruel. He was fun to be with, and we always had a good time.

I understood that Hakan was smart with the sort of shrewd, instinctive intelligence that enables uneducated people to survive against the odds. I was surprised to learn that he had finished law school in Istanbul. Someone less lawyer-like I had never before encountered. He was a businessman through and through, and all that he told me about his life and his family confirmed that he was never cut out for anything else.

Hakan had learned his English during a year at the University of Berkeley in California. He had been a student at the time political unrest over the Vietnam War started on that campus and spread across the US. When we discussed the protest movement, he said that he had been far too busy enjoying himself to do anything as important as demonstrate.

But I found another side of Hakan when I watched him with Steve's children, one of whom was severely disabled, and saw that he was both kind and compassionate. He had a knack for honing in on what makes people tick and a gift for making them feel special. With me, he was attentive and romantic. As far as I could see, about the only difference between us was that he was the more politically conservative one.

As our relationship developed into something serious, we took the decision to live together. Although this would have been considered a bold move - a very bold move - back in the USA, it was, in Swinging 60s London, if not exactly the "done thing", then certainly not uncommon. Free from the constraints of our small town backgrounds, we delighted in the privacy and domestic bliss this arrangement gave us. In the meantime, however, a cloud was forming on his horizon - our horizon: Turkish men must do military service. It is compulsory for all, and citizenship is at stake. Hakan had devoted a great deal of time and energy to postponing the inevitable. When we met, his British visa was expiring, and the Turks were pressing him to return and fulfil his obligations. Not to do so would mean that he could never go home again, not unless he wished to spend time in prison.

There was no choice. Exploiting his talent to influence, Hakan convinced the Turks to renew his passport a final time and persuaded the Brits to give him just one more visa extension. This gave him the period he needed to consolidate his business in London and us, the time to figure out exactly what my role in all this would be. We both had a lot of thinking to do.

Like Hakan's decision to return to Turkey, again there was no real choice. With certain inevitability, we agreed that I would go with him and live with his family, while he reluctantly played soldier. In order to mark this momentous decision, we became formally engaged (complete with a small sapphire and diamond ring), a ritual that would do much to ease my place into his family. Given their cultural views regarding the importance of the bride's purity and the fact that, though sleeping together we were not yet officially wed, a ring would convey the sense of commitment that would make me (hopefully) more acceptable in their eyes. Opportunities for romantic interludes and intimacy would be limited, but not impossible. Over time, we had discovered that we shared the same values and wanted the same things out of life. I trusted him completely. We were madly in love, the thought of separation too painful to contemplate.

And so, in September of 1969, a year after we had first met, we packed up our putty-coloured VW Beetle and headed across Europe to Turkey.

Part One

Into Anatolia
October - December 1969

Chapter 1

23 October 1969

We crossed the Bosphorus into Asia today. All of my senses were on high alert as I stood on the grubby deck of a world-weary ferry, sipped a glass of sweet tea and absorbed the smell of urban port - briny sea breeze with a hint of sewage and a top note of diesel. In front of me was one of the most magical panoramas in the world: the unmistakable domes and minarets dominating the skyline of the place where East meets West. As we pulled away from the European shore, I looked for all the now-familiar landmarks, first spotting Galata Tower, strangely Genoese in this otherwise eastern scene. To the left of it lay Topkapı, comfortably positioned on the Golden Horn. Further out, the extravagantly confrontational Dolmabahçe Palace demanded attention, while the unmistakable domes and soaring minarets of the Blue Mosque presided over them all.

The churning waters were alive with ferryboats heading to various destinations on the Asian side and back, their smokestacks trailing wispy vapours. Mighty cargo ships and oil tankers plied the strait from the Black Sea to the Mediterranean, while sturdy barges bucked its stiff currents. In between these vessels of self-important commerce darted the plucky little fishing boats heading back to Galata Bridge to fry up their catches on the quayside. Kız Kulesi, the Maiden's Tower, lay calmly in the midst of the frenetic activity, enticing passers-by with its colourful legends. The familiar cries of circling seagulls mixed with the vigorous blasts from the horns of passing ships, their distinctive noises cushioned by incessant engine thrum. Along with curls of water slapping the sides of our ferry, they provided the sound track to the view before me. Constantinople, now Istanbul. Roman, Byzantine, then Ottoman and now the greatest city of modern Turkey. Exotic, inspiring and exciting. I can't believe I'm here!

The trip from London has been an eventful one. The ferry departed on schedule from Dover, and the channel crossing was smooth all the way. Once in France, we travelled the length of the country on back roads, meandering through gentle autumn countryside, spending our first night in Lyons. I have one abiding memory of a road junction outside the restaurant where we had our evening meal. It appeared that everyone in Lyons had a motorcycle which eventually turned up at this set of traffic lights. Motors revved incessantly as the local talent tried to impress and outdo each other with breathtaking starts. All attention was fixed on the lights, willing them to change. Sometimes the wait became too long, the anticipated green not coming up fast enough. Never mind, a quick glance around and off they went as if their futures were at stake. We were endlessly entertained and lingered on over the fine food and wine on offer.

The next morning, we moved on southwards to the Cote d'Azur, pausing here and there to take in some of the sights. Cannes turned out to be tacky, a place whose reputed appeal mystified us both, and whose high prices left us nodding knowingly with regard to the empty shops. The fact that it was low season did not register with us at the time. We pushed on and had dinner that night in Monaco (a fish restaurant with sea views - less wine, more atmosphere) and, afterwards, continued on to the Italian Riviera via a truly terrifying drive over narrow mountain roads. I was both speechless and petrified as intrepid Italian drivers overtook us on uncoiling turns and shot around tortuous bends at racing speeds. I guess they thought we were sissies. "This is good practice for Turkish roads," said Hakan, sounding as if we were extraordinarily lucky to have this preparation for what lay ahead. He takes it all in his stride and remains unfazed by most things. Since we were travelling out of season, we had no trouble securing first-class accommodation at knockdown prices, a welcome taste of luxury after long hours of driving.

The next day, we stopped briefly in Genoa, which is "falling by parts" according to Hakan, and then drove through Milan to Venice where we spent a few short hours. Almost as powerfully as Istanbul, Venice grabbed me and begged me to stay. It is a bustling, lively city but also, an utterly romantic one. We browsed in the little shops and bought, somewhat unexpectedly, a typewriter (Olivetti portable). It is just what we need for our business, and I had visions of it coming in handy for personal correspondence as well. We could so easily have delayed our journey, but at this point, we simply wanted to get where we were going.

Unfortunately, after Italy, any semblance of decent roads, edible food and comfortable hotels rapidly fades. It's heads down and travel as fast as possible through the Communist countries: first stop Yugoslavia. On our arrival the border guards, who recognized Hakan from his many previous overland trips, greeted us warmly. Really. They knew that in return for simple items such as western cigarettes, razor blades, stockings and even shampoo, they could ease his way through the formalities of transit travel. He knew this too, and it was then that I understood the reason for an excessive supply of these in our luggage. "Gifts" were made to the appropriate people, and we were on our way again. I have heard that there are some beautiful places to visit here, I think on the Dalmatian coast; but travelling as we did, straight through the centre, the landscape was uninspiring, rolling on and on in endless monotony. The mainly agricultural countryside was flat and almost featureless. The only attractions were the chance to watch medieval farming methods, horse-powered antiquated equipment, and lots of back-breaking manual labour. What kept us awake were the terrors of the rudimentary two-lane road: just one lane there, and one lane back. I found it hard to believe that a major European transit route could be so crude. Since most of the traffic consists of trucks hell-bent on making haste, the drive is a testing ordeal, any entertainment value lost in the frequency with which we passed accidents, and the need to avoid involving ourselves in one.

However, it's not only the roads where conditions are different. We passed towns that I'm sure had once been lovely places but are now the dull, drab shadows of a former life. I can hear Dad saying that he'd like to own the cement business here. This building material alone appears to be in limitless supply. Paint must be unheard of as everything is *au naturel* in concrete grey. It's all so bleak. I found it extremely depressing and cannot imagine what it must be like to live here, and yet, life goes on.

We bombed through Yugoslavia in a day and a half; however, it's not as if there was anything better to look forward to in Bulgaria. It's worse - ten times worse. Even so, I wanted to find something heartening as I knew this was where Hakan's parents had been born and grew up. They came from Shumen where the family had been sent, in earlier times, to guard the sultan's lands and to look after his interests in the region. The Beylers were prosperous Ottomans who took their responsibilities seriously. Hakan's great-great-grandfather built the town mosque, surrounding shops and clock tower, which as far as we know, still stand. His mother's family had been part of the Ottoman rule in Hungary but had migrated several generations earlier to Bulgaria where she also had been born. Hakan's parents married when his father was twenty years old and his mother, merely sixteen. Their first son was born in Bulgaria and was seven years old when they all fled to Istanbul to escape the Communist takeover. They left everything behind and started afresh as did many other European Turks scattered today throughout western Turkey. Hakan says that they tend to stand out because they are, on the whole, better educated and more culturally European than Anatolian Turks.

Whatever its past history, the Bulgaria of the present felt shot through with hopelessness. (We chose to go this route in preference to the route through Greece , which could have been personally harder for Hakan. Due to recent history in this part of the world, relations between Greece and Turkey are always strained, but right now, there is heightened tension over the question of sovereignty in Cyprus.) As we crossed the border, we expected a repeat performance of the scenario going into Yugoslavia. However, what we had not anticipated was the mile-long queue of assorted vehicles waiting to complete the necessary paperwork. Visions of days of interminable waiting unveiled themselves before my eyes. I glanced at Hakan to see how he was taking all this. Just as I opened my mouth to say something, I saw a border guard come pounding up and motion us to follow him. Unbelievably, he too, had remembered Hakan from other trips and pulled us from the tailback.

It was apparent that as far as we were concerned, formalities here would be brief; but while the necessary form filling took place, two very worried-looking young men approached and asked if they could have a word. Hakan turned his attention to the clean-cut Americans dressed in telltale button-down shirts, jackets with college logos and Levi jeans. Shaky voices conveyed the desperation of their plight as they explained that they had been arrested for smuggling. It seems that they had been in India where they had purchased gold and precious stones, intending to sell them in London at a profit. Unhappily for them, they had not declared these items at the Bulgarian border, and the gems had been found during a search of their luggage. They had been arrested immediately and, as far as they could understand, were awaiting transport to the nearby jail. It was clear that they were in deep trouble. Smuggling is a serious offence anywhere, no less so in Communist Bulgaria where the Comrades don't take it at all kindly. No one from their respective families knew of the Americans' whereabouts, they had no language in common with their captors, and no legal representation appeared forthcoming. A stay of indeterminate length in a Bulgarian prison looked like more than a grim possibility, one to be avoided at all costs. The Americans had realized that Hakan had some sort of rapport with the border officials and, desperate for any help at all, wondered if he could assist in some way. At worst, they wanted to get word out to their families.

Hakan listened to their tale of woe with a mixture of concern, bemusement and disbelief that anyone could travel so far and be so naive. He asked a few more questions and then, after giving the matter some thought, said, "I'll see what I can do." He strolled over to the desk of his favourite Comrade and engaged in some light conversation (a mixture of chutt-putt Bulgarian, Turkish, German and English), casually determining what might be happening with the Americans. After a short time, he returned to the three of us. "I think you would like to make a gift of one of your best stones to the official in charge," he suggested, with not so much as a flicker of a smile. But, of course. Without hesitation, the stone was selected and left in the appropriate place; whereupon, as if by magic, charges of smuggling were instantly dismissed as a bureaucratic misunderstanding. The enormously relieved young men fell on Hakan in gratitude. A reward was offered but declined, and the Americans beat a hasty retreat towards Yugoslavia. In the meantime, we had presented our own gifts, though admittedly of a somewhat lesser nature, and we too, travelled on.

If Yugoslavia says "Communist State" all over it, Bulgaria says "Police State". It is very tightly controlled and Dirty Capitalists like us are required to pay $15 merely to travel through their benighted country. It was barely worth stopping for anything even though, like everyone else, we were required to buy a certain amount of *leva* that we might as well spend, as there was no changing it back. There's more than one way to get your hands on filthy capitalist hard currency. The main transit road through the country was merely an extension of the one we'd been on, and it took us to the capital, Sofia. Since we had little in the way of provisions, we decided to head for what Hakan knew to be the best hotel in the city. Here, we could have something to eat and dispose of our *leva* at the same time. The hotel entrance looked promising. Although the building was of questionable architectural merit, at least it was modern and must, as a top hotel, have good catering facilities. Such was our assumption. The immense lobby, largely devoid of furniture or fittings, was nothing more than a murky cavern, heroic murals providing the only decoration in the austere surroundings. It was empty of guests, but a sleepy desk clerk bestirred himself to point the way to the restaurant. We advanced into the silence, assaulted by the sound of our footsteps rebounding from the cold stone floors (imitation marble with swirls) as we made our way down the designated corridor.

A dour looking bleached-blonde waitress of indeterminate age and a table of uniformed officials were the only people to be seen in the blowsy light. Struggling to overcome its dusty demeanour and provide any sign of welcome, the dining room seeped dreariness, the air itself felt second-hand. The sight of the Comrades was almost enough to make us turn and go, but with no other option for eating, we resisted the urge and sat down at one of the vast circular tables. The waitress made her listless way over, to take an order we thought, but she seemed merely to be assessing us in some way. There was no menu. She would bring us what was available that day... and so we waited, struck speechless by the oppressive atmosphere and a longing simply to eat and go.

It soon became obvious that we had entered some gastronomic wilderness. I hope never again to have such poor quality food put in front of me: in this case, a lump of fatty, gristly meat (origins unknown) swimming in a watery broth flecked with globules of lard. There were some harmless-looking boiled potatoes on the side and a basket of grey bread to share. We ate what we could salvage from this pitiful offering, paid up and left.

As we made our way down the street, hoping to find somewhere to spend our remaining *leva*, we heard someone hiss from a doorway. Looking around, we saw the waitress from the restaurant who motioned us over. She made it clear she wanted to change money - our hard currency for a ridiculous amount of *leva*. Were we not in Bulgaria, were it not *leva* in question, the offer might have been tempting; as it was, we had no use for the local currency. Even if we had, we were both keenly aware that the important-looking officials sat just yards away, and that the strictly forbidden transaction she was proposing could land us in a quandary not unlike the one we had witnessed at the border that very morning. We had to refuse. She looked desperate.

In an effort to offer some consolation, I trawled around in my bag and came up with a packet of chewing gum and a bar of chocolate. Without a word, she took them and left. Later we wondered if it might have been those very officials who had put her up to the proposition.

Leva still in hand, we continued the search for a means of spending it, but there was nothing. Absolutely nothing. We were in the heart of the capital, but it felt as if we were in some outpost of civilization. There was hardly anyone on the streets, and those who were scuttled along, heads down, staying close to the grim walls of secretive buildings. The city was as joyous as a funeral in February; the atmosphere was edgy and ominous. We quickly surveyed the few shops that were open, but the only merchandise they had were the few meagre items on display in their grimy windows: a faded artificial floral arrangement, a lacklustre plastic doll, a forlorn china swan of fairground quality and a set of coasters that proclaimed, "Bulgaria is Beautiful" on its imitation leather case. We decided not to waste any more time, returned to the car and plunged on towards the Turkish border.

As we were tearing along the lightly travelled, rough and rugged two-lane road in the middle of the night - in the middle of nowhere - we saw some flashing lights ahead. Not knowing what to expect, we slowed and were hailed to a stop by two soldiers on patrol. Once I had spotted their fearsome automatic weapons, they had my undivided attention. As he rolled down his window, Hakan murmured, "Don't tell them you're American." Our little VW ("Dagmar", to recognize her roots) has German plates, so they asked us, by means of sign language and pigeon German, if we were German. *"Ja"*, we replied in perfect German. He flashed the light around the car and asked to see our passports. Uh-oh. I pretended to fumble in my bag for mine, while Hakan produced his Turkish one. Exclamations amounting to "Welcome neighbour!" were exchanged, and they wanted to find out where Hakan had been. He told them Germany and Great Britain, whereupon they mentioned something about The Beatles. *"Ja, ja - sehr gut!"* we replied and burst into a rendition of "We all live in a Yellow Submarine". Both soldiers responded by doing a little roadside jig, then laughed, stepped back and waved us on. *Danke!*

We arrived at the Turkish frontier early in the morning. Any memory of the ease with which we had completed the formalities at other borders was now fading to reality. The fact that Hakan was a returning Turk necessitated a thorough search of every nook and cranny of both vehicle and baggage. We emptied the car, and I was staggered to see how much of the luggage involved my wardrobe. There was an embarrassment of riches, a mound of belongings that did not escape the attention of the head of customs, a sharp little man who sucked his teeth and eyed us with suspicion. He probably eyes everyone with suspicion.

Item by item, he examined the enormous stack of clothes, asking if we intended to open a store. Although we were innocent of that accusation, we had other concerns. Hidden in the folds of this pile was a stash of mink pelts which we intended to sell in Istanbul. Apart from these, there was also the material for my wedding gown, an opulent length of pale pink silk brocade from Liberty's. The Turks don't care too much about the importation of everyday items, but bringing in luxury goods is a big no-no. I noticed Hakan becoming a little nervous as the customs official must surely be approaching the minks, and about this time, he offered to show the man something worthier of his attention. The official perked up. What could it be? They moved away to the side of the car where Hakan produced my rabbit coat, purchased at great expense the previous winter on the Kings Road. Mr Customs was not fooled and said that coney was of no importance; however, if we felt inclined to leave that bottle of whiskey and a carton of cigarettes on his desk, we could be on our way.

From Edirne at the border, we drove straight to Istanbul, about three hours away. Despite our sleeplessness, the drive was one of sheer joy. What a relief to be out of Bulgaria, to leave all that darkness behind. After several days of nothing but watery light, the vibrant colours of Turkey exploded before our eyes. We blinked in the dazzling sunshine, taking in the earthy smells of the October landscape. Hakan was now on home territory and knows Istanbul as if he had drawn the map. We have shared most of the driving on the trip, but at this point, I was more than happy to hand over to him.

The vast majority of cars are, unbelievably, big and American, while the ancient streets are, unsurprisingly, old and narrow. On top of this, there is only a handful of Turks who has had a genuine driving lesson. The result is indescribable chaos. Hakan had been right about Italian roads being useful training for those in Turkey. Some of the major roads have traffic lights. Some of them work. Few are actually obeyed. The motorcyclists of Lyons are Highway Code role models compared to the drivers of Istanbul who are inclined to pay scant attention to this modern device. As far as they are concerned, traffic lights have been installed only to slow them down, and they are having none of it. There appear to be three rules of the road: (1) regardless of risk or consequence, try to pass the car in front; (2) do not look around; (3) do not attempt to worry about anyone else. The alternative is unthinkable carnage. Since the locals understand the rules and stick to them, they seem to manage. With complete aplomb, Hakan blundered through the city, braking and accelerating, skidding around corners, reversing down busy roads. An outsider would stand no chance. Hakan (to speak of someone who has never had a driving lesson; he just picked it up) coped admirably, though in a manner best described as unconventional. It must be in the blood.

I am writing this on yet another ferry, this one taking us across the Sea of Marmara into the heart of Anatolia, known also as Asia Minor. We have at least another 160 kilometres (about 100 miles) to go on yet more pot-holed roads, but we expect to be there this evening.

Chapter 2

8 November 1969

Having travelled 4000 kilometres (2500 miles) to get here, we have since travelled another 2400 kilometres (1500 miles) on various and sundry matters. Hakan and I are both exhausted from all the running around. But I need to back up a bit.

The drive from Yalova (the southern ferry terminal) to Kavaklı was almost as exciting as manoeuvring around Istanbul. The Turks carry their city driving habits onto their highways, deteriorating and neglected versions of those we had already experienced in Europe. It was a colossal tactical error to have chosen a VW Beetle to bring to Turkey: it plainly doesn't command any respect. If we are foolish enough to find ourselves in such a laughable vehicle then, I'm afraid the feeling is, we deserve what we get. We spent a lot of time getting back onto the roads, having been forced off by impatient bus and truck drivers who bullied us mercilessly. The few cars are mostly the American ones already mentioned and, although there are some from this decade, most date from the 1940s and 50s. Amazingly, there are also a few from the 1930s, making it feel like a time warp for vehicles.

To add to the tension, there is also the fear of the unexpected. We simply never know what will be on the road ahead. During the day, we have rounded a bend to find any number of spectacles, including pecking chickens, dazed cows, shepherds moving their flocks, picnickers (yes, really), broken down vehicles, donkeys trotting along under their vast burdens and - most memorably - a camel caravan. This particular procession consisted of about twenty camels, each one following behind the other, each one bearing garishly wrapped burdens. The animals were bigger than I would have thought, their enormous brown eyes and long feminine lashes in complete contrast to their coarse hides and crusty bodies. They took no notice of us, chewing constantly on some invisible wodge, sashaying along the road, their squashy feet splaying on crumbling tarmac. Their bells, worn for some indeterminate purpose, jangled pleasantly but were useless as a warning to oncoming traffic. I was so excited, I completely overlooked the fact that we had nearly crashed into the rear of the last camel. The caravan driver saw our delight and waved a cheery greeting. All was forgiven, but I doubted that he, or any of the people who use the roads so blithely, had any idea of the danger in which they put themselves - and us.

Such lively roads are a powerful argument for not driving at night. We can be tootling along at a respectable 50 mph and be forced, suddenly, to slam on the brakes to avoid hitting a horse cart (among the other things mentioned). It might be maintaining a decent horse pace, but by comparison with the average speed of a motor vehicle, it is at a standstill. Of course, they have no lights. At best, a small red reflector announces its presence from a few feet away. However, shepherd dogs present the most frightening hazard on night-time roads. They are immense, ferocious and fearless, as effective a deterrent as I can imagine when it comes to guarding the flock. Dagmar seems to pose enough of a threat to be worthy of attack, which the dogs do without hesitation, throwing their muscular bodies at our moving car, while snapping at us with their powerful jaws. I always make sure the windows are shut when driving through the countryside, especially after dark when the dogs are at their most alert. On the plus side, with so much adrenalin coursing around our bodies, there is no chance of falling asleep at the wheel.

And so, we rambled along to Bursa, a picturesque city set at the base of the Uludağ Mountains, the first capital of the Ottoman Empire. It's evident from the imposing mosques, elaborate tombs and fine houses scattered across the foothills that this is a city with an important past. After a couple of days of hard travelling, we were both scruffy. I really did not want to meet Hakan's family without a chance to clean up, and he assured me that I would have a bath before reaching Kavaklı. I suspect now that he had been planning this little surprise all along.

According to tradition, very few people have bathing facilities in their homes, but every little town and village has its own *hamam*, public bath. It's a strange idea in the West but perfectly normal in this part of the world. Bursa is known for its hot springs, a feature that did not escape the Ottomans nor their sultans who built extensive facilities not only for themselves, but also for the population at large. It's here that the term "bath" took on a whole new concept for me.

After arriving at the impressive Çelik Palas Oteli (Steel Palace Hotel, don't ask me why), we were ushered into changing rooms where we undressed and put on our bathing suits. We had wooden clogs for our feet and fluffy robes made of the best Turkish towelling. We then clomped down the hall to the main bath, a magnificent chamber with windows that filtered shafts of sunlight from high up in the dome. We were standing in an ancient Ottoman bath built for the sultans, a place of incredible beauty and calm. The middle of the room was taken up by a round pool with waist-high water in a soothing pastel green, its colour coming not from chlorine, but from the mineral content of the natural springs. The water itself was the source of the steam that filled the room. Marble covered every visible surface. Around the edges of this sumptuous hall were individual basins where we could wash; or for more privacy, there were cubicles off to the side. We were the only ones there, and I felt as if I had been transported to another world, one where someone was about to shout, "Bring on the dancing girls!"

We washed and then we swam in the pool, absorbing an ambience sodden with history. Then we washed some more. I felt invigorated from the inside out, relaxed and revitalized at the same time. As both hot steam and pure enchantment enveloped me, I was overwhelmed by a rush of happiness. I could never be thankful enough for the chain of events that had brought me to this wonderful place. We stayed longer than we should have, succumbing totally to an atmosphere as soothing as a silk-lined purse. Later, while dressing in our respective rooms, we sipped *çay*, tea, and resisted the temptation to rest on the little cots.

I had set aside what I regarded as my most modest outfit to wear to meet Hakan's family. I had ruled out wearing slacks as I was not at all certain how this mode of attire would be received. My Dear Fiancé, excellent fashion trend spotter that he is, manages to be, in the way of most men, comprehensively oblivious to feminine concerns. I found it hard to get any useful information concerning the way in which I should present myself on this auspicious occasion.

"I'm thinking of wearing my black and white dress, the one with the long sleeves."

"OK."

"Is it too short?"

"No, it's good. Everyone wears short skirts." (NOT TRUE!)

"What about the blue one?"

"That's good, too."

"Which would your mother like?"

"Either one."

"What about make-up?"

"What about it?"

"Is it alright to wear some?"

"Do what you always do."

In the end, I chose the black-and-white houndstooth shift, modestly long by miniskirt standards, stopping as it does mid-thigh. But I could wear my thick black tights and black patent shoes and feel fashionable but restrained. I decided on some light make-up, and fortunately, my bobbed hair does not require much in the way of styling. I finished off with some simple earrings and Grandmother's onyx brooch. I presented myself for inspection:

"What do you think?

Big grin. "Not bad for a Yank." (That's a running joke.)

"Thanks. But what will THEY think?"

"They'll think you're a forty camel girl."

"What does THAT mean?"

"It's good. I'll explain later. Let's go!"

We finally arrived at the Beyler household about 9:30 pm and got them all out of bed! They had known we were coming, of course, but not when, exactly. We had a warm welcome from everyone and, after taking off our shoes at the door, were escorted into what would probably be known as the parlour. Having been caught out by our unexpected arrival, they all quickly disappeared to change into day clothes, but as they returned one-by-one, I was introduced at last to Hakan's family. When I met his father, Hayri, and his mother, Bedriye, I knew what to do. Hakan had told me about the importance of hand kissing and that his parents would expect it. Eager to comply, I learned that while holding the proffered hand, I should kiss the back of it and then touch it to my forehead. It's a show of respect for the older generation. It was easy and made the right first impression. Also present were Hakan's slightly older sister, Neriman, and his little brother, Levent, at seventeen, the same age as Peter. I was surprised that Levent kissed not only his brother's hand, but also mine. I have mixed feelings about that. Neriman wasn't involved in the hand kissing, though I had the impression that she might have expected it from Hakan, her younger brother, if not from me. Only the older brother, Sami, was missing as I believe he now lives in Istanbul.

As we (they) sat and chatted, I had a chance to take in my surroundings. The room appeared to be one reserved for visitors as everything was trim and tidy, the decor reminiscent of 1930s formality. The furniture was substantial with walnut frames embracing rust-coloured jacquard upholstery. The walls were neutral and unadorned except for a picture of Atatürk. While there were no lamps, a central light hung low from the ceiling, casting a golden glow over the proceedings. A traditional Turkish carpet covered most of the floor, and there were several nests of small tables. Every flat surface had a doily, while antimacassars sat comfortably on the chairs and sofa. Neriman assumed the duties of hostess, passing around the lemon cologne (this is sprinkled onto the hands and then smoothed over the face and hair, very refreshing) and later, serving *çay* and refreshments.

Hayri, Hakan's father (Baba), is a distinguished-looking man in his mid-fifties. He is shorter than Hakan with soft, rounded features; and like most Turks, he sports a full moustache that matches, in his case, a fine head of silver hair. Neatly dressed and dapper in appearance, he exudes an air of dignified calm, but there is no mistaking the warmth radiating from the small slanted eyes that have passed from father to son. I saw immediately whom Hakan most resembles.

Bedriye, Hakan's mother (Ana), was obviously a beauty in her youth and now has the fuller figure of her contemporaries. Finer featured than her husband, I noticed her unusually rosy cheeks that I suspect bear witness to an earlier intermingling of bloodlines. Her grey hair is bobbed, and she has a shy, girlish demeanour. I felt that she was unsure of me and was watching me closely, with many reservations.

Neriman, an attractive young woman, was busy with her duties and didn't have much to say, while Levent was restless and fidgety, anxious for his brother's attention and eager to contribute to the conversation.

There was so much to discuss that I was happy to sit back and let them talk amongst themselves, something of a moot point since I had no way of contributing anything useful. In fact, since I have no Turkish whatsoever, and since none of the Beylers speaks any English, there will not be any direct exchanges, useful or otherwise, in the immediate future. Even though we all rely on Hakan for translations, it soon became apparent that the family in general, and Hakan's father in particular, was becoming distressed. I hated to interrupt as I could see that they were in full flow. When he could, Hakan began to tell me what had happened. Again, I have to backtrack - this time to London.

I'm sure you know that it is part of Hakan's plan for us to produce some WML coats and jackets here while he is doing his military service. This is partly to provide income for me, partly to help his partner Ken fill orders from London, and partly to help Hakan's father back on his feet after his business bankruptcy. To assist in all this, Hakan had arranged for three fur sewing machines to be delivered from London to Istanbul on the tourist bus driven by his friend, Sid. Hakan had instructed Sid to declare the machines at the border and had given him the money to pay the substantial duties. Sid, however, decided to use his initiative and pocket the money for himself. Since no one at customs had asked him if he had anything to declare, he thought he had escaped detection.

But Sid's assumption was wrong. Officials had spotted the machines in a cursory check of the luggage compartment but let him go on through to Istanbul where he was followed. Evidently they wanted to find out where the machines were going. Enter Hakan's father who arrived, as arranged, to collect them. When the machines changed hands, the policed swooped to impound the bus and arrested both Sid and Hakan's father on charges of smuggling. When the British Embassy got involved, it applied considerable pressure to get Sid released. After the first court session, he was found "not guilty" and permitted to depart with the bus.

This left Hakan's father to face a very serious charge on his own. Of course, we know he is the innocent party. How can he be responsible for a failure on the driver's part - or even know what the driver had done? Nevertheless, he is the one charged with smuggling in a case that is currently before the court. He has not been jailed, but we are concerned that the court will be looking to punish someone, and since Hakan's father is the only one on hand, the focus will fall on him. Ultimately, we are counting on the fact that all the evidence against him is circumstantial, but be assured that we are doing everything we can to bring this crisis to a swift conclusion.

The court has been in recess for ten days but resumes on Monday when Hakan's father, Hakan and I will all be in Istanbul where the case is being heard. This will be our third journey to Istanbul since we arrived in Kavaklı, and there have been trips elsewhere to seek advice and counsel. We really have been on the go.

In the meantime, Hakan has been trying to set up the Kavaklı branch of WML. As long as we're in Turkey, it makes sense for us to have a base from which we can fill orders directly and supply items that Ken needs in London. When we can, we are buying skins (mostly sheep and mohair) and cutting them up ready to sew into jackets, coats, slippers and handbags. Since we don't have any fur machines(!), we have to ship these to London for Ken to complete.

The last few years have been so hard on the Beylers. As you are aware, the oldest son, Sami, managed to squander the family fortune, which means that Hakan's father (he has asked me to call him Baba) lost everything: factory, shops, stock and all. Having now seen two fortunes disappear, it must be soul-destroying to think of starting again. It was devastating enough to be so badly let down by his precious first-born son, but now, with the additional threat of prison hanging over him, it must be too much to bear. And yet, he does. He is such a brave and wonderful man. He is proud and does not want to show how much he suffers, but he does; he would not be human if he didn't. At times, he seems so sad, lost and bewildered.

Baba goes to his office most days (all that survives of Elmas, his shoe manufacturing business) and does god-knows what. There really isn't anything to do, and I'm sure this is why Hakan feels he can best help his father by giving him a renewed sense of purpose and a feeling of usefulness. My heart goes out to him. In the midst of all his own troubles, he has been unfailingly kind to me. Better than anyone else here, he recognizes some of my difficulties and takes every opportunity to explain things to me and help me with my Turkish. When words fail, he just pats me on my head. He has a great sense of humour, and I would paint an unfair picture of all that goes on here if I did not say that we have our share of laughs, too.

When we returned from our last trip to Istanbul, we came, the car packed to her roof with skins. We unloaded these into Baba's office, which has a little workshop above it. Today we set everyone working. Baba is really tired - we all are - but it's a good kind of tired, the kind that comes from work, not worry. I'm trying to learn everything as fast as I can because the day is going to come when Hakan will be in the army and unable to show us what to do. I need to make as much progress in my Turkish as possible. I have learned where to go to buy skins and what to look for, but I can't order. How frustrating!

Having caught you up with all the latest news, I now want to tell you something about my first impressions. Most people here have never travelled outside of Turkey, and they have limited knowledge of anything to do with the West. Stories of Christian crusaders marching across this part of the world, killing Muslims and so-called infidels as they went, linger long in the collective memory. This sombre background is coloured by modern-day impressions of the West which come from salacious news stories, outdated cowboy films and the Americans who inhabit the NATO bases around the country. (Everything about the extensive and slightly mysterious NATO base here in Kavaklı is Top Secret, but it seems to be generally accepted that it is a nuclear missile base.) None of these gives either a realistic or a flattering picture of everyday life in the western world.

Although there is widespread disgruntlement with the perceived failings of the American government, the presence of Americans is tolerated because we are despised far less than Russians and Communists. It's not so long ago that Russia was a bitter enemy of Turkey, and Communism is illegal here. America and all things American are merely the lesser of two evils. Besides, when we Yanks arrive, whether by means of NATO or otherwise, we bring not only money, but our presence which serves as a further bulwark against the Soviet threat, lurking just across the Black Sea at the end of the Bosphorus. Having said all that, and given that the Turks have no particular reason to regard me in a positive light, everyone has been warm and hospitable. They must have their misgivings, if not their suspicions, but they appear willing to give me a chance and remain open-hearted enough to make me feel welcome.

What I find so touching is how much they try to please me and how much they want me to like them. One dear little lady, a friend of Hakan's mother, brought me a package of sweets that had been part of a special ceremony at the mosque. She explained that these were given only to non-Muslims and would bring me good fortune (only to non-Muslims? Who else would she give them to?). I'm certain this was also meant as some sort of inducement to conversion, but that particular aspect was not mentioned. What really amused me was that she also brought some for Hakan. It's funny how so many people think he must be Christian... because he's been living in the West? because he has an American fiancée?

Much to my surprise and discomfort, I am the object of much curiosity. Kavaklı is a small provincial town where few foreign women have ever been seen. Americans from the local NATO base have their drinking hole at the best hotel, but they are all men. I have been told that there is an American woman married to a prominent doctor, and I have heard that there is a Peace Corps worker, but for the most part, we are a rare species. Although the women from the villages dress in the typical baggy *şalvar* trousers and loose tunics with their hair covered, the women in the town (including those in Hakan's family) dress much as western women do. However, women here do not wear short skirts (despite Hakan's fashion advice), nor do they wear slacks in public. Even so, my clothing is unusual as are my facial features, hair and skin, all of which mark me out as "different". I am also the subject of much comment because I drive a car. I am reliably informed that there are no other women drivers in town. (Cars are very much luxury items afforded only by the wealthy. Outside the cities, horse carts still far outnumber motor vehicles.) Wherever I go in Kavaklı, people stop and stare, some in a quite uninhibited manner. They don't mean to be rude; it's merely that their curiosity gets the best of them. It's somewhat unnerving, but maybe I'll get used to it... or maybe they'll get used to me.

Curiosity is not restricted to the people in town. Since my arrival, the Beylers are aware of a noticeable increase in the number of women and children congregating on the street in front of the house. Every once in a while, Hakan's mother insists that I go onto the balcony and wave. I dare not tell her that this gives me a pope-like feeling.

In addition to everything else, there has been a steady stream of guests. Ana, mother, says this is because everyone loves her. At one point last week, Hakan and I counted twelve visitors sitting in the parlour. Good manners dictate that friends, neighbours and relatives must come and welcome me; but the unceasing flow leads us to deduce that all the attention must be accounted for, at least in part, by my novelty value. It's not every day that a son brings home a foreign bride. Entertaining as this might be for the locals, I suspect there is more than a tinge of sympathy as well. The situation is not without problems.

Many people bring gifts. Among other things, I have received numerous bunches of flowers, a basket of grapes and a kilo of milk. A friend of the Beylers sent a platter of two kinds of *dolma.* Half were a rice mixture wrapped in vine leaves; the other half were green peppers stuffed with a lamb pilau. They were delicious and didn't last long.

The most unusual gift came from a neighbour who sent over a dish of what looked like pink meatballs. "Ah - the lady's specialty. How thoughtful, and all for you," was the gist of the conversation around this offering. The family insisted I should have one immediately. They appeared to be raw and I was hesitant, wondering if they should be cooked first, but also reluctant to quibble when the Beylers were all so anxious to see me dig in. I bit and chewed. A warm tingling sensation spread out from the roof of my mouth and increased in intensity until both my mouth and throat were on fire. The burning sensation kept building as I croaked for water. Knowing what was to come, Baba had been standing by but insisted on giving me bread. I was made aware that drinking water would actually make it worse, like adding fuel to the flames. The bread helped to absorb the heat, and I was further soothed with fruit and, eventually, water.

Naturally, they were all helpless with laughter; and when I could breathe, I had to laugh, too. "What do you call them?" I chokingly asked as tears streamed down my fevered face. I needed to find out so I would never eat them again. "They're called *çiğ köfte*, raw meatballs. They don't have to be cooked because the hot chilli peppers in the meat prepare it for eating. They are considered a delicacy and have been sent especially for you as a kind of welcome gift," explained Baba. "What kind of welcome is that?" was my response. In the retelling of the story for the entertainment of everyone they meet, not to mention anyone who happens by, the gift has now become known as *hoş geldin köfte,* "welcome meatballs". I am periodically asked if I would like some for supper.

Most recently, the little girl who lives downstairs wanted to give me a cat. I felt I had to decline the offer as the Beylers have three cats already. At the moment, this little girl is my best friend. Her name is Fatoş. She is two and speaks slightly more Turkish than I do. We have excellent understanding and communication.

I want to tell you a little more about the individual Beylers. I've already mentioned Baba in some detail, so I'll move on to Ana, an easily excitable woman who is still sizing me up. She has been polite and helpful, but she's struggling. She has my sympathy. The culture dictates that the parents decide who the children should marry. Not only has she had no say in the matter of Hakan's bride, but she's had his choice thrust on her. As a package, I must be difficult. Ana is in her early fifties. She doesn't have much formal education, and her life is her home and family. There's nothing complicated about her, and she leaves no one in any doubt about how she feels. The dilemma I present is that she's warming to me on a personal level; she just wishes I wouldn't marry her son. We're trying to find some common ground, which should be eased with her decision to give me a Turkish name. We've agreed that "Zeynep" suits me. Because "food" is neutral territory (or, more accurately, HER territory), it is a comfortable place to meet, and Ana has promised to teach me how to make Turkish dishes.

Neriman is Hakan's only sister. Like her parents, she is both fair and petite. Although they are all of average height in these parts, they are short by western standards. Neriman is twenty-seven, a year older than I am, and a mere eighteen months older than Hakan. She has long, dark hair with the facial features of her mother and the ready warmth of her father. I'm not sure where to begin with her; she's an absolute wonder of a girl, but I am just now beginning to get to know her. Although the official "head woman" is usually the oldest one in the family unit, in this instance, Neriman - I call her Abla (big sister, which is what Hakan calls her) - is really running the household. She sees to everything and is the soul of kindness and efficiency. Whereas Ana's natural tendency is to do the minimum and then go rest, Abla never stops working nor seems to have any time for herself. When she finally does sit down, she is sewing or knitting. I've noticed that with most of the women. They never sit idly when socializing and chatting; their fingers are always busy with some sort of handiwork.

Abla has fallen through the cracks of the culture. Before the bankruptcy, there were many real and potential suitors for her hand in marriage, but no one was ever good enough (according to Hakan). If one member of the family thought a young man suitable, someone else vetoed him. Although Abla would never have been forced to marry anyone she didn't want, I get the impression that she would have gone along with whatever her parents thought best. In any case, nothing happened, the bankruptcy occurred, her options were drastically narrowed, and then narrowed again by her advancing years. She's had a first-class education at the nearby Kavaklı Girls' Institute where she excelled in the domestic sciences. This background helps to make her an attractive proposition as a wife, not to mention her cheerful and accommodating nature.

These have been distressing days for her, going as she has from being an indulged only daughter to chief breadwinner in a very short period. The skills learned at the institute have been the basis for providing much-needed income when the Beylers fell on hard times. Abla has a reputation as an excellent dressmaker, and she is much sought-after in the neighbourhood not only because she is talented, but because she doesn't charge nearly enough. I am acutely aware that my entry into the household is unsettling for her. She's used to being the lone daughter, and now I'm here, hogging the limelight. She has been nothing but friendly and helpful to me, but I wonder how she really feels.

Although the tallest of the Beylers, Levent is the youngest family member. With an open, friendly face and handsome features arranged under thick brown hair and generous eyebrows, many would say he is the best looking of the children. I am finding it hard to get any consistent information about the breakdown he suffered during the bankruptcy. About six months ago, he was hospitalized for a month but is now at home where he spends most of his time since he doesn't go to school.

I like Levent a lot. If he were say, twelve years old, I would think he's altogether normal, but he's not twelve, and his troubles are evident in his immaturity. Always direct in his manner, he has a lot of nervous energy and is constantly on the move. Without a doubt, Hakan's presence here has helped him feel calmer and more settled. He adores Hakan and will do anything he says, which is a blessing as he never listens to his parents. Abla can deal with him, and I haven't had a problem. Levent and I have an agreement: I help him with his English, and he helps me with my Turkish. He is conscientious about this and uses every opportunity to explain things. He has good insight into what I can handle, realizing that I can cope only with basics (unlike Ana who thinks that if she speaks LOUDLY, I'll get the message).

This brings us to Sami, the sole person in all of Turkey whom I've met and don't like. At all. I suppose I'm not entirely objective and have been prejudiced from the start because of all that I have heard about him from Hakan. Probably because I don't respect him, I find him deeply unattractive. He's all edges and sharp angles and has none of the appealing physical traits that run through the rest of the Beylers, nor is his overall appearance helped by a thin face, a weak chin and a receding hairline. As well as displaying a pitiful little moustache that clings to his upper lip like a malnourished caterpillar, he seems to believe that the liberal application of cologne is a substitute for washing.

The first time I shook his hand (I think I was meant to kiss it), his grip was so limp and his hand was so clammy, I would not have been surprised to see that I had clasped a wet washcloth. I should probably try to make allowances for him because he has been through tough times. Then too, I'm sure he's an alcoholic, though no one says this out loud. But however he arrived at his present condition, I can't stand him. Whatever scrapes he has are of his own making, and worse, his irresponsible conduct has landed the whole family in devastating circumstances.

The difficulties begin with the fact that as the oldest - the Number One Son - he has been, in the way of Turkish first-born sons, pampered and indulged from the beginning. After he finished his military service, Baba entrusted him with his substantial business interests, handing over all responsibility and leaving him to his own devices. There had been some talk then of arranging a marriage for Sami, but he sidestepped that and has remained a bachelor. He is - age thirty-five - a spoiled brat.

Sami is completely self-centred. He never smiles or has a kind word for anyone. His usual mode of communication is shouting, his preferred subject is himself, and his favourite pastime is bragging. With epic self-regard, he is always complaining about his life, blaming everyone else for his misfortunes and bemoaning his weighty obligations. He is excessively nervous and never sits down, strutting around the room, demanding attention from one and all. When he comes to Kavaklı - luckily a rare event - he displays all the maturity of a toddler throwing a tantrum. He succeeds in upsetting everyone, making huge scenes and achieving nothing except bad feeling. If he doesn't fancy what Ana has prepared for the meal, he refuses to eat it and demands that she cook something else. To my total dismay and intense annoyance, she complies with this nonsense. He has no idea how his actions have affected the whole family, nor does he appear to feel any shame over his role in losing its wealth. He feels utterly sorry for himself and has no care for anyone else.

I'm trying hard to find something nice to say about him. Nope, I can't think of a thing. (I voice these opinions to Hakan and no one else).

I suppose that last rant was a bit of catharsis for me. So as not to end on a negative note, let me say that there is still so much to tell you that I hardly ever know where to begin - or end - as you can see. Right now, all is peace and calm (Sami has been and gone again). We are all sitting in the salon, the heart of the house. This is where the Beylers congregate, sitting around the edges of the room on comfortable divans, or at the large table in the middle where we have our meals. It's at this table that I set up my typewriter and pound away, while the household continues around me. Just now, they are teasing me about writing so much. With Hakan in his role as chief translator, I told Baba that because I can't talk much, I have to write a lot. Ana is knitting, Neriman is sewing, and Levent is creating affectionate confusion. Hakan is our pillar. We all rely on him.

Everyone sends greetings.

16 November 1969

Many thanks for your wonderful letters which come faithfully. Dad's letter to the Beylers was here when we returned last night from Istanbul. Hakan translated and it went down very well. It is a marvellous letter and the first time we have heard your candid views regarding your future son-in-law. Although you met him for just a few short days in London, I knew that you liked him, but your generous praise is reassuring. It is vital that his parents realize you hold him in high regard, especially since they tend to see him as something of a black sheep. You might presume that role would have been reserved for Sami, but Hakan is so different from most Turks, people here don't know what to make of him.

The court case on Monday was a perfect shambles. It was scheduled for 3:30 pm, but we didn't make it into court until 5:00. At this point, we found out that they had switched judges, and none of those presiding knew what was going on. (There is no trial by jury here. It's similar to France where cases are heard by three judges, one of whom presides and carries the most weight.) The police did not arrive to testify, and the upshot of the whole thing was a call for postponement until the end of December. I thought this sounded like good news, as if they were saying that the whole thing was not massively important and that no one was too excited about it. Hakan agreed, and he should know better than I. This gives us an opportunity to get Ken to produce necessary documentation from London, and then for us to go to Ankara where we hope to pull some strings to make the case go away. The outlook is brighter than it has been for a while, and we are all encouraged by what we hope is a turn for the better.

With regard to our business, we've been busy trying to organize ways and means to export. It's as complicated as it could be, and it's hard to comprehend the sense of this when we might assume that export would have enormous economic benefits for everyone. Nevertheless, we spent the rest of the week in Istanbul chasing from office to office, mostly getting nowhere. I like to believe that all the things we are learning the hard way now, will pay off in the future; that having done all this once, the next time will be easier. The Turks, however, have a deft way of defying logic. Tomorrow, we are going to Izmir to arrange for some forms there, and then we'll go back to Istanbul for more of the same.

It's great to get news from home. Thank you for sending our local "Daily Leader". I wonder how often it can have been sent so far away. For international reports, I've subscribed to TIME magazine. As my Turkish is a long way from dealing with the papers, it will be my sole means of getting any news in the foreseeable future.

It looks as if both Hakan and brother Bill are on tenterhooks over their military service. I'm sorry Bill didn't have the grades to stay in college, but I hear they are cutting back on the draft and that fewer men are being deployed to Vietnam. Fortunately Hakan doesn't have anything like that hanging over him. No. We're merely frustrated at being unable to find out much of anything with regard to when he will start or where he will be sent. He won't know until he begins how long he will have to serve. The standard period is two years, but we're hoping that his service may be reduced. He can only apply for exemptions (mainly on the grounds of education) once he's in. We're not planning to be married until he's done as having a foreign wife could affect his rank and privileges, as well as his exemptions. On the one hand, we want to get on and get this over with; on the other hand, the time has been useful for him to get the business under control, to deal with family troubles and for me, to have a period of transition before he is gone.

I have just come back from the balcony window. I heard something of a commotion going on outside and, on investigating, saw that the neighbourhood had turned out to watch a dancing bear. Really. Led on a short chain by his master, the brown bear was one of the mangiest I have ever seen. When upright, he was taller than the man, but looked far from threatening. Maybe he had been doped, but he looked only malnourished and pathetic. His owner looked much the same, so it is difficult to say who deserved the greater pity. The crowd was oblivious to my concerns about the welfare of both man and beast, simply clapping and applauding the little routines performed by the listless animal. The man collected quite a few coins, but judging by appearances, it hardly seems a lucrative way of earning a living.

The activity on the streets can be an entertainment in its own right. Some days it feels as if a circus is passing, when we have a steady procession of performers, artisans and hawkers, some accompanied by their horses or donkeys to carry the loads. They sell everything from baked goods, to fresh milk, to household utensils and offer a range of services and amusements. One of my favourites is the *şerbetçi,* sweet drink seller, who carries an ancient and exotic container on his back, pouring with impressive ceremony into one of the several glasses he keeps. Like many of the traditional sellers whose trade dates from Ottoman times, he wears a distinctive costume. This is not so much a uniform as a colourful version of traditional dress, the clothes providing an immediate identification of the work.

In the towns, men dot the pavements with their less portable goods and services. You may think you have seen shoeshine stands, but I am confident you have seen nothing that even vaguely resembles the impressive arrangements common on the city streets here. The ornately decorated, shiny brass display stands compete with each other to provide the most comprehensive array of fancy bottles, brushes and accoutrements of the trade. Almost everyone can afford the services of the shoeshine man, and they all do brisk business.

Something else that has caught my eye is the rows of typists who line the pavements, frequently outside a post office or government building. They seem to serve several purposes for they can type a letter to make it look more official, or they can take dictation from those who are illiterate, or they can translate old Arabic script into modern Turkish. One of the many great things the republic's founder, Atatürk, did for the country was to change to the Latin alphabet, thus simplifying Turkish and making it completely phonetic. It has certainly made my task of learning the language much easier.

Currently it's Ramadan, the month-long religious fast, roughly comparable to Lent but much stricter. Virtually everyone fasts from sunup to sundown throughout this period. It's a time of exceptional devotion to Allah, God, symbolized by sacrifice. Apart from those who are exempted from fasting (people in poor health, travellers, pregnant women, the very old and very young), everyone abstains from eating, drinking and smoking in daylight hours. Any form of sensory enjoyment is forbidden. Of course, alcohol is against Islam at any time. Neither Hakan nor I are fasting, though we try to be careful about where we eat when everyone around us is abstaining.

Just now, we are rapidly approaching sundown, and everyone is inching closer to a table overflowing with more kinds of food than we would have at a banquet. The normal evening meal consists of two or three courses, but during Ramadan, everyone goes overboard when there's an opportunity to eat. Bread, the foundation of every Turkish meal, goes on the table first. On this occasion, there is a huge stack of soda bread and special flat *pide* bread as well.

An enormous platter of salad, simply dressed with lemon and olive oil, rests in the middle; everyone will help themselves. This is in addition to another cold appetizer made with green beans and further separate dishes of *börek* (savoury pastries made with meat or cheese), two kinds of *dolma* (such as I had as a "gift" when I first arrived), chickpea purée, yoghurt like velvet and delicate slices of lightly fried courgettes. There is creamy lentil soup and a vegetable dish made with olive oil, eggplant and tomatoes. All of this will be followed by a tasty pilau served with slow-cooked lamb.

If anyone can stuff in anything more, there is fruit for dessert. Later on, tea will be served with rich *baklava* (layers of flaky pastry filled with ground nuts, marinated in syrup), and the heartiest souls will finish off with thick Turkish coffee. We'll indulge in this gluttonous meal and then get up at 4:00 am to eat another that will carry those fasting through the coming day. It is not hard to understand why Turkish cooking is regarded as one of the major cuisines of the world, nor why people do not necessarily lose weight during this period.

Now, I really must go eat!

23 November 1969

For those who are keeping records, I believe we have set one in recent days. With one round trip each to Izmir, Ankara and Istanbul, we have racked up 4500 kilometres (1800 miles) in the week, a total of 11,600 kilometres (7200 miles) since leaving London. Throughout our travels, Dagmar has never let us down. It's true that her windshield wipers work temperamentally, her horn, sporadically and her lights, not as much as we would like; but when we turn the key in the ignition, she starts every time. We've had her serviced twice and carried out some minor repairs, but excluding gas and oil, I don't think we've spent $20 on her. This is a reflection of how cheap things are, especially labour. What amazes me is that nothing daunts our mechanic. If he doesn't have the right part, he makes one or adapts something else. (This must account for all the old American cars on the roads here.) He worked all afternoon and charged us 20 Turkish Lira - about $2.00. Someone told us we were being ripped off because we're foreigners. Somehow, I can't get upset.

The trips to Izmir and Istanbul were for our WML business, but the trip to Ankara we made with Sami to see if we couldn't improve the prospects for Baba's court case, now that we have received all the documents from London.

As you know, Ankara is the capital of Turkey and was established as such by Kemal Atatürk, forty-six years ago when he founded the Republic of Turkey. He wanted a more centrally located hub for the new government than Istanbul, which is to the far northwest of the country and has all that is associated with empire. He selected this site - then a village of about 18,000 - because of its location at the heart of Anatolia. Today, it is a modern city with a population of over a million. Maybe it's because we spent most of our time in government buildings that I thought the city had a western feel to it, but for all its modernity, Ankara has none of the allure of Istanbul. However, we were not there to assess the architecture; we were there to see what we could do to help Baba.

The role of Helper-in-Chief fell to Sami, Hakan was there to deal with the documents from London, and I was along for the ride. One thing I'll say for Sami, he has, undeniably, some mighty impressive connections. We walked right into the sumptuous offices of the Finance Minister who greeted him as if he were an old friend, which I guess he is. Hakan had told me that Sami swings some weight, but I didn't realize how much. Supposedly, he knows Prime Minister Demirel as well, though we did not drop by for a visit.

I am mystified as to how he came by all this. Decidedly not through personal charm. Hakan couldn't fully explain it either. It has something to do with the friends and influence he bought when he had money. He hopes to use these same connections to restore his former fortunes, according to the Beylers who have great faith in his ability to regain their glory days. Money buys power and influence here in a way that I've not encountered before. I suppose we accept it for what it is and hope that it is of some benefit to Baba. I'm not sure what we achieved in Ankara. Procedures were clarified, documents were passed along, promises of help were made and assurances of a positive outcome were given. More wait and see, I suspect.

I haven't been able to follow this second American moon landing as closely as I followed the first from London, though I gather it has been an enormous success. From this vantage point, it's all somewhat irrelevant. When there is so much poverty around, missions to the moon seem to be the indulgence of a rich country where almost everyone has all the basics and quite a few luxuries as well.

I'm sure most Americans have little concept of how very much they have. Even in the relatively comfortable Beyler household, I can easily count the number of electrical appliances: radio, iron, big old Westinghouse refrigerator (the first in Kavaklı!), overhead lights (but no lamps), a small oven and Abla's sewing machine, a real luxury item. No TV, no vacuum cleaner (called an "electric broom" in Turkish), no washing machine. Many wealthier homes have a telephone, but this is an extravagance the Beylers could no longer justify. Although we do have running water, the supply is not to be taken for granted (especially during dry spells), and all the hot water must be heated either by a coal-fired stove or the butane gas in the kitchen. There is no central heating. In cold weather, the lone stove in the salon is used, although the parlour also has a stove which is lit when we have guests.

Nevertheless, even with relative material poverty, I am guessing that almost no one goes hungry. Turkey is agriculturally rich and bountiful. Thanks to a mild climate, crops are produced all year round. The fruits and vegetables would be the envy of the world, if only the world knew about them. As it happens, Turkey has recently started exporting to the Communist bloc, as well as to a few countries in Western Europe. The citizenry complains that the best of the produce is disappearing from the markets as it is skimmed off for export. Even at this time of year, the market stalls overflow with juicy apples, a variety of grapes, rosy tomatoes, black and green olives, lush lettuces and cabbages the size of beach balls. Frozen foods are both rare and expensive, but tinned products are more readily available. Still, why choose these when seasonal fresh produce is so full of flavour, abundant and cheap!

In spite of this plenty, the struggle for existence is a daily reality for many people, mostly those whom the Turks call "villagers" and the wider world would call peasants. These are the farmers who form the majority of the population. Those who are privileged to have a higher education are the elite, but this limited access to learning is changing for the better. Every Turkish village now has electricity and a school. The Turkish Parliament recently passed legislation requiring all children to attend full-time education for a minimum of five years. This is a giant step forward and will address the widespread problem of illiteracy.

I suspect that Turkey represents Capitalism in its rawest form. It's simple: there are no government benefits, so every able-bodied person works (as well as those who are not so able-bodied). I have seen child labourers throughout the workforce in shops, garages and factories. Once they are legally able to leave school, many families simply cannot afford for the children not to work. If they are not employed in small businesses, many will help to work the land. Perhaps surprisingly, I have seen few beggars on the streets, although there are some, and everyone has a few *kuruş*, cents, to hand over. Giving to the needy is a primary duty of Islam.

Hakan has been great, good to me and to us all. Sometimes I think we take him too much for granted. He really deserves most of the credit for my relatively easy adjustment to Turkey. He laid the groundwork in England and has prepared me for much of what I have encountered here. With all he has on his mind, he remains even-tempered and good-natured, though it plainly can't be easy.

Baba has just come home with a turkey. That doesn't mean he went to the supermarket and bought an oven-ready bird hygienically wrapped in a plastic bag. It means he went to the poultry market and selected a live fowl, which he brought home by the feet and is now gobble-gobbling around in the back yard. The poor thing is due for the chop tomorrow. Baba will perform the unsavoury deed; and Ana will pluck, clean and prepare it for our evening meal. This is all in my honour and right about Thanksgiving too, though there is no way they could know this. Hakan told them that the English for *hindi* is "Turkey", and naturally, they thought this was rather odd. They call it *hindi* because turkeys were believed to have come here originally from India, which they call "Hindi". Curioser and curioser.

Happy Thanksgiving to you all!

30 November 1969

If I had written this letter a few days ago, I could have said how pleasant the weather has been. Up until this week, we were having an especially warm Indian summer and were comfortable going out with light jackets or sweaters. They say that such weather is typical of this part of Turkey at this time of year. However, Ankara was cold and my fur coat felt cosy, while eastern Turkey had snow early in the month.

The climate changes as fast as the terrain, depending on whether we are on the coast or inland, how far north or south, and whether there is a mountain range for protection. Izmir, like most places in the southern part of the country, is mild most of the year because it is on the Aegean coast and protected by mountains. The climate there is much like northern Florida (they too, have palm trees). Whatever the norm, we've had a sudden temperature change and it feels like it's down to freezing, though that may be because we've had no chance to get used to it. I have trouble telling what the temperature is since I don't function yet in Centigrade. The good news is that it doesn't rain much, and the sun is nearly always out, so it's a welcome change from English gloom.

Your last letter had some special enclosures. We think Peter's photo is excellent, and all the Beylers agree that he is very handsome. We also passed around Mother's newspaper clipping, which caused much comment. Ana has expressed particular interest in Phyllis. She simply doesn't have a clue what to make of her recently acquired in-laws since she barely knows what to make of me. She tends to believe that you have a sort of Jet Set Lifestyle (you do travel a lot), and the picture from the local paper showing Mother with the other hospital volunteers confirms her deepest suspicions. As I sit here writing, she has asked me to convey her greetings to you, Mother. According to the culture, it would be inappropriate for her to send greetings to a strange man (sorry, Dad).

Last week, we made yet another trip to Istanbul where we spent the better part of a day sending your Christmas presents. Although not export in the business sense, it is every bit as complicated with endless forms to fill, documents to produce and officials to bribe. Really. We don't get anything done if we don't cross the relevant palms with silver, so to speak. Much of this has to do with the fact that government workers are so poorly paid, it is expected that the public help to finance their posts with *bahşiş,* gifts, a custom from the Arab world that spread via The Ottoman Empire throughout the Middle and Near East.

It is illegal to send cash through the post as you have done, but for which we thank you. The problem is that if we were to do everything legally, it would cost 100% in expenses, and then take weeks and weeks to clear through the bank. With the unreasonable laws that exist, it is no wonder there is corruption, as well as a thriving black economy.

During our latest trip to Istanbul, we were able to sell the mink pelts. We had been making enquiries about furriers who might be interested and had no difficulty finding someone who was only too eager to get his hands on luxury fur. Almost by definition, the customers for the resulting jackets and coats are wealthy, and money really is no object in this market. We sold for even more than we had anticipated and felt well rewarded for our trouble. Our nest-egg is replenished, and everyone is happy.

We usually have so much to do in Istanbul that we've rarely had time for sightseeing. Of course, I saw many of the key tourist attractions when I came last year, but this past week, we had to wait for the completion of another order of sheepskins, so we took the opportunity to look around. During every trip to Istanbul, we visit the Kapalı Çarşı, literally, the Covered Market, better known as The Grand Bazaar. This is Hakan Territory, his second home. It's hard by the University of Istanbul where he went to law school. In the midst of his studies, when the family fell into bankruptcy and could no longer finance his education, Hakan was thrown on his own resources. In Turkey, if you win a place at university, the tuition is free; but living in any city is expensive, and Istanbul is no exception.

At the end of his second year, when most of the students went home for the holidays, Hakan stayed on as hostel manager, earning money to continue his studies. Since there were many rooms vacant, he spotted an opportunity to offer tourist groups cheap accommodation, and when he was free, he volunteered to take them around the sites. He loved the contact with foreigners and welcomed the opportunity they provided to maintain the English he had learned during his year in California, and to develop his other language skills.

One day when he was out with a large group of Italian students, they mentioned that they would like to buy some leather goods, so Hakan took them to a suitable shop. He encouraged the students to buy, negotiating ably on their behalf. At the end of the buying spree, the shop's proprietor asked Hakan to come back to see him later in the day.

Curious to know what it was all about, he made his return visit around closing time. As the two sat and chatted over a glass of *çay*, the owner proffered 200TL. Bewildered, Hakan stared at the money, saying, "What is this?" The shopkeeper replied that he had done well with sales to the Italians, but Hakan had bargained hard, and he had not made his typical profit on the merchandise. While saying this, he withdrew another 100TL from his pocket and presented it as well. At this point, the clouds parted and the sun came out. Ah, yes. The man was paying him commission on the goods he had sold to Hakan's

Italians. Never betraying his inexperience in these matters, Hakan shook hands with his new partner and agreed to bring him more groups when he could. His shortage of funds was suddenly a thing of the past.

Throughout the rest of his law school days, Hakan continued to guide tourists and escorted them to stores where he was well rewarded. Everyone was satisfied: tourists, salesmen and Hakan. Following law school, he decided not only that he could he not afford two years of unpaid apprenticeship in a law firm, but that the opportunities afforded by the bazaar were irresistible. In addition to having a real degree of independence, he would also be able to help his family financially. With all this in mind, he quickly acquired his own shop, an apartment on the Bosphorus and a style of living that would be the dream of most young men.

The bazaar is a richly atmospheric warren of tightly packed little shops that goes on forever in an ancient maze of covered streets and alleys. It's a hive of activity, constantly abuzz with people from all walks of life and, undoubtedly, from all corners of the earth. Here, overloaded *hamals*, porters, carry gravity-defying loads on their backs, while tea boys rush from place-to-place, swinging their trays without spilling a drop, deftly dodging foreign tourists and local shoppers alike. The thick musty smells of enclosed spaces mingle with those of tobacco, leather and damp stone. The domed ceilings echo the myriad shouts of vendors, calls to prayer (the bazaar has its own mosque) and the endless invitations of salesmen to "Please come to my shop. I have beautiful leather jacket for you." I am quite certain that if it exists anywhere on the planet, it is probably available to be bought somewhere in the bazaar which has everything from antiques to wash tubs, gold jewellery to kitchen utensils, magic carpets to camel bells. I could write a book about the bazaar and the experiences Hakan had when he was there. But, enough for now.

The Grand Bazaar is a tough act to follow, but in addition to its labyrinthine delights, Hakan took me to some places I had not been before. On Sunday, we drove north along the Bosphorus to the Black Sea (imagine, the USSR on the other side) where we could see Russian ships on their way to the Mediterranean. Turkey controls this international waterway and permits the USSR to send commercial and trading ships back and forth; even Russian navy destroyers are known to cruise through. This is one of the reasons that the US courts Turkey. Well, that and the fact that both are NATO members, although according to the Turks, not enough courting is done. There is a lot of anti-American feeling here because the Turks believe they do not get sufficient recognition for their strategic NATO role. Greater acknowledgment and appreciation of their part in our security would have tremendous benefits. America may be strong, but it is not always smart.

We're as busy as ever. In addition to our standard line of sheepskin coats and waistcoats, Hakan has decided to make embroidered slippers and boots. If these go well, we'll expand the embroidery to the coats and jackets. He has also made up sample waistcoats and handbags which he hopes will be his entrée into a leather business in London. These are very trendy and should appeal to the youth market as some have lots of fringe and beads, while others have the embroidery already mentioned. Our two best customers are taking everything we can produce, which means we're not chasing business, and Hakan is free to develop some new ideas. We're very excited about the leather goods and anxious for reactions from customers in Europe. We're heading back to Istanbul this afternoon to send a big shipment of skins off to Ken. Things are going extremely well, and all the hard work is paying off.

Chapter 3

11 December 1969

I'm waiting in the car while Hakan is off on business, so thought I would take the opportunity to bring you up-to-date. We're parked outside a tannery in a district near the old city walls monopolized by these reeking factories. I'm desperate to distract myself from the viscous stench that clings to everything like a second skin. I swear that the huge clay vats and boiling cauldrons date from ancient times, but the eye-watering amalgamation of smells from rotting flesh, burning hair, biting acids and ripe manure makes no concession to modern noses. Oh, it's a glamorous life we lead!

We haven't been to Kavaklı for over a week, so I haven't read your latest letter. Right now, I am feeling deeply annoyed as I've lost the little Turkish phrase book that has been my constant companion and lifeline. I've scoured the bookstores here but can't find anything I like as much. I guess I'll just have to progress with my Turkish which is, by the way, coming along nicely. It makes such a difference when Turkish is about all I hear.

After almost a year's absence from Turkey, Hakan has come back to find a very different set of business and trading conditions. The sheepskin and mohair that he used to buy so readily are becoming increasingly hard to find. Everyone here wants them for export to the West, and it's become a seller's market. If we can find the skins, they want what Hakan regards as an exorbitant price. So he has decided that WML will now dress its own skins, and this is why it's taken us so long this trip. Our source for the raw skins is here in İstanbul, and we are arranging for them to be transported to Kavaklı where they will be dressed. From the tanners there, we can take them to our own workshop to be cut and prepared for shipment to London. I jokingly said to Hakan, "If we had the sheep, we'd have the whole process from beginning to end." "Why do you think I want a farm in Turkey?" he replied. Did I know he wants a farm in Turkey? I'm not sure I've heard that one before, but as an idea, it wouldn't surprise me. When it comes to business, he's always planning ahead.

This trip I have also - finally - been introduced to Metin, Hakan's best friend from law school days. When Hakan finished his studies, he stayed on to run his business in the Grand Bazaar. But he - like some other people I know - had itchy feet, and when the opportunity presented itself, Hakan made the decision to go to Europe. Meanwhile, Metin had law school to finish and remained behind to continue with that, followed by his legal apprenticeship, just now coming to a close. It was so obvious to me how much the two friends have missed each other and how much they relish catching up.

While we have been busy doing all that we had to do during the day, Metin has been working in one of the city's law firms. But we have all been free in the evenings and have had some memorable times, lingering over drawn-out meals, reflecting on life in general and the state of the world in particular.

Metin has a great sense of humour and is a talented storyteller. His recollections of their university escapades have had us in stitches. I can't remember when I have laughed so hard. According to these accounts, Metin was the reserved and conservative son of a prestigious family, a novice in the ways of the world, not terribly self-assured and not at all certain about Hakan and his impulsiveness. Hakan was, as Metin describes him, "confident, with nothing to be confident about." He was the wild child who was game for anything, anxious to take advantage of every opportunity. Where none existed, he would create one. Hakan would have the ideas, and Metin succeeded to varying degrees - or not at all - in tempering the extremes. If Hakan threw caution to the wind, Metin would point out the pitfalls and then, by his own admission, find himself tagging along, often picking up the pieces at the end. Whatever money they had, they shared, living it up in the bars and restaurants of Kumkapı when their monthly allowances arrived from home, and then eking out meals and entertainment as the month wore on.

Other friends from university and Hakan's days in the Grand Bazaar have also entertained us with food and stories. Everyone is so charming and gracious that it would be impossible not to be completely captivated by the Turks.

We're heading back to Kavaklı today. It's the last day of Ramadan, the end to the month of fasting. Not only is it unthinkable that we wouldn't be home for the ensuing three-day holiday (Ramadan Bayram), but also, there's little point in being anywhere else as everything will come to a halt for the celebrations. Along with everyone else, we will be expected to make the rounds of relatives to kiss hands and pay respects.

I have already met various members of the Beyler clan (mostly in Istanbul) and survived unscathed, but I suspect that the Kavaklı relatives, mainly from Ana's side, will be trickier. Hakan has warned me about Ana's mother and formidable older sister, Hatice Teyze (*teyze* is maternal aunt). I believe they are exceptionally religious and conservative in their views and are unlikely to respond warmly to my presence. Hakan describes his aunt as a "first-class Muslim". We shall see. I told Hakan that we'll go and do our duty. I'm not intentionally giving anyone any reason to criticize my behaviour (I probably come in for enough of that unintentionally). Then if they don't like me, well, that's their concern. I'll do my best, but I can't be responsible for what goes on in people's heads.

There is positively no sensation of Christmas here. The Turks know as much about Christmas as Americans know about Ramadan. On the drive between Istanbul and Kavaklı, we pass an American air force base at Yalova where I can see coloured lights and Christmas trees now. I'm surprised that I find this so exciting. You may recall that we used to come to Yalova across the Marmara Sea via ferry. We have recently discovered that since the Americans established a base here, there is an excellent road to Istanbul. It's possibly the best road in Turkey, built of course, for the convenience of Americans travelling back and forth to the big city. I know you are thrilled to learn that we are benefiting from American tax dollars at work here.

The last time I went home to Kavaklı, I found presents waiting for me: a lovely dress-length of red fabric and an elegant gold bangle. I was really touched - and really torn. They did this to please me. They are so sweet, but they simply cannot afford to make such gestures, so it's a fine balance to express appreciation without encouraging them to do more. Before I left, Abla measured me for the dress she is going to make from the fabric. She doesn't use ready-made patterns; we discussed the style, and she'll custom-make her own pattern using the measurements she's taken. I am so impressed. She told me it would be ready when I get back. Since it is the custom to have new clothes for the holiday, it will be my Ramadan Bayram dress, and I'm anxious to see it.

We're now back in Kavaklı. We stopped in Bursa for another of those fabulous baths which was just as exhilarating the second time around - and all for about $1. This trip Hakan knew the fellow who was working on the desk. He recognized Hakan from having been in high school with him. It seems my fiancé runs into someone he knows wherever we travel. He has one of those faces. Or is it the personality? Is it both? It's just as well he's decided not to live a life of crime. Hakan teases me that I only hang around here in the hopes of another trip to the Bursa baths. There might be something to that.

Once through the front door, I immediately found your fat envelope and tore it open. What a haul of goodies: cold tablets, tissues and newspaper clippings. I have started to receive the local newspapers you've been sending, though they sometimes arrive in batches of two or three. It occurs to me that things like tissues could be rolled up and sent inside the papers. I am a little concerned that fat envelopes could attract the wrong kind of attention. I am enclosing a Christmas card from Ana with this letter. She saw me preparing mine last week and wanted to find out more. Hakan explained the custom to her and left it at that. On our return today, she had the card stamped and ready. It was all her own idea to go out and buy a postcard of Kavaklı, and I was instructed to write an appropriate Christmas greeting for you all. This represents notable progress, don't you agree?

In addition to the welcome mail, I have come home to find my red dress, finished as promised. It is beautiful: a simple shift with long sleeves and a round neck. It fits perfectly. The material is a sort of silk crepe, and Abla has not only fully lined it, but also hand sewn a seed pearl motif around the neckline and cuffs. It's amazing. She's amazing!

The surprises did not end there. Along with everything else, I found a dog waiting for me. Hakan knows how much I like dogs and had suggested that I could have one here. Apparently he said something to Baba and, well, here he is. He's utterly adorable, a little bonbon brown puppy, mostly mutt, but with some claim to beagle parentage, I think. Levent calls him Tarzan.

We have something of a menagerie here these days. I've lost count of the number of cats we feed (they all remain firmly out of doors), but Kaplan is king. He is a mammoth ginger male with a white tummy, the most affectionate tomcat I have ever encountered. We always have a variety of chickens and, at the moment, two turkeys, which will no longer be with us come the end of *bayram*.

Hakan and I bought groceries all along the road to home. Every little village and town has its own specialty, so we made frequent stops to buy a lot (or as Hakan would say, "a lot, a lot, a lot") of gourmet indulgences. Our efforts resulted in a haul of apples, oranges and tangerines, the fruits of the season available at the roadside from the growers. Additionally, we bought homemade yoghurt, oversized loaves of freshly baked sesame bread, all kinds of nuts and dried fruit, plus a selection of cheeses, as well as fancy cakes and sweets. Everyone is very excited and looking forward to the imminent festivities.

Is there any news on Bill's impending military service? Though I know he will be away in California over the holidays, let me wish you all a Merry Christmas.

21 December 1969

We have just arrived home from Istanbul where we spent the last few days in frenzied activity. We're having a more or less last-ditch effort to get organized before Hakan finally goes into the army, sometime soon in the New Year. I hate to think of him going. As well as my sweetheart, he's been my constant companion and best friend, and I shall miss him desperately. However, once he goes, it will be the beginning, and we can start to count the days until his military service is over. I guess Bill is in much the same boat. We fervently hope he doesn't have to go to Vietnam. The reality of sending young men off to war hits home when it's someone close. But of course, every soldier is someone's son or husband or brother. Seen in this light, it becomes almost impossible to justify and certainly, no easier to accept.

Ramadan Bayram has come and gone and, with it, a whole new set of experiences. For the most part, I have withstood the scrutiny of the Beylers' relatives and friends. The noteworthy exception is the previously mentioned Hatice Teyze of the wholly justified formidable reputation. In the way of Turkish families, there was a falling out between Ana and her sister, and the two families have not spoken for many months. However, Abla, Hakan and I decided that we should do our *bayram* duty and pay our respects.

We turned up, unannounced, at their house in another part of town. Teyze's unmarried daughter, Şevkiye, lives at home. She is older than Neriman and is, therefore, Şevkiye Abla to us all. It was she who answered the door and ushered us, with austere cordiality, into a stark white, simply furnished interior. I felt as if I were in the isolation ward of a hospital. Teyze's husband, Murat Enişte (*enişte* is a not-blood-related uncle), sat in the corner of a divan, smiling politely. Teyze, a plainer, older, sterner version of Hakan's mother, entered the room only once and briefly. We were not introduced, nor did she acknowledge my presence - or Hakan's - in any way. (It is rumoured in their house that we bathe in wine.) The daughter, a pretty young woman who would have been even more attractive were she not so severely dressed, saw to all the formalities of the visit: cologne, refreshments, stilted conversation. Everything about the house and its residents seemed sterile.

It was at the point of departure that Ana and Teyze's mother bobbed up. She was delighted to see both her grandchildren, and she let me kiss her hand. Abla suggested that as we had a car, Grandmother should come back with us for a visit. Before anyone could counter the suggestion, and I suspect before Teyze found out what was going on, the elderly woman flew about putting a few items in a little bag and was ready to join us almost immediately.

Looking peevish and far from pleased with the entire situation, Teyze came to the door to see us off. I have to say that I hope it will be a very long spell before I again encounter such naked hostility. But now, what to do? Since we had not been introduced, the usual customs were thrown to the wind, and we were all floundering. I recalled my decision to avoid giving offence, so I approached Hakan's apparently unyielding aunt with what I hoped was my most winning new-girl smile, grabbed her hand and kissed it in the customary way. I was gratified to see her mouth open in sheer astonishment, though I'm not sure what it signified.

I doubt we'll be repeating that little charade any time soon, if only because Ana's temper bubbled over when we got back, and she discovered where we had been. Although she was upset about our visit to her sister, she quickly forgave us because she was happy that we had returned with her mother. Owing to frosty relations between the sisters, the two women had not seen each other for some months.

One of the nicest surprises of our *bayram* has been meeting Nina, grandmother. She is thought to be about eighty-five years old and is so tiny, stooped and thin, that every time she draws a breath, I feel as if it could be her last. But Nina is tougher than she looks and in possession of a robust sense of humour that kept her smiling and nodding as we teased her gently. She wears the long dress and headscarf that the older women traditionally adopt. When Abla last saw her grandmother, she joked that if Nina persisted in wearing her peasanty *şalvar* trousers underneath her dress, Abla wouldn't take her anywhere. As soon as Nina arrived, she briefly disappeared into a bedroom and returned to show us that the detested *şalvar* had vanished. Her legs now encased only in thick dark stockings, she hoped it would be acceptable for her to walk about in the front garden.

It's obvious that Nina is tickled to be here. She's religious in her way but finds her daughter's fundamentalism as tiresome as everyone else. At our house, she's able to engage in such sinful pastimes as playing cards and telling fortunes from either coffee cups or little piles of dried beans. Heady stuff. We rub along quite amicably. When I get up in the middle of the night for my routine trip to the loo, I always ask her if she wants to go, too. Consequently, I'm now her exclusive bathroom escort.

In an effort to say something nice to me, Nina told me the other day that I'm the best typist she's ever seen (that I am undoubtedly the only typist she's ever seen should not in any way diminish the compliment). What a sweetie! This week she told us she's thinking of getting married again. She has no one in particular in mind; she just likes the idea. Maybe it's her means of escaping life with Teyze. It's the custom for her to live with her oldest child, so she'll most likely stay about a month before going back home.

Tuesday evening, when some of the neighbours were here, Hakan and I got into a lively discussion with one of the men who had some interesting things to say about why Americans are so disliked in Turkey. His comments could have been taken from "The Ugly American" because it is something of a universal theme wherever we go. We don't bother to learn the language and customs of the country, offending local traditions in our ignorance. We act as if money can buy everything. We isolate ourselves in our NATO compounds, military quarters and air bases. Also, there is immense resentment because America sides with Greece over Cyprus, a problem about which the Turks are exceptionally sensitive, and a hot potato about which I suspect most Americans know nothing.

I had to agree with most of what he said. He was on a roll which began to disintegrate when he then went on to say that according to his reading, 95% of western children do not know who their fathers are. Everyone is aware of the rampant promiscuity of western women, and marriage does not ensure their fidelity one little bit. He warmed to his subject and continued at length on this theme. Unfortunately, my Turkish is far too limited to reply in any kind of effective way, but I was heartened to hear Hakan defend the honour of women throughout the western world. I found it alarming that an otherwise well-informed individual could hold such views and that many, if not most, would share his outlook.

I suppose it's not hard to appreciate why. Even the most respectable newspapers here are full of sensational tales of promiscuity and depravity from the rest of the world: sex fairs in Denmark, lurid stories from the hippy trail, casual sex in America, the grim murder of Sharon Tate. For the average Turk, the conduct of the foreign women he sees probably confirms what he has read. Western women wear short skirts and reveal far more flesh than any Turkish girl would dare; they are friendly and smile readily at total strangers. I have been guilty of both. Things that are done with harmless intent can be construed as lewd and inviting behaviour in this setting, and it's easy to see how misunderstandings can occur. I have met what must be hundreds of people since my arrival, and apart from Hakan's *teyze*, have encountered no open hostility. In fact, where people have ventured an opinion of me, it is generally agreed that I look like a "family girl", a label which presumably places me in the 5% of children who can identify their fathers. It's all so complex and yet so simple. We - I - have a mountain to climb.

I thought I would tell you a little bit about my home here. Turkey has sixty-seven provinces that, governmentally speaking, are comparable to states in the USA. Kavaklı is the name of the town in the province of Eskişehir, located in the northwest corner of an extensive republic spanning one thousand miles from west to east (Kansas City to Washington, DC), and four hundred miles north to south (Chicago to Memphis). The town is on a plain ringed by distant mountains which, because of their snow-capped peaks, are higher than they might appear. It's remarkable how they change with the light, looking at times comfy brown and mellow; at other times, pewter grey and gloomy; then, primal green and lofty; majestic purple at twilight. In Turkey, the winter landscape is usually green because there's relatively more rain, while in the summer everything turns brown because it is so hot and dry.

Kavaklı (population c.100,000) is a bustling metropolis located 160 miles from Istanbul and about the same distance again from Ankara. Apart from agriculture, the main activity in the area stems from all the military bases: one for the army, one for the air force, plus one for NATO. In the town itself, asphalt main streets have grown up without any discernible plan but seem to accommodate all the many little shops and businesses necessary to the conduct of everyday life. Many of the buildings in the middle of town are three or four stories high, the number of floors dwindling towards the outskirts. Pavements are rare, so the narrow roads are often choked with cyclists, shoppers, horse carts and tradesmen, all vying for the chance to move along the dusty streets.

The Beyler house sits on a hill about a mile from the centre of town, easily accessible by means of the frequent bus service. It's part of a relatively upmarket development of fifty houses, now about ten years old. It was something of a cosmopolitan innovation when planned and built. In the cities and towns of Turkey, there are very few single-family dwellings, and most people live in apartment blocks. Since there is no pressure from the population (at slightly over 30,000,000, it is less than that of the UK) and land is not in short supply, I have not worked out why this should be so; however, even wealthy families live, for the most part, in apartments.

The area where we live - Elli Evler, Fifty Houses - is unusual because each house is built for two families, one upstairs and one down; and every house has its own garden. The Beylers were among the first people to move into the street. They own the whole house and rent out the bottom floor. The upper floor is considered to be the better of the two because it has both front and back balconies and superior views.

After climbing the steps which lead to the entrance, the main door opens into a narrow hallway. This is where we take off our shoes and put on slippers because we never, ever wear street shoes in the house. (I think this is an excellent custom. Although the streets here are dirtier than in the West - horses and donkeys are common, remember - it is still an idea worthy of export.) To the right is the parlour, reserved mainly for entertaining any guests who visit. To the left is another little hall leading to the kitchen and the little room for the toilet. The basin for washing hands and brushing teeth is in this passage.

Back in the main hall, we walk straight ahead into what I call the salon, a sort of combined sitting and dining room. This is where we spend most of our time and have our meals. When the weather is warm, we're on the balcony which runs the length of the salon along the front of the house. This overlooks the street below as well as the further houses and buildings that spill downhill towards the town. The balcony is glassed in so it is snug and dry, but it's never warm enough to sit there in winter months. To the left through a door off the salon is a bedroom (Levent's) which leads onto the back balcony (where we hang the washing). Back at the entrance to the salon, if we walk straight ahead, there is another little foyer off which are two more bedrooms (one I share with Abla; the other is for the parents) and the bathroom.

The kitchen is basic; apart from simple storage, a stone worktop, and a sink for washing up, it contains only the refrigerator, a two-ring gas cooker and a little electric oven.

The bathroom here is, literally, just that - a sort of wet room for bathing - and contains the hot water tank and stove, which is stoked up with wood and coal on bath nights, about every two or three days. The warmth radiating from the stove heats the little room to steamy proportions. The water flows into a stone cauldron-sized container which rests on the floor. The bather sits on a low wooden stool and lathers up, then takes a hand bowl, dips out fresh water from the basin, and pours it over to rinse off. I love a Turkish bath. It's an efficient use of a scarce resource and lots of fun besides. All that splashing! In addition to bathing, all the laundry is done in the bathroom. Everything is washed by hand. I could never begin to tell you what hard work that is.

I cannot conclude this discussion without further mention of the toilet. As a ceramic engineer and manufacturer of "after dinner ware", my father will be particularly interested in this. It's a simple affair, consisting of a ceramic (sometimes marble) recessed tray in the floor. Near the back edge, there is a grapefruit-sized hole which connects to the soil pipe. In front of this are the slightly raised foot rests. Depending on our business (and whether the user is male or female), we either step forward onto these and hover above, or back onto them and hunker down. When we get the hang of hunkering, it's entirely comfortable. Duties completed, we look around for toilet paper. There is a conspicuous lack. Indeed, if there were any to be found, there would be no place to put it, for there is nothing that could be construed as a holder. The only thing in evidence is a little water tap quite close to the floor. Interesting. So I go to my fiancé and say:

"Uh, Hakan..."

"Yes?"

"There's no toilet paper in the. . . uh . . . toilet."

"I know. We use water."

"What do you mean 'We use water'?"

"We don't have paper, so we use water."

"Oh." There is a pause to consider this. "Well... how?" "How what?"

"How do you use... just... water?"

"Well – we take some water in the left hand and wash ourselves."

"You wash with your HAND?"

"No. Only with the LEFT hand."

"Ah." Another pause. "Why does it matter which hand you use?"

"Because we EAT with the right hand, and we WASH with the left hand. It's not hard, once you get used to it."

I was stunned into silence.

Truly, I try to do everything as the Turks do, but I have to admit that this is a tough one. I have been known to sneak furtively into the toilet with a tissue - even some expensively purchased toilet paper - clutched in my hot little hand. I'm wondering if toilet paper might readily adapt itself to rolled up newspapers. What do you think?

I have rattled on for far too long. They'll imagine I've lost my vocal chords. My Turkish is constantly improving and I estimate that my vocabulary is now somewhere in the region of five hundred words, which puts me roughly in the same category as a three-year-old. But I'm gaining!

Happy New Year to All!

31 December 1969

There's time for one last letter at the end of this amazing year. We arrived back in Kavaklı very early this morning, having concluded what we anticipate will have been our last Istanbul trip for a while. Your good letter was waiting here for me. I felt a twinge of homesickness as I read about all the wonderful choral music that Mother had prepared for the holiday season. Although I've not been a churchgoer for years, I do miss singing in the choir. I know it all went well. At this point, Mother, I'm sure you're breathing a sigh of relief and putting your feet up.

I failed to mention Christmas in my last letter. There were too many other matters on my mind, and to be honest, it was pretty much an ordinary day in these parts. Hakan and I cooked dinner, and the Beylers dined western style. It was basic stuff: lamb chops with mashed potatoes, green beans and tossed salad. It was a pleasant family meal, and everyone ate up.

Such excitement as we had that day was generated by the chaos of having two puppies in the house. Tarzan, the first puppy I wrote about, disappeared shortly after his arrival; we still aren't certain what happened to him. The newcomers are sweet little female pups. The first I selected from a litter in a nearby village. I thought I had chosen a male, but a closer inspection at home revealed that "he" is a "she". And I always did so well in biology, too. We changed the name from Aslan, lion, to Aslana, and that was that.

We acquired the second puppy, against my better judgment, about two days later. In this instance, the neighbours had a litter they were anxious to give away, and somehow, my name came up. Ha! This time my selection of a female was intentional as I decided it best to keep life simple.

The two dogs are as different as... well... as their names would suggest: the lioness and the lady. Aslana is a honey-coloured mutt with white paws and a black face. She's beginning to lose her puppy fat and is becoming long-legged and gangly. She's a tomboy. She loves to play and "fight" and has not the slightest intention of becoming a lady. That role belongs to the second pup, a plump, white dumpling of fluff with a few black markings. Her name IS Lady. I'm guessing both are roughly six weeks old, but Lady is about a third of Aslana's size. At the moment, I can hold her in the palm of my hand. I don't think she'll get much bigger than she is now, whereas Aslana looks as if she has legs to grow into.

Everyone adores Lady. She waddles about in her plucky little way, admired by one and all, something she thoroughly enjoys and has learned to manipulate. She's completely vain and, I suspect, silly. I prefer Aslana. She goes about her business, largely ignoring Lady until the latter picks a fight, probably to get yet more attention.

Many Turks are afraid of dogs, including both Ana and Abla, so it is extremely kind of them to let me have them at all. While the weather is cold and the pups are so young, they are allowed to reside on the closed-in balcony.

The Beylers have been very pleased to receive your Christmas card, especially Ana who has taken it out numerous times to show her friends and tell them all about your letter. It was handed around and much admired at Ana's monthly *gün*, held always on the 26th of each month. Most women have a fixed *gün*, day, when everyone knows that the lady of the house will be at home to receive visitors, an excellent way to be available for guests when most homes still don't have telephones. On these occasions, women friends drop by for an afternoon of chat and gossip. Lemon cologne is passed, cigarettes offered, tea and cakes are served. Children may or may not come along. Men, however, make themselves extremely scarce on these occasions, and I was left to fend for myself during my first *gün* last Friday. It's hard work trying to speak Turkish non-stop, not to mention being on display for an entire afternoon. But Hakan was my knight to the rescue when he came along later to take me away on "important business".

Ana has come a long way in her understanding of my limitations with Turkish. She realizes now that I am not going to be fluent overnight and has decided to help by simplifying her speech. Abla is good at this, too. We all have to figure out what works as we go along. Levent tries to use the English he has, so one way and another, we can manage key conversations. Even though Hakan will be leaving soon, I am quietly confident I'll be able to communicate with the Beylers. Sophisticated conversations are still a long way off, but if we can handle the basics, that will be progress.

Our most recent day in court was the 29th, the primary purpose of our last trip to Istanbul. The police gave their testimony - for the prosecution, I presume - but honestly, if they had been paid to do so, they could not have been more favourable witnesses for our side. The testifying officer said that as far as he was concerned, Baba had done nothing illegal and, in fact, had been unusually co-operative and helpful. He even said (so I am told) that he didn't see how the court could find him guilty!

Despite my doubts, Sami's influence appears to have been working. The court had received a personal letter from the Finance Minister saying that he endorsed the machines for legal entry into Turkey, and as soon as his letter has cleared through the Central Bank (don't ask me why it has to go through a bank), the machines should be ours again. They're worth about $4000 each, so we are anxious to retrieve them for more reasons than one. We are daringly hopeful that the next session on the 25th of February will bring this sorry tale to a conclusion and now feel we have grounds to be optimistic about the outcome.

Hakan is winding matters up here. The decision to dress the skins in Kavaklı has turned out even better than we had hoped. The tanner who worked on the first lot has done a beautiful job. Hakan is happy because he is paying less to get better quality skins and is able to get them as he needs them, something that was becoming a huge headache in Istanbul. They are in such demand that we could even sell them on here at a profit. While Hakan is away, much of this end of the business will fall on Baba's shoulders, but he is eager to help. It's a beneficial arrangement all around as it keeps a lot of the money here at home where it is needed, and at the same time, we gain enormously from Baba's assistance and advice. He is an astute businessman. It's easy to see where Hakan gets it.

Our New Year's Eve will be quiet, which suits us fine. We've done so much gadding about recently that it feels good to stay home. 1969 has been my best-ever year, although I say that at the end of every year. But this past one has been truly exceptional. Let's see what 1970 brings.

Greetings from all here (including Nina).

Part Two

Into the Army
January - December 1970

Chapter 4

7 January 1970

Hakan has gone into the army at last. I'm not happy he's gone; truth be told, he leaves a lingering sadness behind him, but it's a relief to get started on this journey. After much rigmarole yesterday, he finally entered the base in Kavaklı which, after all is said and done, is only one kilometre away, about two miles. I had thought that everyone did their boot camp locally, but I am now informed that this, most definitely, is not the case. It is more usual for young men to be sent across the country where they can expect to be out of contact for the first six months. It is only because of highly influential and powerful family connections that Hakan has been granted the extraordinary privilege of training in his hometown.

I don't pretend to comprehend how any of this works; it's all fairly murky to me. Getting a straight answer to anything is almost impossible, so I have decided not to analyse everything to death. In theory, we can expect to see little of him for several weeks, though we hope we might be permitted to visit him at the base for an hour or so now and again. But I don't believe any of this for a minute. Knowing how things work here and knowing my fiancé as I do, I have every confidence that Hakan will manoeuvre circumstances to his liking.

In the meantime, you should see him. His hair, which I've always liked, is without exaggeration, gone! Yesterday - on his 26th birthday - he had his head shaved, something he had to do before reporting to the base. I must say, I have never seen him looking so dismal. No doubt this had as much to do with the prospect before him as with the state of his head. He's absolutely dreading all this, and I can't blame him. With all the distractions after our arrival here, it has been easy to overlook the real reason we've come and just who, exactly, is paying the price.

Baba went to the base today to collect Hakan's civilian clothes and said that he looks worse than yesterday. His so-called uniform is baggy on him, and he is swimming in the trousers. Poor Dear. But - in true Hakan style - Baba found him translating a letter for the base commander (he is the equivalent of a one-star general), the two of them deep in conversation over coffee and cigarettes in the General's office. Already I can hear Hakan spinning tales of "Life in London" for the amusement of one and all. Baba says that he knows most of the high-ranking officers at the base; they are all fine men and will do what they can to make life as easy as possible. I think he underestimates what Hakan can do for himself!

But the days are not so bright without him. There is a big hole in the middle of my life, and I have a constant nagging sensation that something is wrong. Then I remember that he's not here, and I'm left feeling as empty as a Bulgarian gift shop. However, sorry as I am that he is gone, I was not prepared for the onslaught that hit the family. Ana hasn't stopped crying since he went, and Baba has been very grim. Maybe I don't understand parental grief, but it feels to me as if the atmosphere couldn't be sadder if he were dead. They probably regard me as hard-hearted because I'm not sobbing all over the place, but I don't see this as some sort of tragedy, and I surely don't suppose that crying will help anything. I've never been a weepy woman, and now would be a poor time to start. Abla is the only sensible one around at present, and as distractions help me, we've been keeping busy together. No doubt the others will calm down in a day or two.

I feel very lucky to have found myself in such a comfortable position. Of course, there are the minor irritations of everyday life, but we are all making efforts to accommodate each other in a situation that is new for everyone. I am so aware of their many kindnesses, and I hope I convey my gratitude to them.

Apart from Sami, I am fond of all the Beylers, but I am somewhat ambivalent where Ana is concerned. Sometimes I could shake her for letting the others treat her as they do, and then I'm angry with them for not showing her more respect. They have a tendency to talk about her as if she was not in the room, making unkind comments that must be hurtful. Mostly, they just ignore her. She and Abla bicker constantly, whereas Levent takes no notice of anything she says. I feel sorry for her because she loves them all and puts everyone else first, but she is very child-like and unable to stand up for herself in any way. The fact that she has been crying for two days over Hakan's departure shows that she doesn't have much sense of proportion, but it also shows that she is remarkably tender-hearted. She cries when she hurts and she laughs when she's happy, and she does one as easily as the other. No one ever compliments her or says anything nice to her, and I find this bewildering. Whatever her faults, she is Baba's wife, the mother of his children, and deserves better.

I have merely hinted at my observations to Hakan who, I am glad to say, is not part of this picture, but neither is he aware that an outsider might find something disturbing about the treatment of his mother. I guess that's part of the problem. It's gone on for so long that it all seems normal to the point where no one thinks there's anything wrong with it. I have made a secret decision of my own to conduct a campaign to build Ana's ego. Nothing about this is a big deal, but her everyday efforts go essentially unacknowledged and unappreciated, and that cannot be right. I'm not trying to start a revolution, but it would be good to repay some part of all that she does for me.

We really appreciated Dad's last letter which Hakan was able to see before he left. He is tickled to be known as PTB, Poor Turkish Boy. It appeals to his broad sense of humour. As for sending my comments on to President Nixon, I imagine you are referring to my previous observations about the conduct of Americans abroad, particularly those who represent the US Government. No matter where I've been in the world, I've encountered strong anti-American feeling. There were endless anti-Vietnam demonstrations at the US Embassy while I was in London, as there continue to be throughout Europe. Turkey is no exception. The Vietnam War is the excuse, but the feelings are genuine. It's a paradox that people are endlessly kind and hospitable to me, but have strong feelings regarding the failures of American foreign policy. They reject the government, not the people.

Thanks to Dad for sending the Titan bathroom brochure, viewed here with great interest. Although there are western-style bathrooms in some of the more modern buildings in the cities, most people here have seen them only in films, if they have seen them at all. The pictures have caused a lot of comment, and I can only imagine what they must make of them.

It sounds as if Bill has had quite an adventure in California but is now at something of a loose end waiting to hear about his military service. Without question, we appreciate what that's all about. We have had plenty to keep us occupied, but even so, it's hard to commit to anything when the future is so uncertain.

I am enclosing some squash seeds. If you can get them to grow, the resulting vegetables should be bigger than anything I've seen at home. Here, we save the seeds, dry them out, roast and salt them, then eat them as a snack. If you get that far, I can tell you later how to prepare the squash. Ana says you should plant three seeds together and wait for the flower to appear. If it does, it means you're doing well; otherwise, tough luck.

13 January 1970

I saw Hakan, aka PTB, on Monday. Some mail came through for him concerning the court case, so I thought he'd better have a look at it right away. I never dreamed it would be so easy. I drove up to the gate, asked for Hakan Beyler, and he turned up a few minutes later. He has entered the army in a sort of in-between period - that is - he won't start basic training until another group of soldiers arrives in March. The time he's here still counts towards his obligation, and he's supposed to be doing things like kitchen duty while he waits.

But not Hakan. He has landed himself a job as Personal Assistant to the General. This position seems to consist of sitting around smoking cigarettes, drinking endless glasses of *çay* and telling stories all day. Sometimes he does some translating, and occasionally, he types a letter. Honestly, I have to laugh. It looks to me as if this is about as good as it gets under the circumstances.

Hakan has it pretty cushy right now, but when the others come, he'll have to slog it out with the rest of them. He can apply for a commission once basic training is completed, so we are reasonably certain that he will eventually have junior officer status. Standard military service is two years. With a guaranteed six-month reduction for his university education, he will have to serve eighteen months maximum. If a miracle happens, he might get away with only six months, but that is highly unlikely, even with the family's impressive connections. It looks as if we can count on him remaining in Kavaklı for about eight months. After that, he will probably be transferred to one of the metropolitan bases where they will be anxious to make use of his languages and education.

I mentioned that Hakan had correspondence about the court case, and it now looks as if the Central Bank is going to get tricky over the legalities surrounding the fur machines. They want yet more forms, some of which will have to come from the Turkish Consulate in London. Hakan didn't look too thrilled about these latest developments but said that he and Baba will continue to do what they can. What other option is there?

PTB sends his thanks for all the birthday cards. I had forwarded them in the mail so he had lots to open. We celebrated his birthday the day before he left for the army. It all felt a little subdued, but we had a special dinner, and Ana made a cake. However, we didn't have any candles. It's not the custom here, and although I had brought some with me from England, I couldn't find them. I sang a solo "Happy Birthday" while Hakan beamed, and the rest of the family looked on, somewhat bemused by this bizarre ritual. I am in the process of knitting his birthday present, a green mohair sweater. It's been so long since I have knitted anything that I barely remembered how to hold the needles. Like all Turkish women, both Ana and Abla have years of experience in any kind of domestic skills and are on hand to help, a very useful thing for me. It is because of them that I have the courage to try a cable stitch on the front and sleeves, another first.

I am enclosing a photo of Levent which he asked me to send along. It was taken a couple of years ago, and he has changed considerably since then. Of course, he's older now and also much bigger, but he's an altogether fine-looking young man. I know he still has some difficulties, but I feel he would benefit enormously from going back to school. He has no self-confidence and needs constant reassurance, both of which I believe would be helped by having friends his own age. He just needs something else to think about, something interesting and stimulating in an otherwise humdrum routine. Everyone here babies him and lets him get away with what I regard as unacceptable behaviour, which I'm sure can't be doing him any good. But Levent is basically a nice kid who would do anything for me. He calls me Yenge, sister-in-law, and is always offering to run errands and help out. Approached in the right way, he's eager to please and, like most of us, thrives on praise. If he were treated more like an adult and less like a child, he probably would respond accordingly. Well, that's what I think. I have numerous strong opinions (you may have noticed), which I do try to temper for public consumption.

Far from being bored and at loose ends these days, my chief headache is that everyone is afraid that I'll become bored. Hakan must have said something to them about this as I am being bombarded with constant enquiries as to my state of happiness, along with a steady stream of offers to do this and that. They haven't learned yet that I am content to sit on my own and read or write. However, I have let it be known, in my most authoritative manner, that my Turkish studies are sacred. If I don't discipline myself and others on this matter, I'll never get anywhere with my lessons (I brought several textbooks with me), and right now, I feel that my first responsibility is to make progress in the language.

Apart from this study period, which I have set aside each morning after breakfast, I try to do what is expected of me in other ways. I have the dogs to look after, so a lot of time is taken up with cleaning the balcony and feeding and caring for them. At some point in the day, a delegation of neighbourhood children will arrive to play with the dogs, and then we all have to go for a walk. Abla always comes, too. We make an unsightly gaggle of women, children, dogs and bicycles processing the hilly roads, cats and chickens scattering in our wake. It reminds me of growing up in Applewold. It's the same sort of contained neighbourhood where all the kids play outside, and everyone is safe on the streets. The walks are immensely entertaining, and there is normally something to make us laugh. Yesterday Lady was trying to show off, missed her footing, and tumbled off a low ledge and down the hillside. She was furious and barked at us all as if to say it was our fault.

At least once a day, a neighbour or friend drops by, and then we have to rush around and change into nice clothes and serve tea and cakes. Sometimes either Abla or Ana will feel obliged to call on a woman friend, so it's on again with our finery and off to visit. I try to do a fair part of the housekeeping. Abla and I do most of our tasks together, and I do what I can to help her with her sewing. Admittedly, my skills in this area are limited, but I can baste and pick out stitches. She's so agreeable that it's a pleasure to work with her, and we are becoming good friends. Although Abla and I do a lot of the baking, Ana does most of the cooking. I want to learn to make some Turkish dishes, so I usually watch Ana prepare dinner.

In addition to all this, there is a daily trip to the tanners to monitor the dressing of the skins, business letters to write and the accounts to keep. Most days I write a letter to Hakan, and I am catching up on some others that are long overdue. When I do have a few minutes, I like to read, but Ana is bound to see this as a sign of boredom and rushes over to me with a deck of cards, insisting on a game. This can be a bit nerve-wracking. I'm not used to living in such close quarters with so many people, not to mention the cultural differences, but I remind myself that it would be much worse if I lived on my own and had nothing to do. The time flies, and often there are not enough hours in the day.

Tomorrow afternoon, Abla and I are going to the cinema with a friend of hers. I don't think I'm ready for a whole film in Turkish, but Abla said she wouldn't go without me, so I thought I should give it a try. Her friend, Fatma, speaks some English and has said she'll explain things to me. It will be another new experience.

We have been told that Hakan will be unable to leave the base for a month or six weeks, but we are going to visit him on Saturday. My letter next week may be delayed as Baba and I are planning a trip to Istanbul. We'll leave on the 18th and probably be gone about five days. I'll tell you everything when we get back.

Everyone sends greetings!

26 January 1970

Sorry I've been away from my typewriter for so long. I have arrived home to find three letters from you, including one from Bill. It's always fun to open your mail as I never know what I'll find inside.

After five months, I trust you're beginning to feel as if you belong in your new house. We love the photographs, which are of great interest, particularly the ones of the kitchen, luxurious beyond comprehension to the women here. But everyone's favourite snap is the one of Dad snoozing in his new lounge chair. Baba took special delight in that. All the US Dollars you send go into our savings pot, and the packages of tissues, along with the cold tablets, have arrived just as the last batch was running out. Thank you for everything.

Your letters and treats provided a much-needed boost to my flagging spirits, a gastronomic feast after nothing but dry crackers. During this past week, my morale slipped for the first time. But before I go into details of the trip, I have to tell you that PTB came home last weekend. O Happy Days! He had been gone two weeks, but after having been together constantly over recent months, it felt like two years.

Hakan's arrival had been planned as a surprise for me. They all knew he was coming home, but I was told only that we were going to the base to visit. When we arrived, he was waiting for us at the main gate and said, "Let's get out of here," and off we went, though I was somewhat stunned and not sure that I should be following his instruction so obligingly. From Saturday morning until Sunday evening, we had him to ourselves. I'm almost afraid to say that I think the army is agreeing with him. He has put on a little weight and says he's feeling better physically than he has for years. He's not overly fond of army food, but he says he gets so hungry that he eats everything. The meals seem to be nourishing as they have plenty of meat, fresh fruit and vegetables. Everyone calls him "English" and he has developed something of a reputation as an authority on languages.

Since all Turkish men are required to do military service, there are bases everywhere, and the army is massive. There are 18,000 soldiers here in Kavaklı alone. Hakan admits that he is seeing a side of life he had not seen before. Many of the soldiers are villagers who cannot read or write, and yet, they are often more motivated in the classroom than some of those who can. The Turks have a reputation for being fierce fighters and the Turkish army, for tough but effective training. Hakan says this is evident during exercises when all the men want to excel. On one occasion, Hakan was told to inspect the guns, which is rather amusing since he's had a gun in his hands about as frequently as I have. After he gave them what he thought was a thorough inspection, he approved their work, only to be asked by the soldiers themselves if they could have a longer period to do a better job. For many of the men from the villages, this experience is the highlight of their lives, perhaps the only time that they will ever travel away from their homes. They are proud to serve their county and take the whole experience extremely seriously. Though not a "my country right or wrong" sort of person, Hakan has acquired new respect for ordinary soldiers.

Something of which I have only recently become aware is what a roaring business the American government does in the arms trade. Was I ignorant or naive? Since I had no previous interest in the subject, I guess I had no reason to come across this. I suspect also, that this is an "export" that does not get much publicity, politically sensitive as it is. However, since leaving home, I have become increasingly aware of the enormous scale of this trade and realize now that if it were to cease, the American economy would be in serious trouble.

What has most recently brought this to my attention is that Hakan tells me that most things on their base have "Made in the USA" stamped on them, everything from the cutlery on the table to the weapons in the field. Only the uniforms are locally produced (and these appear to have been designed by a committee of monkeys). We are unsure about the explanation for all this. It's unlikely that the Turkish government could afford to buy so much equipment. Perhaps it is, at least in part, the gift of a rich NATO member to another NATO member, acknowledging Turkey's crucial role in protecting western interests against Soviet threats, and policing the strategically important Bosphorus. Whatever the reason, I find it most intriguing.

After Hakan's initial training starts in March, he'll probably be able to secure conventional leave papers, enabling him to come home every weekend. Naturally, there are no guarantees, but I have faith in Hakan. I have seen how he works in the army or, as Dad says, "How the army works for Hakan." We're looking forward to seeing him next on 17 February for the religious festival of Kurban Bayram. We are hopeful that he might get a four-day pass for the full holiday, but we shall have to wait and see about that. Meanwhile, we visit him at least once a week and count our blessings that he is so close and so accessible. The separation has made us both realize, now more than ever, how much we love and miss each other. Absence does, indeed, make the heart grow fonder.

Now about this trip. When Hakan and I entered Turkey, I was given the normal three-month tourist visa to stay. This applied to both me and the car, which has had to be registered in my name (rather than Hakan's) to avoid paying substantial duty. I was told that I should apply for a resident's visa once I was settled; however, whatever visa I have, the car can be validated for only three months at a time. Since I obviously intend to be here for longer, it seemed the easiest way to renew the car's permit was to leave the country with Dagmar and then, re-enter with her to secure the new document. Shortly after arriving here, I wrote to the US Consulate asking for advice, and the replying official said he could see nothing wrong with my proposal.

So last Monday, Baba, Abla, Levent and I set off for the border at Ipsala. I had planned to drive into Greece where I would stay a few hours, return with Dagmar, secure the new permit and pick up the Beylers (who would naturally not be accompanying me to Greece). From Ipsala, we would drive to Istanbul where we had some other business.

We left Kavaklı on a gloriously sunny, spring-like day, all of us looking forward to a pleasant, undemanding drive around the southern shore of the Sea of Marmara towards Greece to the west. A journey which started so full of promise began to deteriorate rapidly as we drove towards our destination. Temperatures dropped, clouds formed and darkened, and a light drizzle turned first to sleet and then to snow. Next, a veritable blizzard delivered more flurries than I had ever thought to see in Turkey. I did not know it could snow so hard or accumulate so quickly. Colour drained from the countryside as the hoary covering snuggled into place.

We had had no warning. The storm came from nowhere and caught all and sundry by surprise. With conditions worsening by the minute, we had to press on; we had to find somewhere to spend the night. Eventually, we were forced to stop at Keşan, a village near the border. Since everyone was stranded, we were exceedingly lucky to find accommodation for the night; but dinner was out of the question as everywhere had closed. So with little in the way of choice, we finished our picnic lunch and turned in early.

In the morning, we were up at first light, desperately in need of some hot breakfast. The only place in the village that appeared to be open was a ramshackle little café, set like a piece of golden amber in the desolate winter landscape. Its welcoming glow pulled us inside where the proprietor was doing a roaring trade in the house speciality which was soup. That's it, just soup. I neither knew nor cared what kind it was; it was exactly what we all needed. By squeezing in, we managed to make room for ourselves at one of the rough-hewn tables, jammed together to provide the maximum seating. The assembled multitude was composed mostly of hardened truck drivers who, with or without snow, obviously had made this place a regular stop. Abla and I were the lone women in the grisly throng. At first our presence caused some looks and nods, but the men soon settled back to their food and conversations.

There was no need to order. The tables were already loaded with baskets of crusty village bread, and steaming bowls were placed in front of us as we sat down. The sharp smell of lemon hit my nostrils as I plunged into liquid ambrosia. The soup was thick, rich and satisfying. We had all consumed two bowls and were preparing for our third before any of us slowed down, and I thought to find out what kind of soup it was. *"İşkembe,"* came the reply. I didn't recognize the word and had no dictionary handy; however, a demonstration of body parts soon conveyed the message. Stomach, tripe. Tripe soup. Ah. Well, bless the many sheep that had sacrificed their stomachs to our well-being that wintry morning. It was one of the best meals I have had in my life.

Fortified and eager to go, we surveyed the situation. It did not look promising. The snow had piled up to twenty centimetres, about eight inches. We had no winter tyres and no chains, nor any prospect of acquiring either. However, the snow on the roads did seem well packed from all the truck traffic. Measured progress might be possible. We decided to try for the border.

Although the actual accumulation decreased as we drove west, the temperature remained well below freezing, and the roads were thick with ice. It was treacherous and slow going. All three of my passengers sat squashed in the back for ballast, and I drove in second gear. We saw stranded vehicles all along the route, but Dagmar kept going, never so much as threatening to slide. I'll never know how or why. When we finally arrived at the Greek frontier, we all heaved sighs of relief and let the tension drain. But this was no time for complacency; we had tricky business ahead of us.

At this point, Baba took over and explained to the Turkish border official what I intended to do. I could see the man baulk. He said that they would not stop me driving through to Greece, but when I came back, the car would be confiscated unless I paid an exorbitant amount of duty (I believe $800 was mentioned). Dagmar is ten years old. We paid $150 for her in London, and even if I had had $800, I could not envision any conditions under which I would be inclined to leave it at the border. What to do? Much discussion, much faffing around.

Finally, the official proposed a welcome compromise: he said he would give the car a one-month extension, but after that, I would have to hand her over to the customs office in Kavaklı or be charged with a criminal offence. None of this made any sense based on what we had been told when we entered Turkey, when we took advice locally, or when I wrote to the consulate. However, the proposal meant that I was spared a trip to Greece, any question of duty was in remission, and I had a further month in which to figure out what to do. It looked like this was as good as it was going to get. We accepted the offer gratefully and completed the always attendant paperwork. It was time to head for Istanbul.

This, as you might imagine, was easier said than done. The weather had not improved one jot while we had been at Ipsala. Since there were no facilities at the border, we felt we had no alternative but to try and keep going. It soon became apparent that the blizzard had covered the entire region, and the roads got worse as we now headed east. Snow had moulded itself to the scenery and appeared in no hurry to depart. There was little traffic in either direction, and conditions deteriorated again as flurries drifted across the exposed tarmac.

About half way to our destination, near Tekirdağ, the snowfall had been exceptionally heavy, and the lightly travelled road had not been cleared. I could see we were headed for trouble, but turning around seemed less feasible than forging ahead. Before we knew it, we were forced to a halt in the middle of the road (insofar as I could actually determine where that was), stuck in a foot-high drift, absolutely unable to move.

No one said a word. The ensuing silence conveyed everything about our plight. I was worried. Really worried. The dilemma was potentially life threatening. We were in the middle of nowhere with almost no passing traffic. We were comfortable enough in a warm car, but we had left home on a sunny day with only jackets and sweaters. We had no coats, no boots, no shovel, no grit, no water and no food. We all understood the implications of our predicament; there was simply nothing to be said.

As we sat, each one of us deep in contemplation, I suddenly saw flashing lights in my rear view mirror. Some sort of emergency vehicle was gradually approaching; I could scarcely believe my eyes when a snowplough hove into view. Very considerately, it swerved around us and began to clear the road ahead. Hallelujah! As I turned the key in the ignition, Dagmar sprang to life and swung into action, following the heavy-duty plough all the way to snow-free roads. How could we ever thank our saviour? Our gratitude was beyond expression. The best we could do was honk the horn (mercifully working... just) and wave our thanks as we left him behind.

That day, the typical three-hour trip to Istanbul took us twelve hours, and we arrived at family friends feeling thoroughly depleted. Although I had done all the driving, I had felt partnered throughout by Dagmar, our utterly reliable little VW. With everything against her, she never faltered. Nevertheless, it had been a demanding trip, and I felt exhausted in every part of my body. Navigating the roads had required intense concentration, heightened by my fear of further snowdrifts and icy patches. Fatigue settled around me like a worn out blanket. A cosy haven had never been more welcome.

In Istanbul we took care of business for Baba and Hakan, and I made a trip to the American Consulate to see what help they could offer in matters concerning the car. The visit resulted in an unbroken record of requests for assistance, followed by their complete inability to provide so much as a helpful suggestion. While I fully appreciate that they cannot interfere in Turkish affairs, I was hoping someone could at least enlighten me as to my legal position. Every Turk consulted offers a different view, and I don't believe anyone has the definitive answer.

After the visit to the consulate, Baba and I made a trip to the bank to deposit some business money and, as we were leaving, got caught up with a group of youths who were pushing and jostling each other on the pavement outside. In the course of the ensuing melee, I was shoved up against the wall and knocked sidelong, while Baba was pushed to the ground by an apparent drunk. After a bit of a tussle, Baba nudged the fellow aside and got to his feet as the three ran off. We checked each other for signs of damage (nothing serious), straightened our clothing and were setting off again, when Baba suddenly realized that his wallet was missing. At this point, he turned around and started running full tilt down the street in the direction of the disappearing men. I tried to keep up with him, terrified that he might get in a fight, but lost him when he darted down an alley in hot pursuit. A few minutes later, he re-emerged, having lost the youths.

The wallet was long gone, of course. Still, it could have been worse. Although Baba had had about 40TL taken, we had just deposited $300, which the pickpockets might easily have stolen had they acted earlier. I cannot imagine why they didn't also grab my handbag and grow slightly faint considering the consequences of that. It contains everything necessary to the conduct of my life here: addresses, money, passport, car documents. It could have been so much worse!

Because we had heard that the roads were bad near Kavaklı, we delayed our trip home until Saturday morning. We had arrived in Istanbul via the western route around the Sea of Marmara, and we returned by way of its eastern shore, following the road through Yalova and Bursa to home. We had travelled full circle. The roads had cleared and we had no further snags - apart from a flat tyre. Never a dull moment. But after all that had already taken place, we took this in our stride. We had made an early departure from Istanbul and, on reaching Kavaklı, drove straight to the base to see Hakan who had been expecting us. After filling him in on everything, we came home. . . and got sick. Since we left Levent with Sami, I have no idea as to the state of his health, but the rest of us expect to make a swift recovery from "the grip".

When I got back, there was a letter from Ken who has a knack for turning the best laid plans into organized disaster. It was a most disheartening report on his business problems in London. Despite all that we have tried to do from this end, he blames Hakan for everything that is going wrong and takes no responsibility for resolving any of the difficulties. I have always felt that while Ken is a hard worker, he has nothing like Hakan's business acumen and, when left to his own devices, is more hindrance than help. After a week that piled headaches on top of obstacles, this was the final straw, and I burst into tears. While I felt much better for it afterwards, I was very sorry to have upset all the Beylers who were very concerned for me. A good night's sleep has improved my outlook considerably.

I don't know what will finally happen about Dagmar. Hakan was as surprised as we were about the trouble I had. We may have to hand her over at the end of February, but I am not convinced that customs are within their legal rights to confiscate my car. For myself, I do not anticipate any upsets over my request to remain here. Baba took me today to apply for a resident's visa, which would be valid for one year and could be renewed if necessary. These are generally granted if there is a legitimate reason to be in the country, but the visas are processed through Ankara, so we can only speculate as to how long everything might take.

Today is Ana's monthly *gün,* so I haven't yet had a chance to get back into any kind of routine. After being away for a week, I am dreadfully behind on everything. While I was gone, three American women came to visit, apparently all Kavaklı residents. The rumour spread that my mother had come, and the neighbours were disappointed when it turned out to be otherwise. The women left their names and addresses, and I am anxious to call on them before too much more time goes by.

I've been saving the best for last because I want to tell you how excited we both are about your decision to come to our wedding. The Beylers have been pestering me for weeks, trying to find out if you might attend. I have been saying "perhaps" and will probably continue with that line as I can pretty much guess what will happen once they hear you are definitely coming. Ana already has all the sleeping arrangements planned and is continually asking about your likes and dislikes. Your visit will be the social event of the year. Nothing is final, but let's cross our fingers that things work out for us all - and that the big day itself is not too far off.

I must stop. At the moment, I'm looking forward to Kurban Bayram and Hakan's four-day pass. Thinking about that, the wedding and your visit have fully restored my good spirits.

Chapter 5

2 February 1970

PTB came home yesterday, just for the day, and brought his superior officer with him. I drove out to the base in the morning and picked them up. As always, it was wonderful to have him here. Selim seemed very young but was agreeable company, and he welcomed a chance to get off the base and into a home. He comes from Konya, and like most of the men, he doesn't get to see his family very often.

I have heard so many stories about the physical punishment of soldiers, I am vastly relieved that Hakan has landed himself in such a favourable position. Beatings are common and, what I would regard as brutal punishments, are meted out for minor infractions. I don't pretend to comprehend why any of this is necessary, but Hakan says it's ingrained in the culture of the military and believed to be the best method of training the mostly young, mostly illiterate soldiers. Whatever the reasons, I am thankful that it's "so far, so good" for Hakan.

I have only just realized (though I'm sure he told me before) that Hakan is a first-rate football (soccer) player. One of his duties this past week has been training with the base football team for a big match with a team from another base. Apparently he kicked the winning whatever it is ... goal?... that gave his team the victory, after which there was much celebrating. He was extremely proud of himself not only because of the win, but also because he had acquitted himself with honour, taking into account both his advanced age and the fact that he has not played for years. He does look good - despite his short hair which is a little longer now - or maybe we're getting used to it. His face is filling out, and he says that with all the healthy food and exercise, he is feeling twenty-one again.

The dogs are extremely entertaining these days. Aslana is the offspring of an enormous shepherd's mastiff (here they are like wolves), and she is growing to a respectable size. She is intelligent, easy to train and has a friendly disposition. She loves to roam around but normally comes when I call or clap. The biggest bother is keeping her filled up, but luckily, this is not an expensive problem. For about ten cents a day, I can buy all the butcher's scraps I want, so both dogs eat well and are healthy.

Lady has grown some, but I can still hold her in one hand, so she's never going to be very big. She trots nonchalantly under Aslana's stomach and through her legs, largely ignored by her friend. Lady can be very excitable and sometimes jumps at Aslana, pretending to attack her. If she notices, Aslana might swat a paw in Lady's direction. But for the most part, they get along well and enjoy playing together. It turns out, however, that Lady is a barker and will persist until she gets what she wants. I'm going to have to think of a way to break her of this as it's driving me (and probably everyone else) crazy.

You asked about our finances. Fortunately, we are not dependent on Hakan's army pay, which amounts to 10TL (about $1.00) per month. Theoretically, he is supposed to receive pay comparable to that of American soldiers. The money is provided by NATO, but since it goes to the top of the Turkish chain of command and drifts downwards, he doesn't see much by the time it gets to his level. In fact to date, he has seen nothing at all. The top brass explain that the money is spent for the benefit of the soldiers; but so far, we have had difficulty trying to determine exactly what those benefits might be, or in what form, they might exist, if they existed at all. The money appears to line every pocket but his.

Now that we are filling WML orders directly from Turkey, we have income from that plus a rainy-day fund of about $300. Money has a different measure here. By western standards, everything is so inexpensive that our cash goes a very long way. We give Hakan's parents a weekly contribution towards household expenses, but other than that, we spend relatively little. I have reduced my smoking to two packs a week, and one of those is given away. Turkish-made cigarettes are so cheap that cost isn't a factor. Apart from stamps, petrol and a few miscellaneous items, I really don't need to spend much, so what we have is more than adequate.

I agree with Dad that the Turkish toilet is the most sanitary type for use in a public place. Who ever sits on a public toilet seat? I was interested in his comments (purely professional, of course) about the growing popularity of the bidet in the US. They are common in European (but not English) bathrooms, an excellent idea where water is in short supply; but for that reason, I cannot see them taking off in America.

Although the bidet is largely unknown here, they have their own solution to water shortages. Both men and women commonly shave off all body hair, and without being more explicit, I mean ALL body hair. Nisa, a neighbour woman who is a genuine character, both outspoken and shameless, felt compelled to enlighten me on this matter, complete with graphic demonstrations. If she hadn't been so earnest, I would have burst out laughing. As it is, I have followed her advice and have discovered there's merit in the method, though it's a bit draughty at first.

We are wondering how soon Bill will be called up now that he has had his physical examination. I did not realize his buddy John had recently returned from Vietnam. He must be overjoyed to be home again. He and Bill will have a lot to discuss. We sincerely trust that Bill won't need John's inside knowledge. Keep us posted, please.

9 February 1970

The past few days have been beautiful, warm and sunny, with a glacier blue sky. The buds on the almonds trees have recently burst forth, and the first snowdrops and crocuses are peeking through the damp winter soil. The air is sweet and as Hakan says, "crispy," and the surrounding landscape is turning the fragile shade of green that hints at new beginnings. The weather has provided the perfect excuse for Abla and me to take the dogs for numerous walks.

At the top of our street, there's a path down the knoll into open countryside. Each time we like to strike out in a different direction so as to vary the scenery. One day we discovered an old Ottoman fountain, big enough for horses to line up and drink. On another occasion, we came across a moss-covered collection of old clay pots, carefully lined up on a stone wall, apparently abandoned and forgotten. Wherever we go, we see weather-toughened shepherds spread across the hillsides, tending flocks of sheep and goats, the sounds of tinny bells floating along on the breeze. Wrapped in their protective felt shrouds, the men stare with both curiosity and suspicion. Strange dogs generally make them nervous, but I suspect they dismiss us as a rather harmless-looking band.

The dogs love these excursions. Aslana especially enjoys the exercise, chasing birds and barking at sheep, feeling very important when they run off. Not brave enough to wander on her own, Lady is just happy to be included in any outing. Yesterday, as we skirted around the edges of a nearby village, we saw a familiar figure waving to us. It was our milk lady at work in her garden, her cow and its calf grazing in the field behind. Together with her neat little house, they made a picture postcard scene of rural charm. Emine comes to the house everyday on her milk rounds, the gigantic metal container strapped in place on her donkey. The milk is still warm from the cow, but as it not pasteurized, we have to boil it to make it safe for drinking. I had always thought that "milk is milk", but this is noticeably better than anything I have ever had before. It gives new meaning to the word fresh.

From a distance, Emine looks like every other village woman, dressed as she is in her colourful head cloth and long dark coat, her brightly patterned *şalvar* flashing from inside the folds of her loose outer clothing. She is of indeterminate age. Her face is sun-baked and brown, her hands are large and work worn, her big chestnut eyes crinkle at the edges when she smiles. She looked delighted to see us and invited us in for *çay*. I had never been inside a village home before, so I was not sure what to expect.

From the outside, the red-roofed houses look like low single-room dwellings. They are made of mud bricks and faced with a kind of plaster that is usually whitewashed. The roofs get their colour from the terracotta tiles that cover most buildings in this part of the world. Some rural homes are shabby and run down, but many, like Emine's, are tidy and immaculate. As we went through the front door, it was immediately obvious that this was a home for both animals and humans. The first bare room, with its packed dirt floor, is where the animals spend the night. From there, we turned left and took off our shoes at another door leading into the domestic part of the house.

Emine's mother greeted us and invited us to make ourselves comfortable. The floor was covered in soft rag rugs, and plump cushions lined the walls to provide seating. Apart from a squat table off to the side (which I presumed comes out at mealtimes), there was no furniture in the room; and since there were no other rooms, the all-purpose living area must become a bedroom at night. A neat stack of bedding in one corner appeared to confirm this. There was a little kitchen area where the *çay* was made, but I was not able to see it very well. I was trying to absorb it all without being offensively curious.

We drank our tea and chatted before Emine invited us to inspect her garden, a term that hardly does justice to that varied, vast and fertile field. I assume they produce most of their own food and take their surplus to the local market. Even at this time of year, the garden was lush and bountiful. No wonder she is proud of it.

We tried to approach the cow and her calf, but they were shy of strangers. The dogs were as unsure of the cows as the cows were of the dogs, so neither got very close to the other. Meanwhile, I bribed the calf with some almond blossoms, and she let me stroke her. She was incredibly soft and completely adorable. I want a cow! As the dappled sunlight faded, Emine insisted on giving us armloads of green onions and carnations. We thanked her profusely, said our farewells and headed for home. It had been a lovely afternoon, a glimpse of another world.

I've started giving Levent more formal English lessons. It was his worst subject at school, and as it's been three years since he last attended, he's afraid he's going to forget everything he knew. He's not very patient and lacks the discipline to knuckle down to the sheer slog of learning. But he has appreciated from watching Hakan that languages are important and that other doors can open for him if he has good English. This is his motivation, and Baba backs us in this endeavour. Happily, Levent is persisting, and we're beginning to see some benefit. I am hoping it will be enough to build on.

Now that Abla and I are spending more time together, I'm getting to know her better. The walks have provided ideal opportunities to talk on a less superficial level. Lately, she has begun to confide in me, confirming some of my suspicions.

Until Hakan and I arrived in Turkey, Abla did virtually everything in the house. As a compliant and dutiful daughter, she obeys her parents in everything, whether reasonable or otherwise. It is clear that Baba adores his only daughter, and they are great companions; however, in the course of day-to-day living, he does not get between Ana and Neriman. The two of them argue constantly, but in the end, Abla always bows to her mother's wishes. Of course, all the housework that she did and still does is in addition to her sewing, which brings in much-needed income. It's only since we came that Ana has taken over the cooking and has involved herself in other aspects of the home, though just why our arrival should provide the catalyst for change, I'm not certain.

Ana can be a tyrant where Abla is concerned. If Abla gets a chance to sit down and read, Ana is on her immediately, insisting that there is other work to be done. When I asked Abla why Ana objects so strongly to her reading, she said that her mother is afraid she might discover "something she shouldn't". God forbid she should learn anything at her age! If she wants to visit friends, she faces a battle royal and, if finally given permission, is subjected on her return to serious questioning about where she has been, with whom, doing what and for how long. The implication is that she's probably been off meeting a man somewhere. This is patently ridiculous. I've only been here for five minutes, and I know Abla better than that.

Ana doesn't interfere with me directly. She would dearly love to order me about, but I'm an unknown quantity, and she's not sure of her ground. It can stay that way. I believe my behaviour is such that I'm in no need of supervision, but then, the same could be said of Abla. Now that I am more familiar with Ana's thinking, there are ploys we can use. For instance, we try to do most things together so that when our work is done, we can read at the same time. Ana is less likely to make it impossible for Abla if I am reading too, though she frequently spoils the quiet with her non-stop chatter, making concentration impossible. To put an end to this, we take our books and go off to the bedroom. This doesn't always succeed as she sometimes persists, knocking at the door with announcements of matters requiring our immediate attention. If there's something we want to do together, I do the asking as Ana never says "no" to me. If there's someone we want to visit, or someplace we want to go, Abla has to come with me as I clearly cannot be trusted out on my own, and the two of us can chaperone each other. Smart, eh?

Abla told me that her parents don't intend for her to marry. Evidently she overheard Baba telling one of his friends that she is too good for any man, and he could not imagine giving her away. To prove her point, she mentioned that at least a dozen young men and their families had approached the Beylers for her hand in marriage. In the end, all had been refused. I gather that there have been two engagements, one called one off by Baba, and the other, by Sami. Neriman had not been consulted about her feelings with regard to any of this.

Abla was not telling me all this to whine or complain, but because she has real concerns about her future. She doesn't give the impression of being overly bothered about not getting married, but she is anxious about the way in which she sees her life stretching ahead of her. She is an intelligent and clever young woman, but she is sorely lacking in any worldly knowledge. Ideally, she would like to get a job outside the house, but this is far easier said than done. All her education has been in the domestic sciences, so she doesn't have any skills which relate to the commercial world where, for instance, she might get a position in a bank. Although I have seen as many professional women (doctors, lawyers, and teachers) here as anywhere, jobs in the commercial world are not usually seen as acceptable for women, banks being the notable exception. Rates of unemployment are high, and generally speaking, it takes connections to get any decent sort of job, let alone the kind of work that would be culturally tolerable for a woman.

This is tricky territory. I have no business interfering with family matters in a culture in which I am the outsider; equally, I can't sit by and do nothing. I advised Abla to have a talk with Baba. I have found him generally open to reason, and they obviously have a close relationship. I think her feelings would come as something of a revelation to him, but I'm sure he would consider what she has to say. Apparently, she did just that because Hakan told me that Baba had paid him a visit at the base, saying he is worried about Neriman and hasn't the first idea what to do about her. They agreed that it would be sensible for her to look for job opportunities in Kavaklı; and also, that if anyone approached the family about a marriage, she should be consulted before any decisions were made. Since that visit, I see that Hakan is taking more notice of what goes on in the house and is siding with his sister when he sees Ana behaving in thoroughly ludicrous ways. Nothing is going to change overnight, but maybe we are moving in the right direction.

We have had some good news this week about the fur machines. According to Sami, we need only one last form to secure their return. He has been engineering the paperwork through the Central Bank in Ankara, so we hope he knows what he is talking about. I have written to London today to see if we can get this final piece of the puzzle, then we'll sit back and see what happens. If we can have everything ready, there is a reasonable chance the court will drop the case when it meets on 25 February. We are desperate for the machines to carry out our work here, so we have everything crossed.

We love the little earrings you sent. I see that Ana is wearing hers.

Greetings from all.

15 February 1970

Thank you for all the valentines! I had entirely forgotten about Valentine's Day as there is no such occasion here in Turkey. The postman has not recovered yet from delivering seven American envelopes in one day. He'll continue to "comment" until I tip him as this is his subtle way of letting me know that he, alone, is responsible for the delivery - or not - of my mail.

Hakan arrived today with his officer friend, Selim. When Hakan comes for the day, they frequently come together now. The two are as thick as matchmakers with a clutch of wealthy clients, such is the enthusiasm with which they plot and plan. Selim has taken a real interest in our business and has expressed a desire to come to London, but we'll have to see how matters unfold further down the line.

You will be as surprised as I was to learn that Hakan has now completed his basic training and passed with flying colours! Considering that he has barely held a rifle or marched around the parade ground, this is an extraordinary feat. It would appear that Hakan has made himself so valuable, no one wants to lose him to basic training for four months. As a result, he was nodded through with the group that finished last week and watched the entire proceedings from his window. He'll be put forward for officer training as soon as the next course opens up, but for the moment, he is proving himself useful in the General's office.

For someone not usually noted for his clerical skills, Hakan has been appalled by the total lack of organization in any of the office systems that are already in place, everything from the bath rota to guard duty, from the office files to the shambles they call a library. There is no discernible logic governing the many neat piles sitting around all over the place, with the result that no one can ever find anything, and important documents go missing. The General has been suitably struck by PTB's hard work and ability to bring order to chaos. High praise for a man who can never find matching socks, who has left most of his wardrobe strewn around Europe, and whose own paperwork would disappear into a black hole were it not for the sterling efforts of his tireless fiancée!

My chief concern is that his noble efforts are going to come to the attention of army headquarters and that he might be sent to Ankara. However, we shouldn't complain as he is being extraordinarily well treated, and we are as lucky as mice in a cheese shop. Tomorrow is the beginning of the four-day Kurban Bayram, but it is not yet certain whether he will get leave for this.

It's been a busy week with preparations for *bayram*. The holiday commemorates the story of Abraham and Isaac, when Abraham proved his love and devotion to God by offering his son as a sacrifice. According to the Koran (as well as the Bible), God ordered him to substitute a sheep instead. Today, those who can afford it slaughter a sheep and distribute the meat to the poor in memory of this event. It is said that the size of the sheep should reflect the size of the owner's sins, though in truth, it probably reflects the size of his purse.

It's interesting how this story pops up in all three major monotheistic religions. Just as Christianity grew out of Judaism, Islam started six hundred years after the birth of Jesus Christ and has its roots in both. Muslims recognize all the Old Testament prophets, regard Jesus as a great prophet and the Bible, as a holy book; but for them, the Koran (dictated by the Archangel Gabriel to The Prophet Mohammed) and its teachings supersede all that came before. According to Islam, Mohammed is not divine, but he is the last and greatest prophet. All three religions believe in the same God (Jehovah of the Jews and Allah of the Muslims).

I have read the Koran and find the similarities between it and the Bible astonishing in places. There are passages which are almost word-for-word the same. I'm not going to try to account for this, but I find it heartening that we are more alike than we think we are. Perhaps that's the answer ... to look for the things we have in common, rather than those that separate us. Sadly, and all too often, we remain largely ignorant of other beliefs and tend to see them as less worthy, less deserving of respect.

Abla and I have been paying some long overdue visits, two of them to women I've been meaning to meet for weeks. Nevin is a friend of Abla's. She's a math teacher who dabbles in languages, and I know she's been anxious to try out her English on me. We had a pleasant afternoon with her at the family home. She's single, but it is unthinkable that she would live alone. If an unmarried woman has living parents, she would continue to live with them; otherwise, she would take up residence with a suitable relative. The pressure to marry arises from the fact that there is no place for an unattached female in this society, but despite this, Nevin appears to manage very well. She has work she loves and a full life outside of school. She's part of a small but growing middle class that, I hope, signals the beginnings of more liberal attitudes toward the role of women in this culture.

Finally, I have met Ruth. You may recall that three Americans came to visit when we were in Istanbul; one of them was Ruth. She's married to a local doctor, has two children and has been here for seven years. That sounds like forever to me; apparently, it does to her, too. She met her husband when he was studying medicine in New York City. He told her that he had to come back to Turkey to do his military service, but after that, they would return to the US. Guess what? I'm still trying to work it all out, but it sounds to me as if her husband, Orhan, does whatever his mother tells him to do.

When Ruth first arrived in Turkey, she and her husband lived with his mother and Orhan's brother, his wife and their two children in a five-room house. They stayed there for five years until finally, the pressure of space, squeezed to the limits after the births of Ruth's two children, forced Ruth and Orhan to move out, taking his mother with them. It is customary for a widowed mother to live with her oldest son, so there is nothing unusual here in this arrangement. It was a relief for Ruth to have more space and, presumably, more peace and privacy, but her mother-in-law is very clear about her role as head woman in the house and the authority this gives her. Nothing gets done without her approval, and Orhan will do nothing against her wishes, nor does he permit Ruth to do so. At some point in the past, Mother announced that she didn't want to move to America, and so the family remains here in accordance with her wishes.

Ruth has been caught in a trap. She loves her husband and children but feels cheated because she has been forced to make her life in Turkey. She is unstinting in her criticisms, doubtless a significant factor in her unpopularity here. As a doctor's wife, and a foreign one at that, she has a high profile in the community, but she says what she thinks and does what she likes (outside the home), thereby committing an Unforgivable Sin.

But all that aside, we had a companionable afternoon. She served American coffee and American ice cream (sheer bliss!), supplied by her contacts through the American PX. We've agreed to get together again in a couple of weeks so I can meet the other women: one, the wife of the US Air Force officer in charge of the NATO base; the other, the Peace Corps worker who has been assigned to the nearby orphanage. Aren't we an unlikely set of comrades? Isn't it strange how such outwardly different people find mutual companionship in foreign places?

23 February 1970

Happy *Bayram* to you! It has been a hectic week with the holiday celebrations and the attendant hordes of visitors. Our sheep has been slaughtered (Don't ask. There are aspects of the culture and its rituals I don't need to know about in any detail.) and most of the meat distributed. The house has been fully occupied by neighbours, friends and relatives, both close and distant, for as much as twelve hours a day. I cannot calculate how much tea has been brewed and served to the assembled guests. I find it tricky trying to work out who everyone is and keeping up with the conversations. Fortunately for me, Hakan has been home the whole four days and is occasionally able to take me away from the unending stream. He refuses to take part in all this "nonsense" as he calls it, so if he doesn't participate, neither do I.

As there was something of a crisis at the base, it was touch and go as to whether he would make it at all. Two soldiers went AWOL and were found dead a few hours later, allegedly killed in a traffic accident. All leave was cancelled. All, except Hakan's. For reasons he cannot figure out, the General insisted he should go home. As Hakan says, "Why should he ca re about me?" But his leave has been my salvation, and we have had some memorable times with as many as twelve around the table, everyone laughing and joking, storytelling and reminiscing.

When things had cooled down at the base, Hakan's friend Selim joined us for a couple of days, along with another army friend, Ali, who came for an afternoon. The latter is an electrical engineer from eastern Turkey. Despite his formal education, he has some extraordinary ideas about women and their place, or lack of it. I did wonder if he was simply stirring up trouble when he made several gratuitous statements such as, "Any woman who is seen in public in a bathing suit will go straight to hell." "A good woman should have no education; she doesn't need this to do her duty to her husband and his family." Comments like that. I guess what I don't understand is why it is acceptable for him to make such remarks, yet if I were to reply (if I were linguistically able to reply), my response would be considered ill-mannered and rude. But then, I am a lowly woman who doesn't know her place.

If my behaviour did not reflect on Hakan's family, I would almost certainly have argued with him. As it was, Hakan saved the situation with appropriate diplomatic noises, while I sat compliantly in the corner (meek little woman that I am), doing a gentle simmer. Ali probably felt sorry for both Hakan and his parents. However, backward attitudes to one side (extremely difficult positioning for me), Ali was genial company. For much of the afternoon he had us in stitches, regaling us with the funny side of army life. There is one, apparently.

Before coming to Turkey, I had never fully appreciated what an art there is to accomplished storytelling. In the West, it doesn't come up that often since we're generally glued to television and rely on that for our day-to-day entertainment. Baba was the first to impress me by his ability to hold an audience with great stories. Hakan's friend Metin has this gift as does Ali, and a few others I have heard. Without television, what do people do in the evenings? In Turkey, they do what people have done for centuries... they sit around and talk, the women usually occupied with some kind of handiwork. Turks seem to need conversation as much as they need air to breathe.

Although all the Beylers have heard Baba's vast repertoire of family anecdotes and traditional folk tales (frequently involving an odd character called Nasreddin Hoca, a wise man who rides his donkey backwards), they ask for their favourites over and over again. Since all the stories are new to me, I have had the added pleasure of hearing them for the first time. The genuinely amazing thing is that language limitations notwithstanding, the tales are so well told that they come alive and are immediate in their simplicity. In addition to their entertainment value, they're important because they tell us where we come from and who we are.

As the narratives have unfolded, we've laughed until our sides ached, held our breaths in anticipation and been close to tears, such is the power of the spoken word in the hands of a gifted raconteur. In the course of one such cosy evening, I learned that Baba, whom I had believed to be an only child, had been the last of eight children born to his mother, Feride. He was the only one to survive beyond childhood. Isn't that impossibly sad? Can we imagine any woman in the western world today remaining sane after such overwhelming loss? It's one thing to hear about this, and another, to find out that it has occurred so close to home. I gather such tragedies were not exceptional at the time. Still, we have to wonder how it could be endured.

On a lighter note, Baba told us how, when he was a little boy, he would eagerly anticipate his grandfather's return at the end of each day. The old gentleman wore the then traditional Ottoman attire, including an abundant length of fabric wound round the waist, a sort of outsized cummerbund. Apart from being decorative, it served the practical purpose of enabling the wearer to use its copious folds as pockets in which to keep a pipe, tobacco, watch and money purse. It was Baba's "job" to unwind the waistband and scoop up the objects as they fell to the floor. Of course, Grandfather always saw to it that there were some sweets or coins for Baba to find. Isn't that a lovely memory? And who would ever hear about it if we were all sitting around in front of a TV? Truly, for every gain, something is a lost.

There had been some discussion about making a trip to the border to sort out the car business, while Hakan had this four-day pass. In the end, we couldn't go as he had day passes only, and it was impossible for him to leave Kavaklı. After putting our heads together with Baba and Sami, we came up with a loophole in the law that could be used to justify retaining Dagmar for a further month. Yet another reprieve.

Speaking of Sami, Old Cheerfulness himself spent the week with us. I hope you don't think I am exaggerating his malevolent influence on the atmosphere here. If he occasionally manages something approaching normal, let alone pleasant behaviour, we can be sure that this is the calm before the storm. He's never happier than when he has everyone dancing attendance around him, the entire household in an uproar.

Sami has an enormous capacity for yelling at the top of his lungs, starting first thing in the morning - if 11:00 am can be called "first thing" - when he shouts from his bed for someone to bring him his *çay*. For the most part, I say little and stay out of his way. As Hakan's older brother and the first son, I am expected to kiss his hand, which he always proffers when we meet. I prefer to shake it "warmly". I cannot bring myself to kiss his hand, though in principle I have no objection to this custom as a means of showing respect. Nor can I bring myself to call him *ağabey,* older brother, which also denotes more respect than he merits.

On the whole, he ignores me as the easiest way to deal with an unknown quantity. But I promise you this: if he ever turns his venom on me, I shall find the Turkish I need to give him the reply he so richly deserves.

On an altogether pleasanter topic, Hakan and I had been hoping that we might be able to start planning our wedding, but the immediate future is still uncertain. We have been fervently wishing that he could get away with a six-month service obligation, but this is highly doubtful, though it is perhaps too soon dismiss the possibility altogether. Our real concern is that he will be transferred to Ankara, in which case he most likely will not be out in fewer than eighteen months. Whatever the timescale, we should be able to give you at least two months notice prior to the Big Day. I get so excited just thinking about it all and wish the army could be more sympathetic to our plans.

With "army" on my mind, what is the latest with Bill? Does he know yet where he will go for boot camp? With his college background, can he apply for officer training? Even though I am unfamiliar with how these institutions operate, I wouldn't be surprised if the inner workings of the US Army are as big a mystery as those of its Turkish counterpart.

Now that I am spending more time here in the neighbourhood, I am getting to know some of the people nearby. Ana has a brother in Manisa (a sizeable town north of Izmir), her formidable older sister whom I met last *bayram,* and a brother living about a mile away in the next village. He is Hüseyin Dayı (maternal uncle), married to

Rukiye Yenge (*yenge* is the term for sister-in-law used here as we would use "aunt"). They have three children: a daughter and two sons.

Dayı is an interesting character. He is generally reserved and quiet, but when he speaks, it is advisable to listen. What he has to say is often witty and reflects a dry, incisive sense of humour. Dayı is one of those people who has dabbled in many things. Like Baba, he had a successful business in Bulgaria, but when the Communists came to power, everything changed. Baba first brought his own family to Turkey, later helping all of Ana's to escape and start new lives here. I have yet to put all the pieces together, but I am under the impression that Dayı started a sausage factory and later, had a little restaurant. Whatever his early enterprises, he seems to have fallen on hard times as their home is modest, and he now works as a chef in a nearby factory. Baba took the Titan brochure for Dayı to see what Dad's work involves. He was favourably impressed and asked us to send you his regards.

I am enclosing a leaflet for TesTape. These are testing strips for our neighbour who is diabetic and uses them to check his blood sugar levels. As they are not available here, his wife has asked if you could find some and send them. Each packet contains enough for about six months, so a little goes a long way.

The Vedats are a wonderful family. Mecit Bey, Mr, is married to Aylin (since she's older, we call her Aylin Abla), and they have three handsome children: two older girls and a little boy of three who is a real handful. According to tradition, Mecit's mother lives with them, too.

Abla and Aylin are good friends who help and support each other with the demands of everyday domestic life. While Aylin provides advice and guidance to her younger friend, Neriman Abla helps in their household with babysitting and kitchen support when Aylin has her *gün*. Most days Abla visits Aylin for 4:00 *çay*. Sometimes I go along, but I don't like to intrude too much on this opportunity for Abla to get away from the house and have time for something of her own. The bathroom brochure has also made its way to the Vedat home. They are in the process of building what will be the first eight-story apartment block in Kavaklı. Mecit Bey was so taken with the bathrooms in the photos that he has asked to borrow the booklet to use for design ideas in the new building. I was tempted to tell him you could supply the Titan fixtures if he really wanted them!

Chapter 6

3 March 1970

The much-anticipated court case has come and gone, and little, if anything, has changed. The outlook remains much the same as it had been before the last session. We are still optimistic about retrieving the machines, but the authorization did not come through for this sitting. The court meets again in April, so we continue to wait, hoping that clearance comes before then so that the process need not drag on.

Bill must be due to leave for Fort Dix. Do let us have his news. We are so anxious to find out what happens next. Hakan wants to know how US Army life compares with his. Somehow, I can't imagine it will be the same. Things work differently here. Also, I am stunned to learn that Peter has had yet another accident with the car. How many is this? Thank heavens none of them involved anything more than vehicle damage, but I'm sure you've all had quite enough of that!

This past week has not been one of my better ones in terms of fitting in with the indigenous culture. The first little upset came on bath night when Ana announced that she was going to give me a bath. I stared at her incredulously, certain she must be joking. She wasn't. I blushed a deep scarlet. Despite her best efforts to get me to the local *hamam*, I have managed so far, to escape this. I am stared at quite enough, fully clothed, to realize that my appearance at the women's baths would cause a sensation. I know from Abla (who won't go either) that it is the custom for the groom's mother, along with other female relatives, to take the prospective daughter-in-law for a bath. As all the women are usually naked, at least from the waist up, it's a chance to inspect the bride and make sure everything is as it should be. Sorry, folks, this is where I draw the line.

Although Hakan was present when this discussion got going, he took more time than I thought strictly necessary to come to my rescue. I'm positive he was enjoying my discomfort and was waiting to see exactly how I would extricate myself. For my part, I was spluttering and speechless, lacking as I do the necessary Turkish to explain myself but not wanting to give more offence than I already had. Ana thought that by not involving her friends and relatives, she was making more than enough concessions, and from her point of view, I guess she was right. But the fact remained that she was not going to give me a bath. Absolutely not. Hakan finally declared that she would have to take me on faith as the practice was not part of my culture, and I would find the experience too embarrassing. While I was relieved, Ana sulked. But the subject is firmly closed.

The second incident came on Sunday morning when Hakan and I were chatting together as I did some ironing. He suggested coffee, which seemed like a good idea, and went off to the kitchen to make it. When his mother found Hakan in the kitchen, she threw a mini-fit that flared like fat hitting hot coals. Presumably, it was shocking enough that he had been reduced to making coffee for himself, but for me as well? Unthinkable.

Luckily, all this rolls off Hakan's back, and he does not feel his masculinity is threatened by entering the kitchen. I can see that Ana regards Hakan as henpecked and feels that I get away with far too much. Sometimes I wonder if he does these things simply to provoke his mother. To understand Ana's concerns, you need to appreciate the highly differentiated roles of the sexes and their relationship to each other in this society.

A Turkish man is the absolute ruler of his domain, whether a sultan on his throne or a farmer in his hovel. He is the provider of everything, and it is the job of the women to serve him in all respects. Serve is the key word here. The concept of marriage as a partnership is unknown. It is the wife's job to do her husband's bidding, indeed, to anticipate his needs. For instance, no self-respecting Turkish husband would dream of stirring his own tea or coffee. One of the women in the household will do this for him and present it, ready to drink.

Another example might occur with a man sitting next to a table where he keeps his cigarettes. He will bellow for someone to bring them to him, whereupon the wife or daughter, most likely elbow-deep in the family laundry or some other chore, will drop everything and hasten to his side, pick up the pack that has been only inches away, and light the cigarette for him. Women light cigarettes for men in Turkey, not men for women, and younger people never smoke in front of older people. Equally, women help men on with their coats, hold doors for men and provide the little courtesies that we play out in the reverse.

There is also strict division of labour. Anything that takes place around the home is "women's work". This category is conveniently broad enough to include working in the fields, while the men smoke *nargile*, water pipes, and take care of world affairs at the coffee houses. In the Beyler household, this covers chopping and stacking wood and bringing in the coal, all of which Ana, Neriman and I do. Levent wouldn't dream of dirtying his hands to help us with such humble tasks, nor is he expected to do so. Oddly enough, shopping falls somewhere between the divisions as traditionally, women did not leave the home, and patently, no decent woman would barter in the marketplace.

But times are changing. Although it is mainly women who now shop for groceries, Levent is often despatched to bring something from town, and Baba will happily buy food for the table. However, it is because of the old attitudes about women not being seen outside the home that there are strong reservations regarding women in the work place. This is looked upon as a "bad thing", a situation in which no self-respecting woman should find herself. The many women in the professions are looked upon as another species and seem to provide no example to those with less education. While Baba has agreed in principle that Abla can look for work in town, it is impossible to engage him in any conversation on the matter. He categorically refuses to discuss it. I'm sure he believes it will reflect badly on Abla and, by extension, on the family, further hindering her chances of a good marriage. Nothing is simple.

It is my considered opinion that the women here are too accepting of their roles, but then, I would say that, wouldn't I? Men can do pretty much as they like without any reference to women at all. The women would never expect to be consulted about anything more important than the quality of the tea they serve, and this seems to suit them, too. Most are poorly educated with few expectations. All have grasped that their world has no role for them unless they are married. Men also need to be married, for all the obvious reasons, but this commitment need not otherwise interfere with their manly pursuits.

Everything is hierarchical so that the head of the house is served first, then the sons. Daughters are not worth mentioning. Whereas age is the usual determining factor in the male hierarchy of the family, among the women it is largely determined by the man to whom the woman is married (or not), and his place in the order of things. Therefore, the wife of the oldest male is traditionally the head woman... unless his mother is alive, in which case, she is in charge. Mothers outrank wives.

The result of all this is a system of complete order, stability and security. Everyone knows his/her place and understands precisely what is expected. The family is everything, and everyone in it will be cared for and protected. In return for this, each member is expected to do his/her duty for the greater benefit of all. Any notion of personal fulfilment does not come into it. Although the men appear to have the best of all possible worlds, I have heard some of them complain that their wives are of no help when it comes to bearing the heavy burdens of familial responsibility. Despite this, they undermine any chance of breaking the cycle by failing to give their daughters a decent education or allowing them the degree of independence they need to become fully-fledged partners in work or marriage. The women are no better than the men when it comes to change.

Having said all this, Baba reflects shifting attitudes because, having come from culturally westernized Bulgaria, he has already experienced a more liberal view of the world. After all, he ensured that Neriman was well-educated, and while he currently opposes her holding a job, I suspect that he could be persuaded if the right opportunity actually presented itself. He has been extremely sympathetic to the modern relationship that Hakan and I have (you are my parents and I am not going any further than that) and has surprised me with some of the more broadminded opinions he has expressed. He has given us permission to smoke in front of him, a gesture we have readily accepted, but I have not agreed that he should light my cigarettes for me. This seems a step too far, even for a Europeanized Turk. I am more than happy to extend this small courtesy to a man who has shown me nothing but kindness and support, and for whom I have the greatest respect.

I must tell you that my family photos have been greeted with immense curiosity here. Everything is passed around the neighbourhood. No one can believe that Mother has turned fifty. She comes in for much admiration, and all the women want to know as much as possible about Phyllis. Honestly, if Jackie Kennedy were my mother, they could not be more interested. They think Mother must be famous since she has her picture in the paper so often. All the newspapers here are produced in the major cities, so the concept of a local paper is not a familiar one.

Once again, I have gone on at length, but now I must go - I really must.

8 March 1970

The first of the tissue packs arrived in rolled up newspaper this week. What is interesting is that the whole lot had been opened by customs and passed without any charges for duty. Hooray! PTB, however, is appalled by the amount you spend on postage and estimates that we are cheating you out of, at least, a pair of shoes a month, given the current rate of expenditure. I am most grateful. Let me assure you that the many things you enclose in your mail make all the difference to me.

Hakan barely managed to get home this week as they are working flat-out at the base with the induction of all the new soldiers (four thousand at his base alone). He has been working twelve-hour days and is as busy as a gardener in a patch of weeds, processing all the forms. The other evening he worked until 9:00 pm and was just finishing when one of the officers ordered him to stand guard duty that night. Hakan doesn't have a military mentality. As far as he was concerned, he was tired and done for the day. Believing the order to be unreasonable, he point-blank refused to obey and walked off, the officer hot on his heels, his all-consuming rage threatening Hakan's very existence. As they rounded a corner, who should turn up but his friend Selim, an officer of higher rank than the one in spirited pursuit. No doubt Selim saved the situation, and Hakan was remarkably lucky not to have been thrown in prison. He knew this full well, but he simply won't be bullied.

Abla has had another recent brush with marriage, in this instance with a high official from Kavaklı's provincial government. He is an older man whose first wife died. It is believed that he has had his eye on Neriman and had put out feelers about approaching the family to discuss a match. Most unusually, Abla not only hit the ceiling, but cracked the plaster and brought down pieces, saying that under no circumstances was she prepared to marry a man old enough to be her father. For obvious reasons, her parents were eager to promote the match; but Abla ranted and raved, making it blatantly obvious that she would have nothing to do with him. Nevertheless, the pressure on her was unrelenting. In the end, she told enough people how she felt that word went around, and the suitor was dissuaded before matters of face and honour got involved. Much to Abla's relief, the subject has now been dropped. Abla may not be worldly-wise, but she plainly grasps how this society works. I trust her totally and would never hesitate to ask her advice. I tease her that she is my *avukat*, lawyer, for all things to do with Turkish customs and cultural practices. She really is my Big Sister.

Amid the other interesting events of the week, Baba took us to the cinema. Back in January, I went to see a Turkish film with Abla and her friend Fatma. The plot was so simplistic that I had no trouble following it, and Fatma, who's English is competent, was on hand to help out if I got stuck. In the major cities, I can see recent Hollywood films with the original soundtrack (subtitles for the Turks), which is perfect; but here in town, any western films are dubbed, and my Turkish is not yet good enough to follow anything more complicated than a cartoon. Baba had tickets for “Chitty Chitty Bang Bang” and, although dubbed, was fun to see as I knew the story anyway. I got almost nothing out of the cowboy film that followed, though it was amusing to see Henry Fonda and Jimmy Stewart speaking Turkish.

On Friday morning, I allowed myself to be dragged into a faintly ridiculous situation. I was not long out of bed when Ana excitedly announced that the Kavaklı pilgrims were returning from The Haj, and she wondered if I would like to go welcome them. No. That’s wrong. She TOLD me were going off to greet them as they arrived at a bus station on the outskirts of town. I was not eager to participate. I didn’t really get what it was all about, but when the distance was mentioned, I thought that she wanted me to drive them there. That much I was willing to do.

Both Ana and Abla were in a state of high agitation and flew around dressing up and getting ready. As we left the house, I headed for the car, only to see them walk off down the hill, re-enforcing my belief that I did not fully comprehend what was going on. As we rounded the bend at the bottom of our road, I saw that a bus was waiting to take us to the site of the anticipated arrival. Thoroughly bewildered, I desperately wanted to back out, but it was too late to do so without causing a scene in front of neighbours and friends.

And so, we all got on the bus, which stopped every now and again along the way to collect more passengers. By the time we got to the station, the bus was straining to the point of rupture with anyone and everyone who might have an interest in the proceedings. Once there, we joined a further throng of people who had gathered from all over the province to welcome the group.

We waited and we waited, until finally, three super buses raced into view throwing up billows of dust, claxon horns blaring “La Cucaracha” amid much cheering and clapping. If the pilgrims had had to endure twenty days on the road with this unrelenting tune blistering their ears, I am sure that this, at least in part, accounted for their glassy-eyed demeanour as, stiff and cramped, they struggled off the buses.

There was a note of hysteria as the crowd swarmed to greet them, treating them with saint-like reverence. Everyone was anxious to show respect by kissing their hands and feet and almost any other available body part. Self-consciously, I shrank to the back of the action, feeling I had no part to play in this drama. Ana spotted me and grabbed me by the hand, ready to drag me into the fray. I baulked. I tried to tell her that I didn’t understand what was going on, and that I preferred to remain on the sidelines. Finally, she got the message and let go. Back on our respective buses, we formed a procession into Kavaklı where our convoy snaked along the streets as everyone turned out to wave a welcome, some catching a glimpse of the bareheaded foreigner. They must have wondered by what miracle of Islam I had been so recently converted.

When it was all over and we were back in Elli Evler, I headed immediately for the house. Ana caught up with me and wanted me to go with her and Abla to the home of some returning pilgrims to welcome them and drink *zem-zem*, the holy water from Mecca. "If you drink this water while praying, Allah will give you whatever you want," she informed me. As gently as I could, I told her that today was not the day to ask this of me; she should go ahead to the pilgrims' house, and I would see them later.

I think the Beylers are under the impression that I am going to convert to Islam, and I'm unsure how to handle this. I have expressed a great deal of interest in learning about their religion. I believe I mentioned that I have read an English version of the Koran in an effort to become familiar with the foundations of their faith, but I have no inclination to convert, and I don't want them to be disappointed.

When everyone was back and things had calmed down considerably, I decided it was time for a little chat. Ana, Abla, and I sat down over glasses of *çay* and I tried to explain, as best I could in my poor Turkish, that while these occasions are important to them, they are awkward for me. I said that in future, they should participate, by all means; however, it was not always necessary or appropriate to include me. Abla understood immediately and helped me spell out to Ana that while they are comfortable in their religion, it was all new to me and very different from what I am used to. "How would you feel if we visited Zeynep in America and she rushed us off to Christian activities?" she asked her mother. Good work, *avukat*. Abla definitely got the message, but I'm not at all certain that any of this hit home with Ana. She listened and nodded but looked a little blank, as if the swirling words were looking for a place to land.

Ruth came to visit this week. We swapped life stories and I have learned so much more about her. She grew up in Brooklyn where she acquired an accent that seems completely out of place in this context, but as she pointed out, I have an English one, which is just as unlikely in Kavaklı. She comes from a big family and had some college education before meeting her husband and moving to Turkey. Although Ruth and I are very different people, our experiences here have given us an immediate connection, and the visits provide an outlet for pent-up emotions. It's bliss to sit and chat in English and not think about how to express myself, nor worry that what I say might cause some unintended offence. But whatever the frustrations, we are agreed that the Turks are wonderful people, open-hearted and generous, and that there is much here to admire.

Ruth speaks fluent Turkish, and of that I am entirely envious. She also speaks it in such a way that I can understand almost every word she says, which gives me hope that I might eventually achieve the same standard. Tomorrow we are going to meet Mrs Trent, the wife of the American air force officer, and then take ourselves out to lunch, a real girls' day out. I wanted Abla to come with us, but she didn't seem overly enthused, so I didn't press her. I guess she wouldn't feel comfortable with strangers in unfamiliar surroundings. I can sympathize as I know exactly how that feels.

To answer your question: the Turks are neutral in the Middle East war. The Arabs resent the fact that Turkey, a country with a majority Muslim population, does not side with them; but apart from religion, they have little in common. Rather than attempt closer links with the Arab world, Turkey is much more interested in looking west and strengthening ties with Europe. Atatürk saw the future of the country in its westernization and sought to bring about the changes that would enable the people to move ahead. Religion was particularly anathema to Atatürk, who founded the republic as a secular nation. He thought that the flaws and weaknesses in the Ottoman Empire had been caused by its adherence to Islam and was responsible for impeding progress.

The vast majority of the population may be Muslim, but the influence of the mosque, its schools and its teachings, was greatly diminished under the new regime. The Islamic calendar was abandoned as was the prohibition against alcohol. The Latin alphabet replaced Arabic script, and universal education was introduced, both reforms resulting in a marked increase in literacy. The traditional fez was outlawed, and men were encouraged to adopt European style clothing. Although the *hijab*, headscarf, for women was never banned, it was discouraged as women too, were asked to follow the example of their sisters in the West. Atatürk wanted them to uncover their hair as a way of indicating that they intended to become fully-participating members of the new society, educated for the first time alongside boys and encouraged to seek jobs in the workplace. Many religious leaders were executed when they refused to support these radical changes and follow the new laws of the new republic.

It is impossible to overstate the significance of Atatürk's influence and vision, or the high esteem in which he is held by every living Turk. Few countries can have been as genuinely and permanently changed by a single ruler as Turkey was by Atatürk. Every town has a commemorative statue; his portrait can be seen in all public buildings, on all Turkish banknotes, in every home. If Turkey had a patron saint, indisputably, it would be Atatürk, a man whose very name is spoken with reverence and whose legacy is never questioned. Social change is always hard, and progress can be slow, but the continuing appetite for modernization promotes and encourages everything that Atatürk set in motion.

I didn't mean to go off on a tangent, but if we want to understand anything about modern Turkey, we need to know about Atatürk.

17 March 1970

We are all so relieved to hear that Peter is now home from hospital. What a scare! No one expects an otherwise healthy teenager to suffer a ruptured appendix. Of course, it's a pity that he has missed the class trip to Washington DC. That is a huge disappointment for him, but at least, he is well on the road to recovery. It could have been so much worse! It sounds as if Mother handled everything in her capable manner. What a time for Dad to be away on business. I shall have to keep a copy of his letter for Mother to read all the wonderful comments he made about her ability to cope in difficult circumstances.

Nothing ever stands still around here. Each week I think I will catch up on all the things I want to tell you, and then a myriad of other things happen, and my backlist gets longer. I finally finished Hakan's green sweater, cables and all. It doesn't look too bad, though it could be a bit bigger all over. But bless him, he says he loves it and insists it is fine. That must be 50% diplomacy and 50% sheer amazement that I managed to finish it. Somewhat buoyed by this, I am now knitting a sweater for Abla. She never has a chance to make anything for herself, and this is something I can do to help out. I hope the results justify both her confidence in me and her enthusiasm for the project. After that, I am planning a pullover for myself and then a cardigan for Hakan. By then I'll probably be too old to see, so I have no further ambitions in this regard.

Sunday morning the sun was out and it was balmy, even at an early hour. Everyone was up for breakfast on the balcony, our first of the season. The weather has changed so suddenly that we had not yet prepared the balcony for summer, but this opportunity was too enticing to miss. We threw open all the windows and let the light and warmth flood in as we set up a makeshift table and lingered over the traditional meal of bread, cheese, olives, honey and tea. A *simitçi* passed by so we bought freshly baked *simit*, a kind of soft round sesame pretzel. Any type of bread is simply the vehicle for a variety of toppings, predominantly cheeses; but on this occasion, we also had rose jam, a gift from a neighbour. It tastes just like roses smell. This breakfast now feels so right to me that I never miss cereal at home.

Last week, army headquarters in Ankara sent Hakan a form to fill out on me. It is no secret that he has an American fiancée, and this information has made its way to high places. It looks like he is being screened for a possible transfer there. Exactly how my presence will affect matters, we haven't been able to establish. Hakan says the army is paranoid about spies, and I guess I look like a possible candidate. Whatever happens, they will be investigating me, though I have no idea what this signifies.

When I went to pick him up on Saturday morning, I had just pulled into the parking lot and was stepping out of the car, when I overheard a soldier telling one of the guards that I had come to see Hakan Beyler; would the guard send someone to tell him. I have no idea who he was, but he did me a great favour. I hate putting in a personal appearance as eyes follow me intently, and I am uncomfortably aware of all the gawking and staring. It seems Dagmar and I are becoming well known in this part of the world.

Thank you for sending the TesTape which we delivered yesterday. The Vedats were pleasantly surprised and very grateful; they send their thanks. They are one of the few families in this area who has a telephone we sometimes use, so this was a practical way to say thank you for that. Both Abla and I are very fond of them all, especially Aylin Abla who is a trusted friend as well as a good neighbour. In fact, she is the street's "good neighbour", the first person everyone turns to for words of wisdom, whether it's colicky babes, straying husbands or troublesome in-laws. She has time for them all.

During the week, Abla showed me her dowry which she stores in two huge trunks. This is the collection of items that every mother starts for her daughter from the day she is born in preparation for her eventual marriage. In some cultures, the dowry is synonymous with "bride price", but in this instance, it's simply the domestic goods (mainly textiles) that every bride is expected to bring to her new home. Because there is so little ready-made merchandise in the shops, it takes years to prepare from scratch all the necessary sheets, pillow cases, tablecloths, napkins and doilies needed to set up a new household, especially when we take into account that virtually everything is embroidered or otherwise personalized. Because they have been handed down through the generations, many of the items are antique. All of them exhibit the most exquisite handiwork.

Abla started making her own contributions from the age of five. I suspect I didn't know how to hold a needle at that age, let alone possess the skills to make anything worthy of preservation. In addition to all the linens, there is clothing for her future husband: underwear, socks, handkerchiefs and shirts; and her children: lots of little booties, sweaters, hats and diapers; as well as a substantial supply of pretty underwear and nightdresses for herself. Anytime she gets anything new, into the dowry it goes. She has a lovely collection; and when we consider all those years, all those hopes and dreams, it really is something special. (Having nothing even remotely comparable in my possession, I represent a poorly equipped prospect for any man; as such, I really shouldn't have much hope.) Neriman is obviously proud of her dowry, even though she says "it isn't much". She clearly enjoyed showing it to me, and my sincerest wish is that she will have a chance to use it in happy circumstances.

I am sorry to disappoint you, but Ana does not make her own bread. We go to the *fırıncı* to buy it, like everyone else. Each neighbourhood has one or more bakeries, and each baker makes his own on the premises (both manufacturing and retail are usually in the same small space). The crisp loaves are baked twice daily, filling the streets with their mouth-watering, yeasty aromas. Turks think that eating warm bread is bad for the digestion, so Hakan and I have to be sneaky if we want it hot. Bread is so cheap that most people buy it, though the villagers probably make their own.

You have asked what Sami does. Well, we have all been wondering that. Family finances are discussed as freely as the price of the above-mentioned bread, so I have discovered that about ten years ago, Baba turned everything over to Sami. I don't mean that he merely gave him his money, but that he legally put almost everything he owned into his son's name.

Despite his reputation as a "good businessman", Sami managed to lose most of the family assets as well as to incur debts to the tune of one million Turkish Lira (about $100,000). He doesn't play small. And it gets more complicated. In order to get credit to try to recoup his losses and pay his debts, he got Baba to act as his guarantor for hefty loans. When he fails to meet his repayments, the banks come after Baba for their money. Obviously, he doesn't have any because he gave everything to Sami. This is the most vicious of circles. As far as I am aware, all Baba has left are this house, another house in town (rented out) and a valuable piece of land in the business district. He is desperate to hang onto these as you might imagine.

The chief criterion for obtaining an export license in Turkey seems to be having a lot of money. When Sami was very rich, he got himself one of these, and his license to export has never been revoked. And thank goodness for that as this looks to be his main way of making money and putting a dent in some of the losses and loans. He is always wheeling and dealing, darting about the country, pulling off transactions here and there. But precisely what this involves, no one is quite sure.

Sami brags constantly and loudly about who he knows and what he does, occasionally sending Baba some money. To be fair, Hakan says that Sami has now paid off most of the immense debt and is nearly at the break-even point. He uses this information to convince me that his older brother is a brilliant businessman... that with his brain as his major asset, he has been able to raise vast amounts of money in a short period of time, and that he is now poised to become a rich man again. What I see is that regardless of how much money he makes, the Beylers will remain dependent on him, a condition I am confident feeds his already over-inflated ego, allowing him to boast of his many sacrifices on the altar of family welfare.

Hakan is most concerned that Baba repays the loans before the banks decide to come after the house. He has advised his father to sell what's left of his real estate, pay off the debts in his name and use the remaining money to reopen what was an enormously successful shoe manufacturing business. There has been a great deal of interest in the plot of land in town, and Baba would be able to obtain top money because of its excellent location.

While Baba grasps the logic of this, letting go of the property would mean letting go of his dream. He bought the site with a view to building The Beyler Apartments there. I believe work on the foundations already had started when financial disaster struck. I'm certain Baba is hoping that when Sami is rich again, there will be funds to fulfil that dream. Perhaps Sami will come through; perhaps he won't. But I'm convinced that Baba is fooling himself if he imagines that he could depend on Sami for anything. He may be a good businessman, but he is a lousy son, and one with the poorest sense of family that I have ever seen. Especially by the standards of the culture here where family is all.

I have heard Sami make endless outrageous promises that no one this side of rational could possibly believe. Of course, he didn't keep them. It seems to me that if he enjoys the privileges, power and glory that go with being the Number One Son, he must also accept the responsibilities attached. That message has been lost on Sami. And yet, hope springs eternal, and the family clings to an unrealistic belief in him. Maybe the alternative would be too painful, but that belief appears to be more important to the Beylers than the independence I would want in similar circumstances.

The planned girls' day out with Ruth and Mrs Trent was something of a mixed venture. As arranged, I picked them up in the car, and we drove into town for some shopping and lunch. The shopping part was fine. Shopping is an acceptable activity for women as there are other women in all the stores. But lunch is another matter altogether. Women do not eat out much and, apparently, never without a suitable male escort. When we were planning this little excursion, I told Hakan what we had in mind, and it was fine with him. When I told Ana, I think a seizure threatened to overwhelm her. Although she didn't say much to me, she went straight to Hakan to complain. Culturally speaking, he should have backed his mother in this, but thankfully, he supported me. After that, she had to fume quietly, although I was left in no doubt as to her feelings on the subject. In the end, shopping completed, we ladies had *çay* and pastries at a popular *pastane*. It didn't feel too daring.

On the way home, Ruth and I stopped in at the Trents where they are busy getting ready for their move back to the US. I can appreciate Mrs Trent's frustrations, living as she has done in the community. She's felt lonely and isolated, but has good things to say about her

Turkish neighbours who have been friendly and helpful. Understandably, both Trents are anxious to get back for their son's wedding in April. Mrs T mentioned that she wanted to have some last-minute sewing done, but that she was having a hard time finding a seamstress. I knew that Abla didn't have a lot of work just then, so I suggested her.

When I returned home and told the family what I had said, I knew I had done something wrong, but I couldn't figure out what. With obvious reluctance, Abla agreed to go, and the next morning we made our way to the Trents. After talking with Mrs T about what she wanted, Abla agreed to do the work but looked as if she was about to burst into tears. Mrs T was oblivious to all this, and before I knew it, she proposed that we have some lunch with them. While a harmless enough invitation, I knew Abla would rather die than eat with a strange man, so I politely declined with some excuse about lunch waiting at home, saying we'd return in the afternoon for the required fittings.

I tried to get to the bottom of the problem, but Abla wasn't giving much away. I thought maybe she felt uncomfortable with so many foreigners, or maybe it was the strange man in the house. I was grasping for clues and desperate to learn what folly I had unwittingly committed.

Eventually, Abla said that she didn't do sewing outside her own home; Baba didn't permit it. Okay. But Baba and Ana had both been present when I told Abla about Mrs T, and no one had raised any objections then. I still felt there was something I was missing. Much as I was inclined to help Mrs T, there was no way I was going to jeopardize my relationship with Abla over the matter.

Explaining that I needed to ring Ruth, I left to use the telephone at Aylin Abla's. In truth, I felt I needed to tell Mrs T that we had to cancel. When I spoke to her, she sounded disappointed and was as baffled as I was. We were discussing the quandary, trying to make sense of it all, when she suddenly had a brainwave: why not invite Ana to come along in the afternoon? Back at the house, I followed up with her suggestion.

If the Queen of England had issued the invitation, Ana could not have been more excited. She hurriedly finished her lunch and rushed around changing into her best clothes, splashing on cologne and fixing her hair. She never leaves the front door without donning a headscarf, and if we are going beyond our garden, she wears a dress-length coat as well, regardless of the temperature outside. In the car, Ana sat up front with me, and the three of us set off for the Trents.

When we arrived, Mrs Trent made Ana feel very welcome and entirely comfortable. (But in these unfamiliar surroundings Ana did not remove her headscarf.) Despite Mrs T's minimal Turkish and my only meagre contributions, the two older women managed to exchange information on knitting and crocheting in which both were interested. While Abla worked, I poured American coffee and cakes into Ana.

We had a nervous moment when Mr Trent came home (strange man... strange foreign man...), but he adopted exactly the right degree of formality. Later, he won them over when he entertained them with his tape machine, recording their voices and playing them back. It all went unbelievably well. Ana came away feeling that Mrs Trent was first-rate, that it would be fine for Abla to continue there until the sewing was completed. Abla seemed happier too, though she mentioned to me that she didn't think it necessary to take Ana with us the following day. She said that she liked Mrs Trent and that she had relished getting away from the house.

I'm still not entirely sure what was wrong and what was fixed, but the dilemma had resolved itself. (That was a deep sigh of relief you just heard.) As Mrs Trent said later, "It was a real blow for Turkish-American relations." The Trents have gone now, but Jill, the Peace Corps worker, has recently returned from a trip to the Middle East. I stopped by her house long enough to meet her and plan an outing together with Ruth. I am anxious to hear about her travels and also, about her work here.

Stay tuned for the next instalment.

23 March 1970

I was so glad to get your letter and to hear that Peter is still making good progress in his recovery. If he has his appetite back, he must be doing well. Dad, on the other hand, sounds as if he has made a sensible decision to have the surgery for his diverticulitis. When he's had several painful attacks and has been on such a restrictive diet, it's time to do something more. I know he wants to get union negotiations under his belt before going into hospital, so let's hope all matters will be resolved quickly.

There have been all kinds of developments on the political front this week, mainly around the current crisis over Cyprus. I'm unsure how much news you get on this subject (since it doesn't directly involve the USA, probably not much), but Turkey is on high alert. Archbishop Makarios (the Greek leader of Cyprus and leader of the Greek Orthodox population on the island) was shot at, and later, a Greek military official was killed. The island is under the control of Greece but was part of the former Ottoman Empire and still has a substantial Turkish minority. The Greek army has strengthened its forces there and has launched fresh assaults on the Turkish population, blaming them for the attacks on their leaders.

The Turks believe that the island rightly belongs to Turkey. They closely observe events there, ever watchful for any sign that could be interpreted as a possible threat to the welfare of their brothers. It's an extremely tense period when people feel that anything might happen. Last week, I heard sirens blowing, the kind that I used to hear as a child when we still had air-raid warnings. I didn't think much of them then, assuming there was some kind of drill going on.

When we saw Hakan this weekend, he said that the alerts were for real, and that all the troops were receiving intensified combat and guerrilla warfare training. They have all been up at 4:00 every morning for field manoeuvres. Even Hakan. He says he did himself proud, considering he's scarcely had any training, and managed to surprise everyone, including himself. They all thought he was a Mama's Boy. When one of the officers accused him of firing too fast, another whipped around and said, "If it comes to battle, you'd better shoot fast!" When someone yelled, "Charge!" Hakan was out in front doing just that. He was picked by the men in his unit to be their leader.

Hakan doesn't feel that the sabre rattling over Cyprus will amount to much. Maybe this is wishful thinking on his part. In any event, he doesn't believe he would be deployed to the island because his division functions as a support unit, rather than as a combat one. At worst, he might be sent to Antalya to help supply the ships and planes that would depart from there. The news on the radio today didn't report much, so I'm hoping that things are cooling off. We have heard that the base is still on full alert.

Somewhat worryingly, Hakan did not receive my last letter. It could be that they are checking my correspondence, or it could be that it got lost. We don't know. But after Hakan has had to fill out forms about me, and with the current security precautions over Cyprus, not to mention Turkish paranoia over Americans, we wouldn't be astonished if someone decided to have a closer look. I can remember what I wrote and don't recall that there was anything in it to interest the Turkish army, but I enclosed one of Dad's letters, and I can't remember what he might jokingly have said about Poor Turkish Boy, or if he made any cracks about army life. We hope there is nothing that could be embarrassing or otherwise, but we'll have to lie low and wait. We're doubtless concerned for nothing. The paranoia of the times is contagious.

And who could blame me for indulging in a bit of paranoia? Sami sent word this week from Ankara that my resident's visa will issued, but only for three months. Everyone had led me to understand that these are granted on an annual basis. I overheard Abla telling Baba that she believes the reason for this reduced period is because the Turkish government doesn't want Americans in the country. She is probably right.

So we have a dilemma: if we get married, the government would be obliged to grant me a proper visa, since I would then be married to a Turkish citizen. But if Hakan has a foreign wife, he would lose his rank and privileges and every good thing he now has going for him. Trust me when I say that you cannot possibly picture what an inhumane place the Turkish army can be for most ordinary soldiers. No. That simply doesn't bear thinking about. Maybe the authorities will extend my visa, or maybe I will go out of the country and come in again on another tourist visa. We have until June to figure this out.

I have finally caught up with Jill. She's an impressive young woman: bright, enthusiastic, energetic and possessed of great common sense, precisely the sort of person you would be proud to have representing the USA in the Peace Corps. She is coming to the end of her two-year commitment and feels that it is an appropriate time to leave. Some of the more radical political groups here are protesting PC presence, and students are boycotting PC (mostly English) university classes. Due to political pressure, many of her colleagues in the urban areas have left already. Unlike them, Jill feels that she has had an unusually constructive experience here in Kavaklı where she's worked in the local orphanage and taught English in the community. Although she knew very little Turkish on arrival, she is fluent now, and that, along with her determination to blend with the local culture, has made her both popular and well respected.

Hakan and I have had some interesting discussions following my meeting with Jill. Despite the fact that the Peace Corps arrives in any country only by invitation of the host government, Hakan feels defensive about its presence here. To him, and obviously, to many other Turks, it's as if the Americans are saying that the local people can't do these things for themselves, that America needs to show them how everything is done. He asked some valid questions about why the Peace Corps is here, why Jill is here. If they want to help orphans or work with children or teach in schools, why don't they do it in their own country? Don't they have any problems there? What's Turkey to them? How would the Americans like it if Turkey sent workers to show them what to do in their schools and orphanages?

I tried to find answers to questions I didn't know existed. It's hard to explain the almost missionary zeal that many Americans feel about helping those less fortunate. Many consider that privileges bring responsibilities, that it is important to give something back. The fact that I could not convincingly articulate this to my own fiancé brought me up short and made me realize that people on the receiving end of all this munificence must also feel as Hakan does: patronized, criticized, defensive, inadequate, and not at all appropriately "grateful". It feels as if we're insisting that ours is the only way and that anyone with any sense will agree. Our arrogance is undermining our benign intentions and clouding our perceptions, so that we end up doing more harm than good.

Whatever the optimism with which it arrived, it is clear that the Peace Corps is no longer welcome and has no future in Turkey.

30 March 1970

You will see from this letter that earthquake notwithstanding, I am fine. We here in Kavaklı are all fit and well. Though I know you don't have much about Turkey in your news, this has been such an enormous disaster that I'm certain you would have heard something. The centre of the *zelzele,* earthquake, was in a rural area nearly five hundred kilometres (about three hundred miles) to the southwest of us, but believe me, we felt it!

There are lots of earthquakes in Turkey, and we frequently experience tremors that last for a few seconds. Sometimes they are not noticeable unless we are sitting quietly, but they are most definitely part of the background. This big one happened Easter Sunday morning at three minutes past midnight, to be exact. The rest of the family had gone to bed, but Hakan and I were still up talking when I gradually became aware of an increasingly loud engine of noise that sounded as if a freight train were about to burst through the floor and streak across the room. Baffled, I interrupted Hakan's conversation just as the house began to shake. At that point, no one could be in any doubt that we were experiencing an earthquake, but unable to fully comprehend the situation, I sat there with my mouth hanging open.

The Beylers were instantly up and moving to go outside. Our soundly constructed house, built on rocky foundations, had turned to cardboard, so flimsy did it seem. The salon blurred with the vibrations. The walls thundered and shook. The windows rattled in their frames, threatening to snap under the strain. The ceiling lights, hanging from cords, swung crazily and hopped about. Surely the heavy tile roof would collapse in on us.

As we were seated on opposite sides of the table, Hakan shouted at me to crawl under. I couldn't hear anything over that terrible roar, but I followed his example and dived with him. We hung onto each other while the quake continued around us for a full minute, undeniably the longest of my life. When the shaking had ceased and we pulled away from each other, I saw that the colour in Hakan's face had drained away, leaving him apparition white. I must have looked much the same.

Struggling to make sound come out as words, we checked each other for signs of injury. None. We glanced around us, fully expecting to see that the house had disintegrated. Miraculously, everything looked to be in place. When I tried to get up, I realized that the bones in my body had melted, and my muscles had turned into marshmallows. My knees were knocking together with the fear that only then enveloped me before sliding away in relief.

We fought our way to standing positions and looked around once more before wobbling to the front door and hanging onto the banister as we descended the steps into the garden. Thankfully, the Beylers were all there. Though badly shaken, everyone appeared to be safe. As we surveyed the neighbourhood, we saw that people had taken to the streets. Like us, our neighbours were anxiously inspecting themselves and their properties for harm. Evidence of damage was minimal: a few toppled chimney pots and the occasional rearranged garden fence.

I called for the dogs who came bounding from the back of the house at the sound of my voice. They were as bewildered as the rest of us. Like sleepwalkers coming to conscientiousness, people who had been stunned and quiet, now began milling around, exchanging stories and discussing the best strategies for protection. Most of the neighbourhood seemed to have fled outside, but we had stayed indoors as Hakan believed we were safest under the table. What do we do for the best when we feel that the earth might be crumbling away from us?

We have been so very lucky here in Kavaklı. Apart from a nasty fright, most people have suffered little. The news you have had has undoubtedly come from the epicentre where they recorded 7.4 on the Richter scale. You may even know more than I do since I have to translate everything from Turkish. Over a thousand people died, and most certainly, this number will rise as bodies are uncovered in the rubble. In one town, only the school was left standing. To add to the misery, the weather has turned cold and rainy; but we have heard that the Red Crescent is doing excellent work, providing food, shelter and medical care for the thousands left homeless. Following the earthquake, there have been many aftershocks, which we are all convinced will turn into yet another quake, a normal over-reaction to the usual tremors which come after such catastrophic events. They make us all nervous. The dogs are especially sensitive to these and start barking whenever they happen.

Before the earthquake struck, it had been a bureaucratic week. I've filled in my tax return for the US Government and completed a census form for the US Consulate. The next item on my agenda concerned the fact that my temporary visa to remain expired on Friday. Since I am supposed to be getting something more permanent from Ankara, I had been hanging on, hoping that this would arrive before the current one expired. No such luck. If I remain with an expired visa, I am here illegally. What to do?

We sat down together with a neighbour who is a detective in the police force. He decided that I must be terribly ill, too ill to travel. Under the circumstances, local officials would extend my visa so that I could remain here and "rest". He helped me get the necessary forms, and Abla accompanied me to the government hospital where, by signing the required papers, I would have six doctors attesting to my poor health. What with one thing and another, we managed five of the six signatures, needing only that of the Chief of Medicine to finalize our mission. We were eventually admitted to his office where he considered the documents I placed in front of him. He looked up and studied me closely before asking us to sit down. Then he surprised me by starting a conversation in accented, but otherwise perfect English:

"Why do you want to stay in Kavaklı?"

"Because my fiancé is doing his military service."

"Who is your fiancé?"

"Hakan Beyler."

"What's your work here?"

"None."

"How many months do you want to stay?"

Three appeared to be the magic number in these parts, so I said, "Three."

"So, you want us to lie for you."

"Well..." I hedged, "... I could say something more diplomatic, I guess, but the truth is that I need your help. By the way, where did you learn such excellent English?"

"I lived in America for five years. I left my heart there, too."

We chatted about America for a few minutes, and then he said, "You've got a bad case of rheumatism, haven't you?"

"That's right," I replied.

"Well, I'd better fill out these forms for you."

Mission completed. I now have another three months during which I hope my visa from Ankara will come. Nothing is guaranteed, of course. I try to roll with the punches.

Meanwhile, the permit for the car has also expired. In the extra month we were given at the border, I have tried to find out what I could do to extend this. The broad consensus is that I should keep Dagmar and live dangerously. In conversation with an acquaintance who used to work for customs, he indicated that the worst that could happen would be a 30TL fine. Naturally, they would also confiscate the car. That's if they catch me, which he thought doubtful as there is no customs office in the town. If I were stopped say, in one of the random road checks conducted by the police, I could always produce medical documents, proving my poor health. Or I could plead stupidity about duty, car permits, rights to remain and all matters related. This would not be as far-fetched as it sounds. I am totally ignorant regarding anything involving officialdom, and there seems to be no definitive answer to any of the uncertainties. There being no other realistic alternative, I have opted to live dangerously.

The ethics here are different. Everyone accepts that bribery and corruption are a way of life. Everyone expects to be part of this system if they want to get anything done. No one really questions if this is right or wrong. It's simply the way it is. It's a kind of dishonesty to be sure, but in other respects, the Turks are morally upright and honourable in ways that stretch our imaginations. Shopkeepers display their wares openly on the streets and pavements, and no one steals so much as a pin. Even at night, when many goods remain in place, no one touches them. They continue to sit out where they have been all day, no one even thinking of taking anything. It just isn't done.

In our town, burglary is almost unheard of, and there's no such thing as a crime rate, though there are lots of fights. Some people will try to take you for all they can if they think you're capable of taking care of yourself, but the vulnerable need have no fear. There's no sport in taking advantage of someone less able. (Note: Tourists are considered "good sport".)

Not much has changed in the difficulties over Cyprus. Both sides claim to be on the verge of going to war, but fortunately, there has been no precipitous incident to push either one over the edge. Let us be grateful for small mercies. The skies have been noticeably busier with all the overhead traffic, some planes on scouting expeditions and some flying protective missions for Turkish ships in the Aegean. Intensive training continues at the base, and the army is still on high alert. We trust Bill is having a less exciting time with his basic training. It sounds like he has settled in and made the best of it. What else can he do?

I had not remembered it was Easter until I received your cards, so I hope you had a happy one.

Chapter 7

5 April 1970

I had a letter from Bill this past week! The shock nearly did me in. Hakan read it eagerly, anxious for his comments about army life, and got a great kick out of my brother's comments. I guess armies all over the world have much in common, for better or for worse. By the way, Bill says he is getting a lot of grief from US Army officials about having a sister in Turkey. And just how do they know?

We have a hectic week coming up. Ken wants a big order of skins, immediately. Of course. We had anticipated this, but did not think it would materialize so quickly. It's caught us about halfway through the order, so it will be all hands on deck to get it finished and off to London. Realistically speaking, "all hands on deck," means Levent and me. Hakan is not around to help and Baba is in Istanbul.

I'm glad to report that Levent and I get along well, and it's beneficial for him to have something worthwhile to do. He's bright and energetic and does little but create havoc at home, largely because he is bored: no school, no work and no friends. The family keeps saying that he is sick and can't be expected to do anything, but this genuine reason has turned into a convenient excuse. He's off medication, and during a recent trip to Istanbul, he was given a clean bill of health by his psychiatrist. It's time to resume everyday life. He likes to work with me in the shop, and obviously, he likes the wages, too. He's a terrific help, and most assuredly, I could not finish the order without him. We have a full week ahead of us.

When Baba returned from Istanbul, he brought two pieces of dramatic news. The first is that Sami may be getting married. The arrangements are far from settled, but if things continue to progress, our dear *ağabey* may pull this off. No one but Sami has met the girl in question, but her Baba has talked to our Baba, and they both agree that the marriage is a good idea. Apparently her father is very rich, with impressive business connections. Sami has managed to convince him that he is his equal in both wealth and influence. The girl herself is said to be intelligent and well-educated; she works as a pharmacist and speaks several languages. I heard that phrase "forty camel girl" again but didn't like to interrupt to ask for more explanation. Sami wants this girl and her father wants Sami. Our father hasn't said much, her mother hasn't said anything, our mother has said A LOT, and no one cares what the girl says.

There's a catch. The family is Jewish. I believe I now have some idea of the firestorm that took hold when Hakan announced he was bringing home a Christian bride. I can't assess which is worse in their eyes, but I have witnessed the ruckus that followed the revelation. In truth, Baba is pretty cool about it all. He has presented the facts without expressing an opinion. If Sami persists in this, I think Baba will do what he needs to do and concede gracefully, perhaps believing that this marriage (any marriage?) might be good for his son.

Ana, on the other hand, is not about to concede anything, gracefully or otherwise. I am certain she mentioned that they already have one foreign bride, which is quite enough for any family, and that if this new girl so much as approaches the house, she will fall down dead from grief. She is in earnest. While the discussion raged, she took me to one side and confided that everyone knows Jews are awful liars. When I gently asked her if she had ever met a Jew, she looked at me as if I were about to contaminate the entire property. I think I missed a chance to reinforce our mother/daughter relationship. But Ana enjoys melodrama, and there is no way this affair will be resolved without histrionics.

Abla is completely practical on the subject. She says that if Sami is going to get married, Hakan and I had better hurry up and go first, or Sami will get the better wedding presents. Levent too, is pragmatic and feels kindly disposed towards anyone who might want to give him a motorcycle. He figures that anyone as rich as this girl will undoubtedly want to do the right thing by him. Where do I stand? I hope - for the girl's sake - that the marriage doesn't happen. As far as I'm concerned, the Jews have suffered enough persecution without inflicting Sami on them. So for various reasons, we are all poised in eager anticipation as we await the outcome of the current negotiations.

As if the above news were not enough, there is now a real possibility that Neriman may go to Istanbul to work. Get ready for contorted logic. For years, Abla has been pleading with her father to go out to work not only so that she can contribute to expenses, but also to save some money towards her very uncertain future. For years, everyone has firmly vetoed the idea as too disgraceful. Imagine, a woman from the Beyler clan holding down a job. Now Baba has decided that his financial situation is such that his daughter will have to go to work not simply to augment domestic finances, but to support the entire family. The idea is so incredible that I have yet to close my mouth. Hakan and I are willing to bet dollars to doughnuts that the idea came from Sami. If he is the source, then it is, by definition, "a good idea". Don't ask me why. All the evidence is to the contrary, but I've already said that logic has nothing to do with any of this.

Abla has been told that she has until the end of this month to finish her work here, and then she will be packed off to Istanbul where employment already has been found. She will, of course, turn over her pay packet to Sami who will forward the money to Baba. (The words "pigs" and "fly" spring to mind.) I can't understand how Sami has the nerve even to suggest such a thing. It is well known that he spends more in a nightclub in one night than it takes to run this household for a month. Yet when Baba approaches this same son for money, the grand and glorious first-born always has some remarkable story about how, just at that very instant, he is without funds.

If Baba would only take more notice of the business suggestions that Hakan has proposed, there would be no need for Abla to go anywhere. It's not that she's opposed to working, but the thought of leaving home and living in Istanbul with Sami brings tears to her eyes every time someone mentions it. Who could blame her? Because she is an obedient daughter, she won't argue with her father; she merely smiles and says, "As you wish, my dearest father." It appears to be much easier to take advantage of an amicable and loving daughter than to require more of the person responsible for most of the current calamities. Hakan is as appalled by the whole fiasco as I am. He's tried several times to talk to his father, but all he gets is stony silence. There are times when I feel as if we're all treading water.

With all that has been happening, our paranoia is running rampant. That missing letter I mentioned a couple of weeks ago has turned up. It had been opened but resealed to look as if it had not. So who is investigating? Is it to do with the secret service, the military or my resident's visa? Are they investigating Hakan or me? And how does the US Army know that Bill has a sister in Turkey? Maybe I should get the CIA to put me on its payroll: if I am suspected of being a spy, I might as well get the benefit.

14 April 1970

I was stunned to get your recent letter saying that you still had not heard from me since the earthquake. I'm sure you have been very worried. When there is no news, we always fear the worst. As you must have learned by now, we are all safe and well. Hakan was not sent to the disaster area to help; none of the soldiers from Kavaklı were. There are so many military bases in Turkey that they had all the assistance they needed from those closer to the epicentre. Help has been pouring in from all over, and everyone has contributed to the relief efforts. Local collections have been made, and those who could not give money gave clothing, blankets or canned goods, whatever they could. It always seems to be those with the least who are hardest hit. It's a mystery.

Strike fever is everywhere these days. The US postal strike has presumably had something to do with my letters being delayed, and now Titan has gone out on strike. I gather this is most unexpected. I am concerned about the postponement of Dad's surgery and the effect of this on his diverticulitis. I hope, for so many reasons, that the union negotiations will be resolved both swiftly and satisfactorily. Dad needs to take care of his health.

The Cyprus situation has cooled off considerably, and the bases are no longer on high alert. Things are more or less back to normal. Hakan was recently selected to be the leader of his unit, which means that he is also the flag carrier. Henceforth, he should no longer be referred to as PTB but as PTFB, Proud Turkish Flag Bearer. While it is regarded as an honour to carry the country's flag, it is something of a mixed blessing in other respects. During battle, the flag must never touch the earth, so the bearer can't "hit the ground" when circumstances and orders might warrant. During training, it means Hakan is able to hold the flag and watch from the sidelines as the other soldiers scrabble about in the dirt, glaring in his direction. He loves being the flag bearer.

With all the talk of Sami's marriage, an interesting story has emerged about events prior to my arrival. Levent was telling me this as we worked in the shop. When Hakan wrote from London to tell his father about me and our plans to come to Turkey together, Baba was worried most about Ana's reaction. He showed the letter to Abla and Levent, and they all agreed that Ana should not be told until the last possible minute.

There was a period of several weeks between that letter and our arrival. During this time, Hakan's mother knew nothing about the impending upset, sitting in the midst of the family like the moment of tension before the starting gun. When Baba found out that we were on our way, he knew the time had come. But before anyone could say anything, Ana pre-empted the announcement with a story over breakfast about last night's dream (she does this a lot). In it, Hakan came home with a blue-eyed blonde who wore glasses with dark frames. She could have been describing the photo we sent. At this point, the family broke the news to her as gently as they could. The shock was enormous, not to mention a surprising confirmation of the validity of her dreams. Levent did not comment on what came next, but I get the general idea from all that has been happening recently.

According to Sami, the number of potential brides has now multiplied to three, all of whom are Jewish and all of whom are desperate to marry him. With so many possibilities, Baba and Ana have gone to Istanbul to investigate more fully. Ana says she will have absolutely nothing to do with a Jewish bride, but I can tell that she is already softening. When Abla had completed a set of sheets for us (my dowry? provided by the groom's family?), she announced, "I don't think I'll be doing the same thing for Sami's bride." Without hesitation, Ana stated firmly, "You will." That doesn't sound like total rejection to me.

Baba is feeling affluent this week. After trailing Sami around the countryside for most of the past fortnight, he finally managed to get a substantial sum of money out of him. Most of it is being used to pay off debts, but some has been reserved to spoil us. He bought a bicycle for Levent who is as happy as an athlete with Olympic Gold. Suddenly he is pestering us to run errands, inventing excuses to hop on his bicycle and ride into town, or anywhere. There have been gifts for Abla and Ana, too. Sunday he came home from the weekly market with an old silver bracelet for me. It's hand hammered and decorated with calligraphy in black enamel. Although we know it has some age, we have no idea how old it might be. It's beautiful and I love it.

Abla says that people are asking what we want for wedding presents, and I have told her to say that we like Old Things. They don't command much respect here. The Turks all want the latest in fashion to use, display and impress. Ready-made clothing and household linens, both rare and expensive, are more highly prized than old family heirlooms or anything handmade. They simply cannot get over my fits of rapture, but seem shyly pleased to have them so admired.

Many people have heard that I love these things, so I am often treated to a show of belongings from dowry trunks. It's impossible (for me) not to be slightly in awe of these breath-taking treasures. Because they have no commercial value to most Turkish consumers, they are easily affordable on the rare occasions that I see them in a shop, and I have been able to collect a few pieces. The other day, when Hakan and I were crawling around in the attic trying to clean out a plugged chimney pipe, we found Ana's collection of ancient pots and pans that have been in her family for generations. One pot in particular is very much like the copper yoghurt pot we sent you for Christmas. Ana immediately said I could have anything I like up there. Since no one else appears to be interested, I may take her up on this.

With a little extra in his pockets, Baba has been indulging his sweet tooth this week. He loves chocolate, and since it is expensive (and frankly, of not very good quality), he has stocked up. Although I love chocolate too, I'm rather less inclined to eat it here as I much prefer the scrumptious pastries. Generally though, we have nuts for snacks, all of which are top quality and produced in Turkey. The huge variety includes hazelnuts, almonds, pistachios, walnuts and peanuts the size of bullets. Specialist shops sell them in their shells or out of them, raw or roasted, salted or plain, candied or flavoured. There are some other nut-like items called *leblebi*, which are dry-roasted chickpeas.

In addition to all of these, we also eat a variety of seeds; my particular favourite is *çekirdek*, pumpkin seeds. These are normally sold in their shells and take some practice to eat. The pointed end must be in the right position between top and bottom front teeth to crack it open in such a way that the seed slips out into the mouth. In theory, the shell remains intact and can be disposed of separately. I am proud to say that I have provided endless amusement for family and friends as they have watched me struggle to learn the knack. In the process, I usually consume as much shell as seed, though it would be hard to differentiate one from the other once the sorry mess has journeyed around my mouth. However, practice makes perfect, and I am almost there.

Something I have eaten for the first time this week is baby goat. It was just as delicious as the antelope we also had. Both were tasty, tender and succulent. Another first was brain. I've seen whole ones (sheep, I think), cooked and served as a starter when the myriad dishes of *meze*, appetizers, have been presented, but I had not tried it before. The Beylers are partial to a bit of brain, and this week Ana sliced and lightly fried it. It has almost no taste but I'd rather not, thank you. Something else that is commonly eaten are sheep's testicles (or sheep's "eggs" in Turkish). I have not tried these and have no intention of doing so. It's all psychological, of course.

One of our neighbours, Nisa, the wife of a Turkish air force officer, has gone to Germany to work. She's a local character who has provided us with much entertainment because of her outspoken ways and flagrant disregard for the usual customs and practices. She couldn't care less about scandal unless she is causing it, in which case she is delighted. She has most recently heaped humiliation on us all by wearing slacks at every opportunity. It's simply not done, certainly not in public, and most assuredly, not here in Kavaklı.

Both Nisa and her husband are wholly unconventional, so no one was surprised when she announced her latest scheme. It would seem she has an aunt living in Hamburg who has invited her to visit for three months over the summer when she can work and earn vast amounts of money to boost their finances here. Nisa is totally candid about their eternal lack of money. I've always had the feeling that Nisa should have been born in the West. Germany will suit her perfectly, and she will have the time of her life.

Yesterday, dressed in her new white trouser suit and waving lavish farewells, she departed for Istanbul in a blaze of gossip and glory. Her husband went with her to see her off. In the meantime, their three children (ranging in ages from eight to thirteen years) were left here on their own.

The first we knew of this was today when I saw the older girl in the garden and asked who was staying with them while her parents were gone. I was horrified when she said, "no one", but didn't let on, thinking I should clear this with Abla before I went further. Unsurprisingly, she was equally horrified, and being parentless ourselves, we invited the three children to spend the coming night at our house. The little boy is too young to care who looks after him, but the two (older) girls were visibly relieved. They had been frightened by spending the night on their own and seized on our invitation to stay. Just now they are sitting here in the salon eating oranges by the kilo and playing card games with a vengeance.

Nisa did not depart without one other upset. She and her husband decided to hold a farewell cocktail party. The fact that alcohol was implicated in the evening meant that no self-respecting woman would attend. We were all invited, but under the circumstances, Abla and Ana decreed it inappropriate for any of us to go. Baba, however, had other ideas.

Although he enjoys the occasional beer, Baba is not much of a drinker, but he decided that he would like to attend this neighbourhood gathering. Abla and Ana were outraged and flew into a frenzy, the like of which had not been seen since Baba broke the news that Sami was about to marry a Jewish girl, probably. It's not often that Abla and Ana are totally united, but when they are, it's a formidable double act. Their feelings about alcohol and anything related are unequivocal; they make the Women's Temperance League look like a refuge for AA dropouts. Although they have understandable reasons for their feelings, they have no sense of proportion, any consumption of alcohol being equated to full-blown alcoholism.

Since the weather was warm, the party was held outdoors, and we could hear the boisterous proceedings as the noise drifted past on a powdery breeze. Obviously everyone was having a grand evening. Meanwhile, Abla and Ana skulked about indoors, acting as if Baba were a lost cause, assuring each other that they would be well within their rights never to allow him to enter the house again.

The man himself rolled home about 10:00pm, pretty merry and only slightly drunk. Whatever his degree of inebriation, he entirely failed to notice that neither his daughter nor his wife were speaking to him. That they were refusing to serve him his dinner was also lost on him as he had eaten his fill at Nisa's and couldn't have cared less about food. We sat in the salon for a further hour as he told us stories about life in Bulgaria and recounted tales of his travels, oblivious to the silent treatment. While I don't advocate heavy drinking, I couldn't blame Baba for a harmless evening out. In view of all that life has thrown at him, it's perhaps a miracle that he's not drunk on a regular basis. After a good night's sleep and a chance for the women to mellow, Baba's sins seem to have been forgiven, and this particular crisis has passed.

Abla and I stopped to visit Ruth during the week. She took us to see the new house they're building. When it's finished in the summer it will be one of the finest houses in town. The American influence is evident not only in the kitchen and bathrooms, but in the overall layout. Although currently a single-story house (with a big basement), they have built it in such a way that more floors can be added above at a later date.

I want to get both Ruth and Jill up here for a picnic soon. It won't be long before Jill leaves, and by then, it will be scorching hot and impossible to do anything out of doors during the day.

22 April 1970

Once again, the court case has come and gone. It remains with us, little changing, rather like a squatter who has invaded our lives and won't budge. There has been no further mention of the machines being returned. Sami was supposed to be shepherding our documents through the Central Bank, but we have heard nothing more.

I don't believe I have told you about a couple, Şirin Abla and Tuncer Ağabey, whom I met during an early trip to Istanbul. He is a lawyer and they are family friends, contemporaries of Sami's. Tuncer Ağabey has arranged to take over Baba's legal defence. He did so reluctantly because this is not an area of the law in which he has much expertise, but as a favour to the family, he has agreed. Baba is happy with this. He feels he would rather put his trust in someone he knows will do his best, than in an unknown quantity of whatever background. None of the lawyers he has had to date have made much of an impression.

The prosecution presents its case first, and it is far from finished. From what I can ascertain, during the last session, no one in the court grasped what the case was about, and each time they appear to start from scratch. Tuncer Ağabey feels that Hakan's testimony could make all the difference to Baba's case, but we have no idea when he might be called. At the rate things are going, we shall most likely be back in England before the prosecution has finished.

Neither Neriman nor Levent are used to having their parents away and, after four days, started to worry. But both Ana and Baba were back on the fifth day, and normal life quickly resumed. In addition to considering possible brides for Sami (an investigation about which not much was said and which seems to be inconclusive), a further reason for Ana's Istanbul trip was so that she could see a doctor. Somewhat predictably, he told her that she has high blood pressure and that she would have to lose weight. He suggested she restrict her diet, cutting down on salt, fatty foods, bread and potatoes. It has been a wasted consultation as she continues to do as she always has done. She eats as she pleases and then wonders why she doesn't feel well. When the family points out to her that she feels poorly because she is not following the doctor's advice, she shrugs and says, "Who listens to doctors? I'm going to die anyway." Hakan says she has been convinced of her imminent demise for as long as he can remember. In some respects, it could be said that Ana enjoys ill health.

This has been a particularly good week for the bureaucracy, first with the court case and now with my visa. Today a police jeep pulled up in front of the house, leaving Ana as alarmed and shaken as if The Inquisition had arrived, and causing such excitement in the neighbourhood as has not been seen since the dogs chased a chicken thief over the hill. The uniformed officer had been sent as a rather extravagant messenger to announce that my presence was required immediately at police headquarters. The urgency of the matter had to do with my application for Turkish citizenship. There was little point in explaining to this envoy of the government that I had applied for no such thing. I thought it best to go investigate and set off for the office of the bureaucrat who was supposed to be overseeing this knotty affair.

Despite telling everyone, over and over again, that I did not want Turkish citizenship, I wanted a resident's visa, it has made not the slightest dent in anyone's consciousness. My man said that Ankara was under the impression that nationality had been requested; that's why everything had taken so long. They had been screening me (and most likely my mail and my movements). But I should not worry. HE would take care of everything. I didn't like to remind him that's exactly what he had said several months ago, and that we were now about to start all over again. I think I showed remarkable self-restraint in refraining from any smart-ass comments, astutely perceiving that they would be counterproductive. I collected an armload of forms that were to be filled in by me, completed by my fiancé, countersigned by the proper authorities and returned to him within the week. I have no intention of doing anything more until Hakan has had a chance to look these over and see what they're all about. It's a blessing I am laid up with rheumatism.

And speaking of Hakan, the light of my life is coming home tomorrow for Çocuk Bayramı, Children's Festival. This is a holiday - always on 23 April - dedicated by Atatürk to the children of the world and involves the ones in Turkey processing through their local communities. We are planning to watch from Baba's office window as it has a perfect view of the parade route.

Last week Abla and I were *çok çalışkan*, very industrious. While Ana and Baba were away, we got the balcony ready for summer. We moved everything out so we could whitewash the walls and cleaned the place from ceiling to floor until it was spotless. We washed all the windows (I never knew that they come up shining using just vinegar and newspaper) and hung new curtains. We had previously laundered the cushion covers and wiped down all the chairs so that the summer furniture was ready to go in place. We beat the carpets and put down new rag rugs. Alas, as our project was nearing completion, the rain came down (our windows!), and the weather turned cool and gloomy for the next few days.

But yesterday the sun came out again, and we have made the balcony our warm-weather headquarters. From here we can see up and down the street, over the houses below us and into the town itself. Nothing escapes us! From this vantage point I got a rather depressing view of Dagmar who was looking unloved and uncared for, so I felt obliged to give her a thorough wash and scrub. While I was doing that, I got stung on the ankle by a wasp. After having been stung by a bee last week, I am beginning to feel that either the insects here are more vicious, or there's something personal in it. This, after losing part of a tooth while eating dinner last night. If bad things come in threes, that should mark the end.

Ruth and I had a day out on Friday. We had decided to do some shopping together and then have lunch. I invited Abla, but as usual, when she learned that we would be eating in a restaurant, she wouldn't come with us. I guess I'm not going to change her in this respect, but since I dine out with Hakan's knowledge and approval, I don't suffer any prolonged agonies of guilt over the matter.

Ruth, Jill, and Mrs Trent have eaten often at the Altın Palas, our restaurant of choice on this occasion. I had heard a lot about the place and was looking forward to an enjoyable afternoon. As we entered the cosy foyer, the Head Waiter immediately recognized Ruth and began to officiate.

I have long been in awe of Turkish standards of service. No task is too menial; no service is too small; no effort is too great. Our Head Waiter turned out to be the ultimate role model for all others. With a warm and effusive welcome, we were ushered to the best table where he seated us, all the while assuring us of his personal care and unwavering attention. We settled into our comfortable upholstered chairs. After handing over menus, he snapped open two crisp linen napkins and presented them with as much ceremony as if they were the keys to the kingdom. He beamed. Opening rituals concluded, HW momentarily left us, and I surveyed my surroundings. I might have been in a quality restaurant anywhere in the world. The interior decor had a warm, lush feel to it; the atmosphere was intimate, hushed and sedate. Each table was laid with a damask tablecloth, fine quality silverware, porcelain china and cut glass goblets. A stylish arrangement of fresh flowers completed the setting.

It was not a very big restaurant. There were twenty tables at most, and only three or four others were occupied by well-dressed businessmen. We were the only women, but it didn't matter here. Apart from the staff, no one paid us any attention.

I was about to turn my thoughts to the menu, when our smiling HW returned, rolling a little table into position beside us. Assuming this would be used to serve the food, I took little notice until I glimpsed some subtle movement out of the corner of my eye. Looking up, I saw that our devoted HW had placed a goldfish bowl to one side of the table. Clearly, there was more to come. He hurried away, returning shortly with a birdcage of impressive size and accommodation for the lone canary inside. I could practically hear the drum roll as he placed the imposing edifice on the table. He radiated. I dared not look at Ruth. He was beside himself trying to determine what more he could do to please us. We thanked him profusely for his considerate and considerable attentions. He sparkled. Then he wondered if he might make a bold suggestion. We held our breaths, hardly daring to think what might come next. Would we permit him to prepare a special meal for us?

Now I ask you, who could resist such an offer? Despite my misgivings about the cost that might now become a factor, we murmured our charmed assent. Relieved of the tedium of ordering, we daringly agreed to indulge in a bottle of wine. A fine Turkish red was produced, opened with a flourish and expertly poured, the liquid velvet furling into our glistening glasses. We sat back to chat ... instead of which, the minute the Head Waiter's back was turned, Ruth and I finally dared look at each other and collapsed in fits of suppressed giggles. We were helpless with the effort of trying to maintain some decorum and remain discreet. It was of little use. Ruth spluttered, "It must be you. None of the rest of us has had service like this before." "Nonsense," I choked, "it's you; you're the regular here."

The meal that followed more than lived up to the expectations that had been so impressively created. Our HW whisked away the ubiquitous basket of bread only to reappear with freshly made toast. Next he brought a selection of *meze* that included little savoury pastries, a selection of olives, grainy humous and grilled vegetables. The *döner kebap*, served with a crisp mixed green salad, was the best I have eaten. Perhaps I shall never again in my life have French fries moulded into a basket complete with a handle, filled with more of the same. Fresh fruit carved in fancy shapes came next. This was followed by crème caramel fit for the gods. Since at this point we could barely move, let alone get up and leave, we were treated to coffee, petits fours, cigarettes and liqueurs "on the house". The presentation of each course and dish had been exquisite, and each time, our HW was anxious to find out if everything pleased. Indeed, we had been pleased beyond imagining. To be any more pleased, we would have had to make our way to Paradise.

The afternoon had passed in a blur of food and drink, but as it drew to a close, we had to return to reality and think of going. When the bill came, it amounted to 25TL, about $2.50. For both of us. Including tip. This has to be the gastronomic equivalent of the Çelik Palas baths!

Jill and Ruth are coming here for a picnic this Friday. If the weather lets us down, we can eat on the balcony. Abla has friends visiting from Istanbul, so I invited them to join us. At first the idea went down like a man at a hen night. Turkish women drink tea and coffee together, and that is about the extent of it. So I've gone ahead and made my plans with my friends, but as I've begun to talk about the menu, Abla has become enthusiastic and has said they might come along. She's offered to make some desserts, so that sounds promising.

Do you remember that green shirtwaist dress you sent me last year? I never wore it as it was too loose through the top, but my talented Abla has tailored it for me and it looks great. She has been such a magnificent support to me, especially in the beginning when I was getting used to everything. Even now, continuing as my *avukat*, lawyer, she always helps me make the right decisions. When I can't understand, she translates - that is - she adapts her Turkish to use the words she knows I can understand. If I get into a tight spot, for instance wanting to refuse an invitation but not knowing how to do so diplomatically, Abla comes to my rescue. She is a true friend and a wonderful companion. I can't imagine what any of us will do without her if she goes to Istanbul.

I am so sorry to hear that the Titan strike is dragging on, and I assume this means that Dad's surgery has been postponed. If the doctor believes he should go ahead, you should be guided by that (don't do as Ana does!). I know Dad hates to leave work before matters are resolved, but it WILL be settled one way or another, and Dad should not jeopardize his health in the meantime.

28 April 1970

You're right. There have been more earthquakes since the big one. Because their source is in the same area, they're all classified as aftershocks. While the strongest of these are in the region around the epicentre, it is not unusual to have noticeable tremors several times a day here in Kavaklı. I am reliably informed that the chance of having another sizeable one in the near future is rather remote. I am counting on that.

I have been completely caught up in the story of Apollo 13 and frustrated at being dependent on everyone else for news. Although I can now just about grasp most of what is said to me in everyday conversation, I still have trouble with anything sophisticated. Radio reports move too fast for me, and the newspapers take such effort. Because Turkish is phonetic, it is easy, in theory, to read; but with so little practice behind me, it takes forever to wade through articles. My TIME magazine arrived, so I finally got all the background, and the family has been very good about keeping me informed. It has been a nail-biting story which I'm sure most of us thought would end in disaster. The astronauts' safe return, against all the odds, is the real triumph of the space program. The Turks have been interested, but not as much as I have. The concept of space travel is too remote for most people here. When TV is only beginning to develop and telephones are still a luxury, travel to the moon is unimaginable.

The weather has been glorious this past week and picnic fever has struck. While Hakan was home for the Children's Festival, we packed a basket of food, grabbed Abla and headed for a nearby village where we had hoped to visit some Byzantine baths. But we didn't get to see them as the road was impassable, having turned into a muddy quagmire as a result of all the rain we've had lately. After fording two streams, we decided that we were pressing our luck and turned back, stopping at another place on the way home. It turned out to be an interesting detour.

We picked our spot for the little stream that cut through a meadow, leaving a swathe of wild flowers and tough grass on its shallow banks. Hakan was full of mischief and took enormous pleasure in throwing both the dogs into the water. Lady took it all philosophically, but Aslana was furious. She raced in circles around her tormentor, barking angrily, stopping only to glare up at him. Hakan just laughed at her, and she would start all over again. Eventually we spread a blanket and settled down to our food, while the dogs, having been fed earlier, turned their attention to some horses and a donkey grazing nearby. These provided a new form of entertainment, but the bigger animals remained largely unimpressed by the dogs' efforts to intimidate.

Some women from the local village came down to the stream to do their laundry. After watching this, I am struck not only by the effort it takes, but by the need for sturdy clothing to withstand all the vigorous pummelling. The women had a sociable time, chattering and teasing each other. When they were done, they laid the clothes on the rocks to dry and sat down to their own picnic some distance away.

We had, with unprecedented foresight, managed to borrow a camera for the day. When we began taking snaps of each other, one enterprising man thought he spotted a business opportunity and approached us, offering to let us take pictures while I was perched on his donkey. The proposition had no immediate appeal. When I looked more closely at the donkey, I was even less tempted. He was dirty and mangy with a fluff of flies around him. Even from a distance, I could see fleas leaping off, a suicidal plunge seeming preferable to life spent in that fetid atmosphere. I declined the opportunity. PTB said I was being a bad sport, but I didn't notice him volunteering to take my place on that poor, miserable beast.

As we were packing our things to go, the women called over to us that we couldn't possibly leave yet. They were heading back to see the local children's procession; we must come, too. Hakan wasn't eager, but I love it when people invite me to see something of their lives. At my insistence, we made our way to the main road of their village.

The children were gathering, full of animated excitement as they lined up in readiness for their parade. They had on the most elegant costumes: the boys, in jackets of heavy velvet, the lush purple trimmed with thick gold braid; the girls, in long skirts with matching jackets and headdresses decorated with Ottoman gold coins. It looked as if the costumes had been handed down and taken out only on special occasions.

Wishing merely to observe, we suddenly became the centre of attention. This probably had something to do with my "picnic outfit", which consists of sleeveless blouse and Bermuda shorts. I'm sure none of them had ever seen anything like it. No matter what the temperature, a village woman never exposes anything more than her hands and face. To add further to the confusion, they saw that we wanted to take pictures and pandemonium broke out. There is something about a camera that provokes and stimulates. The teachers tried to get everyone organized for a group shot, but lack of co-operation meant that plan had to be abandoned, and we settled for taking snaps as we could. Having created unqualified chaos, we felt we should take our leave. With typical Turkish hospitality, the villagers had considered us to be guests and pressed farewell gifts on us. We came away with sweets, nuts and a loaf of freshly baked bread, promising in return to send copies of the photos.

What with one thing and another, it was a busy weekend (lots of visitors and late nights), during which Hakan and I had no time to ourselves. This made him grumpy and put me in a sour mood so that we quarrelled over nothing and parted feeling miserable. Our notes of regret must have passed in the post, each of us full of apologies, each of us determined that there would be no repeats. Whatever else is going on, we must get away from the general hubbub. We can't deal with everything else if we expend our energies being ratty with each other. I'm glad we've cleared the air and can look forward to an easier weekend coming up.

Friday we had the planned picnic with Ruth and her little boy, Eren. Jill couldn't come as she had been called unexpectedly to Izmir. Later, Abla and her friends joined us, so we were six in all. Abla and I had prepared all the food: *börek* (cheese pastries), *köfte, dolma, piyaz* (a salad of haricot beans, chopped onions and olive oil) - as well as tomatoes and cucumbers, olives, the last of the winter oranges, plus a homemade dessert and, of course, bread. Ruth came with some luxury items she had managed to obtain from the PX, including a catering size tin of tuna fish. That, together with a jar of Hellmann's Mayonnaise, meant tuna salad to us. We whipped this up in our kitchen, and although the Turkish contingent took enough to be polite, none of them showed much enthusiasm for it. Maybe it's an acquired taste. Anyway, it won first prize as far as Ruth and I were concerned; between the two of us, we demolished our own generous portions as well as the leftovers.

Yesterday was Ana's *gün*. For a gathering that happens only once a month, it comes around quicker than mosquitoes on a summer's night. We had a busy day, serving nearly fifty glasses of *çay* and endless cakes and pastries. Since Abla and I do most of the legwork, we were worn out by the end of the afternoon. Thankfully, we had had the foresight to prepare the evening meal that morning, so supper was easy.

After that, Baba took us out for ice cream. We went to the Yıldız Oteli, Star Hotel, where the town's elite meet to eat. They have a very good restaurant where they make their own ice cream, among other things. But the point is not so much the food as it is being in the right place to see and be seen. Once inside the hotel, we might have no idea that we are still in Kavaklı. While the building is relatively new and the interior is quite modern, the clientele seem to be from another world. Everyone is immaculately attired in clothing of obvious fine quality, all elegance and latest fashion. This is Kavaklı high society, an extremely rich one, and one which loves to impress. In these circles, there is no such thing as excess, and the smallest details of outfits and demeanour are carefully calculated. Current trends dictate the style of the garments, the colours, the cut. Here, women wear miniskirts and even slacks. The cues come from the fashion houses of Europe, but Turkish tastes give them a cultural twist.

The women are like highly stylized artificial flowers. Most have long hair that has been coiffed and regimented, their make-up faultless, their perfect crimson nails attesting to a life of servants and leisure. Jewellery is not worth its name if it is not ostentatious. Most of the women in Turkey wear jewellery, always gold, and lots of it. When I commented on the fact that many seemingly poor village women often have an armful of gold bangles, it was explained that most of these would have been given at the time of marriage. They are her personal wealth and provide a kind of security against hard times. The women at the hotel had an altogether different reason for wearing their jewellery, which was purely for display and status.

The Turks are a handsome people. Most men have moustaches, but are otherwise clean-shaven and take great pride in their appearance. They are exceedingly good looking, and they know it. The women are their equals. I have seen many ordinary women on the streets of the towns and villages who could easily win a beauty contest anywhere. With their abundant dark hair, earthy eyes and flawless skin, they are absolutely stunning. As we sat out on the terrace and watched our little portion of the world go by, I thought about the natural beauty of the people around me and doubted that it was at all enhanced by the dictates of fashion and wealth.

Chapter 8

5 May 1970

Imagine my surprise when I unrolled the latest batch of newspapers and panties fell out! (As the whole family was watching, I was not the only one surprised.) You are becoming extremely inventive in your search for ever more items that can be folded into newspapers: tissues, cold tablets, tampons, birthday candles, costume jewellery and now, underwear. Mother, you are one impressive woman.

Thank you for these and for the clippings from the local newspaper. I can't believe they published my report about the earthquake. Everyone here is so excited about it, but I can think only of former English teachers reading it and seeing all the faults. Had I but known. Baba is completely captivated by all this, browsing the strange text, pouncing on rare familiar words as if discovering valuable nuggets while panning for gold.

In anticipation of Mother's Day, we have gone to Teyze's and brought Nina home for a stay. I wasn't sure how we were going to manage the transfer: Ana won't go to Teyze's house, Abla was too busy with sewing, and I didn't want to go on my own. In the end, Teyze's neighbour got Nina for us and escorted her to our waiting VW. She is now in the salon, happy as a wasp in a jam jar. She totters about and chatters to us all. I can work out most of what she says, but she occasionally lapses into Bulgarian, and I have to remind her that I don't understand. I teased her that if she didn't stop speaking to me in Bulgarian, I would speak to her in English. She said that would be fine as her English is excellent.

Last night, after two glasses of *çay*, Nina was high on caffeine and attention, and kept us in stitches telling us all the dirty scandals in the family. She was absolutely thrilled to be the bearer of such shocking revelations. I probably ought to clarify that these stories involved nothing more salacious than the cousin in Bulgaria who deliberately inflamed all the local men by wandering around town with her curls escaping her headscarf. And the aunt who never married because of some unspecified defect, which Nina thought was an extra finger. Or the anonymous relative who, it is whispered, had twins, one black and one white... hmmm... Other shockers were hinted at but considered too risky even for Nina's bold tastes. We love having her here.

With every letter now, I am looking for news of Dad going into hospital. I am staggered to hear that the strike continues to drag on, and we are concerned that he keeps postponing his surgery. I am glad he is playing some golf and trying to relax, but this is no substitute for the medical attention he needs. Health first, Dad.

We are also wondering about Bill, now that his basic training is finished. The quagmire in Vietnam and Cambodia looks worse now than it did a couple of months ago. It's all so complicated, and I'm never sure that we're getting the true picture, or even part of it. I cannot believe, knowing how the American people feel about our involvement in Vietnam, that President Nixon has taken us into Cambodia as well. The papers here are saying that Congress is threatening to impeach him for, in effect, declaring war on Cambodia without its consent.

Friday was Bahar Bayramı, Spring Festival, always on 1 May. This is a big holiday throughout the world, especially in Communist countries where it is known as May Day. For most people in this country, it's an excuse for a picnic; but since we've so recently had a few, and since the weather has not been very good, and since it didn't look as if PTB would be able to come home, we didn't plan anything special. All military leave was cancelled because the authorities were on alert for possible pro-communist demonstrations in the bigger towns and cities. Communism is specifically outlawed under the Turkish Constitution, and party membership is illegal; but that doesn't prevent protest marches from taking place, particularly by the student population.

As it turned out, everywhere remained calm, and Hakan was able to come home for the weekend after all. Following his last hectic visit, we set aside some time for ourselves and just did very little, very slowly. As of today, he has finished four months in the army. He is still trying to find a way in which he can finish after six months, but there's only a 50/50 chance he thinks. We aren't discussing it because we don't want to be shattered if it doesn't happen. I can say only that if there's any news, we'll tell you without delay.

This has been Abla's week. A married friend who now lives in Istanbul has been staying with Nevin, their mutual friend, here in town. There has been much visiting back and forth and a lot of gabbing, giggling and great times. One evening, while Baba was in Istanbul, we had the two girls for dinner and an overnight stay. After a huge meal, we sat around looking at old photos and talking. When it came to 11:00 pm, I could see that Abla was fidgety, hoping that Ana and Levent would soon go to bed. Naturally, the girls wanted to chat on their own, and Abla wanted a cigarette, which she could not smoke in front of her mother.

Eventually, Levent got fed up with women and girl talk and said good night. But Ana, who normally goes to bed about 9:00 pm, would not budge. She seemed blissfully unaware that the girls wanted to gossip without her, and she hung on, afraid she might miss something. Wanting to help out, I began to stretch and yawn (normally rude behaviour) and indicated that I was soon off to bed. No response from Ana. More of the same from me while inching forward to the edge of my seat, looking at my watch. Still nothing. Finally I said, "Come on, Ana, let's go to bed. It looks like the girls are going to be up all night talking nonsense. I'm not going to make myself tired for tomorrow. How about you?" Reluctantly, but very reluctantly, she agreed to go with me.

Honestly, Abla gets no peace. Since that evening, there has been more visiting, and Abla was asked to spend the night. She has never, in her life, slept over at a friend's house. Ana has never permitted it. However, in this instance, it would have been impolite to refuse the returned invitation. By western standards, Abla has led an unusually sheltered life. Things that are a novelty for her would be nothing unusual for a sixteen-year-old at home. It would be no exaggeration to say that she was delirious with excitement and full of plans for her first overnight adventure. She actually made new clothes for this august occasion and went off dressed fit for a royal tour. Hakan and I delivered her to Nevin's on Saturday afternoon and picked her up Sunday morning.

However, her joy was not yet complete. Sunday afternoon, she left with Baba for a week in Istanbul. (They asked me to go with them, but trailing Sami around is not my idea of fun, so I begged off). Happy doesn't begin to express Abla's feelings. She and Baba are close, positively lighting up in each other's company. He gives her the support and companionship she doesn't get from her mother, probably hoping that little indulgences might in some way compensate for the things that are otherwise missing in her life. He finds it hard to refuse her anything.

I'm certain that Abla took advantage of this by making herself a pair of slacks - her first ever - and asking to wear them on the trip to Istanbul. Of course, Ana was having none of it, but under the circumstances, the decision was not hers to make. So slacks it was, and very chic she looked. It's easy to assume that it's always the men who hold women back, but from what I observe, it's the women who are the preservers of culture and frequently, are the more conservative in their views. Most men seem shy about "women's problems", preferring not to get involved and to let women deal with these matters themselves. It's the women who need to decide what is in their own best interests, then unite and stand firm.

There is renewed interest in Abla as a prospective bride. Last week, the mother of the young man in question came to meet her. She is the friend of a neighbour, and it is her role to meet the girl first; if she passes inspection, other members of the family come into play. Evidently Abla passed muster, which is a shame as we didn't like his mother much, but we have decided to reserve judgment until we see the son. Abla is thoroughly nonplussed about the whole thing. She says this is the way it generally goes. Her parents are flattered to be approached, but when it comes to the proposal, they always say no. Hardly a week goes by without someone making at least tentative enquiries on behalf of a potential suitor, but nothing ever comes of it because the Beylers won't agree. If Abla wants anything to happen, she is going to have to be thunderstruck by one of the prospective candidates, then get on her feet and fight her corner. To date, she hasn't been so inspired.

I'm becoming aware that part of the basis for all the nay saying has to do with the present lack of money. The Beylers feel they couldn't uphold their end of the financial arrangements that a good marriage would require. According to custom, it's the groom's family who provides the bedroom and dining room furnishings, while the bride's family supplies everything for the parlour and kitchen. We'll simply have to see how things evolve. I haven't heard anything more about Sami's love life. When it comes to matchmaking, this particular family backs off. The reasons are complex, and I don't understand them all.

It's been two years since I've been home and a year since I've seen you all. I am missing everything and think of you all so often. What would we do without mail!

12 May 1970

I am so grateful for your frequent letters keeping us posted on Dad's progress. Strike or no strike, I was not surprised to learn that he had finally decided to go ahead with the operation. Hooray for that! It must be a massive relief to have it behind him and to know that he is already making a speedy recovery. No more special diet, Dad! That alone has to be something to celebrate.

We were so pleased to get Bill's Fort Dix photo. He's looking physically fit and very well. The tough training seems to agree with most men. Everyone here has seen his picture and says how handsome he is. They've also admired his uniform (much better than the Turkish equivalent) and the amount of his pay, a small fortune compared with pay packets here. You have said that he is having further training, but training for what? We are so anxious to find out where he will be sent abroad. Let's hope it's Germany.

Baba and Abla came flying home from Istanbul on Saturday. Literally. I wasn't aware, until they came by way of THY (the Turkish airlines) that they even had domestic flights to Kavaklı. They obviously had a fabulous time and came laden down with gifts for everyone. I gather that Baba managed to get another sizeable chunk of money out of Sami, with a promise of more to come. Most of it will go to pay debts; getting those behind him would make all the difference to Baba's outlook. Meanwhile, Abla has had the time of her life. It's been a long dry spell since she has had the means to splurge, and she did exactly that. In addition to buying lots of new clothes and eating in the best restaurants, she insisted that Sami take them out to all the plays and concerts. I was overjoyed to see two of my favourite people so happy, laughing and joking and wanting to share the good fortune. Undoubtedly, the best gift of all is that Abla will not have to go to Istanbul to work. At least, not now.

Entirely unexpectedly, we have had a letter from a German department store asking for WML samples and prices. Hakan was so excited by the prospect of another new customer that he couldn't sit down all weekend. I'm afraid I am less excited as we are not in a position to handle anything like the quantities that would be involved in an order from a company of this size. With Hakan away, the business is operating in low gear, and I don't see that changing until he is out of the army. If he were here and in charge, I am sure we could handle anything; but without him, I don't want us to take on orders we can't reasonably fill. We have written a careful letter in reply and sent some samples to see what happens. PTB is the eternal optimist; I am - not the pessimist - I am the realist. He's generally trying to pull me ahead, while I'm trying to slow him down. Usually, we strike a sensible balance. At times, his plans leave me breathless, but life is never boring, and I wouldn't have it any other way.

In the workshop this week, Baba and I have been playing around with leather and suede patchwork. We're experimenting to see what we can come up with. Ken has said that anything with a crazy-quilt effect is all the rage in London now, so we're trying out some ideas. WML needs to stay in touch with a fiercely competitive market that is continually changing and moving on. We are so out of it here. The best thing about patchwork is that it makes economic use of a scrap material of which there is no shortage. Baba can stitch the pieces together on the machines he has, producing a sort of fabric from which we can make jackets and waistcoats. As large pieces, they make handsome bedspreads. We are also planning to make maxi-coats and will ask Abla to help us cut master patterns. We want to have a few things ready for Hakan to see and approve before sending them to Ken for his reactions.

The more I find out about Nixon's War in Cambodia, the angrier I feel. Whatever was he thinking? I'm probably getting a skewed view of events from here, but I have the distinct impression that most Americans do not support this insanity. And I am so sorry that my wonderful country is behaving in such a way as to enrage most of the rest of the world. What are we doing there? All this loss of life, for what? I am thoroughly confused and fail to see any logic to any of this. I'm not the only one.

Abla said there were anti-American demonstrations all over Istanbul last week, and that the American embassy is under heavy guard after university students destroyed an American flag just outside the embassy walls. Cars bearing US identification are being attacked and their windows broken. I am so grateful that Dagmar has German plates, a happy accident rather than a cunning calculation. Luckily, the Turks like the Germans and I am often mistaken for one, a little deception in which it can be convenient to participate. But I hate having to do it. I cannot believe that all the violence I read about characterizes the country I left only two years ago and now appears to be a place I never visited. When are the politicians going to stop blaming the demonstrators and start accepting responsibility for their endless mistakes? I cannot imagine returning to all that. What an appalling picture.

Tomorrow we are taking some time off; Baba, Abla and I are going to Uludağ Mountain. Bursa, where we go for those amazing baths, lies in its foothills. We've decided to go by coach so as not to risk being stopped by the traffic police (there are frequent and unpredictable security checks), alerting them to the illegal presence of my vehicle in their country. We'll take a picnic hamper and plenty of warm clothes. The weather here is hot (HOT!), but the mountain is high, with snow at the top. We can take a cable car to the ski lodge where we can have our lunch and then strike out on some of the forest walks. We're all looking forward to this little overnight excursion.

18 May 1970

Such excellent news to hear that Dad is now home from the hospital. Since this marks yet another step on his road to recovery, I'm sure he is in high spirits. I guess Peter loses out in the scar competition. Dad's ten-inch souvenir makes Peter's look amateur. Seriously though, we are relieved and delighted that everything has gone so well. Dad now needs to take it easy and make steady progress without overdoing things. We know he's in capable hands.

Thank you for the "magic" birthday candles. They've arrived for Levent's birthday, and we're going to have some fun with him. Having never before seen candles on birthday cakes, the Beylers have taken to the custom with mammoth enthusiasm. We now have candles on all our special occasion cakes, the latest having been the one we made for Mother's Day. We just sang "Happy Mother's Day" to the tune of "Happy Birthday".

Whatever he's doing at Fort Dix, Bill must be sweltering. I can relate. It sounds as if he has adapted to the additional training and has done well with his promotion and division honours. I hope that his success in these matters doesn't increase his chances of going into combat, though of course, the army will do with him exactly as it pleases.

I can't help wondering what it must be like in the US these days. The killing of the four students at Kent State is beyond tragic. What has become of us? It's hard to be so far away and not have any real sense of the atmosphere, apparently changed beyond all recognition. I am totally dependent on TIME which indicates that the students weren't even demonstrating; they were just innocent bystanders. Even if they were protesting, what are we doing in Vietnam if we don't have democratic rights on our streets and campuses at home? I'm getting to the point where I don't want to know any more. The truth is too awful.

We have had so many *bayrams* and holidays lately that I'm losing track. Tomorrow is another one. It's the National Day of Youth and Sports in honour of Atatürk. It's commonly referred to as "19 May", and there will be extensive celebrations all over the country. As might be expected, the focus is on children and teens who have been preparing for weeks. It is an important event, and everyone will turn out to the stadium to watch displays of gymnastics, acrobatics, callisthenics and the like. I can't say that I am overly enthusiastic about watching amateurs do imperfectly what I myself always did so abysmally. But as it is a holiday, Hakan will have the day off, and at least, it is a further opportunity to be together.

The trip to Bursa had good points and bad. We never did go up the mountain. Due to high winds, the cable car wasn't operating. That was disappointing, but there will be other opportunities. As you know, we had decided to travel by coach. Because Hakan and I have had some nasty brushes with buses, I was not looking forward to this experience. I simply don't trust the judgment of their drivers. Size is everything on the highways, and operators of big, powerful Mercedes buses have run me off the road, literally, countless times. They come roaring up from behind, inching closer and closer, breathing down my neck, impatient with my speed, determined to pass, whatever the cost. If I am too slow getting out of their way, I fear that they will mow me down and drive on without so much as a backward glance.

Highway safety apart, there is a plus side. After the lack of organization so evident in many aspects of life here, coach travel comes as a welcome revelation. This private system of public transport is extensive, integrated and comprehensive. We can pretty much get a coach from anywhere, to anywhere, at almost any hour. And it's cheap, even by Turkish standards. Since horse carts still far outnumber cars, it is no wonder that most people choose to travel by bus. We bought our tickets in advance and had seat reservations for the front rows. I wanted to see precisely what was going on from the driver's perspective. As the four-hour trip to Bursa took place mostly over back roads, there was hardly any traffic and therefore, almost no need to pass (phew!). I took in little of the countryside as my concentration was fixed on both road and driver for most of the journey. I watched him as if he had the last chocolate on the planet and wondered if he could feel my eyes boring into him, assessing his every move. Luckily, my fears were unfounded. On this occasion.

Most of the buses are spanking new, full of the latest equipment and features. And they are spotlessly clean, both inside and out. Stewards, whose duties are similar to those of airline hostesses, offer lemon cologne, serve drinks and snacks, and provide helpful information. But the driver is the captain of his vehicle. He is most definitely in charge and in command. If we picked up passengers along the way, it was at the driver's discretion. If he didn't like the look of the three villagers with their six chickens, he bypassed them, and they had to wait for the next prospect. Once admitted through the rear entrance, the *ad hoc* passengers were told where to sit and to be quick about it as the stop lasted no longer than the time it took for them to get aboard. Without warning, the doors would whoosh shut, and we were off again, leaving the newcomers lurching and stumbling, their baskets and parcels sent flying.

As we progressed towards Bursa, the air in the coach thickened and took on a pungent quality, a mix of garlic breath, sweaty bodies and unwashed clothing. It occurred to me then that the Turks must have economized on one feature: air conditioning. Since none of the windows would open, it soon became obvious that without the introduction of fresh air from some source, we were all in danger of fainting, if not suffocating. Once again, lemon cologne came to the rescue as I doused a tissue with the contents of the little bottle that Abla quite cleverly produced from her handbag. Its biting sweetness provided welcome relief from the enveloping fug that threatened to congeal around us, until we stopped and the doors opened, admitting a brief but much-needed blast of air.

Part of the reason that a three-hour car journey takes four hours by coach is the frequency of stops. Not only did we pause often to take on extra passengers, but there was also an implicit understanding that there would be periodic breaks at key locations. Every town and village along the way seems to have a specialty that requires indulgence. It was obviously expected by the passengers and built into the schedules. Thus, we had stops to buy cologne (I have been converted and now carry my own supply), *ayran* (a refreshing yoghurt drink), *kestane şekeri* (candied chestnuts), salami (beef), *börek*, eggs and olives. We ate and drank our way to Bursa.

Sated and more relaxed as we approached the city, I gasped when I saw the stunning expanses of scarlet poppies covering the fields and hillsides like an exotic carpet. Since some poppies are the source of opium, their beauty can be regarded as a double-edged sword, and their cultivation is strictly controlled by the government. At least, the government tries to control both their harvest and distribution.

Turkey is currently one of the world's biggest producers of opium-based drugs, legally for medical purposes, and illegally for other uses. The difficulties arise because it is a highly profitable crop in a relatively poor country, and it is not easy to persuade Turkish farmers that they should abandon it to raise something far less lucrative. I gather the US Government is applying enormous pressure to halt outlawed production and is willing to provide financial incentives to achieve it, but this is all easier said than done. Cultural traditions, as well as profit, have to be taken into account. Turkey does not have a drug abuse problem, but its farmers are being asked to sacrifice their livelihoods in order to protect the youth of a faraway country. The closer I get to these things, the more I understand that there are no easy solutions.

Once we arrived and realized we couldn't go up the mountain, we decided to stay in town and explore its many attractions. Before Constantinople was conquered and the Ottoman government moved to Edirne, Bursa was the first capital of the empire. As a result of its importance, there are many fine mosques and tombs to visit. I love the mosques. The buildings themselves are quite magnificent with their trademark domes and varying numbers of minarets. It's from these that the call to prayer ("There is no God but God and Allah is His Name") resounds throughout the population to remind it of the requirement to pray regularly. The faithful (by no means everyone - this is a secular country) stop whatever they are doing, unroll their little rugs in the direction of Mecca and perform their *namaz*, the energetic prayer rituals, five times a day. I find something reassuring in these calls which are really half chant, half song, always in Arabic. The voice of one talented *müezzin*, singing from the heart, is enough to inspire the godless and this, from someone who is not a Muslim.

Once inside the mosque (modest attire, hair covered, shoes off at the door), there is an atmosphere of serenity and calm that makes me feel as if nothing bad could ever happen there. They are oases: cool and refreshing on a hot day, warm and welcoming on a cold one. The simple interiors are largely unadorned save for the beautiful carpets which cover the floor. Sometimes the walls have colourful Iznik tiles; sometimes the windows have stained glass; sometimes there is a candle-lit chandelier hanging down from the ceiling. Since the sexes do not pray together, certain areas are designated for women. A niche in the wall denotes the direction of Mecca, and a high podium-like piece of furniture is the place from which the Hoca leads prayers, reads the Koran and delivers his sermon on Friday, the Muslim Holy Day. It's the simplicity that I find appealing. No icons, no symbols, no altars. Nothing between you and Allah.

Baba, Abla, and I played tourist for most of the day, finishing up in the main bazaar. While this is nothing like the one in Istanbul, it is, nevertheless, of significant size with an impressive variety of shops. I was after Turkish towels. Bursa is famous for them, and I managed to find what I wanted without difficulty. Specialty towel shops offer the whole gamut of toweldom, coming as they do in all sizes, thicknesses, colours and motifs - plain or striped, simple or ornate. Abla helped me haggle, explaining that the shopkeepers should not embarrass themselves by asking tourist prices when we were clearly locals. I spoke Turkish to them to emphasize the point. It's always worth it just to see their faces go from bewilderment to delight. Everything helped, and I was pleased with both purchases and price.

After that, I bought a length of material with a typical Turkish pattern that will make a decorative tablecloth. But my real find was some antique textiles. I spotted them in a little shop hidden away, there not being much demand for Old Things. I learned that the long cloth (about three feet long and a foot wide) is a sort of napkin called a *yağlık*. These were in use when people had their meals seated cross-legged around a low table on the floor. Each diner had a *yağlık* that was spread across the lap and legs to catch food spills. The ones I saw were hand woven, only the ends embroidered so as not to spoil the work with greasy stains. The shopkeeper had a pile of these exquisite, yet functional cloths, and I was overcome by indecision. I would like to have bought them all, but in the end, I settled for just two: one with a finely stitched flower design, the other in the same pastel colours, obviously done by a beginner. The work on the latter is coarse and irregular, but it has character and speaks to the earnestness with which a little girl had so lovingly made this piece for her dowry. The cost was 20TL, $2 each.

We spent the night in a hotel in the town. All the hotels there seem to have thermal baths, so we were able to wash away the day's grime in the comfort of our rooms. While resting peacefully on my bed, reflecting on the day, Abla shook me by the shoulder and told me not to get too relaxed. I had to get up and get dressed as we were going out for Bursa's speciality: *Iskender Kebap*. Naturally, Baba knew the best place for this famous dish comprised of *döner kebap* served on thick chunks of *pide* bread with a yoghurt dressing and a spicy tomato sauce topping. Together with a salad, it was a complete and satisfying meal. And well worth the effort.

In the morning, guess what? Another bath. This was followed by a traditional breakfast in the hotel dining room with views over the town. We had one last stroll around the bazaar before boarding the coach for home. I could not have had a better time up the mountain. Baba and Abla are terrific companions, and we all had a marvellous trip.

Last week, we sent the final lot of dressed skins to London. If we want any more, we shall have to buy raw and get them dressed, but we are holding off because we want to see how our patchwork is received. Hakan approved all the samples we had prepared, and they have gone off, too. It would be good to spread our money over the different materials so as not to have all our eggs in one basket, but we need news from Ken before committing ourselves.

Yesterday, Neriman and I took Nina back home. We had strict instructions from Ana that we were to deliver her mother to Teyze's door and scarper. Under no circumstances were we to enter the house or speak to anyone. Regrettably, as far as this plan was concerned, the whole family was sitting on the porch when we arrived. Everyone, including Teyze, made a big fuss of us, and we were invited to sit down. We felt we had to decline the invitation to stay, but we greeted everyone and had a brief chat, during which Teyze's prospective daughter-in-law was introduced. She seemed young, probably no more than eighteen at most, but since her fiancé is Hakan's cousin, in the social hierarchy we are peers. Like Teyze and Şevkiye Abla, she was simply dressed in *şalvar*, blouse and headscarf: no make-up, no adornment. I thought she eyed me warily. I felt she was judging me for my uncovered hair and short skirt, but it may have been purely my novelty value that had her mesmerized.

Teyze herself was a changed person from the only other occasion I had seen her. She was warm and welcoming and actually offered her hand for me to kiss as we departed. I am deeply suspicious that Abla has told them I am going to become a Muslim. While she knows this is not true, it would be characteristic of her to do almost anything to keep peace in the family. Consider it a white lie. And for whatever reason, I have suddenly become more tolerable in their eyes. When we got home, we confessed everything to Ana who hurled verbal abuse at us for the next ten minutes, threatening us with every conceivable torture and punishment for disobeying her orders. Then she promptly forgot the whole incident and promised to make us our favourite *börek* the next day.

I have begun to wonder if we shall be inviting Teyze and her family to our wedding. We were not invited to their son's engagement party, but we have heard that we will be invited to the nuptials. Ana says this is merely because we will be required to give them a present, so she's refusing to attend. Hostilities continue.

I finally got to the Sunday morning flea market that I have been longing to see. In the past, PTB has steadfastly refused to go, assuming it to be of no interest because it's only old stuff, junk really. However, he evidently had a change of heart as, when Baba suggested a visit, Hakan said it was a great idea, and what did I think? I laughed and agreed. Like most markets, it begins early and we were there for the start. Baba has obviously picked up on the fact that I love Old Things and directed us to the stalls he had found interesting in the past. Hakan had been correct in his opinion that there would be more trash than treasure, but I was fascinated because there were so many curious objects that I had never seen before.

The sole problem was that we were as obvious as skiers on a golf course. Hakan was in his London clothing, complete with sunglasses (associated with tourists), and I always stand out wherever I go in small town Turkey. There was no way we were going to get reasonable prices. Everyone assumed we were rich foreigners, and since I seemed to be the only woman in the entire market, we soon attracted a crowd of curious onlookers. We tried to ignore them as we wandered around, gradually acquiring an entourage that forced us to give up. We decided that if we really wanted to buy anything, Hakan would have to go back in his army uniform. Everyone knows that soldiers have no money.

When is Peter's graduation? What has he decided about college in the fall? I trust you will keep us informed about Dad.

26 May 1970

I am in the process of getting a gift box ready to send to you, some everyday items I thought might be of interest. I have assembled some towels and the fabric I bought in Bursa along with tea, tea glasses, lemon cologne, cigarettes, *nazar* or evil eyes (good luck charms), assorted nuts and some dried fruit. If you can think of anything else, please say so.

It was interesting to hear your views on recent news events. I guess we'll have to agree to disagree on most of it. I don't care what the provocation, there can be no justification for the killing of unarmed students on their own college campus. And I cannot support Nixon simply because he is President. To do so would be to give him a mandate to act as he wishes (which he appears to be doing in any case). If people feel he is wrong, dead wrong, then they should let him know. It must be a difference in the generations that enables some to follow unquestioningly anything that the President advocates. I love my country, but am heartily sick of trying to defend the indefensible. We are paying a high price at home for our involvement in Vietnam, not to mention what has happened to our international reputation. And for what? The minute we finally leave that benighted country, the Communists will take over anyway. We need to get out of Vietnam and allow the people to determine their own affairs. And we need to restore peace at home.

On Wednesday, Abla and I had a million things to do, but nothing was accomplished because of guests. Throughout the day, ten different people called in, each one overlapping the other, so that we did nothing but serve *çay* and refreshments as the hours were eaten slowly away. Ana is reassured by all the attention; the numbers confirm her belief that everyone loves her. It felt like a *gün* but was only an ordinary weekday. This is the downside to Turkish hospitality. Everybody is expected to be available and welcoming any time anyone turns up.

Some days it is completely impossible to get anything done, a situation the Turks take in their stride, but one which I find endlessly frustrating. It is impossible to plan anything. Just as I'm ready to hop in the bath (this in itself must be planned in advance because of the need to get the stove fired up), someone arrives at the door. We can never let a guest feel that the visit is inconvenient as this would be rude and insulting, but I must confess to more than one instance when I have dived into the bathroom, pretending total deafness to the doorbell. I can't tell you the number of occasions we have started out the door, only to be confronted by an arriving visitor. There's no choice but to return inside, take off our coats and offer hospitality. I can see why the system has developed, and I have often been on the receiving end of it, but it is something I'll never get used to, no matter how long I live here.

On Friday, I met Ruth and Jill for lunch. We were going to have a picnic, but our May weather has been unusually cold and dreary. Since the salon stove was put away weeks ago, we've been sitting around in heavy clothes and sweaters, trying to keep warm. Under the circumstances, we decided to eat in town and could not resist the temptation to dine again at Altın Palas where Ruth and I had such royal treatment.

Our Head Waiter was there and looked after us just as well this time. It was sheer bliss to chat and swap anecdotes without worrying if we were doing or saying the right things, oblivious to the scandal of our brazenly unchaperoned state. After June, there will be no more Peace Corps workers in Turkey, so we teased Jill about being the last of a vanishing breed. While pressure from the students has had the desired effect, there are also genuine regrets in some quarters as most of the PC workers in the universities have been training virtually all the English teachers. When the PC goes, much of the work will be unfinished, and there will be a conspicuous shortage of qualified English teachers.

Jill had to leave the restaurant before Ruth and I were ready to go, so the two of us stayed on over coffee, and Ruth unburdened herself about her miserable home life. She has a dreadful mother-in-law who constantly undermines her, even working to turn her own children against her. For instance, she won't permit English to be spoken in the house, so Ruth cannot teach it to her children. She is always criticizing Ruth in front of the family and sneering at American culture so that the children learn that anything to do with their mother is bad. Ruth says she is able to redeem some of this negative feeling with the American ice cream and other treats she gets from the PX. But her marriage is under terrible strain.

Ruth realizes that the major consequence of divorce would be losing her children. She is far from ready to quit, but she has almost no one but Jill and me to turn to since there is no support for her either in her home or outside it. Everyone believes her husband is God's Gift to Medicine in general, and to Kavaklı in particular. No one will hear any criticism of him. No matter what Ruth does, she is the villain. It's a tough situation, but about all I could do was listen and sympathize. And be thankful for my own more agreeable home life here.

Among other firsts, I can now add, "wallpaper hanging" to my list. Hakan and I had brought enough with us to paper two rooms; we did that on Sunday, completing both the parlour and the salon. I could not understand why it was important to him to bring wallpaper with us, but they don't have it here, and the one-up-man-ship is worth more than you might imagine. There is tremendous status in being first with the latest in home decorating trends straight from London. Since none of us had ever hung wallpaper before, it took us a while to get the knack, and the first few pieces looked a little patchy. But both Baba and Hakan have extremely practical minds, and it didn't take them long to work out the technique. After that, the work sailed along and we finished in good time. It's Ana's *gün* today, and she is anxious to show off the new decor. I can hardly wait to hear the many comments I'm certain will be made.

Glad to hear Dad has been staying calm and relaxed during his recuperation. If he's really good, we'll let him read tax law for excitement. Meanwhile, it sounds as if everything is on the right track for a full recovery.

Chapter 9

3 June 1970

Congratulations to Peter! How does it feel to be a high school graduate? What are your plans for the summer? When do you start college? I have heard that jobs might be scarce as even some of the recent college grads are having difficulties. It doubtless depends on how picky you are.

Once again I am in trouble, this time in two not unrelated ways. You most likely recall that Ruth, Jill and I lunched last week at Altın Palas; I may even have joked about the three of us eating out unchaperoned. It turns out that there was nothing amusing about the incident. Well, not for the Beylers. We've had the it's-a-disgrace-for-unchaperoned-women-to-eat-in-restaurants discussion before, but apparently, I have compounded the sin by patronizing Altın Palas. Whenever we've met there, it has been a relatively last-minute decision, and since I am fully acquainted with the Beylers' feelings about my dining out with my American friends, I didn't go out of my way to advertise what I had been doing. Besides, I actually thought the restaurant's exclusivity made it a discreet choice. We weren't flaunting ourselves in a public way, or so I believed. But I should know better when it comes to small towns and local gossip.

Word of my lunching escapades reached the family, and I was engulfed in a wave of madness that broke over our little ship. How was I to know that this was the scene of Sami's wicked outrages? Since it is clearly the best place in town, it makes sense that Sami would show off by taking everyone he wanted to influence there, wining and dining them, picking up the tab. This is where he caroused night-after-night, a considerable portion of the family fortune disappearing down the throats of the area big wigs whom Sami was eager to impress. In one sense, he seems to have achieved his goal, for he certainly has managed to open doors in exalted places. However, the cost to the family not only in terms of money, but in terms of the drinking and excesses that resulted in the ruin of their first-born, has made them bitter about the very name of the place.

I had heard the stories of Sami's appalling outrages, but the name "Altın Palas" had never been mentioned. And while I was not being deliberately secretive about my activities, I had not gone out of my way to advertise something I suspected would result in upset. Well, upset there has been, and I am now in the process of trying to earn my way back into their good graces. With Hakan's help, I have managed to calm the Beylers and reassure them of my harmless intent, but for the sake of peace, I felt obliged to promise them that I would never go back. I think it's unreasonable, but I can see their point, too - not with regard to eating out - but in terms of their sensitivity to this particular venue and its unhappy associations. It's okay. I can live without lunch at the Altın Palas. But I'm ever so glad to have had the experience of eating there.

Opportunely, I am able to do penance by continuing to help redecorate the house. Once the wallpaper was up and looked so good, we decided that everything else appeared a little shabby, so we have been repainting all the woodwork and doing some other little decorating jobs that have given the house a lift. Abla and I have done most of the work, but Baba helps out in the evenings and Hakan, at weekends. Levent cannot be bribed or threatened to do something he doesn't like, so he has been noticeable by his absence. After today, the biggest part of the work will be done, and we are feeling incredibly pleased with ourselves.

Last Friday, Ruth, Jill and I went for a picnic in a little municipal park about ten miles out of town. The weather has not been favourable, but we have been trying to do this for so long that we simply disregarded it and went anyway. Each of us had prepared something. I took Turkish food, but Jill had made brownies, and Ruth had made chocolate chip cookies. These are the first I've had since I left the USA. Even England has not discovered such delights. I must have mentioned previously how much I have missed these things, and both girls came through spectacularly. I was delirious and couldn't stop eating. It's difficult to make American recipes here not only because the ingredients are hard to come by, but because I have no American measuring cups or spoons. I tried to do it by guesswork once, but that was not very successful. Jill has a cookbook that converts Turkish ingredients into American recipes, so I am going to borrow that and copy some favourites, like brownies! It would be such fun to make them for the Turks.

We had a memorable afternoon. The park was mostly deserted, so we had the pick of the tables and found one under the trees, which shielded us from the mist and drizzle that started early on. As the afternoon progressed, drizzle became light showers, then the skies darkened, and the rain came down with a vengeance. By the end of the afternoon, we were soaked through to our skins and dripped like overloaded sponges, looking all the while like something nasty that had been fished out of the nearby stream.

We agreed it must be poetic justice. Our little adventure had caused much consternation. Given that we had been trying to arrange this for weeks, the decision to picnic was hardly a surprise. When we had made this last plan, I informed the family and left it at that. Naturally, I asked Abla to come along, but she said, "No"; and Ana said, "Absolutely not." I assumed it was because they don't like Ruth and probably don't approve of Jill. Ana said that I had to get Hakan's permission to go. I agreed and then promptly forgot. I knew he wouldn't care; after that, it never crossed my mind.

The next time Hakan came home, Ana cornered him and told him what I was planning, as if there were some big intrigue involved. I heard them discussing it. I also heard the word *ayıp,* shame, mentioned. When their conversation had finished, I obviously wanted to find out what had been said. Hakan reported that his mother was upset because she considered it a complete and total disgrace for three young women to go off, unescorted, by themselves, on a picnic, in the middle of a forest where anything could happen. Our reputations would never recover. Of course. It's just the outdoor version of the whole restaurant scenario. I don't know why it didn't occur to me.

I explained to Hakan that I had not realized the implications for kith and kin, nor the upset it would cause. In the interests of family peace, and I suspect, family honour too, I was willing to make my excuses and cancel. But Hakan wouldn't hear of it. He supported me unconditionally, saying that they should appreciate that I am a responsible person, and that he trusts me to do the right thing, regardless of where I am, be it England or Turkey or anywhere else. He said that he would tell me if he thought I was doing anything wrong, but as far as he was concerned, I wasn't; I should go and enjoy myself with my friends. Ruth had had the third degree from her mother-in-law, and Jill's Turkish friends had advised that this was not a sensible idea. We had had our way in defiance of all Turkish society. Or so it seemed. Poetic justice, indeed!

I feel bad about having caused such uproar over what I deem to be events of little importance. Even though we saw nothing wrong in what we were doing, whether eating out or in, I really don't want to be the reason for upset and grief, especially when the Beylers have all been so good to me. Hakan, bless him, and Baba too, always back me up. I am only now beginning to appreciate how exceptional this is, and how lucky I am to have both of these wonderful men in my life and on my side. However, I will try to avoid this sort of thing in the future. It benefits no one.

An amusing side note to all this is that if Abla and Ana had not made a point of telling everyone about it, no one outside our immediate families would ever have heard about our scandalous behaviour in the park. It's my opinion that the two women enjoy a little *frisson* of excitement and take a giddy pleasure in the telling of this rather daring tale... and the subsequent sympathy that comes their way as a result. (Not to mention that Nina now has new material for her repertoire.) I believe they think it makes them look tolerant, modern and somewhat long-suffering. Being "modern" and "western" are fashionable and desirable in the upper echelons of Turkish society. But for most people, liberal attitudes are something to be viewed from afar. It's not as if you would want your own daughter to have them.

We are going to miss Jill when she goes. I've known her a few short weeks, but we hit it off immediately. Her work is finished now, and she is spending this week packing and getting ready to meet her parents who will arrive in Istanbul to do some travelling with her before she goes home. Tomorrow, we are meeting at Ruth's house for a farewell lunch.

As you almost certainly have guessed, we have had to give up on any hope that Hakan would get away with only six months of military service. It was never very likely, and we are disappointed but not surprised. At present, the picture looks like this: Hakan will undergo formal officer training here in Kavaklı for four months beginning in July. After that, he will probably be transferred to one of the major cities.

I keep forgetting to tell you that Sami travelled to America with two business companions a couple of weeks ago. He rang one evening before he left to inform us that he was off and would be gone for a week. We haven't seen him since his return, so I haven't found out where he went, nor do I have any trip details. Ostensibly, it all had to do with some important deal at Westinghouse. I would love to hear his version of a trip to America. No doubt he is an authority now. When he got back, he asked us to send Levent, so we have packed him off to Istanbul for a visit of unspecified length. We had a letter from him to say that he is having a great time. Sami spoils him, and Levent basks in the attention. Depending on how long he stays, we are wondering if Sami might help him find some work there.

Just so you are up-to-date, the dogs are now outside. Once the weather warmed up and we had cleaned the balcony for people, four-legged creatures were banished permanently. But they are used to the outdoors now and appear to be perfectly happy. There is a shed at the back of the house where I have made up beds for them. It offers some shelter from the rain, and if the weather is very bad, I can put them on the back balcony. They are no trouble to the household, and everyone has grown fond of them.

Like you, I couldn't figure out why Bill had turned down the chance for a place at non-commissioned officer school. I would have thought that this would be an opportunity to improve his status, but Hakan empathized entirely, saying that such training means more responsibility, and no sane person looks for responsibility in the army. Hakan, unequivocally, hates army life and is going to officer training only because he will be transferred anyway. Whatever he does, he will lose his comfy weekends at home when he leaves the Kavaklı base. If he must be somewhere else, he might as well be in as privileged a position as possible. Also, there is little chance of Hakan having to go into combat. He wholly understands Bill's reasoning.

9 June 1970

It's been a bumper week for books. Your parcel of "printed matter" came through customs with no trouble. Presumably these come under the same heading as newspapers and don't much interest the authorities. Also, Jill has left a trunk full of paperbacks, about a hundred books in all. The Peace Corps provides book lockers which get moved around to the various locations. As the PC has wound down here, Jill acquired four. She let me sort out what I wanted, and the rest are going to the Americans at the NATO base. Making my selections from such a wide variety was intoxicating, as if I could have anything I wanted from a bookstore. How gratifying to obtain these free from Uncle Sam.

When Hakan came home at the weekend, he asked me where I had been the previous Tuesday afternoon. I had to stop and think and said that I couldn't be certain, but I thought Abla and I had been shopping. "Yes," he agreed, "you bought some material and paid 18TL for it." "How did you know?" was my puzzled response. "I saw the report on your movements. It landed on my desk this week." An explanation was plainly called for and it goes like this (but don't tell anyone as this is all top secret! Really.): Hakan is one of four men at the Kavaklı base to have been selected to work in military intelligence (no jokes, please). He has agreed to this not only because the work is interesting, but because it places him well beyond anything available to him as an ordinary officer. Obviously, he will have to receive special training, but before this can go ahead, there have had to be all kinds of security clearances. Apparently, I was one of the major stumbling blocks. Because they weren't sure what to make of me, I have been followed and watched, all my movements detailed in reports for the army.

The irony is that all these go to the powers-that-be through Hakan who is, of course, the General's PA. It seems he has been hearing all about my activities for the past several weeks. Clearly, I had no knowledge of any of this. I expect that whoever followed me had a fairly dull time of it, poor man. All my mail has been intercepted, so that explains a lot. I wonder, are you aware of any of your mail from Turkey having been opened? All of this is totally hush-hush. Hakan has said nothing to his family, and you are the only ones I am telling.

Last week a three-star *paşa,* general, arrived from Ankara to interview each of the new intelligence trainees. He told Hakan that he would like for him to come to Ankara immediately. The base commander, also present, made it clear that Hakan had not yet finished his officer training (in truth, he hasn't even started it). It was agreed that he should finish this and then leave immediately for the capital. From there, he could be sent to Europe or the Far East.

As you might expect, this arrangement did not suit Hakan at all, so he said, "I'm planning to go to Bursa after my training."

"What do you mean," roared the General, "YOU plan to go to Bursa? This is the army. You will go where we tell you to go!"

"Well, sir," said our fearless PTB, "that would be fine if it were only me, but there's another person here doing my military service with me."

"What the hell does that mean?"

Hakan's base commander was, by now, turning various shades of burst-blood-vessel red. Hakan, remaining completely calm throughout, went on, "My fiancée has come all the way from America to be with me, and I have to consider her before I commit myself to travelling around the world with the Turkish army."

"We know all about your American fiancée, and as far as we're concerned, she can come with you to Ankara."

End of conversation.

It looks as if the army has big plans for Hakan. They seem to be completely oblivious to the fact that he has no interest, whatsoever, in anything beyond finishing his obligation as quickly and as comfortably as possible - and then - getting back to London.

A star shines down on us when Sami comes to call. Fresh from his trip to America, he returned home with Levent, bringing a vast array of items from an American supermarket. It's been a very long while since I've seen Heinz ketchup, Scott paper towels, Bisquick, Nescafe and Hershey's chocolate. He's still not saying where's he's been nor discussing anything about this mysterious trip, indicating that everything is Top Secret.

I don't get it. More than that, I am deeply suspicious that he's been to America at all. It's my humble opinion that the American store products were acquired from a PX. I ask you, if you had really been to the USA, are these the only items you would bring back? If you were a man visiting America for the first time, would you head for the nearest supermarket to shop? I have said nothing to anyone else, but his reluctance on the whole topic is so atypical, we can assume that he and I know the truth of this matter.

Whatever the story, Sami appears to be doing very well financially. This is good news because, if things are going well for Sami, they are better for the Beylers, too. Not to mention that improved finances mean a corresponding improvement in his temper. There is talk of him moving to a house in one of Istanbul's better neighbourhoods. But then, there is always talk. Even when he hasn't got a *kuruş* to his name, he's bragging, so nothing can be taken at face value; everything he says must be diluted. However, he does seem to have money in his pockets at the moment as Levent has had a new wardrobe. Since he is off his medication, he has lost a lot of weight and is much slimmer these days. He says he is back for a mere couple of weeks.

Once his brother moves to his new home, Levent plans to join him in Istanbul and work as a shop assistant for a handbag business in which Sami claims to have some stake. There has been no further mention of Sami's proposed wedding nuptials.

We're a little subdued in the neighbourhood this week. Someone complained about a pack of wild dogs that had been hanging around the fringes of Elli Evler. Rather than address the cause of the complaint, the local authorities laid poisoned meat up and down the streets. The children knew exactly what they were up to, and at least ten of them came calling, "Zeynep Abla, Zeynep Abla" (that's me) to warn us to keep Aslana and Lady inside for a couple of days. They were confined to the back balcony until the threat had passed, but not everyone got the word, and some of the neighbourhood dogs have died as a result. Lady was particularly friendly with the little dog next door, one of the hapless victims. Each morning she goes to look for her friend and is obviously missing her. The neighbours too, are missing their dog and have taken to feeding Lady, something about which I am not overly pleased. I haven't said anything but will keep an eye on the situation.

Abla and I have just spent two hours picking all the sour cherries off the two trees in our garden. We also have peach, apple, apricot, plum and almond trees. She's going to make a compote for dessert tonight, and later, we'll make jam with the rest.

16 June 1970

Ever since I unrolled a newspaper in front of the family and a pair of panties fell out, I am more careful about the unwrapping. Like Aladdin's cave, I am confident there will be good things inside, but the approach must be cautious. Imagine my astonishment today when I discovered Anthony and Cleopatra cigars! Hakan and Baba are delighted. I'm sure most of the fun comes from saying that their in-laws sent them all the way from America (we still have cachet in some respects). Baba calls them "Elizabeth Taylors". Levent is longing to smoke one, I know. Maybe he already has, but even though he maintains he has no such intention, he has claimed one to carry around to show off. A little bit goes a long way.

Even if I couldn't tell from the temperature, it is apparent that summer has arrived in full force: we're having water shortages. I'm not certain how it works, but water from some central source here in Elli Evler feeds into individual storage tanks on top of each house. We get so much each day, and when that is finished, that's it until the tank fills up again.

The supply is reliable in the winter, but now that hot weather is here and we have far less rain, there are days when we get no water at all, or so little that it is finished by mid-morning. The tank feeds into both floors, so it's first-come, first-served. The family on the ground floor has three small children, all in diapers, so it's not hard to see where the bulk of our supply goes. I could never have pictured the degree to which water regulates life when it is something we have to plan around.

We have our baths first thing in the morning. We can do that now and not have to worry about stoking up the stove because the water is always warm from the hot sun on the roof. Jobs requiring water - washing dishes, cleaning windows, mopping floors and doing laundry - are done *ad hoc* when we have the means to do them. Turkish housewives have a saying that goes, "no water, no work," a situation that is all too often a reality. I have learned how to have a bath, shave my legs and wash my hair using a mere bucket of water. It CAN be done. It is also at these times that the ubiquitous lemon cologne, a staple of every household, used as it is for everything from antiseptic to aftershave, comes into its own.

When things get really bad, as they did last week when we did not have water for four days, Abla and Levent and I gathered together a car full of pots and jugs and headed for a nearby spring to fill up. Sometimes I find it hard to recall that in America I could simply turn on a tap and find a ready supply - whenever I wanted it - either hot or cold. I could even drink it!

The lease on the ground floor of the house runs out in August, and we are hoping that the family will decide to leave then. Apart from the tremendous strain on the water supply, the mother, Cemile, is altogether hopeless. She goes off visiting and leaves her three tiny children on their own. When the youngest falls down, she smacks the other two and blames them for not watching the baby. The children run wild, and she lets them do whatever they want. As a result, the Beylers can't have flowers or anything decorative in the garden as the little ones destroy it all. We dread to think what the inside of the house looks like. Cemile is positively oblivious to hints and even outright requests. The Beylers ought to ask them to leave at the end of the summer, but they feel that such a step would be *ayıp* and can't bring themselves to take it.

The sequel to the story of Lady and the next-door neighbours is something of a little local drama. For reasons known only to themselves, the people in question seemed to decide that they wanted to hang onto Lady, but rather than discuss the matter or ask us, they have been keeping her in their house. When they let her out, she's come home to me with a full tummy, refusing to eat anything here. I tried to get both Abla and Levent to speak to the neighbours and ask them not to feed her or keep her indoors, but they both refused, saying that this would be another *ayıp*. So I said I would do it myself. I haven't fed and cared for these dogs for the past six months so they could wander off with whoever takes a shine to them.

Accordingly, up the street and into their yard I went. In my broken Turkish, I tried to explain - as politely as I could - what the difficulty was. They all smiled benignly and said they agreed, and anyway, they didn't even want Lady; she was becoming a nuisance to them, and so on and so forth. Fine. A little misunderstanding, or so I thought.

The next day we were sitting on the balcony when I heard Lady crying. I looked everywhere, trying to determine where the sound was coming from and finally spied her on the flat roof of the neighbours' house! It was mid-day and the sun was ablaze, heat shimmering off the tarred surface. I have no idea how long she had been up there, but I knew that poor Lady was past wretched. I could hear her pathetic whimpering and see her panting with thirst. This was the last straw. That dog didn't get onto the roof by herself. I marched directly to the house to get her back.

No one answered the door, but other neighbours told me the children were inside. When I realized they were not going to open up, I came straight back to our house and got a ladder from the shed, intending to retrieve her myself. This was easier said than done. The top rung of the ladder fell short of the roof edge, and I didn't feel nimble enough to make the leap over. A little crowd of local children assembled to advise on the proceedings. Lady was torn between her desire to fling herself into my arms and her fear of the necessary leap. She would come towards me, carefully approaching the edge, but then bark at us all, before backing off again. I couldn't grab hold of her and began to despair, when a couple of the older boys offered to take my place on the ladder and from there, get onto the roof.

I was doubtful about letting someone else's children try to rescue my dog under decidedly tricky circumstances, but the boys were convincing in their assurances that they were the ones for the job. Since I could come up with no alternative, I decided to let them try. The first one up the ladder leapt onto the roof, and while coaxing Lady with a cool drink, managed to grab her. The other boy waited at the top of the ladder and was able to take the dog from his friend, then hand her down to me. I was exceedingly grateful for the help the boys had given me. I was also furious with the people in the house but found no one on whom to vent my feelings. This was probably just as well. Lady is now tied up in the yard. I hated to do this but have no other option at present. I am baffled by the neighbours' behaviour. It is all a great pity because one day I shall be leaving and will want to give the dogs to people who are happy to look after them.

Abla seems to be at the centre of evolving events these days. No, there is nothing more about weddings for either her or Sami. These matters wither away, though whether from lack of interest on one side or the other or both, I cannot say. No, Baba has consented to let Abla go to work to earn her own money, and she has submitted an application to work at a local bank. Though these are coveted jobs and vacancies are rare, we hope that all will be in order for her to start as soon as her papers have been processed in Ankara. It will be a whole new world for her, and she is very excited. After years of doing little more than clean her mother's house, visit her mother's friends and sew for her mother's neighbours, she has a chance to develop her own life. This will be the best thing in the world for her, and I sincerely hope it works out. Compared to most Turks, Baba is reasonably liberal, and now that the decision has been made, he too, is pulling for his daughter.

Ana, however, is fully opposed to the whole idea and never hesitates to say so. Baba is head of the family, so his opinion is the one that counts. What we are afraid of is that Ana will tell Sami, and he will make it his business to scupper the plans. Considering his connections in Ankara, he could easily do this. With total disregard for his previous campaign to get Abla to work in Istanbul, he has decreed that no one in the family will work, especially not Abla. Having never been someone to let a few facts get in the way of an arbitrary decision, he has no intention of changing course at this point. Sami likes everyone to be dependent on him. This situation allows him to be domineering and feel powerful, until he finds the financial responsibilities overwhelming, and he caves in under the pressure. In this, as in everything else, he is unable to see beyond the end of his nose, and that, unfortunately for all concerned, is unlikely to change. Does anyone else grasp the twisted logic of it being acceptable for Abla to go to work for the whole family in Istanbul, but if she wants to work in town, for her own benefit, this is some sort of disgrace?

Next week, Abla is going to Istanbul with her teacher friend, Nevin, to visit their former classmate. Both girls are extremely sensible, and there is no reason why they shouldn't make the journey. Although it is unconventional for two women to travel unescorted, Baba felt it would be acceptable in this case since Sami would meet them at the other end and chaperone them around the city. Everything was fine, and all the plans were underway until Ana got Baba alone and said she would never permit such insanity... that it was all a colossal *ayıp*, that she needed Abla at home, that the girl was becoming lazy and had too many holidays, and on and on. I know this is what she said because she has been ranting at Abla and yelling the same things in her direction since Baba agreed she could go. In the end, Baba gave in to his wife and said Abla couldn't travel after all.

Abla, however, is wise to the way things work. She knew that Baba had agreed simply to get some peace, that he had taken the easy way out, rather than actually having changed his mind. When Nevin came to the house to discuss the latest plans, Abla had to tell her the bad news; at the same time, she proposed that Nevin go to see Baba at his office and have a private chat with him to plead their case. Nevin wouldn't be permitted to go to Istanbul without Neriman, so she had a big incentive to get Baba to review his position.

Whatever she said, it worked. When Baba came home that night, he reported that Nevin had been very convincing, and he had agreed that his first decision had been the right one. So everything is back on track again, and everyone is happy, except for Ana who is doing a silent simmer. But she cools down as fast as she comes to the boil, so I'm not worried. We're pampering her today, and she is returning to room temperature. But I'm telling you, what Abla goes through to get a little pleasure is absolutely pathetic.

I am continuing to give English lessons to Levent, and he is doing very well. He tries to use it as much as possible and is anxious to be able to converse with you when you come to the wedding. Everyone here speaks about "when you come" and all are looking forward to that visit.

22 June 1970

Despite our best efforts, Abla didn't get to go to Istanbul after all. The day before the planned departure, riots broke out in the city. The reports said that something like 60,000 workers were on the streets protesting a new law curtailing their right to strike. When the rioting and violence became widespread, the authorities declared martial law and imposed a 9:00 pm curfew. Given the nature of these incidents, there was only one rational decision, but I felt disappointed for Abla who had been so excited about this trip.

I am proud to report that this week, I struck a blow for American cooking. Me, of all people. After much deliberating, calculating and converting of measurements, in addition to the tracking down of vital ingredients, I made Jill's brownie recipe. It turned out very well, and they have been a huge hit with the family. I also made iced tea, totally unknown in Turkey. When I announced to the family that I was making *buzlu çay*, you should have seen the looks on their faces. If I had declared the imminent arrival of the last Ottoman Sultan, they could not have been more sceptical. They all said they would try it, I'm sure to prove to themselves that it must be as bad as it sounded. Hakan did an outstanding propaganda job. He's a great fan from his California days and was enthusiastic with the advance publicity.

When the drink was ready, complete with fresh lemon and mint, the tasting began. Cautious assessments followed hesitant sips. Before long, smiles broke out, and there was unanimous agreement that this was not good; it was wonderful! There were seconds all around. Abla and Ana are telling everyone about this tasty new drink, and I think I have now provided most of Elli Evler with the recipe. Invigorated with a new catering confidence, I am ready to try more dishes. I have found some cups and spoons that serve fairly well as basic measuring devices, but I am a little leery of using these guessed-at substitutes for more delicate things like cakes. I would love it if you could send me some measuring spoons. I know that cups will be harder… I don't suppose there is such a thing as a collapsible set?

On Sunday evening Abla, Levent, and I went to the farm of some people they know. We went only to stock up on home-grown fruit and vegetables; but in the end, we stayed for three hours and had an unexpectedly agricultural kind of experience. The family members were all working in the fields when we arrived, so we made our way out to see them. They said they needed a break and stopped to chat as we drew drinks from the well. The resident dog had recently had puppies, so we gave them a boisterous game, our laughing voices scratching the serenity of the countryside. Since we were in no hurry to leave, they accepted our offer to stay and help (?) cut the grain, irrigate the fields, pick fruit from the trees and milk the cows.

The family we visited is unworldly; the term "salt of the earth" springs to mind. Like most Turks, they were also extremely hospitable. There were numerous children around, and I'm not sure yet who belonged to whom. The older of the two women explained, quite matter-of-factly, that she had had two children whom she had given away to childless relatives. She had been blessed with good fertility, and it is not uncommon for such a woman to share her offspring within the family in a kind of informal adoption arrangement. Another child, a boy about two-and-a-half years old, had been living with them for the two years that the parents had been working in Germany. They had not seen him since he was six months old. I guess this practice is not uncommon as parents go abroad to find opportunities for work, forced by circumstances to leave their children behind. We have no idea what lives people live.

It was a perfect summer evening, a watered-down version of the day, balmy and refreshing. The smell of new earth and fresh-cut grain hung in the air. Insects rattled in the grass and cows gently lowed as they settled for the night. As darkness began to gather, the work of the day wound down, and we packed our purchases into the car. In addition to two kilos of fresh milk, we bought two dozen eggs and a trunk full of produce. We also came home with two chicks which Levent wants to raise for an eventual *bayram* feast. Sadly, one of them has since died... couldn't digest the feed he had given it, or some such. I admit to a vast gap in my knowledge where animals and their nutrition are concerned.

At present, we are busy getting ready for a *mevlüt* on Friday. I think its best described as a kind of "pray-in", but I will be able to tell you more in next week's letter.

30 June 1970

First of all, let me extend belated "Congratulations" on your wedding anniversary! Staying together for twenty-nine years is no small achievement, but staying together HAPPILY is certainly grounds for celebration. Dad really is a rare romantic: twenty-nine red roses! What could be better? You surely provide us with an excellent model for our own marriage, which I hope will be as long and as successful.

Our weather here has been beautiful - hot to be sure - but here on the hill in Elli Evler, there is usually a breeze (and sometimes it's a wind robust enough to lean against!). As long as we are out of the sun, it feels comfortable. Though I am assured that July and August will be hotter than a baker's oven, the climate is a dry one and is more bearable than the same heat with humidity. The sole thing about which I wish to complain are the mosquitoes, which are driving me batty at night. In the main, it's cool enough to sleep with a light cover, but if any flesh strays beyond this protection, I wake up with a whole new set of bites. (There are no screens on the windows.) I am the only one the mosquitoes bother as everyone else is either immune or hardened to them. My final point about summer in Turkey is that there is no change of time. Consequently, it is broad daylight at 4:30 am. At first, I had trouble sleeping through the early light, but I have managed to adapt and generally get up around 8:00 am.

As previously announced, the major event of this week has been the *mevlüt*. We spent the whole week cleaning the house from top to bottom, getting ready for Friday. A *mevlüt* is essentially a (single-sex) prayer session held for any number of reasons: to celebrate the birth of a baby, to honour someone who died, to give thanks for a special blessing, or in our case, to request divine help. Sami wanted us to hold one for his work and for the court case. He provided the wherewithal as the hosting of a *mevlüt* is a significant financial, as well as a religious undertaking.

We invited about one hundred women; the final turnout was eighty-five, including a few children. ("Babies will be left in the bedrooms to sleep, and the younger children will be turned out into the garden to play.") The house was packed. We had borrowed chairs from all the neighbours, and we managed to seat everyone in three rooms. The balcony, salon and parlour all have partition doors which can be folded back to make one big open space (good, eh?), so everyone had a reasonable view of the proceedings.

The guests began arriving about 2:00 pm. Abla and I served Turkish coffee, but as we could make only four cups at once, it was nearly 4:00 pm when all our guests had been served and settled. Everyone was modestly attired and would have completed the ritual washing that all Muslims perform before praying. No one wore make-up or jewellery, and each woman had her hair covered.

The chief "reader", a woman specially hired for the occasion, sat cross-legged on the divan and took charge of the proceedings. She came with two assistants who would relieve her as needed. The term "reader" is misleading as it fails to convey the significant achievement required to earn the title. In Turkish they are called *Hafiz*, meaning "memory", because they have memorized the Koran and can recite it fully in the original Arabic. Muslims do not have much regard for translations of their holy book, believing that its purity comes through only if read in its original form. Many older men and women (including Ana and Baba) can read the Koran in Arabic because they have learned the alphabet, not because they have any understanding of the language itself. This practice has parallels with the traditional Roman Catholic practice of recitations and prayers in Latin. The fact that no one, not even the *Hafiz,* comprehends what is being recited is not considered important. The recitations are understood on a spiritual level.

The chief *Hafiz* chanted the Koran for around an hour, others breaking in to help her along with the bits they knew, or to relieve her for a sip of water. Intermittently, the assembled rose and faced Mecca or raised their hands to pray. (Islamic hands open palms up, hands side-by-side to express an attitude of prayer.) Everything was done according to prescribed rituals which, of course, were unfamiliar to me. When the *mevlüt* itself had finished, rose water (truly divine) was passed and sprinkled into hands, and everyone received *mevlüt* sweets in designated packages, ordered from a specialist supplier in town. When any group of people individually known to each other gathers for any purpose, it is bound to become something of a social event. The women stayed on, chatting and visiting, and it was 7:00 pm before the last guest left. By then, we were whacked.

Despite all our plotting and planning, I still have not had my permanent visa from Ankara. The three-month sickness papers have expired, and with no sign of the visa, I was forced to go back to the hospital to get the doctors to attest to my rheumatism once again. They were not pleased. It took all my pleading and cajoling skills to get them to co-operate. One man made it clear that he would not sign for me again, so I have until September to get this sorted out, once and for all.

Meanwhile Hakan has started his officer training…just as the weather is heating up. This continues alongside his training for intelligence work. He has put in a request to be relieved of the latter as he is afraid of the consequences if this is taken to a more advanced stage. He doesn't want to become such a valuable asset that they won't let him go. His division commander was not hopeful of him being allowed much choice in the matter. In any case, he will be in Kavaklı for the coming four months. . . we think.

We have now heard from the German company that had requested samples of our work. They are interested in our products and have asked for a trial order of patchwork bedspreads. Baba has gone to Istanbul for supplies, but we're not buying in quantity until we see what results. In London, Ken is frantically filling orders for maxi-coats and suede patchwork. He needs more suede, and Baba is seeing to this as well.

There are a lot of new babies around at the moment, and we've been busy visiting the mothers and offering our congratulations. It is the custom for the new mother to wear a red ribbon in her hair. The baby has a red ribbon together with an evil eye (referred to as a *Maşallah,* a charm to keep bad spirits away) pinned on its blanket or clothing.

Newborns here are swaddled, something I had never seen before. Their arms and legs are bound securely into a blanket and another two or three blankets wrapped just as tightly around them, resulting in a packet as stiff as a wooden plank. The women believe that this enables the baby's bones to grow straight. When I ask to hold the baby, I am presented with something that looks and feels more like a gift-wrapped package than the expected wriggling bundle of softness. Generally speaking, only the face is on show, and often not that, if a cloth has been thrown over the face for protection.

The Turks live in morbid fear of draughts. If there is the slightest whisper of air, someone will eradicate its source immediately. Never mind that the weather is sweltering, and we are all in mortal danger of drowning in our own sweat, the Turks have a greater fear of death by breeze. And so, the babies are protected from every possible contamination that any fresh air might bring. The theory seems to be that the more layers there are, the greater the protection afforded. The temperatures can be tropical, the population limp with heat, and the baby is still swaddled. Ruth said that she nearly threw the entire hospital into a panic when she refused to carry out this practice with her newborns. Even the doctors, some of whom had studied abroad, could not understand her refusal to do this. Tradition dies hard, whichever side of the fence we're on.

I felt so sorry for Hüseyin Dayı's daughter-in-law, Nihal. She and Dayı's son were married last year (she's now seventeen), and she's recently had their first baby. Visiting days at the hospital are Mondays and Tuesdays only. She had her baby on Wednesday, and no one could visit her until the following Monday, not even her husband. No one explained this to her, and the poor girl spent nearly a whole week thinking that because she had given birth to a girl, no one loved her anymore! She was bereft by the time the family finally got to see her.

Nisa, our neighbour who went to Germany, is back. She arrived in a whirlwind of commotion and a flurry of presents for one and all.

Naturally, we had to go and welcome her home. The house was awash with visitors and confusion. What puzzled me most was that no one asked her what she thought about Germany or enquired about her experiences there. When I finally managed to question her, all she could say was that Germany is expensive. Of course it is, especially by comparison to things here. But I have never known anyone to get so little out of a journey, nor seen any group so uninterested in travel as the women who were there that day. It was only the shopping and the gifts that drew them.

Maybe that's how most women relate to other cultures. None of those present had ventured out of Turkey; none of them appeared to have any curiosity about the wider world. I could count on one hand, the number of people here who have ever asked me anything about my own country or culture. They like to hear about my family, but that's it. I guess this reflects their own day-to-day experiences and a world composed mainly of domestic concerns. My assumption that everyone is as nosey as I am is largely misplaced.

Hakan and I have been feeling quite domestic during our recent weekends together and have been taking over the kitchen to prepare most of the main meals. It began as something of an escape from the hubbub of the household and has continued as we discovered the kitchen to be a refuge, a place of relative peace and calm. Here we can simply putter about and have some quiet time to ourselves. It's such a pleasure to be able to chat and joke without constant interruptions. By the way, our cooking is not bad either!

Chapter 10

6 July 1970

It was such fun to get all your birthday cards and little gifts along with your regular letter this week. I had a great time opening everything and sharing it all with the family who likes to see what arrives in the envelopes and packages. I have put the dollars aside for a trip to Istanbul where I'll have more choice for the things I want to buy. Thank you so much. I've had the most tremendous 27th birthday. Only a short time ago, I could never have dreamed that I would spend it in Turkey. Sometimes it still feels a touch surreal.

Everyone has been so kind and considerate. Abla kept saying, "It's your first birthday in Turkey and we want it to be special." Indeed it was. Hakan bought me an old Ottoman gold coin, adapted to wear as a striking pendant. All the writing is in old Turkish, which means Arabic script, which means I can't read a word of it. Baba translated it for me and I have written it all down. I love it and have been wearing it at every opportunity. Baba gave me some white lily cologne; Levent, a little silver ring; and Ana, material for a dress. Knowing how much I like flowers, she also gave me a bunch of gladiolas. I know she was tickled with herself for coming up with this idea, and I was touched.

When we had the *mevlüt*, I had admired many of the beautiful prayer scarves the women used. The one that the chief *Hafiz* wore especially caught my eye. She explained that it was unusual because it had come from Mecca. Abla's gift to me was that very prayer scarf. Isn't she thoughtful? Hakan and I had arranged to go out for dinner, but it soon became clear that the family had organized their own celebratory meal, so we put our plans to one side. The food was delicious, and it was obvious that they had gone to a lot of trouble to prepare it. Abla had made a four-layer (yes!) birthday cake decorated with chocolate icing, garnished with nuts and dried fruit. Of course, there were candles and an ever-improving version of "Happy Birthday" as the family has become used to hearing the song and now join in. For all the right reasons, it was a memorable birthday.

On Saturday morning, Abla and I had our picture taken together. This is something she has been wanting to do for several weeks. I must admit that I have been hesitant as I felt somewhat odd having my picture taken with another girl. I have seen the typical poses for these photos, and they have struck me as being far too lovey-dovey for my tastes. However, Abla has been insisting for so long - having even made us identical dresses for the purpose - that I felt I could not resist further without giving offence, which I sincerely did not want to do. Okay, deep breath, "when in Rome" and all that. We had our hair done especially for the photo, and the results will be ready later this week.

One of the things I have found tricky are the public displays of affection between members of the same sex. Coming as I do from a culture where the opposite is the norm, I have felt ill at ease walking down the street holding hands with Abla or Ana or my women friends. They do this as a matter of course; it's perfectly natural to them. Men do the same, and it is not uncommon to see them walking arm-in-arm or hand-in-hand, meaning nothing more than friendship. The standard same-sex greeting is to shake hands while kissing both cheeks. Unaccustomed as I am to such demonstrativeness, I felt awkward at first but can now get in there to hug and kiss with the best of them. On reflection, I have seen similar displays in France and Italy. It must be we cold-blooded Anglo-Saxons who are the odd ones out.

Poor Hakan. He hates the army and gets frustrated with civilian life here as well. Recent events have done nothing to counter depressing news. Fortunately, a one-man cavalry came to the rescue of his morale this week. Hakan's old friend, Metin, was passing through Kavaklı and stopped at the base to see him. He couldn't stay long, but they had a few hours to catch up. Despite their different backgrounds and characters, the friendship is strong, and the visit did Hakan a world of good.

Nina came to visit when we had the *mevlüt,* and we took her home during the week. Teyze is a little nicer and a little friendlier each time Abla and I drop by. On this occasion, she brought chairs out into the garden and served us coffee. We were having a lovely chat, all memories of my first visit fading, when a neighbour woman arrived. She seemed to have come over purely to snub me. With a face more accustomed to scowling than smiling, she greeted everyone else while keeping her back to Abla and me. She had brought some fruit with her and offered this around, again passing us by as if I we did not exist. Finally, she gave us all a withering look and flounced off, announcing that she could no longer remain in the presence of women who were wearing clothing (sleeveless dresses with, admittedly, short skirts) which was both shameful and an offence to Allah. Aha! So, it wasn't just me who set her off. Abla was guilty too, or at least, guilty by association. I am not letting her forget this!

We are stunned to hear that Bill is training to be a tank driver. Surely he didn't volunteer for this. It doesn't sound to me as if this is the sort of thing he'll much need in Germany. I don't like the omens, and we're all anxiously awaiting further news. Breaths held.

14 July 1970

Oh My Goodness! Is there no end to your inventiveness? International smugglers could learn a thing or two from you, Mother. The secret is simply to put everything into a rolled up newspaper. I hadn't had any of your packets for a while. Sometimes they come within three weeks of mailing; others arrive three months later. I'm never sure what to expect. This week's batch produced a bumper crop. In addition to more cigars, I have unrolled socks, panty hose, band-aids, measuring spoons, and best of all, chocolate chips! If the authorities come after us, I'll bribe them with cookies. I can't wait to get baking. Manna from Heaven could not be more highly prized.

I know you'll let us have Bill's news as soon as there is any to report. If it's hard for us to be patient, I realize it's worse for you... and Bill, though maybe he knows more than he is telling. I'm not surprised that he is unhappy. What's to be happy about?

Since you are aware that Hakan's army career is as predictable as a race involving cats, you will not be astounded to hear that his military life is apparently subject to change at the slightest whim. Orders came from Ankara that he is to stop his officer training immediately. There was no explanation, of course. Baba went to see a friend who is the highest-ranking officer in the Kavaklı region. He said he would try to find out what is going on and forestall a transfer, if he could. Since Hakan is taking what is regarded as an "improvement" course, he said that they couldn't make him stop the training. He is entitled to this, even though Ankara might consider it irrelevant for anything they have in mind. I'm not sure that even Hakan is in a position to argue with headquarters, so we'll have to cross our fingers that this man can do something for him.

Abla's application for work in the local bank is still in Ankara. Any kind of bureaucratic paperwork takes forever. Meanwhile, she has taken up sewing again and is saving all the proceeds. As the word has gone out that the family is not going to arrange a match, there have been no more developments on the marriage front. I sincerely hope a job comes through for her. She needs to get out of the house.

Sami isn't doing much about finding a mate, either. I don't believe he has any intention of marrying. His courting rituals appear to have had more to do with the girl's father than with the girl herself. Do I honestly feel he could be that cynical? Yep. While the girl has faded from view (maybe she rejected him?), Sami and her father are submerged in business deals. On the home front, we have been instructed by Baba to look out for a suitable bride for Sami. The problem is that I don't think there IS anyone suitable for Sami... at least, no one I am willing to set up for sacrifice.

After a busy week working in the shop and getting samples ready for Germany, Hakan was anxious to see what we had done. He arrived home Saturday, and after a bath and some lunch, we headed into town. He was pleased with everything we had done and helped us get it ready for shipping. After that, we strolled around town, browsing. The shops here are different and interesting. Because I simply never know what we'll find, even looking is fun. When I'm with Hakan or Abla, they get tired of me asking, "What's that?" "What's it for?" "How is it used?" Sometime I manage to stump them with my questions. That's amusing, too.

I've recently had my eye on the square cloths the village women wear on their heads. They're cream with darker cream patterns woven into the fabric, all of it overstitched with gold machine embroidery. They're about card-table size and could be used in many different ways. When I mentioned my interest in these, Hakan thought it was ridiculous. Why would anyone want anything so common and so forth and so on. However, he agreed to humour me and have a look at them in the little bazaar. By the time I found what I was after, he had evidently decided that it was easier not to argue. We decided what would be a fair price for half a dozen and, after much haggling, emerged successful.

I was on a roll, determined now to go after some wicker baskets. I don't have to remind you how much I love any kind of basketry. Here, I'm spoilt for choice. After discovering a merchant with a substantial selection, I could scarcely control myself when I found out that the largest item in his stock, a basket big enough for a body, was an incredible 4TL (about forty cents). Having no immediate need for anything that large, I went to the other extreme and bought a little egg basket costing only a few *kuruş,* so little money that I can't be bothered to work it out in cents. Hakan is seriously worried. Now that I have discovered how cheap they are, he's afraid I'll inundate him with baskets. He keeps muttering, "It's not the money, it's the space. How are we going to get all this back to England?" I have time to work on this (him).

The only item we failed to secure was the camel bells I have been admiring since I saw them a couple of weeks ago. They are old and rusty, but appear to be handmade and are positively dripping with character. I must have conveyed too much admiration when I asked the price as it was well beyond reason. Having postponed these negotiations, I urged Hakan to have a go at buying them for me, but this time the price was even higher, and we came away empty-handed. I doubt there is a big demand for old camel bells in these parts, so I'll keep my eye on them and hope that the price decreases through lack of interest.

At the end of the day, we made some food purchases and came home, having decided to eat in the garden. We set out a little table and some chairs and then prepared our feast. We made enough for the others but left them to it, while we took ourselves off to a quiet corner. Well, it was quiet after we chased away small children, curious cats and our own dogs who had to content themselves on the sidelines, waiting for us to throw titbits their way. Long after the children had gone, the cats continued to hang around, tiptoeing in the background, their eyes glowing in the shadows. Eventually they too, had their reward for persistence. It was such a pleasant evening that we sat out until 11:00 pm.

There was another *mevlüt* last week, given by Hüseyin Dayı's wife in honour of their son's first-born. The mother is Nihal, the young woman who believed she had been abandoned in hospital. Although the family is poor and Nihal herself has little formal education, her eyes sparkle with intelligence, and she is full of common sense. And she has her own very definite ideas. No *kundak,* swaddling, for her baby! To the genuine horror of all concerned, her little daughter (one of the prettiest babies I have ever seen) had been liberated in the oppressive heat, her tiny arms and legs free to move about. Thank heavens!

So that we would have an opportunity to visit, we arrived at the house well before the *mevlüt* was due to start. Nihal had recently finished nursing baby Kadriye, and she handed her over to me to hold. I put the baby over my shoulder and started to pat her back, trying to bring up a burp. Nihal asked me what I was doing, and when I explained, she said she had never heard of such a thing and neither had any of the other women. I thought this was very odd, but then maybe the need is not so great with breast-fed babies. Maybe the practice is the result of bottle-feeding cows' milk, which is not so easily digested. I'm sure I really don't know, but each of us was as mystified as the other. However, I felt completely vindicated when I got a very satisfying burp.

I was very much the stranger at this gathering. Apart from relatives, I had not met any of the others who attended. Since I'm not yet familiar with the songs and rituals, I tried to sit unobtrusively in a corner (wearing my new prayer scarf from Mecca), but I fear I continue to stand out like bacon at a Bar Mitzvah. The women were trying to determine exactly who I was and what business I had there. But rather than ignore me, they chose to stare in an uninhibited, open-mouthed, point blank sort of way throughout the proceedings. I can't remember when I have felt so ill at ease, mainly because it went on so unrelentingly for so long. Abla was well aware of my discomfort and suggested that we go, but I decided to stick it out. I did not want to disrupt the baby's day, though it was probably too late to be concerned about that.

Sometimes it's hard to know what to do for the best.

20 July 1970

The current heat is stifling. Since our dependable Elli Evler breeze has deserted us, it feels as if all the good air has been sucked up and stolen away. I'm not sure what the temperature has been... HOT! Hakan says that some places in the country have reports of 45 °C, something like 115 °F. These occur mostly in the south and the east. You can't be more surprised than I was about the lack of screens. Apart from the hospitals, no place has them. Given the variety and wealth of flying and crawling insect life, it is an immense oversight, but the Turks take all this in their stride. I'm the spoiled one who minds.

I have been thinking about Hakan in all this heat. He doesn't complain, but it must be beyond miserable at times. Despite temperatures and vigorous workouts, he is still gaining weight to the point where he has trouble getting into his civilian clothes. When they recently had a physical training exercise, he was the only one to score a perfect mark. He is nothing if not competitive.

I stopped to see Ruth this past week and found her busy sewing and getting ready to move into their new home. While I was there, she took me to one side and told me she's pregnant again. Given the state of her marriage and her personal unhappiness, it's little wonder that she's unenthusiastic about it. I have mixed feelings about Ruth. She complains about her life, but is unable to act on any suggestions that might improve things. She refuses to stand up for herself, and I am constantly baffled by her willingness to put up with treatment I would find intolerable. My role seems to be that of listener as she pours out her heart. Maybe that's enough.

Saturday morning Baba, Hakan, Abla and I drove to Pınar for their well-known weekly market. We left about 6:00 am for the twenty-kilometre drive over horrendous roads, passable only because we have had so little rain lately. The deep ruts had dried as hard as granite and made for slow going. We had set off early so as to avoid the worst of the heat, leaving the house as the sun rose, already ruthless with promise. Pınar is a prosperous village boasting brick houses and, in addition to the customary mosque and school, a little commercial district with a variety of shops, including a barber, a book store and a coffee house.

When we arrived, the market was just getting under way. We had come especially to buy a quantity of eggs but were immediately frustrated at every turn. Although there were eggs aplenty, no one wanted to sell them. It slowly dawned on us that they all had been promised to buyers who were on their way to crate them up and load them onto trucks bound for the cities. Was this the reason for the area's prosperity, I wondered. After we learned the buyers' prices, we skulked about on the road into town, approaching farmers before they got to the marketplace. By offering a higher price, we were able to tempt them into parting with their eggs and eventually accumulated the sixty we needed for Ana's proposed cooking marathon. Job done, we set out for the poultry section where we bought three live chickens for 6TL or sixty cents each, also destined for future meals.

After that, we became a little unhinged with the tempting displays of freshly picked fruit and vegetables and came away with potatoes, tomatoes, peppers, aubergines, onions, cherries, corn, melons and plums, not to mention twenty-five kilos of peaches for preserves. I personally succumbed, as Hakan had predicted, to seduction by wicker basket and bought two for forty cents. Serious shopping completed, we wandered through the various sections of this unexpectedly vast market that as well as seasonal produce, had separate areas for the sale of cloth, second-hand items, household goods and livestock.

I have a recurring dream in which I walk down the street, and no one pays me the slightest bit of attention; I am exactly like everyone else ... just like in the West, just like at home. As we made our way around, and as the day wore on, we began to attract attention. Everyone assumed we were tourists, something of a rarity in these parts. Some of the most curious came up, planted themselves in front of me and stared. When it became impossible to shop, we called it a day. Luckily, we had gone early and had managed to buy all that was on our list - and more!

On Sunday, Hakan and I gave Aslana and Lady their first baths. The family downstairs is away visiting her parents, so we have more water than usual, otherwise such extravagance could not be justified. The heat has taken its toll on both dogs who move around with their own personal clouds of fleas. I had already purchased a quantity of flea powder, but we thought a thorough scrubbing in advance of its application might help prevent the insects from settling again.

Originally, we had planned to do all this outside but began to appreciate that we could make more progress in a confined area. This turned out to be a wise decision. We cleared the bathroom of everything except the washtub and metaphorically rolled up our sleeves. As neither Lady nor Aslana had any idea what was happening, they were both skittish and nervous. Since she is the easier to handle, we experimented first with Lady. Once she had worked out that a sudsy brushing was not a bad idea, she let us get on with our work.

Aslana - always independent - was having none of it. She was suspicious of our intentions before we even got her to the bathroom, where she used all four of her legs to good effect. We simply could not keep her in the tub and wash her at the same time. Eventually, we cornered her and scrubbed her down where she stood. When she too, realized that the unfamiliar had some merit, she relaxed and let us get her back in the tub. Needless to say, Hakan and I got soaked, but as it was a hot day, no one stayed wet for very long. With their scrubbed faces and shiny coats, the dogs are now in pristine condition, their fragrant soapy smells lingering in the lifeless air as they pass.

As well as the dogs, Dagmar also has been in need of some attention. A lot of little repairs have piled up as well as a couple of bigger jobs. Last week I had two tyres recapped, and today they are overhauling the engine, fixing the broken exhaust and repairing the electrical system which works sporadically. The bill will be 100TL, about $10. My mechanic is a genius, and I truly don't know what I would do without him. Our insurance has run out, so I bought new cover here: $14 to insure us both for a year. We have been talking about having the car spray painted. The estimate is $15-$20 if we use Turkish paint and twice that for European paint. Everything is so cheap by western standards.

28 July 1970

Sami came to visit this week and whisked us off to Izmir for a couple of days. He and Baba had some business there and decided to take Abla and me as well. Normally, I would not be complicit in his adventures, but I have to admit to being the teensiest bit bored with Kavaklı at present. As I knew I would not be seeing Hakan in the middle of the week, I agreed to tag along.

Izmir is a bright, modern cosmopolitan city right on the Aegean. Historically of course, it is ancient (possibly better known as Smyrna), but following all the fighting at the end of WWI, much of the original city was destroyed and has been rebuilt in western mould. NATO headquarters are here, and many international organizations have bases in the area. Consequently, there is a sizeable ex-pat community which gives the city its western sheen. The area called Kordon, situated on the edge of the bay, is full of high-rise apartments and sophisticated shops. This is a taste of home, a place where the atmosphere feels familiar, and I can buy the odd American item. As you might guess, this is where most of the ex-pats live. They're always in the most expensive part of any city.

Across the bay is a more traditional Izmir with historic houses, many of them clearly from a different architectural tradition than the ones I have seen in Istanbul. The influence there is eastern and Ottoman; here it is Greek and European, remnants of the recent past. Both here and in Istanbul, these fine old mansions are under increasing threat. Many of them fall derelict while in dispute over ownership; others are neglected through lack of funds. Since the Turks don't much value Old Things, they need only the slightest excuse to tear them down and throw up skyscrapers (or sky-crappers, as Hakan calls them) in their place. They desperately need some strict planning laws with designated and protected conservation zones.

The first stop on the morning after our arrival involved Sami's business, so I had hoped that Abla and I might be excused to go window shopping. But Sami had other ideas, and we were told that we could indulge after the meeting was finished. Apparently, we were not to be trusted out on our own. But that said, I'm glad I didn't miss the experience that followed.

Since I take as little notice as possible concerning anything to do with Sami, I was initially uninterested in the proceedings and still could not tell you who we visited, or why. From our hotel, a short walk took us to a most extraordinary penthouse office at the top of an equally imposing office block. Ever one to grandstand, would Sami have taken us anywhere else, I asked myself.

The person on whom we were calling had an extensive executive suite roughly the size of a school gymnasium. It was divided into sections for work, relaxation and hospitality by variations in gilded furnishings, lush carpets and gaudy chandeliers. Sami's arrival was greeted with much enthusiasm, while the rest of us were introduced to his "associate", Hakkı Bey. I could almost hear the fanfare as we were ushered to the hospitality area where The Number One Assistant hovered. After he had issued the orders for refreshments to another waiting attendant, cigarettes were passed. Abla and I declined, but the men all had one each. As a rule, the person offering the cigarette will light it as well, but I saw no such service about to be offered and wondered if an inexplicable lapse of etiquette had occurred.

I need not have concerned myself. After depositing the gold cigarette box on a highly polished mahogany table, The Number One Assistant glided across the room and activated a discreet control, causing the bookcase to slide back and reveal a wall safe. Utterly riveted, we all stared intently, breathless with anticipation. The Number One Assistant quickly spun the combination, opened the door, rootled about inside and dragged forth a lighter, so big and so heavy, he struggled to hold it with both hands. The solid gold device, reminiscent of Aladdin's lamp and roughly the size of a gravy boat, was deposited with a flourish on the lustrous table. The second assistant was summoned to hold the lighter, while The Number One Assistant flicked the flint that ignited the flame. With grave attention and much ceremony, the cigarettes were lit one-by-one, after which the almighty treasure was returned to its resting place.

Well, now. There's something we don't see every day.

If anyone wanted a second cigarette, would the same ritual ensue, or was it strictly one performance per group, I wondered. Hakkı Bey looked around the room to make sure we were all suitably impressed, while at the same time, assuming the modest air of deep humility affected only by politicians and the self-made super rich.

I was glad that Ruth was not with me; we would have dissolved into fits of hilarity. Hakan would have been similarly amused, but he would have found some subtle way to mock the proceedings. As an act of sheer ostentation, it would be hard to match. I doubted I would ever see the like again, and I wouldn't have missed it for a truckload of chocolate chips. It is completely appropriate that I should have witnessed this pomposity in Sami's presence, and says more about him and his cohorts than I could ever explain.

On an entirely different topic, I find public transport to be exceptionally good in Turkey. Although train service is limited, there is the extensive coach system which serves the entire country; and in the urban areas, both buses and taxis are plentiful and affordable. In addition, there is something unique called a *dolmuş*. This is sometimes a big old American car, more usually a minibus, which travels over a predefined route, dropping off and picking up passengers anywhere along the way. In short, it is a kind of shared taxi. More flexible than a bus and cheaper than a taxi, it is a popular way of getting about. Before coming to Turkey, I had never heard of these, but I think they are an excellent idea. Like taking shoes off at the front door, this is a concept worthy of export. Since I have so often had the car, I have not had much experience of the *dolmuş*, but having gone to Izmir by coach, we used them extensively to get around.

We were away three days, and while it was a welcome break from routine, I have vowed never again to travel with Sami. The price is too high. Everything must be done his way, or he sulks. I don't know now what possessed me, nor why I thought a trip with him would be remotely tolerable, let alone a sensible idea. However, anyone can make a mistake, and I have learned my lesson.

Tomorrow is Abla's birthday, but we had our main celebration on Saturday, when Hakan was at home. I made her a birthday cake, which didn't turn out very well (I'm guessing I didn't bake it long enough); but I made up for that with a super-duper chocolate frosting that helped camouflage some of the damage. She looked happy with my efforts. Hakan and I bought her a gold bangle, which may seem a rather extravagant gift in our present circumstances, but she has done so much for us both, without even mentioning all the sewing she has done for me, that it struck us as an appropriate way to say thank you. She was genuinely surprised and pleased, which is what we had hoped. I am going to take Abla and Ana to the Yıldız Oteli for cake and lemonade tomorrow afternoon. Quite daringly, we are going without a male escort, something of a brave new world for them. I'm looking forward to treating them both.

So who is happier about Bill being at home, you or Bill? It's a special occasion for all. He must be enjoying home cooking and the break from army life. Presumably he hasn't said anything about his next posting. We wait with bated breath.

Chapter 11

10 August 1970

I could see it coming from a long way off, but I am still thunderstruck by Bill's posting to Vietnam. Somehow I assumed that if we studiously ignored it, the inevitable would go away. I guess that's what we've all been hoping. I am so glad that he had a good two weeks at home and was able to go camping with his buddies. Since all the news centres around the troop withdrawals, it is strange to learn that more men are going out there. I am under the impression that his tour of duty will be twelve months. Let's trust that there will be an end to all of this, for both Bill and Hakan, by this time next year. I know how I'm reacting, so I can only imagine how the rest of you feel. Obviously I want his mailing address when you have it.

Baba and I have recently returned from Istanbul where I had hoped to meet up with cousin Jean and family. They were travelling from their UN posting in Manila for home leave in the US and were scheduled for a stopover in Istanbul. I thought I would try to meet them, but we got our signals crossed, and the reunion never came off. When we got back home, there was a letter from Jean to say that the recent Istanbul riots and the martial law that is still in place had made them change their plans. Since they couldn't know precisely what was happening here, I didn't blame them; but most of Istanbul is back to normal, and it would have been fine for them to come. Only bad news makes the headlines. But either way, Baba had to go to Istanbul for his next court appearance, so it wasn't a wasted journey. For my part, I love any excuse to travel to Istanbul. It pulls me like a magnet, and I discover something new during each visit.

On Monday evening, Baba took me to an English language film, the first I've seen since I was last here with Hakan in December. Though the film was nothing special, it was a treat to see something in my own language. Following that, we met up with Sami who improves neither with time nor distance. Malice seeps out of him as if contained in every pore. Already molten with rage, his opening gambit was to yell at his father for turning up early and for bringing me along. Among other things. There is so much to complain about when the whole world is against him. Without exaggeration, he did nothing but rant and rave for the next half hour, his spittle-inflected speech yet another indicator of his toxic personality. I didn't see any reason for either of us to stand there and take his abuse, so I announced that I was tired and was returning to the hotel. Happily, Baba also decided to call it a day and came with me.

The following morning, we met with Baba's lawyer, Tuncer Ağabey, to discuss the court case. After that, we spent the afternoon visiting several of Baba's relatives, and then went on to dinner with Tuncer Ağabey and his delightful wife, Şirin Abla. Our host has a dry, droll sense of humour and thoroughly relished telling jokes about Americans. I knew he was teasing me, and I found the jokes as funny as he did. The atmosphere was pleasant and relaxed. Şirin Abla, one of my favourite people in Turkey, had outdone herself preparing a mouth-watering meal with a wide variety of superb *meze* to start. It was a perfect evening. Until Sami arrived. He had been drinking and turned up in a filthy temper. Powerful 90-proof fumes rolled off him like steam from a cooking pot. He did not miss a beat as he took up exactly where he had finished the previous evening. He said terrible things to his father as he went on and on about what a dreadful drain Baba was on his finances, declaring that he was an interfering old man and announcing that he was not going to give him any more money. It was painful. Baba sat quietly throughout this tirade. When Sami finally wound down, Baba simply said, "Unfortunately, it is plain to see that I haven't taught you anything. Obviously, I gave you nothing at all."

The next day, Sami behaved as if nothing had taken place. I couldn't imagine how he had the nerve to face his father and not offer so much as a humble apology, but I suppose he had no recall of an evening that presumably passed in an alcoholic haze. Like many drinkers, he pretends that nothing has happened and that each day is a new beginning. Not that this is a reason. Such behaviour is inexcusable and unforgivable.

The strange thing is that relatives and old family friends like Tuncer Ağabey and Şirin Abla (she is the same age as Sami), who have known the Beyler family for years, all regard Sami as a prince of a fellow, a rare jewel in the sultan's turban. Somewhere along the line, he developed a reputation as an astute and talented businessman. Everyone admires the Sami of old. Surely the scales fell from our hosts' eyes during last night's performance. It could not be clearer that the Sami of today has been addled by alcohol, and I have no way of ascertaining how much of his previous reputation is deserved. If even a portion of what they say is true, Sami has thrown away his not inconsiderable gifts. The whole thing is an epic tragedy.

As if all that were not enough, Sami's latest campaign is designed to turn the family against Hakan. With his knowledge and approval, we have used his export license to send goods and orders to Ken in London. Once the money to pay for these arrives, the license holder, in this case Sami, needs to fill in the correct forms and submit them to the authorities to show that the transaction has been legally completed. Ken has always sent the required funds, and we have always fulfilled our obligations in this matter.

Familiar as he is with self-inflicted wounds, Sami has acquired a taste for them and is refusing to fill in and submit the end forms. For his own contorted reasons, he prefers to say that he hasn't had the money, or that Hakan has been short-changing him when nothing could be further from the truth. Thanks to his own negligence, Sami has been summoned to court for his failure to submit the correct papers. We believe that the future of his export license is in the balance, and he is blaming Hakan for everything. Frankly, it's nothing to do with Hakan. Baba understands this, but Ana doesn't; she is siding with Sami and giving Hakan a hard time about why he has landed his older brother in such a mess. Wouldn't you assume that even Sami would have had enough of court cases? The man defies belief.

On the day of the current case, Tuncer Ağabey and Baba went off together, while I had decided to make another trip to the airport on the off chance that Jean and family might turn up on one of the rare Manila flights. Şirin Abla is a teacher, and as it is summer vacation, she elected to come aong. Even though we didn't find any relatives, we had a lovely morning. We sat on the terrace overlooking the runway so we could watch arriving aircraft. Having comfortably ensconced ourselves at a table with a suitable vantage point, we spent several hours drinking cokes, eating cheese toast, trading stories and smoking as if cigarettes were vitamins. She and Tuncer Ağabey don't have any children and spend most school holidays travelling in Turkey, so Şirin Abla is knowledgeable about the country's geography and sights. We talked about life in Turkey as well as a variety of other topics, including Bill's posting to Vietnam. She understood so much, refreshing in itself, as most of the Turkish women I encounter haven't a clue about world events. Ana thinks Vietnam is a city in the United States, so she can't figure out what all the fuss is about. While we were sitting there, Süleyman Demirel, the Prime Minister of Turkey, arrived, so we were able to see the ensuing hullabaloo.

Nothing much happened in court. Tuncer Ağabey explained to us that his strategy is simply to draw everything out for as long as possible. He's looking ahead to 1973(!) when the republic will celebrate its 50th anniversary, and according to tradition, there will be a general amnesty for this type of case. It sounds like forever to wait for a result, but Tuncer Ağabey regards this as the best way to proceed. He believes that if we were to force a conclusion, Baba would receive a prison sentence, most likely a light one, but that any conviction would be too much. He is absolutely right! Time spent in a Turkish jail doesn't bear thinking about. Prison here makes army life look like a pleasant pastime. Although having the prosecution continue to hang over him is a less than perfect situation, the alternative is insupportable. After learning about his lawyer's plans, we are all feeling a little more relaxed. Baba is happy with Tuncer's decisions, and based on experience, it doesn't appear as if there will be any difficulty stringing things out in court.

On the drive home, we saw another camel caravan, the only one I have seen since Hakan and I narrowly missed hitting one. We drove a little distance ahead and pulled over to watch it pass. Baba was as captivated as I was. He leaned out of the window to ask the driver how much a camel cost. "2000TL," (about $200) came the reply.

"So, Baba, that's a lot of money isn't it? A camel is a very valuable animal."

"Very. In desert areas an entire family can live from one camel."

"And if a family had forty camels, it would be very rich indeed."

Baba looked at me with a little grin. "That's right."

"And if the bride price was forty camels, that would mean she was a highly prized bride."

"Only the very best girls could achieve such a price. In the old days, that was the most anyone would pay for the fine daughter of a noble family."

"But that custom no longer exists, right?"

"Well, not in modern Turkey, but the sentiments are still there. We have always had forty camel brides in our family." He looked at me and grinned again, "Always."

This made my day, my week and my month… maybe my whole stay!

The horrible heat is taking its toll on man and beast alike. Although the flea population has diminished, the dogs are wretched and sluggish with the effort of constant panting. The sun burns fiercely white from first light and everything is slick with heat. The temperatures have been over 100°F. with not a whisper of air. As I'm typing on the balcony, I can look out over the garden and see total stillness, not so much as a single leaf stirring on the trees. It's a strange phenomenon in this typically windy spot.

We have had such a water shortage of late (no rain for over two months) that Abla and I tired of economy washing and decided to splash out, literally, with a trip to our local *hamam*. Neither of us is big on the idea of public bathing, but she assured me that we could get a private room. We packed our bathing suits and off we went.

The place was crowded, swarming with women and children in all states of undress, but we secured the room we wanted and got down to business. Using a rough-textured *loofah*, a sort of vegetable sponge with all the abrasive qualities of a Brillo pad, we began scrubbing in earnest. Nothing was spared as the fibrous material dug into every crevice and pore, and we dislodged disgusting amounts of dirt. After this, we soaped down, rinsed off and started over again, repeating the procedure twice more. Then we washed our hair five times. With pauses for refreshments to keep up our strength, not to mention our body fluids (the process is exceedingly dehydrating), the whole operation took us about two hours. Once we had ceased our ablutions, we rested on the little cots provided before dressing to go.

For many women, the *hamam* is a community centre and provides a social occasion as well as a bath. Children and relatives in tow, they come and spend the whole day, bringing with them vast picnics to share. Many engage one of the bath staff to wash them, and most will have a professional massage on the marble slab in the middle of the main chamber. But both of these involve rather more public exposure of flesh than either of us care for.

The whole performance sapped our energy but left us peaceful and serene. I could get used to this say, once a month, but I wouldn't be interested in going more often. It feels like an awful lot of effort just to bathe. The price was twelve cents each for as long as we liked. No wonder the cost of the Çelik Palas bath is prohibitive for most folks.

It's now about 3:00 in the afternoon, and I finally feel like eating a little something. It's been so hot that I've lost my appetite. Imagine. The intensity of the mid-day heat tends to lessen about now, and some fruit sounds appealing. When I visited Ruth this morning, she served American coffee and cake, but that's all I've had so far today. The poor girl is suffering in the heat and not sleeping well, which showed in her face. In the course of our conversation, we were talking about the foods we miss, and what we wouldn't give for a cold tuna fish salad - or even a hamburger! She has pregnancy as an excuse. Deprivation is mine.

24 August 1970

There is so much to write, I hardly know where to begin. I'll start with the good news. We made a last-minute decision to go to Edirne to sort out the illegalities with the car. I have taken enormous risks by driving her at all and have been lucky so far, but I cannot continue to count on favourable fortune alone to protect me. Dagmar is my salvation, and I cannot do without her. Finding a way to legitimize her meant finding a customs office, so Baba, Abla and I set off for the Bulgarian border last Monday. There, for a $50 bribe, the officials were willing to overlook the fact that I had just left the country and returned with the same vehicle only a few hours later. All was attended to with efficiency and importance, and the car is legal for another three months. I gather that all the gold in Christendom is insufficient to secure a permit for longer than the sacred three months. However, it's one thorny quandary at a time, and now I can think about something else (until the current permit expires).

At the moment, Dagmar is more legal than I am. Since I have yet to hear anything from Ankara, I merely assume that some bureaucrat is sitting at his desk, awaiting my visit and the bribe that will ensure the swift completion of my papers. This is all terribly dishonest, and I feel guilty colluding in the system, but I'm not knowledgeable enough to find another way to accomplish these things. Sometimes I really "give it up," as Hakan says.

Just as every town seems to have some historical significance, so the same places all seem to harbour someone known to Baba. I don't think we have been anywhere that we have not stopped to say hello to a relative or old friend; Edirne is no exception. Everyone appears genuinely pleased that we have unexpectedly dropped in to stay a night or two. It's the custom of hospitality that carries over from an era when there were no hotels, and caravansaries were few and far between. A traveller can be certain of a welcome wherever he stops. And so in Edirne, we met old friends from Bulgaria, a husband and wife, both teachers.

Although I have sucked up conversational Turkish as if there were a language vacuum in my brain, I frequently find myself floundering when it comes to serious topics of discussion. However, in this instance, I found the exchanges with the other dinner guests easy to follow and extremely interesting. I wasn't even conscious that all the other women had drifted away from the table when the meal was over. They are never interested in politics and current events, but I lingered to enjoy the discussion. As I became aware of their absence, I also heard their mutterings about my bad manners in remaining with the men. I realized that once again, my disgraceful behaviour was the cause of adverse comment. I looked quizzically at Baba to ask if I should excuse myself before further humiliation was heaped on all our heads, but he smiled and asked me to remain, "if I would". If I would? What a man!

On Thursday morning, we left for Istanbul, picked up some things for Hakan and paid a mercifully brief visit to The No 1 Son, before heading back to Kavaklı. That night we stayed with some of Baba's relatives who live in a stunning house right on the Marmara Sea outside of Izmit. With the water before us, calling loudly on a hot day, it didn't take us long to get into bathing suits and enjoy a swim. This was followed by late afternoon *çay* in their lovely garden. The setting was almost paradise, and we were all totally at ease. I worked out the family blood lines when we brought Hala, paternal aunt, back with us to her home in Kavaklı. She had been visiting her son, so Baba and our host are cousins. I always like to understand the connections, but they don't seem overly significant to the Turks. Family is family.

We took the long way back and stopped in Bursa where Baba wanted to visit yet more relatives. At this point, I had had more than enough of driving (and relatives), and all I wanted to do was get home, but it is beyond me to refuse Baba almost anything. As we were leaving the city, we came as close as it is possible to come without actually being involved in a major road accident. Bearing in mid that we were travelling along a crude two-lane road, there was no place to go when I found a truck had come to a complete standstill in the middle of our lane. As there were vehicles oncoming, I slowed to a halt, leaving a couple of car lengths between us. Unaware that we were stopped, another truck roared up the road from behind and, to avoid hitting us, swerved out into the path of an oncoming tractor-trailer. The two collided and, quite literally, bounced off each other, one landing directly behind us and the other, directly in front. I can't begin to think about what might have happened if I had not left that gap. Perhaps the most amazing thing of all was that no one appeared to suffer serious injury. Both truckers walked away from their vehicles, and we drove on. It's all part of the rich tapestry of life on the roads in Turkey.

We arrived home Friday evening to find Ana hysterical and Levent on the verge of mental collapse. He had seemed to be doing so well, but the idea of returning to school this fall has created a great deal of anxiety, perhaps causing him to backslide.

Prior to our departure, Levent had been unusually active. He had been overweight and sluggish when he was on medication but, since coming off, has lost his excess pounds very quickly. He took up weight lifting, which undoubtedly contributed to the loss; but additionally, he has been hyperactive. He can't sit still and has driven us mad with his incessant singing, humming, talking and general noisemaking. He has been out of school for over two years, and the thought of returning to a situation in which he was having trouble under better circumstances - and where he will be well above the age of his classmates - was possibly asking too much of someone in a fragile state.

Before going back on medication, Levent neither slept nor ate but is doing both now. However, he is becoming agoraphobic; he does not want to leave the house and will do so only after much persuasion and for very good reason. He is also surly and uncommunicative. If we question him, he often won't respond, or he'll say he doesn't know or can't remember something obvious. He is almost incapable of making decisions (what shall I wear? which pastry shall I eat?) but likes to feel important and powerful by strutting around giving orders to Abla and Ana, even threatening physical assault on occasion. There is no question that he is difficult to handle, and no one is sure what to do for the best. Psychiatric help is available only in Istanbul, and I am not reassured by what we have seen. Their solution to everything is either medication or hospitalization, both of which are means of control, rather than effective treatment. At present, we are hoping that the pills will help stabilize him and provide an atmosphere in which we can offer encouragement and support. But we are not professionals, and I have no idea if this will be helpful, let alone enough.

On top of all this, Sami has lost his export license. This in itself is not a shock; we all saw it coming. The surprise is that when he went to court, it not only revoked his license there and then, but also instigated proceedings against him for failure to comply with his legal obligations. No one can understand why he has allowed himself to get into this position. If he did it to spite Hakan, he has paid a heavy price, cutting off his own nose in the process. But yes, it means we now have to look elsewhere for means of export. This will be expensive for us, possibly prohibitively so.

In the meantime, a friend of Ken's is driving a tour bus to Istanbul the first week of September and will be able to take goods back to London for us. Although clearance through customs will be complicated without a proper agent here, at least the transport will be cheap and should help make up for the difficulties. To this end, Abla and I are working flat-out to get some of the jackets and waistcoats embroidered. In addition to these, we want to send a supply of dressed sheep and mohair skins, so we have a lot to do. Things have a way of working out. Sometimes is just takes longer than we would like.

I don't know whether you would have heard that the Turkish Lira has devalued. We used to get 9TL to the dollar, but now it is 15. This is bad news - very bad news - for everyone. Overnight, most prices have gone up by 50%, mainly because imports are based on the value of the US Dollar; and petrol prices, among others, affect the wider economy. But since our business works in foreign exchange, and Ken always pays for the shipments in US Dollars, we are able to offset the domestic consequences. We are lucky; most are not in such a fortunate position. People are outraged, and Prime Minister Süleyman Demirel is not a popular man, I can tell you. Let us hope that the prize is worth the pain.

Although it's been only two weeks since Ana's birthday, it feels like ages ago. I'm glad you remembered to send her a card, otherwise it would have been a disaster. She never gets any mail, so she kept looking for it as it meant a lot to her. Ana has her limitations as I'm sure you have realized. It's impossible to separate what might be a family tendency to mental frailty from circumstances that might have led to it anyway. Since I knew none of them before all the latest life-changing traumas, it is impossible for me to assess their impact on individual family members.

Hakan, however, was alarmed by the transformation he saw in his mother when we arrived in October, the first opportunity he had had to spend any time at home in recent years. Ana has gained a lot of weight, but that in itself is not a cause for major concern. It's the emotional toll that has been noticeable, I think. Both Sami and Levent resemble their mother in the way that they deal with difficult situations. None is emotionally robust, and all lack the tools needed to cope with testing times. Ana is largely capable of handling the routines of everyday living but, at the slightest provocation, says she is sick and goes to bed for days on end. Sami and Levent do exactly the same thing. It's almost as if Ana is happiest when she is unhappy, bringing everyone else down with her. Maybe this is the one aspect of her life in which she feels she is in charge, but I also understand that none of this is calculated. She does what she does from gut reaction, not from any intent to be malicious.

Whatever the cause, the results are measurable in terms of the despondency in this family right now. The mother is the hub of most homes, and Ana's misery casts a pall over the whole family. Abla in particular pays a high price. Ana constantly nags her and argues with her. Nothing anyone does is right, and Abla, especially, can never do enough to please her. I can't imagine how she retains HER sanity. But if Levent and Sami resemble Ana, Hakan and Neriman are Baba's children. They appear to have rock-solid foundations that see them through whatever is thrown at them. Ultimately though, the family feels fragmented, and this is not a happy home. Each member has problems, and each has withdrawn to a private place to contemplate them alone. Certainly that is how it feels.

While I am an observer, I am also a participant, and it is a strange position. Quite unfairly, we all turn to Hakan for answers, and I am afraid that we put terrible strains on him. But he is at his best when everything is in turmoil. A mantle of calm seems to envelope him, and he draws on some unseen source for the strength to bolster us all. He says that he wouldn't know what to do without me. I hope that is true because the feeling is mutual. I would not like to think that my being here didn't make things easier for him.

That's enough of that. I want to complain about the weather for a while. Do you remember I moaned a couple of weeks ago about the heat, but really had no idea of the local temperature? It turns out that it had been 50°C, about 120°F! It's probably just as well I didn't realize it, as even now I get hotter merely thinking about it. We set a nationwide record for top temperatures that week, a forty-year high for the town. In addition, the water shortage gets worse and worse. Sometimes the tank fills only every four or five days.

When I lived in the US, I never connected the amount of water coming out of the tap with the amount of rain going into the ground. Here, the connection is all too obvious. Last week, the scarcity of water in Istanbul was so bad that barbers were giving shaves using soda water. It's true! I'm currently making regular trips to the vet in an attempt to keep the dogs' flea population under control. The hot weather has aggravated a particularly virulent strain that my shop-bought remedies can't keep in check. To add to the general tenor of things, Lady is in heat, and I suspect Aslana is soon to follow. I'm trying to keep them both under my watchful eye, but I see puppies on the horizon.

About wedding ceremonies: the only legal ones are civil ceremonies. Many people have a religious ceremony as well, but that is optional. Interestingly, a few diehards in the eastern part of the country still choose to have more than one wife (Islam allows for four) and can achieve this by marrying in religious ceremonies several times over. Since Islamic rites have no legal status, no laws have been broken, and the traditionalists are satisfied. Where there's a will...

No news from Bill, yet. I know you will fill me in as his letters come through to you. Peter is bound to be getting ready for college, or will it be a case of throwing his stuff in a suitcase at the last minute?

Take care of yourselves.

31 August 1970

After outdoing myself in the last letter, I feel I don't have much to say this week. The weather has cooled off, so that is our headline news. In fact, the temperatures have dropped so quickly that we are suddenly under eiderdowns. I can't believe this will last as it is unseasonably cold.

However, speaking of seasons, that for fur and leather garments is upon us, and we are working hard to fill the orders that are popping up from all over. The patchwork maxi-coats have had an incredibly favourable reception, and we have requests for those from Germany, along with all the usual items. After a sparse summer, it's good to be busy again. Baba and I are going to Istanbul later this week to hand over the shipment that the tour bus will take back for us.

Yesterday was an exceptionally significant day in the history of the Turkish Republic. Known as Victory Day, this anniversary commemorates Atatürk's conquest of his enemies at the end of WWI, when he drove them out of the old empire and secured the territory that became the modern republic. This is a big occasion for the military, and we knew that Hakan would be participating in the day's events. We went to the shop and worked until the parade passed in front of Baba's office. With so many soldiers marching by so fast, I didn't think I would be able to find Hakan, but he stands out in any crowd. We were close to the town square where all the important officials were making speeches, and I was somewhat alarmed to hear one impassioned speaker burst into tears. Abla said it was only for show, but I know how emotional and sentimental Turks can be, so I wasn't convinced that it was purely theatrics.

After I found Hakan in the march-past, I lost all interest in the endless displays of soldiers, hardware and vehicles. I could only believe that all the money spent on the military could be better spent on schools and hospitals. I could say the same for my own country. However, while the literacy rate here is just 60%, the government maintains an army that is 2,000,000 strong, the largest in Europe. It is slowly being acknowledged that if Turkey wants to move ahead, such military strength is a luxury that it can ill afford. There is some talk that those with higher education would not serve their full obligation as soldiers but would be sent to serve on community projects. Professionals such as teachers, doctors, agricultural advisers and engineers could use their skills for the benefit of the general public. It sounds like an idea worthy of further consideration.

Meanwhile, the money used to maintain this gigantic military machine could be used to advance the country as a whole. Turkey is not going to give up its army, but the entire operation could be scaled down, and neither national security nor NATO obligations need be compromised. Turkey's infrastructure is in desperate need of modernization; there can be no serious economic growth without more sophisticated methods of communication and better roads, not to mention enhanced energy and water supplies. This is a land of huge resources with a population hungry to progress. Turks are capable, hard-working and enterprising, but these talents can take them only so far without government backing. The politicians need to recognize this and work in the best interests of the voters who put them in office. Sadly, there is an enormous stake in keeping things exactly the way they are. The Turkish military probably has greater power than the government, and it is not willingly going to decrease the significance of its role, its importance or its impact.

Levent is about the same as when I last wrote. Following that letter, there was a spell of dreadful days when it was virtually impossible to talk to him without being yelled at. He stomped around the house in an awful frenzy. It reminded me precisely of Sami. Make of it what you will. When his medicine began to kick in, his bad times got shorter as his good periods got longer, a trend which may or may not last. The drugs make all the difference, and when he refuses to take them, which he sometimes does, the least thing can spark a terrible rage. Because Hakan is extremely patient with him and provides the solace and understanding that elude the rest of us, Levent responds positively to his older brother and is much calmer when he is at home. Hakan has a rare gift for understanding how to handle people, and Levent is completely in his thrall.

For better or for worse, Levent is not now going to go to school in September. Despite my theory that the thought of it might be the source of much of his current anxiety, he willingly went off the other day to register for the new term. Unhappily, they rejected his registration, saying that he is too old for the classes he has missed. It is my impression that he was vastly relieved at this decision, but again, I may be wrong. In any event, he cannot go to school now, and it is not his fault. As a result, his future is looking very uncertain.

I had not seen Ruth for a couple of weeks, so I stopped by to find out how she's getting along. She looked dreadful and surely doesn't take care of herself. She has too many late nights, too many demands on her time and too little rest as evidenced by her thin face, pallid complexion and sunken eyes. Her mother-in-law was out, and the housekeeper was entertaining the children, so we were able to sit uninterrupted at the kitchen table and swap news. Apparently, she is no longer pregnant. I'm under the impression that she had a termination but was reluctant to spell it out. I was a little surprised as she is a devout Roman Catholic, but abortion is relatively easy here; and it would not have been difficult for her to arrange one, especially as her husband is a doctor. Whatever the case, she seemed relieved not to be having another baby. I didn't stay long as she was preparing for guests arriving later that day. She is always preparing for guests.

I loved Mother's comments about the US trying to solve the problems of the Middle East when we can't handle the Vietnam negotiations. I'm so anxious for Bill's news; I'm counting on you to tell me as soon as you hear anything.

Chapter 12

8 September 1970

One good turn deserves another, and I am pleased to hear that the Turkish cigars are doing the rounds, making a hit with the men at home. Since I have never tried any of them, I couldn't possibly comment on the quality or variations. Even if I had smoked them, I don't think I would be able to distinguish one from another. But it is true what you say about the cigarettes. They really are much better than the American ones and deserve their reputation as the best in the world. It took me awhile to get used to them, but now, I much prefer them. Undoubtedly, this is due as much to the high quality of the tobacco as to the fact that it is not mixed with a lot of fillers, a practice I have heard is widespread elsewhere. And yet, it is American cigarettes that everyone here wants to be seen smoking. Despite being much more expensive - or maybe because of it - they have cachet. Marlboros have the coolest reputation wherever I go - even England - which just proves that fashion has nothing to do with common sense.

Levent continues to have his ups and downs. To paraphrase: when he is good, he is very, very good; when he is bad, he is unbearable. Overall though, the tolerable periods are gaining on the insufferable. It's hard to know why he is improving; is it pills, time, or something else? Hakan makes a point of spending an hour or so alone with Levent whenever he is at home. I think this special attention has as much to do with his recovery as anything else; he's always better after seeing Hakan. At the very least, he appears to have overcome his agoraphobia and now goes out. Apart from periodic temper tantrums, Levent seems to be returning to normal. I believe even these would cease if Ana would stop provoking him. I realize that she only wants to help, but she has no sensitivity to his moods and doesn't know when to stop "helping" him, when to leave him alone. I can see his temper building as she nags and fusses at him, all too aware that if she simply left him in peace, there would be nothing to aggravate him. Totally oblivious to the effects of her actions, she continues to plough on until there is an almighty explosion. Then she wonders why Levent is angry with her. It's so easy to see this from the outside.

Since it is obvious that he is getting better, we have to believe that the improvements will continue, and that a period of relative stability will provide a turning point. He has youth on his side, and we hope that this will be enough to see him regain his balance over the long term. In America, no one thinks anything of seeing a psychiatrist, but here, the stigma of mental illness is huge.

According to what I call the "beefsteak index", the family's financial position is relatively sound at present. I judge this by the number of times we have fillet steak, the most expensive cut of meat. Although the subject of money is discussed freely within the family, and often in society at large, I'm not entirely certain where Baba gets his income these days. He may have funds left from money that Sami gave him, or he may have had some stashed away, or maybe he sold something. Hakan and I pay him for all the work that he does for our business. This has been slow over the summer months, but is looking much more promising for the coming season. We have it in mind to give Baba an official company role once we return to London. We'd like to let him run things here and make his own money from the work and transactions he carries out on our behalf. Of course, Ken would have to be consulted, and the realization of such plans is still some way off. We DO have to contend with this military service interfering in our lives, all our lives.

Baba and I had a two-day trip to Istanbul to deliver the London order via Ken's friend with the tourist bus. Disappointingly, Ken failed to send many of the items we needed; but in return, we could deliver only a portion of the order he wanted. We understand the bus will be back at the end of the month, and we'll try to have everything ready for that trip.

We paid a mercifully brief visit to Sami only to find him still in bed at 11:00 am. Baba was so disgusted that we left after five minutes. Business accomplished, all I wanted to do was get back to see Hakan who would be arriving home on Saturday morning. I drove through the night on Friday, not a wise move, since I gave myself a sharp fright by falling asleep at the wheel. It could only have been for a split second, but I realized that I had closed my eyes as I drove into a curve, only opening them again as I came out of it. After that, and doubtless to Baba's annoyance, I sang aloud the rest of the way home (my extensive repertoire of flawlessly rendered show tunes). We got in about 3:00 am, having developed a faulty (and noisy) exhaust and having suffered a flat tyre on the road into town. There's forever something to keep us on our toes.

I've about given up on the chocolate chips you say you sent ages ago. They haven't arrived, and I suspect they didn't make it through customs. Maybe someone opened them and ate them.

15 September 1970

It was exciting to open your letter this week and find one from Bill as well. It's such a relief to have news, any news at all. I found it reassuring to read his report of the relatively secure situation where he is at present. I know there is no room for complacency, but given some of the nightmare incidents we have heard about in the recent past, we are all bound to fear the worst. I shall start writing a weekly letter to him just as soon as I finish this one. I don't suppose I'll recognize him when I see him next; I barely knew him in the photos you sent. He looks so grown up.

My heart positively skipped a beat when I read your suggestion that I should go home for a couple of months. Apart from being with Hakan, there is nothing I would like more than spending some time with you. It sounds better than Christmas morning. I miss you all very much, and it would be wonderful to see everyone after so long away. But - you could probably hear the "but" coming - we have no idea what the approaching weeks and months will bring. Until I know more, I don't feel I can commit myself to any kind of travel, however enticing.

Everything hinges on where Hakan will be posted when he finishes here. If it is far away, which seems unlikely, he might be so inaccessible as to make a break most welcome. On the other hand, if it is one of the more likely locations in Bursa, Istanbul or Ankara, Hakan would still be close enough for us to have frequent visits, and I would not want to leave. We are in this together. He has said that I too, am doing my military service, and while it is nothing like as difficult as his, simply being in the same town feels like moral support during these demanding days. I think Hakan would feel disheartened if I left. He hates the army so much and feels so out of touch with his own people and culture that I think it would be a genuine blow to him if I just took off. Everything is up in the air. I appreciate both the thought and the offer and will fill you in on what's happening as soon as we hear anything at all.

Lady has disappeared and I am forlorn. She never strays very far but has not been seen for two days now. Despite a thorough search of the neighbourhood and countless enquiries, we have been unable to find any trace. We think that someone has made off with her. She is generally regarded as a most attractive little dog, and it's possible she might appeal to someone intent on making some money. Well, that's what Levent says, though I'm not sure I understand why she is such a potential goldmine. I'm anxiously hoping she may turn up yet, but it's all rather mysterious.

So, my hometown is about to get a new bridge. They have been talking about it forever, rather like the bridge that is finally being built over the Bosphorus in Istanbul. If ever a bridge was sorely needed, it's that one. At present, the only means of getting from one side of the city to the other is by ferry, a time-consuming process that has long needed replacement. I gather the Bosphorus Bridge will take three years to complete and will be ready for the 50th anniversary of the republic. It will link Europe and Asia and will be the longest single-span bridge in the world. Sorry. I didn't mean to steal your thunder.

The weather has turned autumnal of late, a most welcome change from the oppressive heat of only a few weeks ago. It's still warm and sunny, an altogether pleasant transitional period before cold weather sets in. It's now that I miss the Pennsylvania hillsides with their dramatic change of colour. I used to think that autumns everywhere were more or less the same. It's only since I've been abroad that I realize how very untrue that is. England has colour in places, but overall has neither the cold temperatures nor the bright sun needed for spectacular displays. The foliage there goes from green to yellow, whereas here it turns from yellow to brown. Still, there's a crisp, smoky edge to the air and a feeling of optimism that I have always associated with September and the start of a new school year.

Alas, the change has not brought much rain, and our water shortages are as severe as ever. Everyone here says that this has been the hottest and driest summer in recent memory. As the water coming from our indoor taps is not fit for drinking, we rely on the water seller who comes around once a week to meet our needs. He has a sturdy horse cart filled with giant glass water bottles encased in wicker baskets. These not only protect the glass but also keep the water cool. We buy enough to last us for the coming week, storing it in large ceramic jugs where it stays fresh. A week's supply costs about fifteen cents.

Did I mention that Cemile, the tenant downstairs, was expecting her fourth baby? She has three girls already, so they were desperate for a boy. They have finally had their wish, and naturally, they are all thrilled. Personally, I find her one of the most annoying women on the planet, about as agreeable as a swarm of gnats, but I wish her well and hope that baby Erol uses water only in proportion to his size. Ha!

I don't know if you would have had any news of the cholera that is in the area. It has moved across the Middle East into Asia Minor and is threatening Europe. Most affected countries now have strict quarantine laws; no one who has not had a cholera vaccination can cross the borders. There have been scattered cases reported throughout Turkey, but it is much more widespread in southern Russia and Syria. Because so few people are automatically vaccinated against this awful disease, it spreads quickly when it gains a foothold. We are watching the situation closely but feel there is no reason for panic.

It transpires that Levent is going to go back to full-time education after all. Although his old school refused to admit him, he was able to enrol in a private one. More than ever, I am convinced that many of his current problems are connected to anxieties surrounding his studies. He had had a good week prior to this recent acceptance, but since then, life has been like a car on a caravan track: lots of ruts and potholes with very few smooth places. He has redoubled his efforts to establish himself as the family dictator and marches around barking orders at everyone. When he gets in one of these moods, it is impossible to communicate with him. It's as if he shuts himself away in another reality, and nothing we say or do seems to penetrate. He blocks off all attempts to get through by simply talking and yelling over anything else being said.

School does not open until 25 September, so it's anyone's guess as to whether he will be fit to start. I don't see how he can learn anything in his present condition, but maybe it is best to encourage him to go. Since reality cannot be as bad as he fears, perhaps he needs to address his anxieties in order to overcome them. Is this asking too much of him in his current state? Who knows? We're totally ignorant about what to do for the best. In the meantime, he is driving us all crazy with his incessant hyperactivity. He refuses to take his meds because he doesn't think he is sick. If he doesn't take them, I'M going to! Let us hope that we all survive, mentally intact, until the 25th.

You have excelled yourselves in the squash-growing department, and all the Turks are mightily impressed with your resulting 22-pound squash! What a magnificent result, originating as it did from the donated Turkish seeds. This has been a truly rewarding international effort, and credit is due to one and all. May it be the start of many more co-operative programmes between our countries.

Congratulations! (Picture required ASAP.)

22 September 1970

This has been a week of bountiful blessings. It's raining. The weather is cold, gloomy and miserable, and we are overjoyed! (There's a sentence I never imagined I'd write.) The showers have continued long enough and hard enough to make all the difference to our water supply. Super! It can stop now.

The next piece of good news is that Lady has returned to the fold. We found her, entirely by accident, when I was taking Baba to visit an old friend. We took a wrong turn, and there she was with a pack of dogs, foraging around in a pile of garbage. I called to her; she picked up her ears, looked around, made a beeline for the car and hopped straight in. Then she began whimpering and crying. I don't know which of us was happier! She had been missing for five days, so we all assumed she was long gone. Evidently she wandered too far from the house and got lost. Or maybe she followed some other dogs or children and couldn't find her way back. At any rate, everyone was glad to see her.

More good news: the blessed chocolate chips arrived in perfect condition. Can you believe it? After all these weeks and the summer heat, I expected that they would be a lumpen mass, if they arrived at all. The measuring cups came in the same package. I paid a ridiculous 40TL duty for both, but it was money well spent from my point of view. The chocolate won't be around long, but the cups are ideal and will last a lifetime. My baking attempts have been reasonably hopeless, so I'm relying on the transforming power of the cups to produce the required results. No prizes for guessing what I'll be doing this afternoon. The postman also delivered a big batch of newspapers which I had not had for a long while. The news is stale, but I still enjoy reading them as they keep me informed about events in the hometown. Thank you for everything. Your thoughtfulness is appreciated more than I can tell you.

The household is expanding. Of course, there is baby Erol downstairs, but we have recently realized that both of our dogs are expecting. And in addition to our fluctuating mammal population, we now have eleven chickens. Following previous unsuccessful attempts to raise poultry, these are Levent's latest project. He built their coop and is conscientious in his care of the birds, which though still young, should eventually produce eggs for breakfast. I hope he has more luck with this flock than earlier ones.

After a truly awful week, Levent is now much calmer. The chickens have provided a soothing and convenient distraction to his worries. School starts on Friday, and it will be a relief to have the waiting over. Baba and Abla took him to buy a new suit, which should help boost his outlook and confidence. For our part, Hakan and I are buying all his books and supplies and will contribute to his school expenses. Additionally, Hakan has been working closely with Levent, helping him get his room organized for study and encouraging him with useful advice. After this, we simply sit tight and wait.

Abla is still looking for work, but there seems to be an obstacle at every turn. She has been promised the receptionist's job at the local law association, but she can't start until the present girl leaves, and she is waiting for a permit to work in Germany. She could be going anytime soon or not for two years. Abla's applications with the banks have come to nothing. These are regarded as plum jobs, and it takes string pulling to get them. Baba has pulled a lot of strings but plainly, not the right ones. There are many feelers out but no luck so far. More wait and see. This family could certainly use some uplifting news. Sometimes I look at Baba and see a remarkable resemblance to a man called Job.

Cemile had a *mevlüt* for her little son yesterday. She had her hands full with all her children and guests, so Abla and I volunteered to serve the refreshments. It gave us a good excuse to sit in the kitchen, out of sight. I don't mind *mevlüts* per se, but all the staring makes me self-conscious. One of Abla's friends came to join us in the kitchen. We had an agreeable afternoon chatting very un-*mevlüt*-like amongst ourselves, and the afternoon passed quickly.

In the evening, we went to a wedding reception given by friends of the Beylers whose son has recently married; it is not uncommon for the civil ceremony and the reception to be held on different days. This was a typical affair held in a *salon*, a room big enough to take the vast number of guests for, according to custom, everyone - and I do mean everyone - is invited. No acquaintance is too casual; no connection too vague; no relation too distant not to be included in this rite of passage. Upon arrival, each guest was seated at a table amidst the general hubbub that comes with the celebration. Excited announcements as to the whereabouts of the happy couple meant that we knew the bride and groom were arriving long before they appeared. They were roundly applauded as they entered and immediately took up their positions for the first dance. Expecting the gentle strains of something romantic, I was stunned to hear the little combo lurch into the latest Turkish pop song, a number both screechingly loud and impossible to dance to. They struggled bravely.

The bride was a picture of confection in white lace and sequins. The local beauty parlour had provided her with the extreme hair and make-up inevitable on these occasions. Although she resembled nothing so much as a 1950s bride doll, I'm sure a pretty girl lurked beneath the camouflage. Custom requires that the newlyweds and his parents (who are the reception hosts) must greet everyone individually, not easy when there is no such thing as a receiving line and the numbers, well into three figures. However, there is a tremendous incentive to make the rounds, as this is when the invited guests present their gifts, usually something gold. The variety of suitable items ranges from small token gold coins, to the standard gold bangles, to impressive sets of jewellery. The groom rather loses out to his bride in this matter (what she receives remains legally hers), but by way of compensation, he is normally presented with an ostentatious watch from the bride's family. Both will have paper money pinned to red sashes worn across their bodies for that very purpose.

This particular couple chose to break up the greetings with intervals of dancing. Or were they breaking up the dancing with intervals of greeting? The first half of the evening was devoted to pop music with only a limited number of younger dancers on the floor. Unmarried people dance with same-sex friends, so it's common to see girls dancing with other girls and men the same, though the latter tend to reserve their masculine displays for the folk dances. At one point, the bride and her uncle broke into an enthusiastic set of gyrations and were obviously having a great time. We could see disapproval register on the groom's face as he sulked and then ignored his new wife for the next half hour. When he left the room, Abla and I surmised that he had gone off for a drop of whiskey. He was definitely in better spirits (heh, heh) when he re-appeared a little later at his bride's side. Apparently all had been forgiven.

When the musicians stopped for a break, we had wedding cake (no rituals over this) and sodas. A wealthier family might provide more, up to and including an elaborate meal. The band turned to folk music for the second half, and this brought far more people onto the dance floor. These are the traditional tunes beloved by all ages, and the area soon became crowded. My family seemed to be the only group with no one participating. Hakan positively hates this kind of dancing; the others are uninterested. I have joined in at some of the women-only affairs, and although I am not very good, I think it's fun.

The festivities looked set to go on into the small hours, but shortly after this, we made our excuses and left. All this has me wondering about the nature of our ceremony and reception. If we ever get to that point. What I might have in mind and what the family might expect could be two very different weddings. I don't think Hakan has any firm views, though to be honest, we haven't really discussed it in much detail. It has felt like tempting fate to plan anything before we have jumped over more hurdles.

Like the rest of us, Hakan was relieved to read Bill's first Vietnam letter. We're all keeping our beady eyes on him and the situation there. I am going to drop him a line now.

Please send our greetings to Boy Wonder at Ashland College!

29 September 1970

How very strange to find you in the warm, sunny place and us, shivering around the stove here in Turkey. Your trip to Cape Hatteras sounded perfect; I'm so glad you've had good weather. It has turned unseasonably cold in these parts. I don't remember it being this bitter when we arrived at the end of October last year. The notorious Elli Evler wind whips around the houses and streets, making it feel even colder.

We were glad to get Bill's second letter. They don't waste any time getting into the thick of things, do they? Still, I am reassured by his tone. He appears to be entirely sane in an insane world. Under the circumstances, it's a healthy attitude to have. As you say, considering events elsewhere, he might have been sent to the Middle East, potentially as dangerous a place as Vietnam, and one with neither compromise nor resolution in sight.

The Turkish papers have little news from Vietnam, so I'm always at least a week behind as it takes that long for my TIME magazine to arrive. You mentioned in your last letter that Syria had invaded Lebanon, an event about which I have heard nothing. I want Hakan to fill me in over the weekend. When the two planes were hijacked to Jordan a couple of weeks ago, he told me that the army had been on alert status, but we do not think that there is any imminent prospect of Turkish involvement in regional conflicts. Turkey is neither an Arab nor a Muslim state and wants to identify with Europe, rather than the Middle East. I don't believe the government would take any military action whatsoever, unless directly threatened. As far as I am aware, the country has no territorial ambitions and would have nothing to gain by embroiling itself in complex problems that have existed for centuries.

Hakan finishes his officer training 8 October. We understand that the transfers have been finalized, but no one has yet been told. One of his superiors informed Hakan that he is being sent to Istanbul, but we are reluctant to trust this until it's official. When he leaves, he will have spent ten months in the army, with eight to go. That means we'll be on the home stretch!

As expected, Levent started school last Friday. So far, they don't seem to have done much except get organized and not much headway has been made in that direction. He still doesn't know who some of his teachers are or when his classes meet. Although it is an established school, it's almost as if no one there has done this before. Maybe they have a lot of new staff.

The children here go to school for half days only. I'm not clear whether this is due to tradition or to overcrowding. Levent starts at 8:00 am and finishes by 1:00 pm, giving him plenty of opportunity for both study and relaxation. He has his work cut out for him. He has had no schedule to follow, no duties, no discipline for over two years. The adjustment will be a demanding one. Hakan has done all he can to help Levent realize that he must assume responsibility for his future. He has told him that this is "the last train". If he doesn't catch this one, there will be no other. We are all prepared to do whatever we can to assist, but ultimately, the only one who can make this a success is Levent.

The chocolate chip cookies I made were a disaster. Well, 50% disaster. I followed the packet recipe precisely, forgetting that there is a vast difference between American and Turkish flours. I really needed to add much more of the latter. That we were using an unregulated and largely uncontrollable wood-burning stove didn't help either. We put the first batch in when the oven was far too hot and came away with a gluey mess. We let the oven cool down, but the second batch still came out runny. At that point, Abla and I decided to chuck in more flour, resulting in something resembling the cookies I remembered. Since chocolate is expensive here, it is rarely used in baking. Anything that looks chocolaty is probably only colouring and tastes of nothing but sugar. Consequently, any of the baked goods I produce, using large amounts of real chocolate, are a stunning success. Just before the chips arrived, I made a real chocolate cake with butter-cream icing that turned out very well. Hakan said it was the best thing I had ever made, but the cookies are unique and disappeared quickly. I am hoping that you will send me more chocolate chips (hint, hint). While awaiting reinforcements, I shall experiment with flour proportions, using nuts and raisins instead. Chocolate chips are too precious to waste!

Despite my eternal griping about the weather, Saturday was a beautiful autumn day, and for several reasons, not least of which was pure desire to escape the ensuing *gün* at our house, Hakan and I took ourselves off for a picnic. We packed some apples, cheese, olives, nuts and cookies, and we stopped on the way for *simit*. We headed for the picnic grounds a short distance out of town and had the place to ourselves.

Although it was cool enough to wear heavy sweaters, the sun was warm. Summer heat had turned the grass to straw and baked the earth until it cracked. Leaves crunched and dry branches snapped beneath our feet as we made our way through the pine groves. It wasn't exactly Pennsylvania in October, but not a bad substitute either. We took the dogs with us and spent most of the afternoon trying to keep them off the blanket... when we were not pulling them out of the nearby creek. But overall, it was a peaceful, contented sort of day. Eventually, the bleached-out sun of late September sank low in the sky, and the fungal air of evening settled around us, signalling time to go home.

The dogs took up their standard positions in the rear of the car, their heads out of the windows as we drove slowly through town. When we stopped to buy some eggs, I realized that Lady was not in the back seat. No matter how hard I stared and no matter how disbelieving my eyes, she simply wasn't there.

"Hakan."

"Yes?"

"Lady is not in the back."

"What do you mean, 'she's not in the back'?"

"I don't know. She's just not here."

Incredulous, he turned and looked. Still not satisfied, he got out of the driver's seat and searched around as if there were a space in which she could hide. We stared at each other, bemused by the improbable situation and mesmerized with indecision.

We had no idea at what point Lady had gone missing, nor where she could be at that precise moment. It seemed unlikely that she would fall out, but whatever had happened, she wasn't there. Slowly, we retraced our route, looking for a silly little black and white dog. Searching for Lady was beginning to have a somewhat familiar feel to it. Before we went too far, some little boys called out to us that they had seen a dog fall out of our car. Sure enough, there was Lady standing in the middle of the pavement, looking totally bewildered. I guess she was as stunned by events as we were. What a character!

The two expectant mothers are currently reclining on the porch in their new beds. In anticipation of family expansion, I decided to enlarge their sleeping facilities. Baba made the frames for me, and I stuffed new cushions to line the boxes. The dogs are no longer allowed in the house, so I am preparing for the winter months. They are fine where they are just now, but later on, I will move them to the little brick house in the back where they will have more protection from the cold and wet.

On Wednesday, Ana's brother, Hüseyin Dayı, came to visit with his daughter Zehra, daughter-in-law Nihal and their babies who are about the same age. We had a lovely afternoon, and as it ended, Dayı invited Abla and me to have supper with them at their house. Without hesitation, we accepted and thought no more about it until Ana came into the room and vetoed the whole idea. She said we couldn't possibly go until Baba had given his consent.

Even by Turkish standards, this is absurd. It makes no sense to require two women, ages 27 and 28, to seek permission for a meal with their uncle and his family at their home. However, rather than argue about it, Abla went to Aylin Abla's to use the phone and obtain the required assent. Baba gave it, of course. So that was settled, or so we assumed. Then Ana decided that I couldn't go unless I had Hakan's consent. As with vanishing dogs, this conversation began to feel like familiar territory. Without thinking, I burst out laughing.

She knew perfectly well that I was not going to go to the base to ask Hakan's permission. Besides, who would give me permission to go ask him? This is how ridiculous it gets.

As on previous occasions, I told her that I wouldn't dream of bothering Hakan for such a petty request, and that I would take full responsibility for my actions. I think Ana feels that as the oldest woman in the hierarchy, she needs to assert her authority. Even though her demands are unreasonable and what she proposes is total nonsense, she acts in a manner that she regards as tough and restrictive to demonstrate her position. Unfortunately for her, I am not playing this game.

Did I tell you that she took to opening my mail? When I had been out one afternoon, I came home to find that she had inspected everything that had arrived in the post that day. I looked at her quizzically, and she said that it was her duty to investigate her prospective daughter-in-law's mail... in case I get up to nefarious activities, I suppose. I was incensed, but decided not to say anything because I realized that it was all a charade. She can't comprehend a word of English and wouldn't recognize a nefarious activity if it announced itself. In due course, she grasped the futility of trying to scrutinize papers written in a foreign language, and the intrusions ended.

Ramadan starts in another month. Since there will be no visiting during this time of fasting and abstinence, we are currently engaged in a frantic round of social calls on people we have been obliged to see for eons.

Always something to keep us busy!

Chapter 13

6 October 1970

We have passed the halfway point in Hakan's army career! We're on the downhill run. If all goes according to plan - and a plan is not a certainty - he should be out in July. To mark this milestone moment, we've been kicking around ideas for the wedding. Hakan favours the spring, but I am inclined to wait until he is out of the military, so we can do things our own way. I believe we are giving the army too much power over us if we try to organize something while he is still committed. We've waited this long, a little longer doesn't bother me if it means being able to do it right. Anyway, it's all just talk at present. And we've still had no official word on his new posting.

Now that cold weather is here - much too early this year - we are stocking up on items for winter. This week, Baba bought one ton of wood and two tons of coal, now loaded into their storage bins. After a fair amount of coaxing and persuading, Levent agreed to help. This morning, we went to the bazaar and bought sixty-five pounds of onions, as well as several kilos (about twenty-five pounds) of *salça*, tomato paste. This is handmade and much denser and richer than the store-bought variety at home. Since there will be no fresh tomatoes in winter, *salça* is widely used as the basis for flavour in many dishes.

Living in the West where so many produce items are available year round, I had never before thought about foods having a season. Naturally, I knew this, but I didn't understand it, if you see what I mean. When something is in the market here, we eat all we can because we know it won't last forever. When it's done, it's gone. Already the fruits and vegetables of summer are disappearing, and the few tomatoes, melons and peppers that are left, purchased for mere *kuruş* a couple of weeks ago, are now prohibitively expensive. However, no one need mourn their passing. We ate our fill and now look forward to the apples, grapes, onions, potatoes and squash that are appearing. We'll have the "infamous three", as Hakan calls them, throughout the winter: spinach, cabbage and leeks. We will have winter lettuce from the south and, of course, excellent citrus fruits. As far as Hakan is concerned, the best thing of all is chestnuts, roasted and eaten warm. Delicious. Ana says that because both quince and pomegranates have been plentiful this year, we are in for a long, hard winter. I hope not.

Abla and I have developed a habit of staying up once the other Beylers have gone to bed. They frequently retire about 9:30 pm, and then we have the house to ourselves. It's bliss, all peace and quiet with no interruptions and no compulsion to do anything more constructive than sit and talk. Since she never smokes while her parents are around, this is a chance for Abla to have a cigarette. It's not a matter of being secretive; it's a matter of respect. If there is yoghurt in the house, we might make ourselves some *ayran*, but generally, we have tea. And we always nibble on nuts and pumpkin seeds. Finally, I have mastered the knack of eating them and have found them addictive.

The other night, we were settling in for a relaxing chat when we realized that our supply of *çekirdek* was alarmingly low. This is as bad as running out of cigarettes. Some things cannot be substituted, and nothing else would do. We both had a craving that would not be ignored. What to do? "Let's drive to town and buy some more," I suggested, looking questioningly at Abla to see what she might make of this bold idea. It was late and dark and quite unacceptable for two young women to be seen driving around in a car on their own. She hesitated, the decision finely balanced, and then said, "Let's."

We knew a nut seller with a little kiosk in the town centre who would oblige us by bringing our order to the car. Since we would not have to get out, we decided to remain in our nightgowns and threw jackets on over the top. Aslana and Lady, alert to the possibility of an adventure, followed us to Dagmar and were allowed to chaperone. When we arrived at his stand, the proprietor recognized us and came over to the car to see what we wanted. Both Abla and I rolled down our windows, and Abla, on the pavement side, gave him the order. So as to sniff all the novel town smells, both dogs had their heads out of the windows, and before we knew it, Lady had jumped out and was off like a goat after grain. Something had caught her attention, something that needed to be barked at! Abla and I sat stunned... and stuck.

Although my nightgown was not diaphanous, it was still, clearly, a nightgown, and I had no desire to hop out of the car and run down the street in such a state. I called to Lady, pleadingly, frantically, but she had a one-track mind, and I was nowhere on her radar. And she was scampering further ahead all the time, attracting bemused attention. If I did not want to abandon her (it would serve her right!), there was nothing to do but go after her. Luckily, there were only a few people about, and while the sticky light of the street lamps meant I was relatively shrouded, I still had to run past several astonished men before I was able to scoop up my sassy little miss and run back to the car. I kept my head down and looked at no one, hoping this made me invisible.

We certainly had a lot to discuss once we got back home. Ever mindful of the way news and gossip spread in a small town, our chief concern was that the family would somehow hear of our escapade. We were already dreading the repercussions that would inevitably follow. After mulling it over, we concluded that confession would be the wisest course and decided to tackle Baba, usually up before Ana, early the next morning. Abla must have been worrying all night as she was up at first light, waiting for Baba to emerge. By the time I made it out to the salon, Abla and Baba were chatting in the normal way. I saw the relief on Abla's face as I cast a glance in her direction to see if she had revealed our sins. Baba looked at me and chuckled. We all agreed that this was something we need not tell Ana. Happily, the matter has ended there.

Earlier this week I met Ruth and together we called on Betty, a new American in town. Her husband is something at the NATO base. Aren't they all? They'll be here for about a year, and like American women before her, she is finding it tough to live in a community where she doesn't speak the language and has little interest in the culture. It makes me wonder why they bother to come. Betty managed to find Ruth right off, and they have been friendly since her arrival two months ago.

The first thing I noticed when I entered her living room - in obvious pride of place - was an enormous autographed picture of George Wallace, that racist thug who calls himself the Governor of Alabama. Betty and I are not going to have much in common, I thought to myself. This turned out to be true. We didn't have many shared interests, and I found conversation a struggle. Ruth seemed oblivious to any awkwardness and kept everything humming along with her easy chatter.

Betty had invited us for lunch. I took some Turkish bread and *baklava*; and in return, she gave us potato salad, baked beans, pork sausages and bacon. Bacon! It has been ages since I have had any pork. It tasted like the food of the gods to me, and I must admit that I wolfed everything down. Without a doubt, the very best thing about Betty is her access to the PX. It was surreal to walk into her kitchen and see all the familiar American food brands and household products. I felt dislocated. However, even the lure of these temptations will not draw me into a friendship. It was an interesting afternoon, but I think I shall leave Ruth and Betty to their own devices. I have come to the realization that shared nationality alone is an insufficient basis for friendship… even in a foreign land.

Meanwhile, other visits continue apace. In addition to the pressure to fit in what we can before Ramadan, there is the further social responsibility incumbent on the Beylers to introduce me to everyone they know. It is an expected courtesy to do so. I have been here for nearly a year now, and apart from close relatives and friends, I have never visited the same house twice. There seems to be a never-ending list of people I am obliged to meet. I do not think a two-year stay will suffice to see them all.

16 October 1970

I can't believe Dad is in hospital again. What a shock! I hope that he has had our cards and is now at home. Maybe kidney stones are in the air. I never knew much about them, but during the past month, I have heard of several people who have suffered, including Ruth's mother-in-law. I understand they are just about the most painful thing around, so I'm glad Dad passed his quickly. I imagine he has had to endure some teasing about being sick again so soon after his vacation. Obviously, we all wish him a speedy recovery.

A second, and altogether more agreeable surprise this week, came in the form of a letter from Bill. Oh, I was excited! I had been hoping that he was getting my letters without really expecting any response. I had no idea if he was in a position to write, but apparently, he was having a "leisure" period in the camp. He has such a calm way of explaining the situation there, making everything sound much more comfortable and secure than it must be. I presume this version has been edited for family consumption. As I'm sure you are aware, he is driving a truck at present. This he describes as a "cake" job. It must be his perception. But it was great to get his news first hand. As he points out, his tour of duty is expected to be twelve months, and it is going to be a long year.

Hakan has finished his officer course; he came top of the class. Naturally. He's a spirited competitor, in case you had not noticed. He is now known as Hakan Çavuş, Sergeant, his title as a junior officer. However, our big news is that he is being sent to Bursa! We have heard that he really had been assigned to a base in Istanbul, but at the last minute, the long arm of influence worked in his favour and he was given his first choice. Hakan is nigh on ecstatic - we both are! We know that we are unbelievably lucky as many of the men are being sent to the east, some to the Russian border. By contrast, Bursa is a few hours away. We have heard that the base there is small but noted for its modern facilities, while the city itself is lovely, one we have both enjoyed visiting. All things considered, his new location could not be better for us. Since petrol prices have soared recently, we shall probably do most of our travelling by coach as it will be far cheaper than taking Dagmar. He will be leaving on Monday the 26th, but it is unclear whether he will be able to get home before then. There's a strict quarantine at the base because of the cholera scare.

This brings me to my next news. I think I have already mentioned that over the summer, we had a few isolated cases of cholera in the country. Just as we were thinking that this deadly disease had largely passed us by, we heard of outbreaks in Istanbul. As of last week, that city had reported over a thousand cases, and others are starting to appear throughout Turkey. We then heard of a few incidents in Bursa, which means it is only a matter of time until it strikes in Kavaklı. No one, apart from me, seems to be concerned about this. Bearing in mind that I have never been vaccinated for cholera and have no natural resistance (if there is such a thing), I decided to take myself off to the local hospital for vaccination. When I invited the Beylers to come with me, they looked as if I were proposing a trip to the moon. They made it plain that they thought I had unwarranted fears, but I have a healthy respect for killer diseases and was not about to be put off my mission. Perhaps more unexpected than their reluctance to have injections was the fact that no one felt I needed either a guard of honour or a companion. I am pondering the significance of this.

I left after breakfast and made my way to the government hospital in town where I knew there would be vaccine, if any were available. We have heard that supplies are short, and I was not certain of success; but I felt I had a better chance of getting a vaccination at this stage, rather than waiting until an epidemic was declared and finding myself caught up in a panic. Without any trouble, I found the clinic where the injections were being administered. Along with a few others, they gave me mine, free of charge. As cholera comes closer, the Beylers are taking sensible precautions. Since this is a water-borne disease, we now boil all our water, a right royal pain, but absolutely essential. Also, we don't buy any fruits or vegetables that cannot withstand being washed or prepared in scalding water. I sincerely hope these safety measures are not needed.

Baba and Abla left for Istanbul this morning. Baba has his court case tomorrow, and Abla went along to keep him company. They are such dear people. I wish they could put all of this behind them, but I suppose the case will continue to drag on, with or without cunning manipulation.

It's a constant source of amazement to me how much control parents here retain over their children's lives, even into adulthood, even after the children have married. A child is always a child and is never regarded as the equal of the parents, whatever the age. It's especially true for women who live under the control of men, moving from father and brothers, to husband and even sons. For a girl like Abla, who is never allowed to leave the house by herself, never permitted to go out in the evening without her father, the concept of working and living away from home is freedom and independence beyond comprehension. And probably something she wouldn't want anyway. I don't believe she envies me at all.

When we have spoken about her having an arranged marriage (an arranged marriage, not a forced marriage... people on the outside confuse the two), Abla is completely accepting, saying that since she has had almost no contact with men outside her family, she would have no means of judging a suitable husband. She considers that such matters should be left to her father and brothers to determine what is in her best interests. Under the circumstances, she is undoubtedly right.

Of course, all this begs the question about the wisdom of keeping women so sheltered that they are unable to make these decisions for themselves. But this is the traditional way of doing things, and if we accept that it is fine for women to be dominated by men, then I guess the system works. Certainly divorce statistics indicate a greater degree of success in cultures that arrange marriages, than in the West, where we pick our own partners.

Thinking about it practically, it makes sense to let those with our welfare at heart make calm, sensible decisions about our long-term happiness, rather than making the same life-changing choices based on unpredictable and often illogical emotional highs. Ah - but logic does not allow for the chemistry of attraction, a vital ingredient in any relationship. Either way, I simply cannot imagine what they make of me. More and more I understand what a gigantic leap it has been for them to accept not only someone about whom they've had no say, but also a young woman who is a stranger, a foreigner and a Christian into the bargain. I have renewed respect for them all. None of this is easy.

It's a busy week. We've had an unexpected order from our regular customers in Berlin. We sent a big shipment only two weeks ago, and they reported that everything sold as they were unpacking it. The patchwork suede and leather maxi-coats flew off the rails, and they want everything in more sizes. This is easier said than done. As we had not anticipated the demand, we are working flat-out to get the materials together to meet this sudden - and most welcome - order. These items are the fads of the moment and will not last, so we want to capitalize as much as we can, while we can. WML strikes again!

I have recently learned that Cemile (downstairs) has never seen the inside of a school. I knew she was an ignorant woman, but I hadn't picked up that she can neither read nor write. She brought us all little gifts the other day: a prayer scarf for Ana, a baking pan for Abla (which she immediately whisked off to her dowry. She puts everything in her dowry. We were missing two chickens last week, and I wouldn't be astonished if they too, are in her dowry) and a plastic fridge box for me (I'd put this in my dowry except I don't have one). We couldn't figure out the reason for the gifts. There were no circumstances we could think of that warranted presents. We finally concluded that these were "thank yous" to Ana and Abla who had both read her coffee grounds and predicted the birth of a son, and for me as I had brought her home from the hospital.

I've had another letter from Bill. He was out in the field when he wrote, struggling with the muck and mire that make everything such hard going. The numerous rats don't help either. Let's hope these are the worst that he encounters.

26 October 1970

I am so happy to hear that you were able to enjoy your planned trip to New Orleans. It's the right season to head to the sunny south and a pleasant way for Dad to ease into things, though it sounds as if he is back to normal now. Long may this continue.

Here in cold, wintry Turkey, the wheel of fortune keeps on turning, and I can only guess as to Hakan's whereabouts today. Theoretically, he should be in Bursa or heading there, but arrangements have changed twice already, and we have said good-bye as many times. On Friday evening, he made a telephone call to Aylin Abla's asking if I could meet him at the base at 10:00 on Saturday morning. Could I! Since I knew the base was still under strict quarantine, with no one permitted to leave for personal reasons, I didn't understand how it was going to work. When I pulled up at the gate, Hakan jumped in on the driver's side, and we made our escape via a back way, through fields and over dirt tracks, to avoid being spotted in any road checks. He said he had "cover" at the base, which I later worked out must be the General; but he was technically AWOL, and I worried about this constantly. On this occasion, he was home for a few hours before I took him back.

We had assumed that would be our last visit in Kavaklı, but the following Saturday morning, Baba rang from his office (what would we do without Aylin Abla's telephone?) and asked me to come to the shop, bringing civilian clothes for Hakan. When I arrived, there he was, once again having gone AWOL with cover. This time, he had arranged to be home overnight, giving us a chance to sort out some business matters which desperately needed his attention before he left. I smuggled him back to the base early Sunday morning, and as far as I know, he has now gone to his new post.

The cholera outbreak rumbles on. None of the soldiers have had their injections, which concerns me greatly, especially as Hakan will be based in a known cholera area. We have heard that the American government sent a huge shipment of vaccine that, we have also heard, sits in customs because the Americans are demanding too much money for it. I cannot believe this is true. It's incomprehensible that the US would send needed drugs and then hold them to ransom. It makes no sense whatsoever, but this gives us some idea of the contempt in which our government is held.

Earlier today, I went back to the hospital for my second injection and saw, literally, dozens of boxes of vaccine all over the place. They were all labelled in English and had come from American sources. The supply seemed sufficient even for the lengthy queues already forming. I was alarmed to see that they were using the same needle repeatedly. When my turn came, I insisted that they use a new one. They may have thought me awkward and demanding, but they complied without fuss. I wonder how many being vaccinated for cholera will get hepatitis instead.

Baba and Abla have re-evaluated their original decisions and have agreed to let me drive them to the clinic for injections tomorrow morning. Ana and Levent want no part of it, and we can't force them. I am planning to meet Hakan in Bursa mid-November. If he hasn't had his vaccination by then, the first thing I will do is drag him off to get one!

Now then, about your decision not to come to the wedding. I have to say that it's not completely unexpected. I am extremely disappointed but not surprised. For different reasons, I had been thinking along the same lines myself. Obviously, we were conveying more to each other than I thought. I have missed you all dreadfully but have begun to realize that your visit here would probably be unsatisfying on many levels. We would want an opportunity to visit and catch up and that, quite plainly, would not be possible. Your very arrival here would unleash hoards of visitors, the like of which this town has rarely seen. I assure you that everyone within a twenty-mile radius would turn up to greet you.

All this commotion, on top of the wedding preparations, sounds like a recipe for total chaos. Everything would be complicated by the fact that you don't speak the language nor understand the customs, so you would feel bewildered and confused. In all honesty, I don't think you would enjoy the occasion, nor would you see the best of all the wonderful things I want to share with you here. It pains me to say all this, but I believe it is better to be realistic now than to have regrets later.

If the above were not enough, I am concerned about the mental health and unpredictable behaviours of both Ana and Levent. Both are struggling these days. I used to think that "growing up" would take care of many of Levent's problems. Now, I am not so sure. It's hard to draw a line between making allowances for his illness and indulging him unnecessarily. The family makes no demands on him, blaming everything on his condition, but I find it hard to excuse him for belittling his father and pushing his mother and sister around. I know he is not so ill as to be unable to discriminate between acceptable and unacceptable behaviours. That he pulls none of his shenanigans with either Hakan or me, leads me to conclude that he does much of what he does simply because he can get away with it. He is sick and he does need help, but I don't believe indulgence is the answer.

Ana is also deteriorating. Lately she has been making irrational demands and accuses us all of plotting against her. At her insistence, Abla and I moved some furniture around in preparation for this month's *gün*. Ana got up in the middle of the night and fell over a recently moved chair, breaking a tooth. Then she blamed us for purposely placing the chair so that she would hurt herself. And at the last minute, she demanded that we entertain her guests in the family salon, rather than in the parlour, as usual. At present, she isn't speaking to any of us. Between Levent and Ana, the house is in constant uproar with little peace for anyone.

So all things considered, I think your travels here are best postponed until a later date. Meanwhile, let's look forward to a reunion as soon as possible after we get back to London. I really want a leisurely visit with you. And I promise to bring you to Turkey at a more opportune time.

Just as I was concluding that all interest in my dubious activities had gone away, I find I am being investigated by the Turkish equivalent of the FBI. I think it has to do with my application for a resident's visa. Although such a document appears to exist in principle, I'm doubtful that any are ever issued as the government assumes it must be Turkish citizenship that is required. If I am marrying a Turk, I must want to become one. Even the Beylers have not realized that, no thank you, I don't want to become a Turkish national. For some reason, the authorities find this suspicious and have decided that I must be up to no good. Or maybe it has to do with Hakan's security clearances, though we thought those had finished. Either way, certain officials have been asking around town about me. I feel like some kind of *femme fatale*, a sort of Turkish nemesis. How divinely glamorous. And how very different from my daily life.

We are deeply worried about Bill. The reports of heavy fighting in his area give every cause for concern. We hope that his unit will be able to pull back to secure territory, if there is such a thing. This is where it all becomes starkly real. It's frustratingly hard for me to come by the sort of detailed information I want. His safety is uppermost in our minds and – more than ever – we are desperate for your news.

On Thursday, I celebrated the first anniversary of my arrival in Turkey. It seemed entirely appropriate that as on my first day, I couldn't speak on the anniversary, either. Of course, a year ago it was due to ignorance; on Thursday, it was due to laryngitis. For reasons unknown, this has happened a few times; and although not otherwise sick, I lose my voice entirely. The Beylers have never seen anything like it, but I have been able to reassure them that apart from being unable to talk, I am fine.

The year has gone by in a flash. Without doubt, it has been the most entertaining, frustrating, absorbing, stimulating, fascinating, bewildering, satisfying, humbling, maddening and broadening year of my life. Another year here - even one with a wedding - cannot top this. I've had my ups and downs, but I would not have missed any of this. The whole experience has greatly strengthened my relationship with Hakan and enhanced my life in ways I could not have predicted.

I cannot wait to see what the coming year brings!

31 October 1970

This is a quick note to let you know that Baba and I leave tomorrow for Istanbul. We'll be gone a few days to buy more materials for the orders we have.

We'll be taking Hakan with us as far as Bursa. He transferred there on Monday and came home Wednesday for five whole days! At the current ratio of two days at the base to five days at home, I may be sorry he didn't transfer there sooner. Hakan is not certain why he was given such generous leave when he had only just arrived. Even he would not have had the temerity to make such a request. It must be partly because of the recent four-day public holiday, partly because there was no work for him and partly because he has been an instant hit with his latest commander.

His new boss was in Kavaklı yesterday. Hakan's old commander here reported to Baba that the new general couldn't stop raving about him. This is an excellent start and bodes well for the immediate future. I have no idea what Hakan will be doing in Bursa. It's all Top Secret. I'm happy to remain ignorant on this point and will ask any questions once it's all over. Hakan is delighted with his new assignment, as well he should be. He came home full of enthusiasm. There are only sixty men on the base, so there is an atmosphere of freedom and informality not possible on the larger bases. I gather he will be doing some travelling in his new job and is already scheduled to go to the border 15 November on military business. That is the same date we had thought to make our own trip to sort out the latest car permit. With this in mind, Hakan has obtained authorization to take care of personal business while he's there. Things have an astonishing way of working out.

Hakan says there are only a few cases of cholera in Bursa, and it appears to have stopped spreading. However, he tells me he will have a shot on Monday. That's what he says. In any event, it seems that the outbreak will not develop into an epidemic. The Turks have done a marvellous job containing the disease, and given how very contagious it is, this comes as a massive relief. I hope we are not speaking too soon. I heard that 350,000 people died of cholera in India last year. Can you imagine?

Lady has had her puppies. I had thought she would have them later but only recently learned that the gestation period for dogs is fifty days. That works out about right. I suspected something was up the other evening when she retired in the afternoon and wouldn't get up for her supper. I checked on her before I went to bed. Still nothing. It was Aslana who gave us all the big news. She came to the front door at 6:00 am where she scratched and banged around until we were all awake. Then she herded everyone outside and around to the back to show us what Lady had done. Lady looked extremely pleased with herself. Given her tendency to the inane, she is turning out to be a better mother than I had expected. She won't leave her pups even to eat, so I have been giving her meals in bed. The puppies are too new to be cute; at present, they resemble hairy worms. Three are jet black and two look like Lady, white with black marks.

Know anyone who wants a puppy?

Chapter 14

8 November 1970

This has been an extremely busy week. We went to Istanbul and back in three days, and since then, it has been work, work and more work to get the goods ready for Germany. Although we had to buy more materials to complete the order, we've sent what we had finished and want to have the rest ready to go when Hakan and I travel to the border. Prior to leaving Istanbul, we called on Baba's aunt and brought her back with us so she could visit her sister here. We also made the rounds of various banks trying to get them to pay up. We have had no problems with Ken, nor any of our customers, sending the payments for their orders. No. The problem has been trying to get the banks to release the funds once they arrive. Their systems are designed to hang on to any foreign currency for as long as possible, and they will use every ruse, trick, lie and deceit to delay paying out.

It is difficult for the banks in Kavaklı to handle these transactions, unfamiliar as they are with international banking. Staff here advised us to go to their head office in Istanbul to secure payment. They confidently assured us of the central bank's ability to pay out on presentation of the cheque in question. Sounds good, right? Well, it may sound good, but the advice, typically, contradicted the reality and turned out to be wrong. Despite having a certified cheque in US Dollars, authorizing immediate payment to the bearer, the bank's head office would not comply. We heard the familiar tale of the need for weeks to process, all delaying tactics and feeble excuses, of course. Their tenacity in holding onto money (MY money!) makes a sucking leech look noncommittal, each encounter ending, as it inevitably did, with the suggestion that we make further enquiries at another office.

At our last stop, I sensed a chink in their armour and decided to probe it without mercy; I would not leave until I had my cash. Whatever happened, whatever it took, I was determined not to go away empty-handed. Baba had come along to humour me and remained quietly at my side, convinced I was going nowhere, fast.

And so once more, I presented the cheque, made my case and then listened wearily to the clerk's story of how they had insufficient dollars; how it had to be cleared through New York; how I would have to wait three weeks. When he had finished, I said I wanted to speak to his manager. A worn little man with moist beige skin and a conspicuous lack of charm appeared and reiterated their procedures. When it was my turn, I eyeballed him and told him, in my best Turkish, that I was an important exporter of fine Turkish merchandise to companies all over Europe, and I would not be deceived by their stories nor deterred from getting money that was rightfully mine. As advised by the local branch of their bank, I had travelled a long way, at considerable expense and inconvenience, to arrive in Istanbul to cash a cheque that would have been paid out immediately anywhere else in the banking world. He would do well to keep me happy as I expected to be conducting a great deal of business and would use all the influence at my disposal to make sure that the proper authorities would hear of any complaints I had regarding his conduct. I am proud to say that my Turkish proved equal to the BS I needed to take command of this particular situation.

Undeterred, the manager redoubled his efforts to explain the facts of banking life to me, telling me that what I wanted was out of the question, utterly impossible and completely unheard of in the entire history of Turkish banking. A cheque issued in foreign currency could not be cashed on demand. Not under any circumstances. Not for anyone. In sheer frustration, my eyes filled with tears, and my voice began to rise. People began to stare. Realizing that an emotional display was having more impact than reasoned argument, I decided not to hold back. After further considering my teary face, my emboldened voice and the resolution in my eyes, I saw inner conflict reflected in the manager's expression. Suddenly, there was a means to do my bidding. While it seemed that Turkish banking could withstand any number of assaults on their illogical procedures, it could not withstand an emotional display. Having shamelessly exploited the hapless man's inability to cope with feminine tears, I left the bank with the money in hand and received Baba's enthusiastic congratulations outside. He couldn't believe it. Quite frankly, neither could I. I was weary but victorious.

Ramadan is here, and I am fasting with the family. It is an interesting experience, one I entered into voluntarily. The Beylers put no pressure on me and did not expect me to join them, but I know they are pleased that I have decided to do so.

To be honest, it was the easy option. It's much harder to eat and drink and smoke when no one else can participate. I probably told you last year that Ramadan lasts for thirty days and is followed by a three-day holiday or *bayram*. The fast lasts from sunup to sundown, which means that it is currently easier than in the summer not only because the days are shorter, but because we do not get so thirsty in cooler weather. Since the Islamic calendar differs from ours by ten days, the fast comes around ten days earlier each year and, over the course of time, rotates across the seasons. Currently, we are getting up at 4:00 am to have a big meal before dawn at about 5:00 am. This is substantial enough to carry us through to the evening meal about twelve hours later. It's rather like having an early breakfast and no lunch. It takes some getting used to but is not unbearably hard, despite all the fuss that is made.

Regardless of custom, it would be impossible to avoid getting up once the drummer arrives to make sure that everyone is awake and on the move. When I say drummer, I am struggling for the words to describe the evil sound that emanates from this instrument called a *davul*. I hate it. I can't bear the sound it makes: dark, menacing and full of foreboding. If the end of the world were being announced, this is the instrument that should accompany it. But I appear to be alone in this opinion; no one else detests it the way I do. I wonder if the day will ever come when an alarm clock replaces this tradition. By comparison, that would be a musical interlude.

When we were in Istanbul, we saw Sami who is much improved for fasting. During Ramadan, no one drinks any alcohol at all, not even after sundown, so if he really is abstaining, he is doing well. It also means that he is not in bed for half the day, nor hung over when he gets up, so he proved to be almost pleasant, almost human on this occasion. But… There is always a sting in the tail with Sami, and the permutations of difficult are endless where he is concerned. We have never told him much about the business Hakan and I conduct here. He's aware that we buy skins and make up items of fashion clothing, but he's never seemed particularly interested in the details. We were wrong in that impression. Apparently, he has made it his business to find out precisely what we are doing and has secured his own orders for our ideas and designs.

To add insult to injury, he also has had the audacity to ask us to help him produce the goods. He thinks that we all owe him some kind of fealty, that we'll all simply do whatever he wants. His assumptions are stupefying. Hakan is not going to believe this. On second thought, maybe he will. I think Baba feels that since he has helped Hakan, he cannot refuse to do the same for Sami. Personally, I don't intend to lift so much as a little finger on Sami's behalf, paid or otherwise. We expect competition in the market place. Our ideas have been ripped off before, so we have learned to be careful, but we didn't expect to have a knife inserted in our backs from within the family!

All this talk of Sami's new business has prompted me to wonder about our fur machines. Last spring there was a lot of speculation that these were about to be returned to us. Allegedly, Sami was guiding the formalities through the central bank on our behalf. There were many assurances then about needing just one more form, just one more signature, and the machines would all be handed back. Although it looked then as if we were on the brink of recovering them, we have heard nothing since. Not a word. It occurred to me to ask Sami about them, and he said that the machines had "disappeared"; that indeed, the necessary paperwork had been successfully completed, but that when he went to collect them, they were not where they were supposed to be. No one knew anything about them. So he said.

Sami maintains that he told us all this at the time, but if he told Baba or Hakan, they have no recollection of the conversation. Given the value of the equipment and the nature of things, I suppose we shouldn't be astonished; but seeing as how Sami has unexpectedly started a similar business, I am more than a little suspicious that he is using our machines to produce his own goods, somewhere out of sight. I certainly wouldn't put it past him. The frustrating and depressing result is that – wherever they are – the machines are unlikely ever to be available to us. In that respect, all our plans have come to nothing.

Lady and the puppies are doing well. At ten days old, the little ones are beginning to open their eyes. They are growing like ivy in summer rain and are as plump as fresh berries. It intrigues me that Lady knows instinctively how to care for them. She gets very nervous if anyone but me tries to approach, snarling fiercely even at Aslana. Although, physically, she's not showing much sign of her pregnancy, Aslana must be due any minute. Maybe it's because she's bigger and carries her pups more discreetly that she looks almost normal. She has been digging an impressive tunnel in the hillside behind the house, so it looks as if she is preparing a place to give birth. Lady had tried to do the same thing, but the effort of the dig was too much for her, so she gave up and had the pups in her bed. And why not? I think Aslana is jealous of all the attention Lady has been receiving. The two have been snappy with each other since the birth. Good around here, isn't it?

Thank you for your offer of financial assistance for the wedding, but we are planning to do it all ourselves. We are not rich; it won't be the wedding of the decade, but we hope a medium-sized celebration will be big enough to include all the people important to the family, without necessitating the hire of a stadium to accommodate the reception. We would never be forgiven for having a small, quiet affair. I doubt the concept even exists here. I like your idea of sending out announcements, rather than invitations, for all those in the USA. It's silly to invite people to an event they have no hope of attending. One thing we had not budgeted for are the photos, and I might let you contribute to those. This is something I haven't investigated, but I will find out more and let you know. I agree that we want lots of photos!

20 November 1970

Sorry this letter is so late. I had hoped to write before I left for Edirne, but there was a last minute change of plan, which meant leaving a day early. Nisa, our neighbour, hitched a lift to her sister in Istanbul, and we were returning Baba's aunt to her home there as well. After stopping in Bursa to pick up Hakan, we were full to capacity. During Ramadan, travellers are exempt from fasting and we all, except for the aunt, had snacks along the way. Fortunately, we arrived in time for her to have the sundown meal, after which we delivered Nisa to her sister, and then we checked into our usual hotel near the bazaar.

Sunday morning, we made our way to Sami's place. He seemed like a different person that day. For a start, he was less moody and bad-tempered than customary. Perhaps this had something to do with Hakan's refusal to argue with him, sidestepping all the obvious provocations and jollying his brother along. Despite the relative serenity of his disposition, there was no mistaking Sami's wretched condition. Unable to concentrate on the conversation, he kept repeating himself and lying so glibly that it appeared to be a compulsion over which he had no control and little, if any, awareness. For the first time ever, I felt genuine compassion for him. He is plainly as sick in his own way as Levent is in his. Probably more so. It is a sad, sorry state of affairs.

After that brief visit, we drove on to Edirne where we completed Hakan's military business and secured the new car permit within a few hours. Then it was back to Istanbul where our top priority was getting some items for the wedding, chiefly, the wine-coloured material for Hakan's jacket. Luckily, we found exactly what we wanted without any trouble, and he'll have it made up in Kavaklı. I wanted to shop for new civilian clothes as well, but Hakan said we should wait until he is discharged. His weight is still fluctuating, and he's not certain where it will settle. Although he put on twenty-two pounds in the early months, he lost half of that during his recent training.

Peculiar things are going on with Aslana these days. Because she had come into heat together with Lady, I assumed that she too, was expecting. However, instead of growing larger or giving birth, she is actually getting thinner and behaving in strange ways. I think she has had a phantom pregnancy. Clearly, there is some sort of hormone crisis going on, the cause of which I have yet to determine. She has continued to dig the hillside tunnels where she sometimes beds down, and she's not eating well, which is odd. Despite her lack of appetite, she is possessive about her food and growls at Lady if she comes anywhere near her dish. At the same time, she has become extremely motherly, largely taking over Lady's pups. This entirely suits our flighty little madam as she'd much prefer to swan around than attend to maternal duties.

Lady has never learned to pick up her pups properly (I stand corrected; everything is not instinctive), and most of this sort of care has now been assumed by Aslana. She has taken to sleeping with the pups, while Lady lounges resplendent in Aslana's bed. If the pups fall out, Aslana puts them back in place, licking them and loving them to bits. It's mad, isn't it? The puppies, by the way, are now nearly four weeks old and too cute for words. They've begun to play and yip and are completely endearing. Many have said they would like to give one a home, but we'll see who actually comes forward in a couple of weeks.

I hope by now that you have had some news from Bill. Since you said he was moving around and would have a new address, I have not written lately. Obviously, you'll let me know what you hear.

This week I have saved my best news for last. The other night I dreamed in Turkish for the first time. I was so excited! It was the first thing I remembered when I woke up in the morning. I can even recall the dream, as nonsensical as most, but vivid to me for its linguistic significance. Not only am I absorbing the language, but I seem to be taking in some of the gestures as well. When the Turks mean "yes", they nod upwards, just like we do. "No" is also an upwards nod but with raised eyebrows, sometimes accompanied by a little "tsk" sound. For an outsider this can be very confusing, but it's amazing how quickly I have become accustomed to these and have taken to using them as shorthand for spoken words. (But whatever you do, don't use the American sign for "okay" with the thumb and index finger making a circle... very rude here.) I feel I have truly arrived!

Happy Thanksgiving to you all! It's coming up soon, and I imagine Peter will be home for a break.

Chapter 15

3 December 1970

Fantastic news about Bill! How very much in the current family tradition to find himself a plum job in such dire circumstances. His assignment to Division Headquarters as a driver for the big brass must be the cake job with frosting! The best news is that he will be in the field only when he takes officers to the firebases. Since they are hardly likely to go out of their way to endanger themselves, I guess Bill will be as safe as anyone can be. We are selfishly thankful for this tremendous break. I think Mother is right: this family is full of operators.

Most of my news this week has to do with Ramadan Bayram. Hakan arrived home for ten days' leave, so there was much for us personally to celebrate. Although I was here for the festivities last year, I wasn't really part of things in the way that I feel I am now. On the morning of 1 December, the men were all up early to go to the mosque for the ritual prayers that mark the end of the fast and the beginning of the holiday. When they returned, we had our first family breakfast for a month. After that, it was into our new clothes, ready for the round of visitors and visiting.

Hakan had his own agenda and took me to call on a former teacher, Temel Bey, who is the art instructor at the local college (the equivalent of our high school). His wife is the gym teacher, but her particular interest is folklore and folk dancing. Their teenage daughter entertained us with some of the routines she is preparing for the national holiday in May, and later, both mother and daughter performed some of the popular folk dances. As well as an artist, Temel Bey is also a talented musician and played a selection of classical Turkish pieces on the traditional instrument called a *saz*, which resembles an outsized mandolin. With special performances just for us, I felt myself an honoured guest and sank back into the comfortable informality of this open and friendly family. They struck me as people who are entirely at ease with themselves.

As we left the house, Hakan told me that they are Communists. If he had said they were Druids, I could not have been more astonished. Nothing in my background had prepared me to think that Communists are anything other than three-toed demons whose main purpose in life is to plot the violent overthrow of governments, mainly mine. Rationally, I know that is not true, but I'd never before met anyone who claimed to be a Communist. If anything, the Turks have a stronger anti-communist bias than Americans do. Because of their declared politics, and because Communism is illegal here, both husband and wife have served time in prison and have only tentative grips on their jobs. While readily acknowledging their warmth and charm, I now had to acknowledge their courage and integrity. It is never easy to row against the current, and their personal convictions come at a cost most of us would be unwilling to pay. At this point, it occurred to me that Communists, like the rest of us, just want to go to work, pay their bills, educate their children and get on with life in general. All of this has given me much food for thought.

In the afternoon, a contingent of Hakan's friends from the Kavaklı base came to the house. The men had a wonderful time, swapping stories and exchanging news. They could hardly drink their tea for all the laughing and joking, and it was great to see. In the evening, Ana and Levent waited at home to receive any visitors, while the rest of us went to pay some duty calls. Our first stop was at the home of Hakan's former base commander, a good friend of Baba's. Several visits later, we found ourselves next door to Teyze's house. With Baba's agreement, the three of slipped over to say a quick hello to Teyze and the family. Unfortunately, they were not in, but Nina was there, having been locked in the house. She couldn't let us in, so we chatted through the window. She looked delighted to see us and promised to tell Teyze we had come. On these occasions, it is important that the young call on their elders to pay their respects by kissing their hands. For the children, there is the promise of *bayram* money and sweets to make the ceaseless rounds more appealing.

Alas, we did not have the unmitigated pleasure of Sami's company this *bayram*. For reasons too convoluted to understand, he wanted all of us to visit him in Istanbul. Since he has no place to put us up, it would have meant staying in a hotel, which is too ridiculous for words. When the family insisted that he must come home, he refused, saying that he was offended because we had turned down his invitation. During the first half of *bayram*, everyone argued about who might be dispatched to spend the holiday with him. When no one volunteered to go, Ana spent the second half in tears because Sami was all alone. I gather he's sulking in Istanbul. So, what's new?

We've lost one of Lady's puppies. When I went out for my morning inspection yesterday, I found the smallest, weakest one had died. I think he must have had some deformity as he did have a strange look about him. Perhaps Aslana smothered him in a fit of maternal enthusiasm, or maybe there was an accident, I'm not sure. Lady may be silly, but she can count. She kept looking for the fifth one, and I had to show her its lifeless body so she would realize what had happened. It had been getting to the point where Lady could not get into bed to nurse the puppies because Aslana had taken over. In the end, we moved Lady's bed to the shed and constructed a doorway big enough only for her. The pups can be weaned in another week and not a moment too soon. Lady, only a small thing herself, is becoming a bag of bones due to the increasing demands of her litter. I feed her constantly but the strain is taking its toll. The little ones are so sweet and appealing that I am confident I will have no trouble finding homes for the males; the females will be harder.

Further welcome news is that Aslana is returning to normal. Now that she no longer has direct access to Lady's brood, she is behaving more like her old self. I tell you, being a "grandmother" is not easy!

8 December 1970

Now that *bayram* is over and Hakan has returned to Bursa, the house feels as empty as an abandoned playground... and as quiet.

While he was here, Hakan made a point of visiting Levent's school and meeting the staff, all of whom were full of praise for their new student. Some very clever teachers have been extraordinarily sensitive to the potential pitfalls for Levent as by far the oldest member of his class. With this in mind, they have made him their "special assistant". This has given him a position of status and respect, and his classmates look up to him. Apparently, he is popular and well-liked, all of which has bolstered his self-esteem. Levent says he has never been happier in school, and the teachers report that they are pleased both with his behaviour and with his grades. This is terrific news and much better than we had dared hope. Levent is a different person these days. He is still capable of throwing immense wobblies, but I think a lot of that is typical teenage stuff. We all put on our best faces in public, then come home and blow off steam within the security of the family. No. I think Levent has turned a corner. Let's hope so.

The gloomy news is the mysterious disease which has attacked Levent's chickens. We have had to slaughter the lot so some would still be edible. Any kind of poultry is expensive eating in Turkey, so in one sense, we have been living it up with a steady stream of chicken on the menu. Still, after the ninth or tenth one, the diet loses its novelty value, and the thought of eating another three or four no longer holds any appeal. Although Levent obviously felt bad about losing his birds, I think there was also an element of relief. Their continuing care was becoming burdensome, especially now that life holds other things for him.

Is it possible that a small puppy can be a chicken substitute? Levent has declared himself the new owner of one of the males from Lady's litter, the sweet black pup called Kömür, coal. The others are still seeking homes. Hakan said if we can't find anyone else, he'll take one to the base. I think he should have at least two, so they will have each other for company.

I am trying to get into an appropriate mood for Christmas. It's an uphill struggle when no one around me has any real knowledge or interest. If asked, I have learned to reply that Christmas is a kind of *bayram* during which we decorate trees and exchange presents. This seems to satisfy. If I attempt any kind of religious explanation, eyes glaze over. Part of this can be explained by the steady stream of anti-Christian propaganda delivered in the Friday sermons at local mosques. Here I believe it is the fashion to extol the virtues of our common human bond in one breath, then to harangue against Jews and Christians in general, and Americans in particular, in the next.

Regrettably, there are few educational requirements for becoming an *imam*, and the lack often shows itself in the dissemination of ignorance, by no means the exclusive preserve of Muslims. I think I can safely say that the dissemination of equally alarming misinformation goes on in Christianity, something I have witnessed in my own religious past. When the leaders - of any religion - speak authoritatively, their words can betray the origins and intentions of the faith itself. Those who follow blindly may be unable to make distinctions. The result is that all too often, people assign ill-founded significance to these words and use them as a basis for belief and action. It is not faith and religion that are to blame, but the manipulation, ignorance, fear, and superstition that surround them. This is the main reason Hakan no longer has any interest in attending prayers at the mosque. I think you are aware that it is much the same for me with the church.

I did not mean to go off on a tangent. I had more to unload than I realized.

15 December 1970

It's like Ramadan Bayram all over again with all the goodies that have arrived this week. Thank you for the dollars which will go into the fund for wedding photos. Thank you too, for the family snapshots, especially the one of Mother and Aunt Sally wearing their new slacks. I'm glad both sisters are keeping up with the times, though I am not certain to what extent this may scandalize the Turks. One of Mother's previous photos caused Ana to comment, "She's not wearing a miniskirt!" If you could see what appears in the Turkish newspapers, you would understand why she might think that every woman in the western world, regardless of age, shape or size, wears short skirts. As it is, I almost never wear slacks. It's simply not acceptable here in our provincial town, not even for the young.

Before I forget, I must tell you that along with the other items, a package of chocolate chips has arrived. However, I was not prepared to pay the extortionate 25TL duty that the postman was required to collect. I instructed him that the bag should be returned to the sender, but I doubt it will ever be seen again. It's impossible to predict on what things the officials will declare duty payable, and what they will regard as inconsequential. It's not necessarily consistent, either. Rolled newspapers are still the most likely way of escaping unwanted attention, as is almost anything sent by airmail.

To answer your questions: although there are relatively few men where Hakan is based, they are located next door to a commando training centre, which is much bigger and has facilities he can use. I have no idea what Hakan does. Apart from the fact that I know he travels, he doesn't discuss his military duties with me, and I don't ask. We both believe this is best. I am aware that he is busy, unlike Bill who is now complaining of boredom. In his situation, this strikes me as far better than the alternative.

Recently, I've been extremely social without much to show for it. Ruth stopped by one afternoon last week. As she wanted a second opinion on some curtains and items for the new house, we organized a shopping expedition for the following day, as well as a further day out merely to gossip and trade news. When I wasn't with Ruth, I seemed to be with Abla and Fatma. Ana and Baba had gone to Istanbul for a couple of days mid-week, and Fatma's family were in Izmir, so we took full advantage of their absences. Not that we got up to anything too, too scandalous, just some girl fun.

With no one to answer to, we bounced between Fatma's house and ours, eating, drinking (tea and sodas) and smoking our way to sloth, obesity and lung disease. We even - gasp! - dared to spend one night at Fatma's, a rare treat for Abla who, as you are aware, has rarely spent a night away from home. Fatma is going to Canada in the summer to visit her sister who lives there. Although her English is good, like most people here, she lacks practice and is always eager for me to help her with slang and colloquialisms.

Two of the puppies have gone. Our postman stepped up and asked for a male pup. I said he could have one, provided he took one of the females as well. I didn't give him much chance to refuse, so both pups were quickly packed up and went off in his big bag. Now we need one more home for the remaining female. I had not named any of them as I felt it would be easier to say good-bye if we hadn't put our labels on them. If you see what I mean.

Abla has not yet started to make my wedding dress. She says we must leave it until the week before so that it will fit perfectly. I don't think my weight fluctuates much, but I can see her point. We only have one shot at this. Hakan is convinced that he will be out of the army in July, so we are thinking about setting a date in early August. Most weddings happen here at very short notice, but even so, we probably need to reserve a venue for the reception, if we want our first choice.

22 December 1970

By the time you receive this, Christmas will have come and gone, so we hope that you have already received our cards and packages. We've heard reports that there has been a lot of snow and wintry weather in the USA but have no idea to what extent you might be affected. There is currently some snow on the mountains around us, though we have had no flurries in Kavaklı yet. Hakan says they have been inundated in Bursa, good news for the skiers.

PTB sent a message to say that he will be coming home on the 24th. I hope so. It has been three weeks since I last saw him. Considering all that we have been through and the circumstances in which we find ourselves, it is incredible that we have never been separated for longer. We understand this and are thankful... but I'd still like to see him Thursday. We knew in advance that he would have several days off over Christmas and had thought of having a break at Uludağ, but I think Hakan has had enough of Bursa, so he hinted at a revised plan. Wherever we go and whatever we do, it will be fantastic to get away on our own for a few days. I'm not fussy about the destination and can be packed in an instant!

Now that the pups are weaned, I find myself rushing out to feed them three times a day. I have taken over from Lady in maternal duties. I am only marginally better at it, with no prospect of losing a similar amount of weight. Damn! The two that are left are adorable. They are perky and full of fun, playing and barking and bounding around one minute, then without warning, collapsing exhausted in a heap. I have decided that I really must do all I can to prevent Lady from becoming pregnant again. It has taken everything out of her. She is thin, run down and suffering with a bad cold. As well as the puppies, I am feeding her throughout the day in an effort to help her regain her strength. Aslana is fully recovered from whatever it was that ailed her. She chooses to eat only bones but seems to thrive on them. Her coat is sleek and shiny and her weight is back to normal. The cold weather suits her as she is constantly on the move, checking that everything is under control in the neighbourhood. Already I have begun to realize how hard it will be to leave the dogs behind when we go. They have been my faithful companions, and I shall feel like a rat for running out on them.

The week's major news concerns Cemile whose brother was involved in what is euphemistically described as an "honour killing". These are common in eastern Turkey where Cemile and her husband (who are cousins) come from. The whole affair is said to have started when her brother failed to pay off a gambling debt to the satisfaction of a "friend" who shot him seven times. (I am simply repeating the story I have been told.) When her brother miraculously recovered from his wounds, other so-called friends placed a gun in his hands, imploring him to avenge his honour. Having killed his attacker, he is now in jail for murder, the code of honour having been fulfilled.

I have never heard of anything like this happening here in western Turkey. I understand that the tradition of honour killing features predominantly in tribal groups such as the Kurds. It is part of their culture and a custom which most Turks find as reprehensible and abhorrent as we do. Many of these executions involve women who are held accountable for the family honour and killed without a second thought if they fail in their obedience to that code. According to this, a woman's murder can be justified, indeed is required, if she disobeys her father, dresses inappropriately, rejects an arranged marriage, runs off with her lover or, incredibly, even if she is raped. It becomes the duty of the men in the family to kill her for the sake of their supposed honour. I cannot begin to comprehend the twisted logic that makes women responsible for the mistakes of men. However, I can see why ignorant, uneducated men have a stake in maintaining this perversion. The need for schools in the eastern Turkey is a desperate one.

We're not quite at the end of the year but will probably be so when you receive this letter. Have a Happy New Year! Let us hope that 1971 brings good things for us all, including a wedding in Turkey and a family reunion in London.

30 December 1970

Thank you for all the many gifts that found their way to Kavaklı for Christmas. I was going to put the money aside for wedding expenses, but instead, we put it towards our trip this past week. As expected, Hakan arrived home here on the 24th. I would have been extremely disappointed if he had not as I was more than a little keyed up to see him.

We had nothing in particular planned for Christmas Day, but Ruth appeared on our doorstep late in the morning. Despite her adherence to most of the religious customs of this country, Ruth is foremost a staunch Roman Catholic, and the holiday means a great deal to her. She had had her hair done, and she was dressed up for the day. Her mother-in-law does not permit any acknowledgement of the occasion in their house - no gifts for the children nor any Santa stories - so she turned up here hoping for some shared culture. I was glad she did. Hakan finally met the friend about whom he has heard so much, and of course, Ruth met my fiancé after all this time. She stayed for lunch and the afternoon. Ana could not have been sweeter, continually bringing us tea and refreshments. She wanted to make the day a nice one for us, something Ruth and I especially appreciated, given the attitude of her own mother-in-law.

Saturday morning, Hakan and I were up early for our drive south. We had toyed with the idea of going to Istanbul, but as we've been there so often, we opted for somewhere new. It's a long drive to Izmir, but from there, we continued on until we found a hotel at Kuşadası, about ten miles from the ruins of the ancient city of Ephesus. Many places were closed for the winter months, so we felt lucky to find this particular hotel, located right on the Aegean and only recently opened. Kuşadası is an old town (aren't they all?) with a picturesque yacht harbour and an impressively restored caravansaray at its heart. The area is quiet now, but we could tell from the facilities that in season, the town bustles with a wealthy international clientele.

There is so much of interest packed into this historic region. Ephesus was one of the most important Roman cities and a hub of pagan worship, as well as a significant seaport and commercial centre. One of the Seven Wonders of the World, the Temple of Artemis (Diana), was the main attraction during the period of religious tourism that flourished in its heyday. Excavations so far have revealed three streets, two theatres, a palace, several temples, a gymnasium, baths, marketplace, town hall, a brothel and the magnificent library.

Hakan has been particularly interested in investigating the area as the woman largely responsible for initiating the recent digs is Iris Love, a wealthy American woman who has been using much of her own money to lead an international team of archaeologists. Having met her in Istanbul in 1965, Hakan subsequently became her personal guide whenever she visited. As the dig began in earnest, he was needed to change money, establish contacts, organize equipment and help deal with the many matters arising from the work of the expedition. The results are breathtaking, the restoration of The Celsius Library among the most striking in the world. However, Ephesus is not just about impressive buildings. Here it is possible to get a feel for the life of the ancients. We could walk their streets, peer into their houses, visit their baths and visualize their market place. Because the ruins are a rarity in respect of their size, it was a stunning experience on a grand scale. Much has already been achieved, but much, much more remains to be done.

Sadly, The Temple of Artemis will have no such restoration. The building was the largest in the ancient world and without parallel in its splendour. In the nineteenth century, what remained of the site was looted and dragged off to The British Museum where the vestiges of this world marvel are currently on display. Today, the setting of that unique monument to Diana is a swampy bog referred to, appropriately enough, as "the Englishman's pit".

The next day we drove to Denizli looking for Hakan's friend, Metin, who finished his law studies in Istanbul and has returned to home territory to start his own practice. When we didn't find him at his office, we went to his parents' home, only to learn that he had just left for the office. His mother invited us to wait, but we declined, saying that we wanted to visit Pamukkale and would return later in the day. She assured us that Metin would be there for dinner and insisted that we join them for the evening meal and spend the night. We accepted with pleasure.

With the best part of the day still ahead of us, we easily drove the distance to one of the most extraordinary and dramatic natural wonders in Turkey - or anywhere. Although there are Roman ruins here, the real attraction is the terraced hillside formed over centuries by calcium-rich deposits from hot springs flowing across the landscape. From a distance, this brilliant white phenomenon makes it seem as if there has been an unexpected and isolated snowfall. Closer up, the bleached-out terraces with their scallop-shaped basins and frozen waterfalls appear to be made of cotton, or maybe ice. Where hot water flows into the fairytale pools, wisps of steam rise up and melt into the air. Although there are thermal baths in the area, we had not come prepared for a swim and contented ourselves with paddling in the shallow ponds, enjoying the surreal landscape.

As we headed back to the car, a little boy rushed up to Hakan saying, *"Antika, antika."* At first, we didn't let on that we spoke Turkish, allowing him to lead us off the path to a secluded spot where he surreptitiously produced a few little relics from his pocket. Hakan looked them over and said he wasn't interested, but the boy persisted and said he would take us to his house where there were better objects to see. I was suspicious, but Hakan's curiosity was aroused, so we told the boy to hop into the back seat from where he directed us the short distance to his home in a nearby village.

A sun-toughened man, short and squat, with a wall of a chest and a face dominated by a generous moustache, came out to greet us and invited us in to see his antiques. This was a typical village home where we took off our shoes at the door and made ourselves comfortable on floor cushions. Amidst all the initial palaver required in the circumstances, the villager, dressed in baggy *şalvar* trousers with a traditional wide cummerbund around his waist, withdrew a pistol from the many folds of cloth and laid it on the low table in front of him. My attention galvanized, I was now firmly fixed on the business at hand.

The father instructed his son to bring the "special box", apparently secreted away in another room. The boy returned with a gnarled wooden container, an object of interest in itself. Watching us closely, the man began to remove the contents, carefully unwrapping his precious trinkets, one-by-one. He claimed to have found an old Roman burial ground, which he was excavating in secret, these relics being a portion of his find so far. We were intrigued. The items looked ancient and seemed to fit the period of the ruins in the area, insofar as we were able to judge this.

Throughout the meeting, I remained as quiet as a stone, a mere observer of the aggressively masculine negotiations taking place in front of me. As always, Hakan stayed cool and gave nothing away. He scrutinized each object in turn, displaying no obvious preference for one over another. Having completed his examination, all were returned to their places on the table, and the haggling began. When no conclusion was reached, we drank coffee and spoke of other things before the negotiations resumed. Intermittently, the man picked up his gun and toyed with it. I think he meant to look dangerous, but there was little in his demeanour to indicate either imminent threat or loss of control. However, not wishing to take anything for granted, I kept my eyes riveted on both our host and his pistol.

At the end of the proceedings, we had acquired a little oil lamp, two goddess figures and a Roman tear cup, the oddly shaped little cup used to collect the tears of mourners during a funeral procession. We bought the lot for 25TL, under $2. Hardly a king's ransom. By now, we both understood that the items were fakes, a matter of some relief, as we knew only too well that dealing in antiquities is strictly illegal. Apart from that, I would have felt guilty acquiring something that rightfully belonged in a museum. As it was, we had had an entertaining afternoon and bought some clever little souvenirs for less money than the gaudy trinkets sold to tourists. Bargain, indeed!

That night we had a delicious meal with Metin and his parents at their home back in Denizli. As the evening wore on, Metin made it clear that he wanted to get away from the house, so he invited the two of us out to the local *pastane* for tea and cakes, which we did not need, having just stuffed ourselves to the point of explosion at his mother's table. But it was good for the friends to have a chance to talk together more privately. Well, more privately than if his parents had been there.

When I had last seen Metin in Istanbul about a year ago, I knew something like twenty words of Turkish. On this occasion, he was gratifyingly astonished by what I had learned in the intervening months. Undoubtedly, this meant that he could not speak as candidly as he otherwise might have done in his conversation with Hakan, but I settled back with my *çay* and gave them a chance to chat without interruption. The next morning, we said our farewells, but not before we were laden down with vast quantities of the oranges and bananas now in season and locally grown. Cotton is another big crop in this region, and Metin's mother insisted on giving me a length of fabric suitable for a summer dress. Such generosity never ceases to astound and humble me.

On the return circuit, we drove straight through Aydın, past Izmir and on up to Bergama (ancient Pergamum), the site of yet more ruins. (In Turkey, there are so many sites of so many ruins from so many different civilizations, there is no end to the amount of money and effort that could be allocated to their excavation.) Little remains of the once splendid city whose architects drew inspiration from Athens and The Parthenon. The locals discovered parchment and used it to create a library of over 200,000 scrolls, second only to the great library at Alexandria. Regrettably, Anthony gave it to Cleopatra in a fit of sycophancy, or was it lust? Though there is nothing here today to reflect the glory of a previous era, the ruins on the plain below are another matter altogether. It was here that the people of Pergamum developed an impressive medical centre, a community unto itself, portions of it still intact or restored.

From Bergama, we drove to Ayvalık on the Aegean coast where we found a little *pansiyon* (comparable to B&B accommodation in England) and had fresh sea bass for dinner. Throughout our journey, the weather had been unbeatable: low 20s Centigrade (low 70s Fahrenheit) and sunny. Not only had we managed to avoid the overbearing heat of summer, but we had avoided the crowds as well. It was the perfect season to have made this trip. We were up early the next day to complete the drive home, feeling refreshed and invigorated after our break.

There was one little cloud over the holiday. We arrived home only to discover that the remaining female pup had died in our absence. The weather here has been cold and rainy, and I'm guessing she caught pneumonia and died before anyone realized there was something seriously wrong. It happened quite quickly. The surviving male,

Kömür, is a sweetie. He's a fussbudget like his mother - won't eat anything unless he is hand fed - preferring milk and bread to anything else. We are going to have to persuade him over to something more substantial as, at two months old, his days of pampering are ending. I say that, but absolutely melt when he looks at me with eyes like little black olives. Who could say "no" to him?

We have nothing festive planned for tomorrow evening. There are several possibilities for celebrations, but I think we'll wait to see how we feel. I'm getting used to making last minute decisions.

Happy New Year!

Part Three

Into a New Year
January - July 1971

Chapter 16

4 January 1971

The weather here is like spring. It's as warm in Kavaklı now as it was during our trip south, sweater weather and positively exhilarating. It won't last, so we are determined to enjoy it while it's here.

Hakan returned to Bursa last night. We had him home for ten whole days, which should hold me until he gets back again in early February. After that, it will be Kurban Bayram, and then we have to go to the border again. It could turn out to be an excellent month for us.

We dithered and debated over what to do on New Year's Eve. There were lots of celebrations at the clubs and restaurants in town, but none of them appealed. Levent went to Istanbul to spend the holiday with his brother, and the rest of the family had special cinema tickets.

With the house unusually empty, it was too tempting not to stay home and have a romantic dinner for two. So, that's what we did. We made a trip to the shops to stock up on our favourite things. While I fixed a plate of *meze* and a fancy fruit salad, Hakan cooked steaks in the bathroom. Yep - that's what I said. That bit was not particularly romantic, resulting as it did in the most unexpected smell of charcoaled meat lingering in our towels and laundry. But my beloved had a longing for grilled meat, so we took coals out of the stove, put them in a pan, placed a grill over the top and let him cook away to his heart's content. We had some very good Turkish wine and to finish, *baklava* and *kaymak*, cream made from the milk of the water buffalo, so thick we could cut it with a knife. We turned on the radio and listened to music from the clubs in Istanbul as they played in the New Year. Hakan was disappointed only in the fact that the lottery ticket he had purchased earlier in the day did not result in a win.

Temel Bey, the art teacher, and his family came to visit the other evening. They are such interesting people, knowledgeable on a wide variety of topics and well-informed about current events, both domestic and foreign. They had fun teaching me some Turkish idioms and slang, followed by a lengthy discussion about the sites we had seen during our trip south. This time, we also met their son, Kamer, a student at the prestigious Middle East University in Ankara. All the classes are conducted in English, so anyone attending quickly becomes fluent in the language. At present, there is much student unrest on all the university campuses, particularly those in Istanbul and Ankara. Last week, seventeen students were killed in demonstrations. It is unclear how many of the deaths were due to violent clashes between left-wing and right-wing groups, and how many were down to the police allegedly trying to keep order. I say "allegedly" because it is believed that a conservative government supports the protestors on the political right at the expense of the socialist students on whose side all the casualties happen.

When we spoke about the current campus turmoil, Kamer struck me as cool in his attitude to the recent student deaths. He is a Socialist - or rather, as he clarified for me, a Maoist - and said that the price is one they are willing to pay in the fight for their cause. He appears to be heavily involved in all the demonstrations, including the anti-American ones (truth be told, probably mostly the anti-American ones), and is proud of his radical stance. In addition to protesting, Kamer goes out to the villages to promote the Maoist cause. He said that his political activities are more important to him than his studies, and he hinted that something bigger than mere protests is being planned. He is as tenacious and committed as a hound dog in pursuit of its quarry, and the detached way in which he spoke gave me the chills.

While I have sympathy for some of the socialist causes Kamer supports, I cannot see how Communism, let alone Maoism, provides a model that anyone would want to imitate. I tried to point out that the majority of people in the USA have far better lives, in whatever way we wish to measure them, than people in Russia or China and questioned why he would want to drag Turkey backwards. The problem is that Kamer wants to compare the reality of life in the West with the ideal of Communism, and that's like trying to compare apples with orange blossoms. Socialism is a model that looks fine on paper but takes no account of the way the world actually works. Nevertheless, I sometimes think we do more harm than good by outlawing organizations, giving them the glamour of the forbidden. If nothing else, opposition shows us that all governments would do well to pay more attention to the causes of political unrest. The Socialists are deadly serious. The rest of us should be, too.

While Hakan was home, we attended several weddings. Normally, he would do almost anything to get out of these, but as our own hovers on the horizon, he has become more interested in seeing what other people do. The one we went to last night had both civil ceremony and reception under the same roof. I had not realized that the ceremony could be conducted anywhere but the official state venue, a barn of a space that has about as much atmosphere as an army barracks.

Although we are only gathering ideas at this stage, we haven't been able to inspire the rest of the family. Because most weddings here are planned at relatively short notice, the concept of looking ahead six months seems incomprehensible and unnecessary. Still, I come laden with my own cultural baggage, and I want to start outlining things. However, I have made one very firm decision: I am not going to get upset over any of this. I refuse to be a nervous wreck on my wedding day, and that begins now. In order to achieve this, I am simply going to have to accept that culturally speaking, it is the custom here for the groom's family to organize these events. The Beylers have the experience of the traditions, so I am going to sit back (as much as I can) and let them take charge. After all, this occasion will be as much for them as anyone. I genuinely want no upsets, least of all for me.

I'll put away my soap box and leave now...

11 January 1971

Hakan wants me to say a Big Thank You for all for the birthday cards you sent. Since we knew he would be back in Bursa on the day itself, we celebrated on the Saturday before he left. I bought him an old silver cigarette case that I had seen in a local shop. It won't be of much practical use, but it is vintage Ottoman and something of a collector's item. The day before his birthday was the first anniversary of his entry into the army. It really does feel as if we can see the finish line, and it's exciting. Anticipation probably accounts for the feeling that as the time gets shorter, the days pass more slowly.

Since Hakan has assured us that he will be out of the army sometime in July, we have mentally picked 5 August, a Thursday, for the big event. The most popular day is a Saturday, but since weddings are always held in the evening, I don't think the day really matters.

Everything is up in the air. I think I have mentioned before that whole populations expect to be invited to weddings here. People of only slight acquaintance can be offended if not included, so the venues are usually enormous and packed to the rafters. Hakan and I had a rough tally of about three hundred in mind. When the Beylers sat down to do their calculations, they came up with a list of six hundred! And these were off the top of their heads. I'm confident more will be added as we go along. Yikes!

This news has resulted in something of a stalemate. Hakan and I simply don't feel we can afford to pay for guests in such numbers, nor do we intend to go into debt trying to do so. The Beylers are insistent that everyone on the list must be included or there will be loss of face and huge offence taken. So there we are. The situation is as tricky as the hierarchy in a harem. It goes almost without saying that I will never have met most of these people, while Hakan maintains that he can't remember the ones he's supposed to know. Personally, I'm beginning to feel less like a bride and more like an exhibition in a sideshow.

I had a real heartbreaker this week. Our last puppy, Kömür, died. As with the other one, it was all very quick and completely unexpected. Monday evening, Levent and I played in the garden with him, and he was fine. When I went out Tuesday morning, he was obviously very sick. He wanted to get out of bed but just couldn't manage it. When I picked him up, he howled as if his whole body hurt. I quickly made a little portable bed and took him to the vet who was mystified. Our weather has been warm and dry, so it wasn't pneumonia, but it wasn't anything else identifiable, either. The vet gave him an injection and prescribed pills and vitamins. Then I brought him back to the house where we kept him warm and pampered him all day.

That evening, Kömür seemed somewhat better, even getting up for a little stroll; but when I checked on him early the next morning, I found his lifeless little body. It was very upsetting. I gather from the Beylers that this was more or less the same sequence of events that surrounded the death of the female pup.

Taking everything into account, I have to say that I think Cemile poisoned them both, and I don't think they are the only ones. She hates animals of all kinds and has complained constantly about ours. More than once, I saw her kick the puppies, and she laughed like she was demented when Ana told her that Kömür had died. It makes me sick. In addition to being extremely sad over losing our dear little pup, I am seething with rage and frustration.

Of course, I cannot accuse her; I have absolutely no proof, but I am as positive as I can be that she is the culprit. When we look back over the past year and count the number of our animals that have died "mysteriously", we cannot come up with any other plausible explanation. All the neighbourhood chickens scratch around together, but it has only ever been ours that died. Kaplan, our favourite cat, vanished during the summer and another cat is missing, too. Either we are the most unfortunate and irresponsible owners of animals in town, or there is another explanation. This realization has made me genuinely fearful for our remaining two dogs and two cats. I cannot keep them locked up in the house, but Cemile is plainly not to be trusted. I am going to find some way to let her know that I KNOW what she has been doing.

Meanwhile on the plus side, Lady is much better these days and has regained her vigorous good health and girlish figure. Our cats adore her. I believe they think she is one of them as she is more their size and gentler than the other dogs. They have all taken to sleeping together, and the cats will always seek her out. It's crazy here.

I have decided that since we don't have a camera, I should gather together all the memorabilia I have accumulated during my stay and make an album. Actually, I'm making two albums: one will be a wedding present for Hakan with photos and items that are personal to us; the other will be more of a memory book about Turkey, trying to give a feel for the customs and culture using postcards, magazine cuttings, leaflets and whatever else I can find. I love working on the project and putting everything together.

The last time Ken sent goods, he included a coney jacket and bedspread. Since these are hot items in London, it is hard to get ahead of the demand and make extra; but he managed to send us one of each, intending them as samples, I suppose. Anything fur is regarded here as a luxury. Because they have so little of it, the Turks don't make much distinction between mink and coney; it's all fur to them, all highly desirable. We could sell everything we could get our hands on, but since our fur machines have "disappeared", we have no means of sewing pelts. Ken is too busy with his own orders in London to supply us, so we're not sure why he sent samples; maybe he just wanted us to see what he's producing. (You can see why we feel we have been knocked badly by the loss of the fur machines.) In any case, we decided to give the bedspread to Hakan's former base commander here in Kavaklı. It seemed little enough as a show of appreciation for all that he did for Hakan when he was stationed here.

The jacket was another matter altogether. Knowing Abla would have the contacts to sell luxury clothing, Hakan told her that he wanted 500TL, but any price she achieved beyond that was hers to keep. Abla is more of a businesswoman than you might imagine. Although I have never believed that she charges enough for her sewing, she has understood, better than I, what the market will bear. She certainly has a feel for what the market thinks of fur, even in our small town. She sold the jacket for 750TL, and her appetite has been whetted.

Inspired by the newspaper clipping you sent, Baba has been experimenting with suede handbag styles. Abla has sold all of these, with a nice commission for herself. Now that she has discovered this profitable little trade, she is badgering us to make all we can. I can see that it wouldn't take much for the family to re-establish itself in a successful business. It's the same everywhere; it's a case of being slightly ahead of the mainstream so that when the trend catches on, the organization is there to seize the opportunity.

When not out earning her title as Saleswoman of the Year, Abla has been doing a lot of sewing for us. Among other things, she has made two sets of hand-embroidered sheets and pillowcases. They are beautiful. While I feel embarrassed that she does so much, she keeps pestering to do more as this is the sort of work she most enjoys. With this in mind, Abla has announced that she wants to make my *trousseau*. We already have several lengths of suitable material, including some rather lush lavender silk, which will make a fine dressing gown. Abla is very good about consulting me and will always do what I want, but where possible, I like to let her decide. She has excellent ideas and is capable of carrying them out. Hakan is pleased to hear that Mother has taken up sewing again. He figures he has it made on my clothing expenses with Abla to sew for me in Turkey, Mother, in the USA and Baba to make my shoes. This is too easy!

Here's something I just found out: Sami used to be the head of MIT, the Turkish intelligence agency (something like the FBI) for the province. Every province has its own Bureau Chief, and he held that position here until sometime recently. This explains his numerous contacts in high places and his influence in Ankara. Or is it the other way around: he got the job because of whom he knows? Hakan tells me that the position is a Very Big Deal, and the identity of the top man is always a closely guarded secret. Baba discovered all this by accident when he found some Top Secret papers with Sami's name on them. He told Hakan about it, but he has not told anyone else in the family. Apparently, Sami used Baba's business as his cover, which sheds light on why it performed so poorly under his control. I am not moved to speculate as to why he no longer has the job. The answer seems obvious to me, but that does not mean it is so.

19 January 1971

It's been a bumper week for underwear! The slips you sent for Abla and me arrived before the letter you sent telling us they were coming. You posted the package on the 11th and it arrived on the 14th. Miraculous! Even more miraculous is that it came through unopened, un-inspected and "undutied". You never know. Abla is delighted with her lovely pink slip. She is short and it is too long for her, but that didn't bother her at all. She said she's never owned a slip she didn't have to hem and whisked it away to deposit in her dowry. She is practicing her English so she can write a little thank-you note.

We had a wonderful surprise the other day as Abla and I started to town, only to see Hakan coming up our street. Abla saw him before I did and let out a yelp. I'm glad he caught us as there was no one at home, and he would otherwise have been sitting on our steps all afternoon. He said he had been working flat-out to get forms ready - something to do with New Year statistics - and his commander had rewarded him with a welcome weekend off. These visits are good for morale, both his and mine.

We talked a lot about the wedding. The long and the short of it is that we will simply have to accommodate the six hundred guests. The Beylers have made it clear that it's an "all or nothing" proposition since there would be no point in having a celebration that manages to alienate half the town. Hakan says we'll find a way. He's confident that we can hold a reception on the money we have. I'm not so sure. He has so little interest in these things that I don't think he realizes what is involved. However, in accordance with tradition, I am taking a back seat in all this and letting the Beylers go ahead with whatever they think is best. I will not be upset... I will not be upset… I will not be upset! I don't blame Hakan. I don't blame anyone for that matter. I'm just feeling resentful that this day appears to be for everyone but us. It feels like a fat trap and we are the mice… or are we the rats?

Abla has had her hair cut very short, a little shorter than my bob. I think it looks more modern and up-to-date than her old style, which was long and rather shapeless. She was fed up with taking care of it and had it cut off in a moment of impulse. She says she is going to collect her hair until she has enough to make a hairpiece. Undoubtedly, there is a little shop where we can have this done. There is almost nothing we can't have made from scratch here. Because labour is cheap, everything seems possible, and most services are affordable.

There is much excitement this week over the big bank robbery in Ankara. Thieves got away with about $10,000, a vast amount by Turkish standards. The thrill factor is compounded by the fact that bank robberies almost never happen here, AND that the suspects are Maoists from the Middle East University! I can't help recalling my conversation with Kamer and some of the things he said that evening.

It is claimed that they stole the money to buy guns and ammunition. After a week of chasing them around the country, the police have arrested two suspects, but I think there are others still on the loose. The university has been closed while investigations continue.

I haven't said much about Bill lately because I assume you get regular letters from him and are receiving much the same information. He writes to me as time and circumstances allow, which means every couple of weeks since he has had his cushy new posting. May it last to the end of his tour!

26 January 1971

I can well imagine that you do not want another Christmas like the past one, with Bill in Vietnam and me... well, not exactly in danger but certainly a long way from home. I can assure you that Hakan and I will do everything possible to be part of a Christmas reunion in Applewold this year, but it is all too far away for me to commit myself to anything yet.

As if life were not complicated enough, Ken has decided to go silent on us. We've had a copy of the company's year-end accounts, and while everything looks to us to be in order, Ken is upset about something he perceives to be a misappropriation of funds on this end. I had a garbled letter from him and could make no sense of it. I forwarded it to Hakan who has replied, unperturbed, explaining what he thinks concerns Ken; but weeks have passed, and despite having sent samples and other items, we have had no response. We have no choice but to continue to wait. Whatever Ken decides, there is precious little we can do about it from here. If the business collapsed, it would certainly make it that much harder for us to return to a country that owes us nothing. We see our future in England and have never really thought beyond that. That the British might refuse to grant us permission to stay doesn't bear thinking about. So I won't.

No matter what kind of weather we're having, everyone tells me it's remarkable for the season. According to the locals, we're meant to have snow in January. I wonder. I've been here two winters and have yet to see so much as a snowflake in this town. However, it now appears that we have missed winter altogether and are skipping straight to spring. The early bulbs are pushing through and the grass is already sprouting. Along with buds from the almond trees, we have a vase full of forsythia on the table. On Sunday, Abla and I took the dogs for a long walk through the fields along the back way to Dayı's house. It was a sun-drenched day, all the more special for being unexpected, and we were able to sit outside to drink our tea with the family. This morning, we took chairs into the garden and did our knitting there. Later, Ana came out with rice and lentils to sort, so we made a pleasant morning of our chores. Everyone is wondering how long this can last... and what it means for the summer months.

I met Ruth for a marathon four-hour lunch last week. We had not seen each other since Christmas, so there was much to discuss. Yesterday, Abla and I gave the house a thorough clean in readiness for the monthly *gün*. That's as stimulating as my life gets at present, about as exciting as keeping pot plants.

I wonder if you saw the quotes column in this week's TIME. In it they printed the words of a soldier in Bill's division who said that the men in Vietnam are the unwilling doing the unwanted for the ungrateful. How very true.

Chapter 17

2 February 1971

We are knee-deep in preparations for Kurban Bayram, which starts on 6 February this year (the rotating calendar, remember?) and goes on for four days. Although we are not having a *kurban,* sacrificial sheep, we can hear their perpetual mewling from neighbouring gardens, the sheep already decked out in their brightly dyed coats and festive ribbons. Tomorrow, we'll be baking and cooking. Ana is going to make *baklava;* most certainly, I will be on hand to help!

Sami has written to say that he would like to come home for the holiday. He hasn't been here for over a year, so the family is looking forward to his visit. I am keeping my mouth shut. Hakan has indicated that he will have a two-week period of leave when he comes, but I'm not clear when that begins. With this amount of time at our disposal, we need to make the tedious trip to the border to deal with Dagmar's recurring permit problems. If she weren't such a lifeline, I would think her a mixed blessing, but there is no question that Dagmar is well worth any trouble she generates. I simply don't know what I would do without her.

I loved all your comments about the wedding. Since I've only ever wanted a small one, I guess it is in the nature of things that mine should turn out to have a cast of thousands. You've raised some questions that I shall try to answer. Turkey is a secular country, and as such, the only legal marriages are those performed by designated civil servants. Some people choose to have a religious ceremony as well, but that is optional and has no status in law. Just as I imagine you would like us to have a church wedding, the Beylers also would like us to have a religious service, but Hakan has said a firm "no" to this, and there the subject rests. We're planning a civil ceremony only, to be held in the same place as the reception (as yet undecided), so everything will be under one roof, both on the same evening.

There is no custom for having a honeymoon. However, there is the delicate matter of the bride's virginity, which is expected to be not only intact but provable, with the so-called "tokens of virginity" being presented to the groom's mother and other female relatives after the couple's first night together. Nisa, with a nudge and a wink, took it upon herself to inform me that more than one chicken has laid down its life on behalf of a young bride's honour. Even so, I could not believe that this ancient tradition is still being carried out today. I think it is positively barbaric that a girl should have to prove herself in this way - absolutely outrageous! I am still spluttering with indignation. Please file my response to this, along with the likelihood of my compliance, under the same heading as that of my prospective mother-in-law giving me a bath.

The wedding invitations go out days, rather than weeks before the ceremony. Anyone who does not attend will be expected to turn up at the home of the parents with a suitable gift sometime in the following weeks. Even those who attend on the day will be expected to pay a further visit to convey their congratulations. It would be a serious breach of etiquette not to do so. The mothers open the gifts (these come to the family, not to the bride and groom) and decide to whom they will be given, if they are passed on at all. No one here ever thanks anyone for a gift, nor is it ever opened in front of the giver. It all happens without a word of acknowledgement on anyone's part. However, the unwritten rule is that there will be reciprocity in the future.

We may joke in the West about weddings being for the families, rather than the couple; here it is a very real fact of life. The bride and groom have virtually nothing to say about any of the proceedings. Sometimes they have had very little to say even about who their intended spouses will be. The groom's family will determine everything from the printing of the invitations, to the style of the bridal gown, to where the couple will live. In these family matters, sons are expected to be as compliant as daughters, and parental wishes must always be respected and obeyed. The etiquette surrounding the various gift exchanges and the role each family member should play in events leading up to the wedding is a minefield of opportunities to give and take offence, intended or otherwise. It is not uncommon for everyone to fall out immediately after the whole affair is over. Family is all. Whether we are talking about marriages or anything else, it is the family, its honour, its welfare, its greater good that should be the ultimate consideration in any decision the individual makes. This prevailing attitude can and does produce painful personal dilemmas.

Levent brought his report card home this week. The Beylers are elated with the results, which are average. I can't say whether he could have done better, but I agree that he is to be encouraged, and I have praised him warmly for his achievements. I have a problem though, with the expectation that he should automatically get money purely because he has brought home his grades. I know that he cheats as I have seen him making crib sheets for his class exams, and I refuse to reward that. His parents and Abla have given him money, and he is cross with me for failing to do so.

Hakan and I are as generous as we can be at *bayram*s and birthdays, not to mention our continuing help with his school expenses; but I'm not feeling particularly charitable towards him right now. Apart from the cheating, his behaviour at home is atrocious. He is rude and ill-mannered to everyone and assumes that he can do exactly as he pleases with no adverse consequences. When it was coming up to Hakan's birthday, Abla suggested to Levent that it would be nice if he sent his brother a card. Levent said he wasn't interested and couldn't be bothered. After all that Hakan has done for him, all the many ways in which he has encouraged and supported him, I found his attitude inexcusable. No. I'm sticking to my principles on this one. Hakan can do as he sees fit when he comes home.

You'll never guess what. My resident's visa came from Ankara. Almost a year to the day after first applying, the Turkish government has come through. Nevertheless, I would have known nothing about this if I hadn't gone along to check on its progress.

"Oh, yes," the clerk reported, "a visa for one year has been granted, but we cannot issue it until you have paid the 250TL costs."

"Fine, but I shall have to get the money and return later."

"Hurry up! This is very important."

Well - no kidding! If it's so monumentally important, why has it taken one year to secure, why did I have to come to you to find out about it, and what, exactly, do you think I've been doing in the meantime? I have had to restrain myself from giving knee-jerk replies on previous occasions, and once again, I was forced to control myself in the interests of a greater good. However, I am not sure now what I want to do. I get my passport automatically renewed when we go to the border for the car, so I'm not convinced that I actually need the resident's visa. Baba says I should get it because it is essential to have, though I don't know who is ever going to care, or check that I have it.

I'm going to delay the decision until Hakan comes home and we have a chance to talk.

16 February 1971

Since my last letter, Kurban Bayram has come and gone, we've been to Edirne and back, and Hakan has returned to Bursa. The days have sped by.

Bayram was a complete fiasco. The only agreeable thing that happened was that Hakan came home. He arrived on the Thursday, and as expected, Sami appeared the following morning, the family having assembled for this august occasion. But along with the brothers, the holiday also brought cold weather, and just as we thought winter had bypassed us, we were jolted by bitter winds and freezing nights. The weather probably accounts for the fact that this *bayram* has been much quieter than others. Or maybe it's simply that my star value is waning. Whatever the explanation, we remained indoors and spent most of the holiday arguing. So cosy. There is nothing like a family reunion with everyone feeling miserable, and it is no exaggeration to say that the Beylers spent the entire four days fighting and yelling, courtesy of Sami.

Whatever the difficulties of the household, they are magnified by Sami's presence. I tried to stay out of the thick of it and went to bed early; however, it got so bad one night that I was awakened by the commotion. Judging by the uproar, I felt confident that someone was about to be murdered and rushed to the salon to find Hakan standing between Baba and Sami, only barely managing to keep them apart. That was the low point of the holiday. I don't think there was a high point. Sami was unbearable the entire time, foul tempered and drunk for most of it.

Despite my attempts to remain in the background, he decided to single me out for special attention his last night here. He started telling me what a nice girl I am (actually, he said that Americans were not good people, but I was all right) and making clumsy attempts at charm. Since this is not something that comes naturally to him, I took it all as seriously as I take a Disney cartoon. I know that when he starts making overtures, it's because he wants something. I sat and waited. After a lot of nonsensical drivel, he concluded by saying that while he accepted there had been trouble between Hakan and him, for the sake of our impending wedding, he was willing to forgive us. How gracious of him. Then he gave me 500TL and told me to use it as I saw fit for the wedding; there would be more to come.

To say that this was possibly the most unexpected gesture in the universe would not be an exaggeration. If asked, I would have said that Sami would live on bread and water for the rest of his life, rather than contribute so much as a farthing to our big day. Yet, and yet. Was I going to have to revise entirely all my negative opinions and harsh judgments about this man? Apparently not. The fleeting doubts I had suffered regarding my ability to assess Sami were firmly routed the next morning when he - shamelessly, I might add - asked me to return the money. He said it had all been a joke. And that should answer your queries about any roll that Sami might play in our wedding.

No amount of frenetic activity, fine speeches or wild promises can disguise the evidence that Sami is all surface; there is nothing underneath. He pulled out all his nasty cards for this trip home. Having previously promised to lend us money for Baba's lawyer fees (until we could get back to England to earn the money to repay him), he has reneged on that, and most of the money we had put away for the wedding will have to go now on legal expenses. It is no longer a case of the wedding anyone wants, but of what we can afford, which won't be much more than a simple ceremony and some cake. And this is not, I repeat NOT, a subtle appeal to you for financial help. You have already contributed substantially, and I am adamant that I do not want you sending any more money for an event you cannot attend and in which you have no say.

No. Hakan and I have chosen this path, and we'll deal with the situation as best we can. Much has happened that we could not have foreseen, but then, that's life, isn't it? We've managed to survive without much work for nearly two years, and we've done all right. We've paid our way here and helped the family as much as we could. In the total scheme of things, we've not done badly. Considering the obstacles we've had to overcome, I'm rather proud of what we've

accomplished. We've benefited in ways that don't show, and I am not going to get upset over a change of plans. I never wanted a big wedding anyway!

But it's Sami's threat to stop Hakan from returning to London that is more worrying than any of the above. To be precise, he said that he would not give his consent. According to the family hierarchy, Hakan does, technically, need his brother's agreement to leave the country. Apart from the fact that we have no regard, whatsoever, for either his opinion or his consent, he might just have the necessary connections to prevent Hakan from getting his passport renewed. This he will need to do once his military service is completed. I wouldn't want to test Sami in this matter as we have absolutely no reason to trust him. We shall simply have to be quicker and cleverer than he is. It's extremely sad, but now, more than ever, we are determined to hide our plans from him. I surely don't want him turning up at our wedding. I am confident he would do everything possible to ruin the day for us, whatever sort of occasion it might be.

During *bayram* I was on the receiving end of several interesting lectures. As a woman, I still do not understand or accept that men are, by definition, superior to me in every respect. I must admit, I have not entirely given myself over to making progress in this department. As you are aware, Muslims do not eat pork. It is strictly forbidden, the result of quite sensible dietary restrictions that originated in a hot country (and which resemble the dietary laws of the Jews, for the same reasons). These are still universally observed in the Islamic world and are now enshrined in religious law.

When Sami arrived from Istanbul, he brought some sausages that I suspected were pork. I couldn't believe that even Sami would eat these if he knew that's what they were, nor could I imagine where he might obtain them, unless from a PX. However, they not only looked like pork, they tasted like it, too. I was convinced and voiced my opinion to the family, purely because I assumed they would want to be told if they were about to eat something forbidden. My observation was totally ignored, and the family had them for dinner, all except Abla who assumed I might just know what I was talking about. During the meal, Sami explained to me that they couldn't possibly be pork because - as everyone who has not eaten it is aware - pork is extremely greasy. Since these delectable sausages were not greasy, they could not possibly be pork. I never said another word on the subject. Hakan privately agreed with me, but ate them anyway. He's not particularly fond of pork (I think it's difficult to overcome an ingrained cultural prejudice against certain foods, like us eating tripe or brain), but he has no objections on religious grounds and will eat it if it appeals.

My second lecture came later in the holiday when the neighbours visited, and the men started a conversation about some of the more puzzling aspects of Christianity. And let's face it - the concepts of Trinity, Jesus being both human and divine, the Virgin Birth - these are all unique and bewildering ideas, even for Christians. But the assembled men had no interest in trying to unravel thorny theology. No, their interest in the subject lay in making the most fanciful pronouncements about what Christianity is and is not, helpfully clarifying it all for me. You would not have recognized your religion from some of the gnarled descriptions they gave concerning basic beliefs. My contributions were not required as, being men, they clearly knew more about the subject than I did. One valuable lesson I have learned here is that there is no point in talking if no one wants to listen.

For Americans in Turkey, the current political atmosphere is hot, and getting hotter. Thanks mostly to the continuing activities of the Maoist student movement, the campuses are in perpetual uproar. I don't know if anyone is studying any more. Another bank in Ankara has been robbed, and a few days ago, students broke into an American PX in the city. A sergeant on guard duty has been kidnapped, and the US Ambassador has demanded his immediate release. American cars are increasingly the targets of attack. Once again, I am grateful for my German car, registration, name and looks. If ever I regretted not living in one of the major cities here, now is my chance to retract that and count my blessings.

The trip to Edirne was relatively easy this time around. I guess practice makes perfect. We took Sami and Abla as far as Istanbul, dropping him at his place and Abla, with a relative (sleeping away from home is getting to be a habit with that girl!). *Bayram* being what it was, everyone felt in need of a change. The weather in that northwest corner of the country is always cold and snowy in the winter, and bearing in mind our trip last January, we were wary. Although we saw some flurries, there was no snowfall of any consequence; nevertheless, we completed our business and left as fast as we could. Unbelievably and unaccountably, they gave me four months on both passport and car permit. Who knows why, or what, if anything, has changed? Who can fathom it? Who can explain? Who cares? I'm well past trying to understand any of it, thankful merely for small mercies. The happy result is that in June, we shall make our last trip to the border!

In Istanbul we shopped for wedding things. Hakan bought shoes and is having a shirt made. Can you believe this is cheaper than buying ready-made? Both his jacket and trousers are being tailored in Kavaklı. Abla assured me, yet again, that she can finish my dress within a week, and Baba will use leftover fabric to make matching pumps. My outfit has been easier than Hakan's.

We picked up Abla on our way home on Saturday. We were about fifty miles from Kavaklı when a passing truck kicked up a small stone which hit our windshield, causing it to splinter into a million pieces. It being shatterproof glass, the pieces stayed firmly in place, but the multitude of fracture lines made it impossible to see anything. It was a shock, and it took a few seconds to register what had happened. Of course, we were out in the middle of nowhere with no realistic chance of a local repair, so we had no choice but to continue towards home.

Unfortunately, it was getting dark, the weather was turning colder, and we still had quite a few miles to go. Hakan picked out enough of the broken bits to see the road ahead, but it was tricky trying to decide whether to drive fast and get cold but get home quicker, or slow down so as not to feel the biting air and take longer getting back. Hakan had a difficult job with all the cold hitting him directly on his face and chest, but we made it without too much delay. As soon as we got in the door, we lit the fire so that he could have a hot bath, and we doctored him up, trying to fend off any risk of a cold. Luckily, he suffered no ill effects, and the glass has been (expensively) replaced. Our exhaust system has a hole and the brakes are bad, so I am taking Dagmar to the garage today to have all that work done. When I got home from the market yesterday, I slammed the car door shut and shattered the window on the driver's side. When it rains, it pours!

We have decided to go ahead with my resident's visa. Hakan thinks it is better to be safe than sorry, and he is right. But I find the whole thing galling. I have had some pictures taken for the visa, and I'll let you have one in the next letter.

PS - just received your latest letter as I was finishing this one. BAD news about Bill. We are really worried about his involvement in heavy fighting.

23 February 1971

I have spent the best part of the week thinking about Bill. Our news of the war here is patchy and unreliable, and I have no real idea what is happening. Neither does he, according to his letter of 10 February. He said his division is spearheading a drive for the Vietnamese Army to go into Laos. They pulled him out of his nice, warm office and put him up a cold, wet mountain at Khe Sanh where his division is providing air support, or would, if they weren't hampered by poor weather conditions and communication snags. He sounds bright enough, but all I can think of is, "What the hell is my brother doing up a mountain in Vietnam?" The war in all its larger aspects doesn't interest me anymore. I just want my brother out of there!

It has been a week of birthday celebrations here, not in the family but amongst friends. Ruth rang last week (at Aylin Abla's), first of all to find out if we were all right. She had heard that we had been involved in a terrible road accident and were in hospital. The rumours must have spread because of the shattered windshield. After assuring her that there really had been no crash and we were fine, she moved on to invite me to her little girl's third birthday party. Thinking that this would be a typical children's affair, and that she might like some help with the food and so forth, I readily agreed. However, further conversation revealed that Nilüfer's birthday was something of an excuse for an evening bash for their friends.

Since Ruth's husband is generally regarded as the top doctor in town, their social life revolves around the upper echelons of Kavaklı society. I have met some of the wives of the local elite and have found that I have less in common with them than with almost anyone else here. They are, on the whole, rich and privileged women, living lives of such ease that their biggest dilemma seems to be which outfit they will wear to the next social event. Their preoccupations are, in no particular order, their clothes, their hair, their nails, their jewellery and their servant troubles. My overall impression is that they are beautiful hothouse blooms, well suited to husbands who appear to have required nothing more than good looks and immaculate grooming when picking a mate.

I had no interest in attending. Even if I had, Ruth has been in Turkey long enough to appreciate that it would be unacceptable for me to go to such a function unescorted. At least, not in the circles in which I move. Can you picture the family's reaction if I announced that I was going to a mixed gathering - at night - on my own? It's simply not possible without causing the biggest kafuffle, and I didn't want to go badly enough even to consider it. But having already accepted, I now had to dig my way out. I decided to be candid with Ruth and remind her how poorly my attendance would reflect on the family and on myself. I felt I was telling her something she should already know. I think she does but doesn't care. I suspect that the upper reaches of the culture are little concerned with matters of so-called respectability as defined in my neck of the woods. But regardless of what I said, I couldn't get through to her, and she wasn't taking "no" for an answer. The discussion had gone on for too long, and my extended use of someone else's telephone was becoming embarrassing, so I agreed to attend merely in order to end the conversation. I would have to reflect on a way out of this.

Meanwhile, both Fatma and Nevin have had birthdays. We celebrated Nevin's on Friday and Fatma's, the following day. Nevin would normally be teaching on a Friday but had the afternoon off, so Abla and I visited with her at home. Though she is quite independent and does a lot of things Ana would never permit, she is restricted in another aspect of her life because her mother is very religious and insists that Nevin must cover her hair at all times. I don't believe she does so when teaching as I think it would be frowned on in a public role, but she does cover up whenever she goes out with us - even when she is at home. The various permutations of "respectable" fluctuate more widely than I had first thought.

On Saturday, we all met at Fatma's house, expecting a rather subdued birthday as her father has been in hospital with a serious heart condition. However, we arrived to find him at home, feeling quite cheerful. We visited with her parents for a while, and then her father sent us off for what he deemed to be a proper celebration at the local "in" place, a new *pastane* so "in" that it has been specifically forbidden to Abla and, by extension, to me.

I'm not sure what Ana objects to. It appeared to be a harmless enough location at which to meet friends and eat pastries, but I could see that some teenagers had appropriated this as a meeting place and were having a jolly get-together at the tables in the rear. Heaven forbid, I think there may have been some mingling of the sexes, possibly even some flirting! Honestly, they made me feel old, far too old to have any activity there reflect poorly on Abla or myself. Nevertheless, I felt like a child sneaking sweets when we set off for a destination we knew would cause problems if Ana found out.

In the course of an afternoon spent drinking tea and indulging in the most delicious cakes, I found out more about Fatma than ever I had imagined. It seems that her mother and father are not her real parents but her grandparents. Her mother is the "older sister" she is hoping to visit in Canada. Fatma has always referred to her as "Abla" and will continue to do so, at her mother's insistence. I gather that her real father died when she was young. Her mother remarried but did not want to be encumbered in her new life with her daughter from the old one (my words, not hers), so she left Fatma behind to be reared by the grandparents. Apparently Fatma has three half-brothers whom she has never met. I really didn't know what to say. Fatma's grandparents are lovely people who strike me as having done a far better job with their granddaughter than with their pea-brained daughter. Maybe there's more to this than meets the eye, but as Fatma's friend, I have trouble understanding a woman who abandons her child to go off with the latest man in her life. Fatma has huge expectations for her Canadian trip, and I sincerely hope it works out for her. She deserves to meet her mother again, if that's what she wants; but at the same time, I hope she is not disappointed.

I am finding out that these convoluted relationships are not uncommon and, undoubtedly, not restricted to Turkey. For various reasons, grandparents often rear their grandchildren. Sometimes the parents have gone abroad to work; or the mother has died; or as in Fatma's case, the mother has remarried and the new husband wants nothing to do with another man's child. There are many instances also of a fertile sister giving one of her babies to another sister who cannot have children of her own. Adoption, where it occurs, is forever a matter of secrecy and shame. Attitudes to this are quite Victorian, as if any of the circumstances could be the fault of the child. An adopted child is always regarded as inferior, less than a fully-fledged member of the family. In this case, blood is not thick; it is positively glutinous.

By way of concluding this discussion on birthdays, I just want to add that I went to Ruth's the day before her party. Since she was not at home, I left my gift for Nilüfer with a note of apology for being unable to attend.

For someone who did not quite grasp the concept of "dowry" when I first arrived, I now modestly believe I am something of an expert on them. Aware of my interest in their customs and culture, the Turks are very good about including me in things, and I have been invited along to many dowry displays, when everything is on show prior to the wedding. In the best examples, everything will be in place, ready for the couple "to take up housekeeping" (a phrase I recall from my own grandmother) as soon as the ceremony is over.

The other day, Abla and I were invited to a neighbour's house to see their new bride's dowry. They are a wealthy family, and obviously their son is marrying someone of equal status as I have never before seen such an exhibition. While not normally given to jealousy, I have to admit to the teensiest bit of envy on this occasion. Not only had the families provided the house itself, but also everything required to carry out daily life, right down to the pins in the sewing box. It was astounding. There was even an elegant bag for dirty laundry. The furniture, kitchen fittings and household items were all of the finest quality. The interior of the house looked like a model apartment straight out of the latest magazines. The bride's closet was filled with a completely new wardrobe, as was the groom's. Nothing, but nothing, had been overlooked. I don't believe there was anything less than perfect in the entire house. The bride is seventeen years old, and he is twenty. I hope they have some level of appreciation for this exceptional start in life; equally, I hope that the marriage will be a long and happy one.

I'll conclude this week's report with a few other titbits to keep you up with the latest in the family. Although there has been no further news on the job front, Abla has decided to take up typing. She borrowed Fatma's course book, which explains the basics and provides practice exercises. She had thought that she could use my Olivetti, but this won't work as the differences between the Turkish alphabet and the characters on my typewriter are too great to be of benefit. She's going to look for a suitable course later in the spring.

Meanwhile Sami has let us know that he is not speaking to Hakan or Abla or me since we didn't look him up after dropping him off in Istanbul. Following his quite stunning performance over *bayram*, why he imagines that anyone would wish to see him again is beyond me. Also, "looking him up" means investigating all the bars and drinking places in Istanbul, not something any of us cared to do.

Chapter 18

2 March 1971

I'm somewhat relieved to hear Dad's assessment of Bill's current situation. I guess on a support mission he would not expect to be involved in actual combat, but I question whether the enemy is aware of the difference and suspect there are no guarantees that he could not be attacked whenever he is in the field. I can't take anything for granted about his circumstances. I don't know if his promotion is a good thing or not; it's most likely a reflection of the fact that he's in a war. Doesn't that sound awful! The only consolation I can see is that he is on the better (shorter) half of his tour.

By opting out of Ruth's party, I evidently missed THE social event of the Kavaklı Season. Everyone, but everyone my dears, is talking of nothing else. Ruth came by a couple of days ago to fill me in. I think she was astonished by all the fuss, having unintentionally pulled off what appeared to be a colossal social *coup*. She was stunned by the gifts that came for Nilüfer. Among the most extravagant was a live lamb, bathed and groomed to glittering perfection and decorated with flowers.

Betty had been drafted in to secure snack foods from the PX, so things like potato chips, pretzels, crackers and other items unusual for Turkey had the crowd gasping with pleasure. In addition to these, Ruth had little open sandwiches that are possible to make only with our airy American bread. More admiration, not to mention extreme appreciation for an unlimited supply of American cigarettes and whiskey. The crowning glory was the extraordinary sculpted cat cake, with so much work and detail, it had taken Betty two days to make. Ruth was still high with excitement. She didn't say what Nilüfer had made of her party.

Ruth and I are trying to plan a lunch out on Friday (not Altın Palas). I say "trying" because we normally have to make several attempts before succeeding. It's harder for her with children and the responsibilities of a home, and almost inevitably, someone comes to call or something crops up at the last minute. Consequently, we don't see each other as often as we would like. Already it has begun.

As soon as I told Ana that I was going to meet Ruth on Friday, she invited some women friends to call at the same time, and then insisted that I had to be present or it would be *ayıp*. She did go on and on about it until I told her, politely, that I had made my arrangements first, and unless Ruth had to cancel, I would be going as planned. I know Ana acts this way because she doesn't like Ruth and doesn't want me to see her. I also know that she will run to Hakan to report my bad behaviour the minute he next comes home.

Ana has a memory like an elephant. Truly. Though she remains largely uninterested in the wider world, she has a tenacious grip on every date that has the slightest significance within the family circle.

As well as the important holidays and *bayrams*, she remembers all the minutiae of minor religious occasions and the birthdays of all her family, whether they are currently speaking or not. She can recall those for all of you, too. She knows when Hakan left for London and when we arrived, when we went to Istanbul and on what matters. She remembers dates from Levent's school calendar, when items arrived in the post and an endless stream of things that are quite beyond me. She ought to be a whiz at telephone numbers, but that's a talent rather lost in the present circumstances.

Ana also tries to be manipulative, though her efforts are somewhat obvious. One of her favourite strategies involves comparisons: "Do you love Baba more than you love me?" "Do you love your mother more than Hakan?" "Do you love Phyllis more than you love me?" (I'm clearly meant to prefer my mother-in-law; it's the nature of the hierarchy). "Who do you love the most?" I usually say something about everyone being loved for themselves, that it isn't a competition, but this doesn't always bring the subject to a close. Last week, she asked if I was afraid of Hakan.

"No."

She looked puzzled. "You don't respect him?"

"Of course, I respect him, but I'm not afraid of him. I wouldn't marry someone I feared."

More puzzlement. Plainly, fear and respect are inextricably linked in her mind.

One day, when we were playing the comparison game, she got me. Well, SHE was playing the game, and I was trying to read. After persisting with her endless questions, she concluded by saying, "If you really love me, you would send me on The Haj (pilgrimage to Mecca)."

I looked up at her and said, treading carefully while hoping to put an end to it, "I'd love to send you on The Haj - one day when I can afford it."

"Do you promise?"

Uh-oh. It was no longer the game I had thought; I knew she was serious. "Why do you ask?"

"I'm not asking Hakan because he won't agree, but if you promise, I know you'll keep your word," she announced, inadvertently giving me what was probably the biggest compliment I was ever going to get from her. I paused, and then said that I would promise to do that for her if she would let me decide when I could afford it... and stopped asking me questions! She ceased to listen after the "if".

"Baba, too?"

"Yes, certainly."

She sprang to her feet and shot off to the kitchen, beaming and humming as she went. I got my peace and quiet but at quite a price. I know she will not forget. She has a way of manipulating information to suit what she wants to believe; that then becomes her truth. In this instance, she got exactly what she wanted simply by manipulating me. I don't think I need to mention this to Hakan - not just yet.

9 March 1971

There are all kinds of stories in the news these days. First of all, we were enormously relieved to hear that Bill had been given some leave and was out of harm's way, if only for a short spell. I had mail from him today, and his spirits seemed better than they have in the last couple of letters. He says that while everyone around them has been getting artillery fire, so far his unit has escaped any action. Long may it last - and may the gods forgive me for my selfish attitude. He mentioned that they only get biased news reports about anything to do with Vietnam. Although he gets TIME magazine there, it is the slanted military version, so I have been sending him clippings from mine to give him a broader picture. I get what is called the Atlantic Edition, different again from yours. It does make me wonder how many versions of "the truth" there are.

Things have gone from bad to worse in Ankara this past week. As well as the increasing number of attacks on American property, there also have been attacks on our citizens, the most recent of which resulted in the kidnapping of four American servicemen by a Maoist student group. I heard this morning that the four have been released, unharmed. But what happened in the capital following their capture was ugly.

The government suspected that Maoist students were behind the kidnapping and sent soldiers to the Middle East University to conduct searches. The students barricaded buildings and resisted all attempts by the soldiers to gain entry, resulting in several days of gun fighting, with casualties on both sides. The papers here reported President Nixon as saying that the American government would not intervene; they regarded the problem as a Turkish one and were willing to let Ankara handle it. Apparently, a ransom had been demanded, but the Americans refused to pay. Quite right, too. I can tell you that ordinary Turkish citizens have been outraged by these events. If the Americans had been hurt or killed, the students would have done themselves more harm than good, and any sympathy anyone had ever felt for them or their cause would have evaporated overnight. They may be mad, but they are not stupid.

We have long contented ourselves that such incidents have little relevance to life here in Kavaklı; what happens in the big cities could not happen here. We were rudely awakened on Sunday when we had an unsettling incident of our own. Evidently the local teachers college has its own Maoist radicals who thought it would be a fine idea to hand out anti-American leaflets on our town's main street. One young recipient of this literature read it and then tore it up in front of the Maoists who took offence and started to punch him. When the boy's friends, who outnumbered the Maoists (so the story goes), realized what was going on, they went to his rescue and started to return the blows. By the time the police arrived, the Maoists had been badly beaten and were taken away to the local jail. When the police closed the school to search for prohibited literature and weapons, the students threatened retaliation; but in the end, all they did was stand around in front of the entrance and chant slogans.

Since a substantial cache of dynamite was discovered hidden under a nearby bridge last week, I suppose it is not unreasonable that the local police have begun to feel that urban activism is moving our way. No one appears to have any sympathy for the students. Heaven knows there is no great love for Americans in Turkey, nor would I be shocked to hear that most Turks want all Americans to leave their country immediately, but they all - well, nearly all - abhor violence and resent the way in which the students claim to speak for the average citizen. Everyone blames the Communists. It's the same in America. When students behave in a radical way, some elusive communist plot gets the blame. Personally, I don't think we have to look that far for the causes of unrest, nor do I think it is helpful to find scapegoats.

Hakan surprised us all with a weekend visit. We had been expecting him the following Saturday, but after the events in Ankara, he wanted to come home to reassure me. It worked. It's always good to have him here, whatever the reason, but his appearance was particularly welcome after a tense and difficult week.

The weather right now is warm and pleasant, inspiring us to take the dogs and get out for walks. With the arrival of spring, we are beginning to realize that Hakan's military service really IS going to end. In addition, we are becoming excited about the wedding and then, our return to England. None of it can come too soon. You have asked about the timing of our departure and will not be shocked to hear that my response is the typical, "we'll have to wait and see". I wish I had 1TL for every time I have said that. My understanding is that once Hakan finishes his military obligation, it will take twenty to thirty days for his release papers to be processed. Then he can apply for a new passport. Sami continues with his threats to block Hakan's departure from Turkey. Since we are fully aware that this is entirely within his capabilities, I have become as jittery as a June bug worrying about it. We are desperately hoping to be back in London by the end of September at the latest, but who knows?

Once again, your airmail package arrived before the airmail letter telling me it was coming. The timing could not have been better. With such gloomy news around, it lifted my spirits considerably to open your parcel and find it full of frilly underwear. Fantastic! Naturally, I passed on to Abla the items you included for her. She absolutely adores the things you send. They make her feel quite special, which she is. She is currently working on a set of embroidered napkins as a gift for you. I will let you know when we have posted them.

16 March 1971

You would never guess that I have just come in from a snowball fight! We've had a sharp blast of wintry weather, resulting in an accumulation of several inches. This remarkable phenomenon brought all the kids, including me, out into the streets to build snowmen and throw snowballs. We quickly divided into sides and pasted each other for about twenty minutes. Abla and Ana watched all this from the balcony, almost certainly wondering if they should disown me now or later. I believe the battle ended in a draw, though that might depend on who we ask.

It would be no exaggeration to say that the political situation here in Turkey is a mess. Although there have been no more kidnappings, anything American is a potential target for radical bombs, and bank robberies are now almost commonplace. Because Prime Minister Süleyman Demirel has failed to get to grips with any of this, and because there has been general discontent with his government over a longer period, the army has asked him to step down. Although it is said that he has resigned voluntarily, it is generally accepted that he has been forced to do so because of pressure from the military. No doubt the outside world would regard this as a military *coup d'etat*, for it was certainly sudden and unexpected; but in the context of Turkey's constitution, it was not illegal nor has it been violent.

Hakan has told me repeatedly that it is the army that really runs Turkey. It is a legacy from the early days of the republic when Atatürk charged it with the responsibility for ensuring the continuation of secular democracy within the country. To most western ears, it sounds like an oxymoron to speak of generals dictating politics in defence of democracy, but that's the way it works here. The concept is not strange to the Turks. In fact, most people, including Baba, think that the army has done the right thing and high time, too. If nothing else, this attitude confirms the unpopularity of the Prime Minister who was re-elected to office about eighteen months ago after a relatively successful first term.

Since then, however, the Turkish Lira has devalued, prices have soared, and there has been a significant increase in the amount of radical militant activity throughout the country. Hakan feels that the devaluation was probably necessary for economic stability, but when people are hit in their pockets, the government is bound to be blamed. There is also the unanswered question of how the economy came to be in such a dire state in the first place.

In addition to fiscal woes, the Turks are alarmed by the increasing violence on their streets. Undoubtedly the military has its own agenda in all this, but Süleyman Demirel has long complained that he couldn't accomplish anything because he had to contend with the army constantly looking over his shoulder, monitoring everything he did.

The military has said that it will announce the appointment of a new Prime Minister tomorrow. After that, we shall see exactly how things will change. I'm sure that rounding up the radicals will be a top priority for the new government, and I don't think anyone is under any illusion as to how they will be dealt with.

It is hard to resist comparisons with the military junta currently running Greece. Consequently, my major concern is the length of time the army plans to remain in charge, and whether it intends to hand back power via democratic elections. Hakan says similar situations have arisen in the past, and the military has always stepped aside when political tensions have eased, and circumstances are right for the return to democracy. We shall see. Meanwhile, Hakan writes that all the bases are on 24-hour alert.

At the other extreme on weekly news, I have knitted a beret for Baba. He likes to wear it at night to keep the cold off his head. When he puts it on, he pulls it to one side, then looks in the mirror and compares himself to General Montgomery. He thinks he looks quite fetching. Of course, we all agree. In the meantime, I have finished the sweater for Abla and have started knitting baby garments out of bits of leftover yarn. Nothing goes to waste here, and nothing is left to the last minute. Even baby clothes - perhaps I should say, especially baby clothes - are part of most dowries.

I see that Pennsylvania has now introduced state income tax. Since I continually read that it is on the verge of bankruptcy, I guess they have to get more money from somewhere. Turkey has income tax too, but precisely who pays and how much seems a bit vague. I am under the impression that hardly anyone pays the full amount. With little enforcement of the regulations, there are many ways to avoid it. No one likes to pay tax, but Turkey needs these revenues - particularly from those who can easily afford it - to build up a desperately inadequate infrastructure. This is a country of remarkable resources and untapped potential just waiting to be unleashed. The right kind of government initiatives could make all the difference to future advancement. I am making a case for paying tax that probably would not be welcomed in many places.

I hope that there will soon be something from Bill. I don't know whether his mail is delayed because he has been on leave, or whether it's because he's in the field.

23 March 1971

It was fascinating for me to read your news clippings about recent events in Turkey. They largely confirm what we have been hearing on this end of things, though maybe all the news comes from the same source. Hakan's little base is concerned with intelligence matters, and he claims to have the inside scoop on the story behind the story. According to him, the secret service uncovered a communist plot to overthrow the Ankara administration. The military felt it had to take over to contain the threat and protect the institutions of democratic government. It has lingered on in the capital while the new Prime Minister, Nihat Erim, settles in, but Hakan does not think there is any serious likelihood that the army intends to remain in power on a permanent basis. He believes it will secure the situation and bow out, leaving its appointee in charge.

Hakan likes what he has heard about Erim, a man who deserves much of the credit for the industrial progress achieved in recent years. He thinks Erim will take a firm stand against the radical socialist movement and be aggressive in moving the development of the country ahead. We often joke that someone just needs to get this country organized. It bites close to the truth, and we sincerely hope the new PM will be able to deliver. Turkey could do with a break.

The 24-hour alert continues because of the communist takeover threat. If there are no further incidents, it most likely will be called off by the end of the week. Hakan says that the chief effect on him through all of this has been a staggering increase in paperwork. As secretary to the base commander, he has been inundated with new orders to process, each order generating its own forest of paper.

Selim, Hakan's best friend from the Kavaklı base, dropped by the shop to see Baba the other day. His tour of duty has finished, but they won't release him until the current crisis has passed. He is going mad with frustration. Right now, he only wants to get home to his family in Konya but has said that he will keep in touch. He has continued his interest in WML, but once he returns to civilian life, no doubt any thoughts he has had to go abroad will begin to fade, especially as he mentioned that his family is in the process of finding a bride for him.

The postman brought separate letters from Bill for Hakan and me today. I didn't open Hakan's, but the news in mine was routine and nothing to do with the present fighting. He seems more concerned with what he is going to do after the army than anything else just now. I think he is planning some major R&R in Australia before returning home, but after that, he'll be kicking around ideas. I think it is safe to say that his plans are as up in the air as ours.

And - finally - a letter from Ken. I know there has been a postal strike in England; nevertheless, it has been five months since we last heard anything. Although addressed to Hakan, I tore it open, only to find that Ken wrote as if we had spoken last week. He's obviously had no idea about our concerns, and my worst fears have not been realized. He did not "skip out with the loot" and appears to be continuing as usual. The fact that he is simply continuing at all is what I really needed to hear; that things are going reasonably well is a plus.

Ken, like Hakan, is not sure he wants the partnership to continue, but he has said that he will wait until we return to England before making any decisions. I suspect that sooner, rather than later, there will be a split. Each is too disenchanted with the other for the business to flourish. Ken is an honest man and a hard worker, but as far as I can see, he doesn't do anything for Hakan that a competent foreman couldn't do. It's more "wait and see".

I don't believe Lady has been in heat since she gave birth, but Levent insists that she is putting on weight and must be pregnant again. I have been keeping a close eye on her, ready to pen her up if circumstances warranted; I don't think I have missed anything. I sincerely hope not. On the other hand, Aslana is most definitely in heat. I'm letting her go not only because I'm assuming she's infertile, but because there is no way I could keep her enclosed for two weeks. She would go wild and take us all with her. She is used to her freedom and loves it.

30 March 1971

As of yesterday, there have been additions to the Beyler menagerie, and we now have two adorable lambs. We visited Dayı recently, and after seeing his lambs, all cute and fluffy, Abla has been pestering Baba to buy one for her. Yesterday morning, Baba took us to the Monday Bazaar, a weekly fixture for buying and selling livestock of any kind. Villagers come from miles around to look and trade. At this time of year, baby lambs are abundant and cheap, so we were confident of an easy purchase. Most go to butchers for the obvious reason, but we had a kinder option in mind, at least in the short term.

When we arrived at the market, Baba thought it best if we waited for him in the car. He returned shortly, bringing the animals with him, saying that since he has two daughters, he had to buy two lambs. What a dear man! Abla and I spent the rest of the day looking after the brothers, helping them settle in. We think they are about three months old and, as they are still having some trouble understanding what grass is for, appear not to have been weaned. I think we can avoid going the baby bottle route if we work with them and encourage them to eat from a dish. They spent most of the day maa-ing for their mother, and given the least opportunity, trying to escape to look for her.

The other animals have taken their introduction with an inquisitive calm. The lambs make a beeline for Aslana if they see her. As the biggest animal around, I think they hope she might be their mother. Even though she doesn't meet the requirements, they like to follow her around the yard. For an infertile female, Aslana surely projects strong maternal appeal. She has decided the lambs can stay as long as there is equal affection for all. Lady has taken a different approach and has concluded that since the lambs are bigger than she is, disdain is the right attitude... unless they are completely out of range, in which case she barks her head off, just to let them know who is boss. She came into heat this morning and is now confined to the back balcony where she rules, if not happily, at least supremely.

Sometimes Ana does nothing but infuriate me, and other times - well - I feel guilty for reacting that way, then shamed by her kindness. As you are aware, Hakan's family lived originally in Bulgaria where, prior to the takeover by the Communists, the Turks and the locals seem to have co-existed for decades. The Muslim and Christian communities integrated to a certain extent because Ana's best friend came from a Christian family. Most of the Bulgarian Turks grew up learning the local language and are familiar with Bulgarian customs and culture. Apparently they too, celebrated Christmas and Easter alongside their neighbours, baking the festive breads and cakes traditional on these occasions.

Ana remembered that Easter came last year on 30 March (her phenomenal memory for dates). Today I awoke to the smell of baking bread. When I enquired, Ana said that she was making Easter buns. She wasn't sure when Easter came this year (neither was I), but she wanted to do something special for my holiday. The buns are delicious and it was extremely considerate of her to do this for me.

Because the 24-hour alert continues, there has been very little news from Hakan this past week. The situation in Ankara is much calmer now. If this continues, the alert could be lifted anytime, meaning that Hakan could get home for the weekend. By then it will be a month since I have seen him, the longest we have been separated. I'm missing him dreadfully. We all are. Yesterday Baba suggested that we hop in the car and drive to Bursa. I wasn't convinced that this was a wise move. It meant at least a six-hour round trip, with no guarantee that we could see him once we arrived. I'd rather wait a few more days and have him home here where we can visit at leisure.

I hope it will be soon!

Chapter 19

5 April 1971

The big news this week is that Hakan came home for three whole days! It was touch and go with the state of affairs in Ankara still keeping everyone as vigilant as a sultan under siege, but if anyone could manage it, Hakan would be the one to do so.

The political situation has cooled considerably, and everyone is feeling optimistic about the latest government. The new PM announced his agenda on the radio the other night. The proposals sound good, but as we are all aware, talk is one thing and action is another. Nihat Erim said that everyone must be realistic about what can be achieved and how long it will take, but his overall strategy was to follow the ideals of Atatürk. This was a politically astute ploy since the very name evokes the ultimate in patriotic feelings.

Atatürk was not only the founding father of modern Turkey, he was the very saviour of the nation. Without him, there would be no Turkey today. While the Allied powers were trying to carve up the lands of the failed Ottoman Empire at the end of WWI, Atatürk, single-handedly roused the pathetic remnants of the Ottoman army and inspired the Turks to drive out their enemies and preserve their territory. Of course, the old empire was lost, but Asia Minor (Anatolia) was preserved intact, thanks to the sheer determination of this one man. He was a benevolent dictator who dealt mercilessly with his enemies, both within and without the new state. Thanks to him, the Turks dragged themselves out of the past and created one of a handful of successful Islamic democracies in the world today. Although there is still much to be done, the Turks are justifiably proud of what they have achieved in such a short period.

In the tradition of Atatürk, the new government has closed down every *medrese,* mosque school, where religion is taught to the exclusion of almost anything else. No qualifications are required to teach in these, and many who do so reflect ignorant backgrounds and little formal education. Some of the ideas that they pass on in the name of Islâm are dubious at best, and not unlike some I have heard advanced in the name of Christianity. I recall the little girl who informed me that I shouldn't let a dog in the house or keep one as a pet because it might steal my soul and sell it to Satan... according to the local *Hoca*.

Although Ana is upset and says that Nihat Erim is anti-religion, most people regard his appointment as a positive step. Hakan is extremely enthusiastic about the choice of new Prime Minister and optimistic about this government's capacity to make the required changes.

While Hakan was here, we went along to the tailor's to check on the progress of his wedding jacket and trousers. Both are nearing completion and a final fitting should do the trick. He was in especially good humour throughout this visit. I think he was glad of the chance to unwind and do very little. During the alert, he was so busy that they moved a bed into his office, so he could be available during the night to answer the telephone and deal with orders as they came through. His life may have been hectic, but he clearly wasn't getting any exercise as he gained eight pounds during that period.

Barring unforeseen incidents (ha!), he is hoping to get off during the first week of May so we can travel to Izmir together. I need to go to the US Consulate to renew my passport. While I'm there, I will also get the documents I need for our marriage license. Getting married here generates a mountain of paperwork, the nature of which is greatly complicated by one of the party being a foreigner. Because of all the ex-pats in Izmir, this particular consulate seems especially geared to dealing with these matters, and they have assured me in correspondence that they can provide the affidavit and other forms required by the Turkish authorities. I could go on my own if I had to, but it would be much nicer to travel together, if we can.

Last week we heard that Nina had moved out of Teyze's house and was living with a neighbour, so Ana, Abla and I went to investigate. Like Nina, the neighbour is also an elderly widow woman. Her husband died several years ago, and her children have grown up and moved away. Since she has no one to keep her company, she asked Nina to live with her. The move has benefited everyone. With no one to interfere or tell them what to do, the two women are as happy as children in candy land. They please themselves and appear to be extremely compatible. I have never before seen Nina looking so well - completely at ease and content - and even a little heavier than I remembered. Now that she is no longer living with Teyze, we can visit as often as we like, and that makes us all happy.

In an attempt to find work, Abla is planning to take the civil service exams later this week and has been frantically cramming so she can do well. Although I'm certain that she will pass with high marks, I have my doubts that any job offers will be based on merit. These are more likely to depend on the right connections than on exam results. Such work would provide an excellent opportunity for her, but I have to say, I don't think the omens are good. Abla has become restless this past year and has vowed that she is going to change her life by finding work, getting married or going to England with us. Ana is totally against Abla leaving the house for any reason, but when she considers that her daughter might actually go abroad, she quickly renews her interest in finding a suitable husband as the least of the three evils on offer.

For a long time, I considered employment to be her best option, but given the realities of the situation, I'm now re-evaluating this position. If she had a job, she would wind up supporting the whole family, undoubtedly looking after the house as well, everyone still telling her what to do. I suspect that the most favourable outcome would be for her to find some nice, respectable man to marry. At least she would have a home of her own and, depending on circumstances, maybe a greater degree of independence, too. Although we are not in a position to take her back to England with us when we go, we could send for her once we are settled. But, realistically, this is the least desirable option.

I know that I'm regarded as a troublemaker and that my example is blamed for the changes in Abla. But for my presence and encouragement, she might never have been emboldened to think of these things or to act on them. She is trying to take responsibility for her life and to stand on her own two feet. She deserves to be supported in this bid for independence, whether anyone else here thinks so or not. We've both been up and down lately. When I've been low, she perks me up; when she has been depressed, I try to do the same for her. We are both waiting, both living with uncertainty. Some days are easier than others.

We are anxious to hear Bill's news now that the planned invasion of Laos has been cancelled. Hakan says he heard that the Viet Cong are attacking across the Demilitarized Zone into the south of the country, but I shall have to wait for this week's TIME to get a better picture. I hope Bill has not been chucked out of a blaze and into a firestorm.

12 April 1971

I hope you all had a nice Easter! I didn't know the date until Mother wrote that it was on the 11th of April this year. Ruth came by on the 10th to wish me a Happy Easter, which was thoughtful of her. We probably would have spent the day together except that Easter is on a Sunday, and her husband would be at home. Whatever the day, women don't visit each other when husbands are around.

When I got up yesterday, the family announced that I would have to find my breakfast. Abla had hard-boiled some eggs, and the Beylers had hidden them all over the house (a custom they knew from Bulgaria). It tickled them to see me crawling around, poking things, searching high and low. Levent proved especially inventive with his hiding places, but I found all the eggs in the end. Then we sat down to eat. It was an unexpected start to the day, and we all had a good laugh.

The excitement of the week is all around Abla. A neighbour woman brought her friends to meet her the other afternoon. One of the women has a son for whom they are trying to find a match, and the neighbour recommended Abla. The 38-year-old son is an accountant (a highly regarded job in Turkey), and he has his own home in Istanbul. So far, everything we have heard about him makes him look like a worthy suitor. It seems that Abla made a favourable impression as we heard that the family is planning a return visit with their son.

Baba is enthusiastic about the prospects for the match, and I'm convinced he will go ahead if Abla agrees. Ana, however, is having fits. Without actually saying so, she makes it crystal clear that she does not want Abla to leave home. Who will do all the work? She is flattered by the positive attentions that her daughter attracts, but she is capable of derailing the plans and has done so before. Although Baba has told her to keep quiet and stay out of it, all she has to do is inform Sami, and he can meddle like Mr Champion of Interference. Abla is sitting back and watching it all happen without making much comment. It's as if she is an observer and none of this has anything to do with her. She says that she has been in this position so many times before that she doesn't believe there is any likelihood of anything significant taking place. She just keeps sewing.

Meanwhile, Abla has had her exams, and as expected, all her hard work and preparations seem to have counted for little. She says she's confident she did well, but the first job went to a man. The results of the second have not yet been announced, but there were ninety-six people taking the exam for one lone job, so her chances of success are slim. Abla has voiced her determination for change to several people. I have to admit that their encouraging responses and words of support have surprised me. I had thought other women would be telling her to back off, but there appears to be general agreement that she has been cooped up for too long. They are all cheering her on as she explores the possibilities for change.

Everyone loves Abla. I have never heard a word spoken against her. Even Ruth, in a better position than I am to pick up gossip, says that she has never in all her years here, heard anything remotely derogatory about Neriman. In fact, it is the general consensus that the family who wins her for their son will be hitting the jackpot. A forty camel girl! All this from a society where it is possible to be denounced for the slightest failing. This is high praise indeed and richly deserved.

Fatma, however, is the one with a new job. Her uncle is the manager of a bank in Istanbul, and this connection secured her a position in their Kavaklı branch. Unlike Abla, Fatma didn't want the job and does nothing but complain about it. She has been a greatly indulged only child, allowed to do pretty much as she has wished; but she is no longer in school and needs something worthwhile to do with her days. She took up the highly prized job at her parents' insistence, but it has come as a rude awakening, and she is not pleased. On the plus side, she has heard from the Canadians about her visa application and they want to interview her. Since there is no embassy in Turkey, it means travelling to Beirut or waiting until a representative comes to Istanbul. Although it will take longer, she is planning to wait for the representative.

I have not mentioned the infamous court case recently because there has been nothing much to report. In terms of stringing things out, I presume that this could be construed as good news. On his way back from Istanbul where Baba had been for the last session, he stopped in Bursa to see Hakan. He says everyone, but everyone, knows him there, and it is obvious that he is both liked and admired. Baba said he felt like a film star with all the special attention he received purely because he was Hakan's father. He also says that Hakan looks quite handsome in his new uniform. Now that he is a junior officer, he has a proper uniform of much better quality, one that actually fits. Baba thinks he should have his picture taken, but Hakan is completely against it, saying that once his stint in the army is over, he doesn't want anything to remind him of these two years. (I've never seen him in it as he always comes home in civilian clothes.)

Lately, I've been joining Abla for afternoon tea at Aylin Abla's house. Her family doesn't have dinner until late in the evening, and she says that she gets a second wind with some end-of-the-day refreshments and a natter with friends. We've gotten to be much better acquainted since I've been tagging along.

Aylin is a handsome woman with generous black hair and a robust figure. She is smart, gracious and warm, someone I like enormously and hold in high regard. She has the normal amount of education for a woman from a prosperous family - the equivalent of junior high school - but it is her abundant curiosity that sets her apart from most people.

Although not much concerned with the big topics of religion and politics, in almost every other respect, she is eager to learn and is a rare example of someone interested in the world beyond her own experiences. Many of her ideas are well ahead of those of other women in the community. She alone has asked me about my life in America and is open to the new, the different and the modern. Such attitudes are reflected in her home where she is eager to adopt the latest trends in everything from interior decorating to methods of cooking. Her house is immaculate perfection, full of practical ideas, many of them gleaned from western magazines and limited contact with foreigners. She is well known for her liberal but sensible ideas which people find acceptable because they recognize that she is an astute and discerning woman. Wise beyond her years, she is also delightful company. If I did not have a perfectly good Abla of my own, I would not hesitate to seek her advice on almost anything.

Having said all this, there was a little hiccup in the afternoon routine a few days ago when Ana suddenly became awkward about our visits. It's not clear what set her off, but she had been behaving strangely anyway. That morning, amidst the customary household tumult, I heard the sound of splashing water and ran into the salon to find that Levent and his mother were having a water fight. Yes - that's what I said - a water fight. The room was drenched and the floor was awash. The two of them stood there, dripping wet, glaring at each other like naughty children. Both refused to clean up the mess, so I did it. You wouldn't believe what it's like some days.

Anyhow, when it came to 4:00 pm, the usual time for us to head off, Ana said we couldn't go. She was only being petulant, but it meant having to stop and make sense of her objections. This in itself is an impossible task because, when she is in one of these moods, there is rarely any logic involved. I think she resents the fact that we go off without her and feels upset at not being included. In the end, we smoothed her over, promising a trip to her favourite *pastane* the next day. When we arrived at Aylin's later than normal, she wanted to know if everything was all right. Abla gave her a rundown of the situation, after which we continued with our tea and gossip.

The next morning, Aylin Abla was on our doorstep with an invitation (for Ana, Abla and me) to go to the cinema that afternoon. Ana was thrilled to be asked and immediately accepted. It was then that I began to appreciate just how perceptive and considerate Aylin Abla is. She had been sensitive to the feelings of hurt and jealousy and was out to make amends. One in a million, she had judged the situation perfectly. As far as the Turkish film was concerned, for the first time ever, I understood every word. I guess my Turkish has come on enough to adapt to different forms of expression, and I'm gratified that my second language is clicking into place. Ana had a marvellous afternoon. She sobbed her way through a heart-wrenching drama of love found, love lost and love restored, doubtless the film maker's ideal viewer. Aylin Abla's gesture was a stroke of genius, and once again, peace reigns.

Back in the real world, all that I have read about the Mai Lai massacre sickens me. Is it true that Lieutenant Calley is regarded by some as a kind of hero? If so, what have we become? If he's being treated as a scapegoat, some serious questions need to be asked. Whatever his role, he didn't commit this atrocity alone.

A sorry note on which to end.

19 April 1971

Postal miracles. The rejected packet of chocolate chips has been returned to you! With only a few left in the bag, it seems as if all the postmen along the way have helped themselves. Confirmation, if it were needed, that everyone is partial to a bit of chocolate. That it has turned up at all is beyond my wildest expectations.

Now that our days in Turkey are numbered, I find them dragging along. Things that had novelty value are no longer new, and without work, I find boredom to be my chief enemy. Until a couple of months ago, I never had this problem, but now I confess to a restlessness that won't go away. I had thought that the lambs might prove to be diverting, but I have long since lost all interest in them. They look sweet and appealing but are as stupid as the grass they eat. They don't even know their names. Abla and I were congratulating ourselves that they obviously identified us as their owners, thinking that because they followed us around, we must be important to them. We quickly learned that they follow anything that moves. What a blow to the ego.

Abla is coming in for a lot of attention these days. The women who visited last week keep popping up unannounced, trying to catch us unawares to see what we are like without advance warning. So far, Abla seems to have passed inspection as they have said that they will call one evening when the son can come from Istanbul. We have heard that they are making numerous enquiries around town. I don't know how Abla stands all the scrutiny. I think her nerves are somewhat jingly at present, but she does remarkably well. When anyone comes to call, she simply remains herself, which is the best way to be. Her attitude is that it they must accept her as she is. If they like her, fine; if not, nothing is lost. Good for her!

All of this makes for riveting viewing and endless speculation. I hope something truly good comes of it. It would be such a relief to leave for England with Abla settled in a life satisfying to her. I still think this is a heck of a way to find a mate, but it works for them and is unlikely to change in the near future. Abla - and everyone else - says it's *kısmet*, fate. Along with many other concepts that strike me as lunacy, this one comes from Arabia and is typically said with a knowing shrug.

I can't bear it that people should be so resigned to life's events - that they don't feel they should, or could, do anything to improve their lot. It's as if they deserve whatever they get and are helpless in the face of the gods. Nonsense. I think the gods expect us to help ourselves; that's why we have brains. After we've done what we can, perhaps then we have earned the right to sit back and blame the fates. But we can't cave in at the first sign of trouble, excusing further effort with an indifferent shrug. Hakan and I have endless arguments over this. He defends *kısmet*, saying that we don't have any control over what happens to us; but I think he, almost more than anyone else I know, proves the exact opposite.

And speaking of PTB, he's coming on Wednesday with a five-day pass over the national *bayram* on 23 April. It will be good to have him home after a dry spell that has gone on for far too long. I'm hoping the weather will finally settle into something resembling spring so that we can be outside while he is here.

Have you heard anything from Bill? With the Mai Lai massacre in the headlines, everything else about Vietnam has been wiped from the news.

We celebrated Baba's birthday with cake and presents on Friday. He sends his thanks for your many cards.

27 April 1971

In typical Hakan fashion, god's gift to the spontaneous arrived, not as expected on the Wednesday before *bayram*, but on the Monday evening. He spent almost a week here, returning to Bursa on Sunday. He will be back again on Friday for the 1 May holiday. It's during his next leave that I want to make the trip to Izmir.

We aren't doing much in the way of work for Ken these days, relations being what they are and everything so uncertain. Hakan is using this period of relative calm to develop new ideas and make up samples in the workshop. In the meantime, Baba has started a little handbag business using leftover scraps of leather and suede to produce groovy fashion bags. They have caught on with the local students, and he is doing well with them. Little successes like these provide a much-needed boost when yet another court case has reared its ugly head.

Sami incurred substantial debts several years ago, debts for which Baba had, unthinkingly, agreed to act as guarantor. In those days, Baba signed whatever his son put in front of him. Sami has never finished paying off the debts, while maintaining that he has, and is refusing to have anything more to do with the matter. And so, the court has come to Baba. Of course, he is extremely worried. Who wouldn't be? Sami keeps saying there is nothing to worry about, but Baba is not a fool; he is afraid that since he cannot win, he will have to either come up with the money (unlikely) or prolong the case for as long as possible. Knowing how the courts here operate, the latter shouldn't be hard to manage. It's a nasty business not only because of the implications for the family, but also because of all the hard feelings created within it.

After all is said and done, Baba is not without assets. He owns two houses and has a valuable piece of land in the centre of town. I can appreciate his reluctance to dispose of his last remaining possessions, but when the word "money" comes up, everyone looks expectantly at Hakan. I don't know where they get the idea that he could possibly have any money, not having worked for nearly two years. We're already footing the legal bill for the case in Istanbul at the expense of our own wedding. But the trouble is, he's forked out for this and paid out for that until our savings are gone, but no one believes it.

I don't begrudge the Beylers a thing, but they have to realize that soon we shall be setting up a home of our own. Right now, apart from the frilly underwear in my dowry, we have nothing in the way of assets between us. (That's what Hakan gets for marrying a girl with no dowry!) When we have money, we'll do what we can to help them, but I feel no obligation to take over Sami's debts.

And speaking of Mr Turmoil, his creative fictions have reached ever new and astounding heights. When Baba saw him in Istanbul last week, the Number One Son had two black eyes and a variety of cuts and scratches on his face. He said that students from the Kavaklı hostel (at the University of Istanbul) attacked him because his brother Hakan is a Dirty Capitalist married to an American. And so forth. And so on. Ho hum. I don't believe a word of it. I think it's more likely that he got drunk and fell downstairs, or even that he was beaten up over a gambling debt. He clearly made up the incident to save face. This was a particularly good story because it enabled him to blame Hakan, yet again. Sami has long maintained that Hakan is the true cause of all the misfortune and hardship he has ever had in his life. For better or worse, everyone looks to Hakan.

Sometimes I don't know how he puts up with it all. Being in the army is difficult enough, but then he comes home to a family which expects him to solve all their problems, and a fiancée who struggles with the most basic aspects of his culture. The fact that he deals so calmly with everything is a source of constant amazement to me, but Hakan appears to have a vast reservoir of patience and understanding for us all.

Throughout the entire time that we have been here, he has never once criticized me for the way I've done things. He's never even so much as suggested that I might do something differently. From the day of our arrival, he has allowed me to find my own path and has given me the leeway to make my own mistakes. It surely hasn't worked out in every case as he might have liked, but I have never heard about it from him. When there have been family disagreements, he has sided with me on every occasion. This has given me incredible "face" in his culture. Without his backing, my position here would have been untenable, and I almost certainly would not have stayed. But that gets us into territory I don't even want to think about.

Today is a big day for Levent. He is taking entrance exams for the local teachers college. This year he finishes junior high school, and he needs to think about what comes next. There seems to be a general consensus that he is not clever enough for the local *lise*, high school, as it is academically quite demanding. After much discussion, he thought he would like to try to become an elementary school teacher. If he passes the exam, he could start the four-year course in the fall. (Higher qualifications and university degrees are required only for teaching junior high and above.) The education is free, and since money is a factor, this is a reasonable option for him. We are all hopeful.

You will not be shocked to hear that there have been no further developments on the marriage front. We have heard no more since the last flurry of interest. No wonder Abla is blasé on the subject. It must be without precedence in this society that so many tentative approaches have been made with so little result. Since we assume that there is no fault with Abla, we must conclude that other members of the family are a cause for concern, either because it is now believed that they don't want to see her married, or because some aspect of the family is putting people off. (Maybe it's me!) There are so many possibilities. In a matter as delicate as this, it is easy to find pitfalls without even trying.

Finally, some news from Bill. It's a relief to hear that he is back at base in Quang Tri. That sounds safe to me - well - safer than the alternative. Since he wanted the extension to stay on in Vietnam until end of September, I'm glad he got it. As he says, the extra time there is worth it (to him) to get out of the army altogether five months earlier. And he will have R&R in Australia to break things up. Still, I'm sure the remaining 179 days will drag.

I know the feeling.

Chapter 20

7 May 1971

We've been incredibly busy lately. Hakan arrived home last Friday and had nearly a week's leave. Despite the holiday, we had a quiet weekend here and then drove to Izmir on Monday, so we could get to the consulate early Tuesday morning.

Without a hitch, we were able to get my passport renewed and to obtain the documentation we needed for the wedding license. I like to think that all my prior correspondence and preparations for the trip paid off. I'm so used to things being delayed or going wrong, I had to keep checking and re-checking my papers to make sure that I really did have everything, that it really was all in order. Of course, we're not done yet. There are still the Kavaklı officials to deal with. Since we had had no way of determining how long everything might take, we hadn't planned anything else and found ourselves with a free half day. The weather was perfect, and we decided to hire a *fayton*, a horse-drawn carriage, to take us along the shoreline and tour the more scenic sections of the old city. After a brief stop in the bazaar, we headed back home via an overnight stop in a little seaside town beyond Izmir. It took us the best part of Wednesday to get back to Kavaklı (the roads are mostly appalling), and yesterday, Hakan returned to Bursa.

I said that it had been a quiet weekend. What I meant was that we didn't do much in the way of celebrating the *bayram*, immersed as we were in wedding plans. We collected Hakan's wedding outfit from tailor Ahmet and it looks very smart, as will he!

Saturday afternoon, we discussed wedding venues. The already agreed six hundred people will be invited, but as many live far away, we expect only (?) four hundred to turn up. Baba had been to Çınarcı, a nice restaurant with facilities big enough for a reception, located on a hill overlooking the town. The proprietor would be more than happy to have us, for a price, naturally. The Yıldız Oteli and the Kule Kulübü are generally regarded as the top spots for these events, but I'm positive we can't afford them.

We were concluding that Çınarcı looked like the best bet, when Hüseyin Dayı dropped in for a visit. He works as a chef at Kaplan Yem Fabrikası, the local animal feed plant. Does that sound a little weird? Unlikely as it may seem, this is the location of one of the best restaurants in the area. Although technically only for the plant's employees, their families and guests, it's open to almost anyone who cares to visit. Despite all superficial indications, it's a busy and popular place.

Dayı had come along with a proposal. He wanted us to have our wedding reception at Kaplan Yem Fabrikası where he would prepare a feast for close family and friends. He felt he could do us a grand meal, including a whole spit-roasted lamb, for about forty people - and keep us in budget. Food for thought (no pun intended). We could still invite everyone who needed to be invited to the civil ceremony at the town hall salon (it holds 250, but that's not my problem), but keep things more intimate for the celebration afterwards. I didn't need to be persuaded. Everything about the idea appealed to me, and I know it appealed to Hakan; however, in order to allow everyone to have their say, we thanked Dayı for his wonderful offer and told him that we would let him know ASAP. While we're deciding, he said he'd check on the dates as he was unsure what events might already be booked.

I think the family likes the idea. We discussed it at length after Dayı left. Since money is a factor, we have to be realistic. Whatever venue we might pick to entertain the four hundred guests, we'd only be able to offer a soft drink and a slice of cake as hiring a band and other attendant expenses would quickly eat into most of the funds. With Dayı's plan, we can invite everyone to the ceremony at the town hall, give them all wedding favours as they leave and then have an informal family affair afterwards. Honour would be satisfied on all counts, we could stay comfortably within our budget, and we would spend our time with the people who mean the most to us. No final decision has been made, but I think this is where we're headed.

As far as the honeymoon goes, there won't be any prizes for guessing that it will be at Çelik Palas Oteli. We won't be able to afford more than a couple of nights, but it is still our idea of paradise, and even though Hakan would love to get away from Bursa altogether, the hotel is in another world compared to his army base.

We've had some good news from Ken. He says the business is going well, and he seems upbeat about everything. This is most unusual for him, the only optimistic letter we've ever received from London. I told Hakan this would be the perfect opportunity to ask him for a loan from the business as we could do with a little cushion. I think our present finances are well allocated for our remaining months and wedding expenses, but we have not yet begun to think about the money we shall need to get back to England. Still, one step at a time.

As I become increasingly aware that the end of my stay is in sight, I have resurrected my earlier campaign to bolster Ana, but now I'm including Levent as well. Their constant squabbling wears me out, and I have decided that the atmosphere here could do with a change. I let Levent's English lessons slide when he started back to school, but I'm renewing that effort as these are a place where we can agreeably meet.

Now that he and I are already on better terms, he has magically produced a stack of Hayat magazines that he had apparently been hiding from me. Hayat means "life" in Turkish, and the magazine is the Turkish equivalent of our LIFE magazine in that it is largely a photo news weekly. It has lots of useful illustrations and pictures for the albums I'm making, not to mention all the society gossip and news. Abla and I love to read them together, picking over the clothes and pretensions of the rich and famous. We're particularly fond of ex-PM Süleyman Demirel's wife, Nazmiye, but since he is no longer in high office, her position too, is less exalted. We miss her.

Anyway, getting back to the subject, Ana is both harder and easier to deal with than Levent. She responds immediately to any sort of praise or approval, but there is little residual effect. She quickly forgets what's been done lately, and for me, it's a matter of remembering that she needs constant attention. This in itself is wearing, but the results are more worthwhile than allowing the ceaseless bickering and complaining to go on and on. I'm trying to do everything she asks of me because 80% of it is acceptable. Then, when I have genuine reasons not to do the other 20%, she won't have to feel that I'm in constant opposition to her.

Well, that's the theory. I'm trying to have the patience it requires. I don't want to look back and feel that I did less than I could. I'm marrying into this family, and if it is going to find me unacceptable, I don't want it to be because I haven't made my best effort. After that, whatever they conclude about me will be up to them. Although I can't be responsible for what anyone thinks, I'm aware that the nature of my relationship with my mother-in-law is almost entirely in my hands.

Poor Ruth... we met today for a picnic at the park just out of town. The weather wasn't very nice and it seemed to pull her down. We were talking about my return to England, and she burst into tears, saying how much she will miss me. I will miss her, too. In a different situation, we might never have been good friends, but here, we have supported each other through some dark days. I think separation is often harder on those left behind.

On the political front, the security situation has not improved since the new government took over. Süleyman Demirel, who is still in parliament, is feeling understandably smug because the new military-backed regime is experiencing more kidnappings, bombings, bank robberies and student unrest, than he ever did. I think part of the problem is that with so many universities and colleges closed, students have been left with nothing to do and now have all the time in the world to cause trouble, if that's their intent. The college that was closed here in town a few weeks ago, remains closed. It makes no sense to me. With the continuing and increasing violence, Hakan has assumed a new role in the army. For three days each week, he wears civilian clothes and strolls around Bursa, keeping his eyes and ears open for gossip about possible demonstrations and any potential threats.

Poor Turkish Undercover Agent!

17 May 1971

Family crisis! Did I hear you mutter, “Another one?” Hüseyin Dayı’s daughter, Zehra, has announced that she wants a divorce. This is as unthinkable as it is scandalous.

I don’t believe I’ve told you much about Zehra. She had only recently married before my arrival here and lives with her husband and his family in a house in town. She and Nihal, Dayı’s daughter-in-law, had their first babies within a month of each other. I’m not clear about the reasons for her unhappiness, but given the implications, they must be serious. Zehra asked her father to go and get her, but Dayı came first to Baba to discuss the situation. After that, Baba went to Mehmet, Zehra’s husband, and had a chat with him. Apparently he’s no more pleased with his wife than she is with him, but he doesn’t want to separate. Then Ana went to talk to Zehra, and when her mother, Rukiye Yenge, heard that Baba and Ana had been “interfering” in their family affairs, she spontaneously combusted.

I’ve never known quite what to make of Rukiye Yenge. She’s had little enough to say when I’ve been around, but I have had the feeling that this was due more to moodiness than timidity. She always looks as if she has a bad smell under her nose. I’m under the impression that she resents our family, though I’m not sure why. It was Baba who brought them all over from Bulgaria and has done his best to help them over the years, but she seems embittered by life. She gave Dayı a dreadful tongue-lashing in front of us all; in fact, she nearly hit him in the course of her wild accusations and assignment of blame. In the end, peace was restored only with difficulty, everyone made up, and Zehra has agreed to stay with Mehmet, though she has returned to her parents for two days “to settle her nerves”. You can’t say things are ever monotonous around here.

Saturday, we attended *sünnet*, circumcision, festivities. Although I have been here many months and these events, like weddings, go on constantly, this was the first I had witnessed. When Hakan is home on the weekends, he refuses to go to any of these functions, so in some respects, I’m still getting acquainted with the rites of passage.

Most boys here have a *sünnet* between seven and eleven years of age. It reminds me a little of the Jewish custom of Bar Mitzvah as the event marks a sort of official entry to manhood. The rituals usually start in the afternoon with the boy, dressed in a special suit and cape, feted at home with a little folk band and dancing before being driven around town. Today, there are processions with cars, horns blaring; but in times not too far in the past, horse-drawn carriages made up the parade, the band accompanying the revellers. The processing finishes at a venue where the invited guests have assembled for a banquet and entertainment, much like a wedding. Similarly, the degree of grandeur is reflected in the amount spent, the spectrum running from humble to sumptuous. Most people go down a middle road.

Sometime after the meal, the *sünnetçi*, the man who performs the circumcision, arrives to do the deed. I'm not sure just how aware most boys are about what happens next. Prior to the day, there will have been a lot of teasing and joking, and the boy would have been told that he will have a red ribbon tied around his penis. I suspect that the older the boy, the more he understands, but ignorance is doubtless the best option under the circumstances. The procedure is performed in a side room with the male members of the family in attendance (to hold the boy down - no anaesthetic), but it's all over in a jiffy after which the boy returns, triumphant, to the assembly. At this point, he will have exchanged his finery for a white nightgown and hat, and is enthroned in a fancy bed decorated for the purpose. Then the entertainment begins as a way of taking the boy's mind off his pain. While all of this is going on, the guests come, one-by-one, to congratulate the boy and give him presents. Gold coins feature prominently.

PTB had two circumcisions. The first he had together with Sami when he was only two years old. He says the job wasn't done properly the first time, so he had another when he was nine. Since he couldn't remember the first occasion and rather liked the idea of having a round of presents to himself, I'm certain he would have pressed hard for this. I don't know what I think about it all. Any kind of surgical procedure without painkillers seems completely barbaric to me. I much prefer that if circumcision is going to be done, it's done in the hospital when the baby is born. However, when I have told the Turks that this is how we do it in America, they look at me as if they don't believe that anyone other than Muslims are circumcised, that assuming I'm telling the truth, our way sounds extremely dull. They are surely right on the latter point.

My being here has been a mixed blessing, if blessing at all, for Abla. It's rather like sending poor children to summer camp to show them what they've been missing, then returning them to deprivation. My stay has offered glimpses of other worlds and other possibilities without providing any realistic means of attaining them. That she has become dissatisfied with her life is not in question. I'm not sure how much my presence accounts for it. I'm guessing that the discontent had been bubbling away under the surface and that my arrival simply sparked a measure of awareness. She has struck several blows for more freedom, which is good, but she remains frustrated in any major attempt to gain a life of her own. Every job opportunity evaporates as soon as it turns up.

Part of the problem is that the road to independence requires that she fight her corner and be able to stand up for herself. Abla has been brought up to be compliant and respectful of every one else's wishes, particularly those of her parents. For instance, when she went to enrol in her typing course, Abla was turned away because the instructor told her she was too late. So she left and came home, feeling dejected and discouraged. When I asked her what had happened, she said that even though there were still places in the class, the teacher wouldn't talk to her. She shrugged her shoulders and said it was *kısmet*; it wasn't meant to be.

Saying this was like the bank telling me I couldn't have my own money, and I launched into a lecture, saying that if she wanted something badly enough, she would have to learn to be more assertive. And so forth, and so on, for about ten minutes. Later that day, when we visited Aylin Abla, she too, wanted to find out about the enrolment. Following Abla's by now contrite explanation, her friend proceeded to give her a similar lecture. We must have fired her up as the next morning she went off again, this time getting herself enrolled. That little victory made her day. So much for *kısmet!*

When I first arrived, Hakan made it plain to his mother that she was not, in the manner of most Turkish mothers-in-law, to tell me what to do. For the most part, she has restrained herself. She gets angry with me when I read or when I go off to visit Ruth, but knowing I have the support of both Baba and Hakan, I merely ignore her on these subjects and go about my business. Abla has obviously picked up on this and has begun to disregard her mother in some matters. This has made Ana furious, and naturally, I get the blame. That bit is okay. I can understand it, and I can handle it, but in terms of getting Abla to a more satisfying place in life, I'm not clear how productive all this is. I suppose it's baby steps, a few at a time. Years of tradition are not overturned without some pain being involved. Ana becomes hysterical at the mere mention of anything that might take Abla away from the house. Considering that she is opposed to something as culturally obligatory as marriage, it follows that she is never going to accept anything as groundbreaking as employment in a public place.

The concept of an "independent woman" is still too alien for most Turks, men and women alike. Complete freedom would be too hard for both Abla and her family. Where all this will end, I have no idea, but I would dearly love to have everything resolved before we leave. Once we've gone, I'm afraid any progressive steps she's taken will be lost. I suspect she'll revert to the "anything for the sake of peace" mentality and, without backup and support, will be inclined just to give in. I cannot adequately describe the stifling cultural conventions under which most Turkish women and girls live. And how weary I am of them.

We're off to Izmir bright and early tomorrow for Baba's court case. We are supposed to be meeting Sami there. Baba is more distressed about this case than the other one because the possible consequences could be more immediate. Although he has made this trip before on his own, he specifically asked me if I would get permission from Hakan to go with him. At first, I thought he wanted me to ask Hakan to go, but it turns out that he wanted me to go and was making sure Hakan wouldn't mind. I ask you. As if I would not do such a thing for Baba. As if I would need to ask Hakan. Without hesitation, I assured him that it would be fine, but said that I would mention it to Hakan. Might as well play the game if that's all it takes. We are taking Abla with us. She can use a break from sewing and chores, and we'll spend two nights in Ayvalık, sort of on the way home. It's a well known Aegean seaside resort (Hakan and I stopped there on our way back from our Ephesus trip) with a rare sandy beach. We are all hoping the weather will perk up.

Industrial action has gone international these days. You've had a lengthy dock strike, and now I see where US teachers are taking action also. England has had a postal strike, and things are simmering here. Since the recent government took over, general discontent is filtering down from the Maoists to the workers. Labour unrest is not new, but it has been gaining strength in recent weeks. Although I wouldn't mind if it affected things like court cases (ha!), I'm increasingly aware that it could have a definite impact on events like our wedding.

I'm so glad that you think I've done the right thing in coming here and spending nearly two years familiarizing myself with my future husband's country and background. I'm positive that the experience will enhance and cement our relationship. And, yes, we also want a get-together with you in London as quickly as we can fix some dates. When I mentioned this to Hakan, he said, "The sooner, the better."

24 May 1971

I believe I last left you as we were on the verge of heading off to Izmir for the court case. That evening, Sami rang to say that he would not be attending... something about having too much work to do, which is utter drivel. I think he was afraid that he would be arrested, doubtless with some justification. Sami's failure to appear in court had both good and bad repercussions. It was good for Baba because it meant that the proceedings were delayed, but the judge was furious and said that if Sami doesn't turn up for the next hearing on 15 June, he will have him arrested. If he wasn't in trouble with the law before, he surely is now.

I think the judge wants assurances that the Beylers are taking the case seriously and are attempting to pay off the debts. Hakan has talked with his father and has suggested that he scrape together whatever he can and offer it directly to those who are owed, as a settlement on all the debts. Maybe they will be happy to take something as opposed to fighting a lengthy legal case which might produce nothing but expenses. Baba is considering this as a way out. There is no point relying on Sami for any help in the resolution of this nightmare.

Although we were planning to spend the night at Ayvalık, Baba wanted to stop on the way to see a relative who lives in Bornova, a suburb of Izmir. İsmail Bey is head of the Beyler clan and as such, should give his consent for our forthcoming marriage. I did not know this at the time.

When we turned up at an unexpectedly modern residence in what was obviously a wealthy neighbourhood, a vivacious young Scottish woman greeted us at the door. I'm not sure which of us was more startled. She knew nothing about me, and we knew nothing about her. She introduced herself as Kate, ushered us to seats and went off to find the head of the house. While she was gone, I studied a home so fashionable it would not have been out of place in California. A clever combination of traditional and contemporary designs, it was built around a courtyard, simply planned, everything trim and clutter-free. On reflection, the up-to-the-minute style probably owed more to the owner's years in Sweden than to any American inspiration for it was all sliding glass doors, light woods and native stone walls. The main room of the house was open plan with areas for sitting and dining defined by their spare blonde furnishings. Only a long counter separated the very western kitchen from the other sections. It was beautiful and functional.

Eventually Kate returned with İsmail Bey, all anyone would expect in the head of a clan... well... the twentieth-century version. Handsome in the way of a distinguished older gentleman, he was tall and well built with thick salt-and-pepper hair, a ready smile and dark eyes that knew how to get to the heart of a matter. Immaculately dressed in expensive casual clothing, he exuded confidence and radiated a vigorous sense of self. The only thing that surprised me about him was the lack of a moustache. It is rare to encounter a clean-shaven man in this part of the world, but I suspect that his years in Europe had had their influence. We all - everyone of us - kissed his hand. He was warm and welcoming and made us feel that there was no one with whom he'd rather be sitting at that very moment.

As the men chatted through the preliminaries and courtesies of the visit, I discovered that İsmail Bey owns a big ceramic tile business, established in the five years since his return from Sweden. He had had a similarly successful business there, but after many years abroad, Turkey called him home again. Interesting as all this was, I only wanted to find out about Kate but could not converse across the room to her without being rude. After a few moments, Kate, struggling in Turkish, asked us if we would like *çay*. We agreed that this would be very nice, and she said she'd do her best but making Turkish tea was not something of which she'd had much experience (this latter part was in English to me, and I translated). It seemed that the lady of the house and its other members were all out but expected home soon.

When I went to the kitchen to see what I could do to help, Kate and I had our chance to chat. She is married to one of İsmail Bey's two sons and her husband is in the army in Ankara. They met when they were both studying at university in Germany, and though she has been here just a few weeks, it seems they are already planning to make their future in Turkey. Apart from the fact that her husband is in Ankara, she says she is happy with her situation here. Of course, she is extraordinarily lucky to have married into so westernized a family.

When we were in the kitchen, Baba seized his opportunity to discuss our marriage. Under the circumstances, İsmail Bey could hardly refuse his blessing, but when we returned with the tea, he was gracious in his remarks and complimented me on my Turkish. In conclusion, he said that it was high time the Beyler family had some new blood. Official business concluded, we all sat back and relaxed over our refreshments. But with some miles to drive before dark, we had to excuse ourselves and leave before the other family members returned. Baba declared the visit a great success.

Anxious about the car's electrical system in general and the lights in particular, we made haste to Ayvalık where we found a little *pansiyon* for the night. The next morning dawned sunny and bright, as if to order. We had brought bathing suits, and though it wasn't quite warm enough to swim (not for me), we relaxed on the sandy beach and whiled away the day. I managed to overdo it and paid the price at the end of the afternoon, but it's been so long since I have had the chance to sunbathe, I got carried away. Abla and Baba had had the wisdom to find some shade and spared themselves the indignities of the lobster look. We stayed on another night and came home after breakfast the following morning. I think the little break did us all good, and Baba's morale had improved considerably by the time we got back.

The only reservations I had had about the trip to Izmir concerned Dagmar. She's been having a lot of trouble lately, and I hated to take her on a long trip before I had a chance to organize repairs. These couldn't be arranged ahead of the drive, and the day after we got back was the 19 May holiday. However, I got to Cengiz Bey's garage early the following morning and threw myself on his mercy, cataloguing as I did a rather long list of problems.

Cengiz Bey brought in an electrician to repair those faults, while he tried to figure out why the car was temperamental about starting. Meanwhile, he fixed the pedal so that the gas now feeds evenly. He repaired the transmission so that both the clutch and gear box work like new; he adjusted the brakes, cleaned the engine and even managed to get the horn working again (sort of). The two men worked for seven hours - yes, a straight seven hours - and charged me a grand total of 50TL. They said they knew my husband was a soldier, and they were happy to give me a special rate. I was overwhelmed. I could never have imagined that it would cost so little, and I'm eternally grateful.

At the same time, Cengiz Bey warned me that I'm going to have to be careful and should not drive over 50 mph maximum. Given the nature of most of the roads, this won't be difficult. He also said that the motor is getting old and is starting to burn a lot of gas and oil (true, true). He wants us to bring her to him for regular checkups (sounds like a doctor), and then he will go over her completely before we make the return trip to England. He said after that, we should get rid of her. To my ears, this sounded more than a little heartless, but then, he cannot possibly know what Dagmar and I have been through together. Despite the social conventions and the fact that Cengiz Bey is a man, he has been a true friend to me.

Sami wants Levent to spend the summer holidays with him. Levent is dying to go, but I hear that Baba will not permit it. It's not hard to understand why.

Chapter 21

2 June 1971

It's good to hear that the May birthdays have been successfully celebrated. Levent sends his thanks for your cards, and we know Dad also has had a big day. Congratulations to him on his promotion at Titan! Neither of you are overly thrilled about the extra travelling he will be doing, but the work sounds as if it could be satisfying.

There is some sad news here: Nina is very sick. We got word of this on Tuesday, by way of Teyze's neighbour who informed us that Nina had moved back home. (You may recall that she had been living next door.) Ana wasn't around when we heard, and Abla and I weren't sure what to do as we hadn't been told how serious it was. We went first to Baba at his office to tell him what had happened and to get his permission to visit.

Although I have almost no experience in these matters, it seemed clear to me that Nina was very poorly. Her bony hands, speckled with age, rested peacefully on the bedding, but her breathing was quite shallow, and she couldn't even take water. I really didn't think she had long to live. We returned home to wait for Ana who had been out to a *mevlüt.* Naturally, she became very upset on hearing the news, but even then, we had to persuade her of the need to visit. Finally, the fear of not seeing her mother before she died overcame her reluctance to enter Teyze's house. In the event, the two women never exchanged so much as a glance, let alone a word during the hour that Ana sat with her mother.

Meanwhile, the house filled with visitors as Muslims take seriously their religious duty to visit the sick and pray for them. While Teyze's daughter, Şevkiye, was kept busy making *çay*, a *Hafiz* sat in the corner quietly chanting the Koran. As we left, we gave Teyze Aylin Abla's telephone number so that she could ring us if anything changed. Abla and Ana are quite emotional, and everyone is feeling low.

What surprised me in all this was that no one thought a doctor should be summoned. There appears to be a kind of general acceptance that anyone of such advanced age (and no one, including Nina, knows exactly how old she is), in such fragile condition, ought to be allowed to slip away. If her time has come, then it is the will of Allah, and none of us mere mortals need intervene. I guess there is something to this, but I was still uneasy about the lack of medical advice.

Yesterday morning, Abla and I went back to Teyze's, and Nina was doing better. She recognized us and spoke a little. She drank some lemonade and her colour was much improved. But she is very weak, and I do not see how she can make anything like a full recovery. Of course, she could go on in this way for weeks or months. The situation is hard on everyone, and I feel genuine sympathy for the sisters who are on the verge of losing their mother.

I'm so sorry that we have kept you in the dark over the final plans for the wedding. Although we already had agreed in principle that we would have the small family reception at Kaplan Yem Fabrikası, we have been waiting for Dayı to confirm the date for us. After much cogitating, we have had to settle on 3 August, rather than 5 August, as previously planned. Due to standing commitments on Thursdays, the restaurant cannot give us the space we need for our party, so we have had to change the wedding day. You may take this as the most concrete confirmation you are ever likely to get and, on that basis, go ahead with your order for announcements. We too, have needed to get to grips with a date so that we can book the hall and order invitations. As we want a Tuesday, I don't think there will be any trouble about availability. In fact, my only real concern is Hakan's final release date from the army, but that is in the lap of the gods. We'll just have to close our eyes and cross our fingers.

Abla has received the most amazing present, one that has given my skin a distinct green tinge. A neighbour woman for whom Abla has done a lot of sewing has given her a beautiful Ottoman lady's caftan. It's a traditional *bindallı* made of penetrating dark blue satin, embroidered with heavy gold thread. It's one of the finest I have seen. I have been looking everywhere for one in reasonable condition, one that I could afford. They're not easy to find, but I believe this one came from the woman's own dowry, and Abla is greatly honoured to be the recipient of such a special gift. I think I'm more excited about it than she is. Maybe she would rather have had the money, but I think she's on the winning end of splendid good fortune, acquiring as she has, an exquisite antique gown in return for making two summer dresses.

While out running some errands today, I dropped by to see Ruth. If I call in on her unannounced, I try to do so in the morning when there will be no visitors. I can generally find her in the kitchen with her servant, Huri, cooking up a banquet for their household and its interminable guests. The two women work together like good companions, rather than mistress and servant. Huri treats us both like naughty children she needs to keep in line. She despairs of our American informality and insistence on drinking coffee at the kitchen table. She's extremely warm-hearted and makes us laugh as she tuts over our lack of regard for what she considers to be important social conventions. For our part, we enjoy the easy atmosphere after being hemmed in by the formality of stiff sitting rooms and the rigid rituals that accompany the most innocent glass of *çay*.

In Turkey, there is a custom for everything. Because the culture is so old, there has been time for strict guidelines to develop around almost every facet of daily life. For instance, take knitting: I can think of at least three customs around this somewhat ordinary pastime:

1 - If I'm visiting, I can knit

2 - If I have visitors, I can't knit

3 - If there is a baby in the house, no one can knit.

When it comes to dealing with guests, there is endless etiquette; consequently, every guest is treated in exactly the same manner and knows precisely what to expect and how to behave. The language and order of greetings, the terms of respect, whose hand is kissed - all of these are of vital importance - and people are easily offended if the protocol is not observed. Etiquette is a minefield for outsiders. Although the system leaves nothing to the imagination, there is comfortable security in familiar routines. At the monthly *gün*, it is the custom to serve a glass of tea with a plate of pastries, both sweet and savoury. Guests must always have at least two glasses of *çay*. They must never eat all the pastries. Each circumstance requires the correct comment and an equally correct response. No deviations, thank you.

I finally remembered to borrow Ruth's English Koran. Although I have my own copy, hers is a different translation, and I wanted to compare the two to see if I can get to the bottom of some of the things that I'm constantly being told are part of Islam. It can be very hard to separate the religious from the cultural, and I would like to read something authoritative, rather than simply take the word of people who can't actually understand the very language they are "reading".

While we're on the subject of religion, I have to say that I have been taken aback by its fundamental role in daily life here. In the West, religion is for Sunday and, outside of churches, doesn't get much mention. Here, it is an integral part of everyday language, which is full of Koranic phrases such as "God (Allah) willing." "God's blessing be upon it." "God go with you." "Thanks be to God." Here's another for you: *Bismillahirrahmanirrahim*. (I can't tell you how long it took me to learn this one.) This is translated as "In the name of God, the Compassionate One, the Merciful." Of the 114 Suras, chapters, of the Koran, 113 of them start with this phrase. It has subsequently crept into common usage by devout Muslims as a sort of invocation at the beginning of any activity, whether it is getting out of bed in the morning, opening a prayer or starting a journey. As well as in language, the duties of Islam - the Five Pillars - are reflected in daily life:

1 - SHAHADAH is believing and saying the affirmation of faith, "There is no God but Allah, and Mohammed is his Prophet."

2 - SALAH is praying five times a day. There are set prayers which Muslims should say, and set times at which they should perform them. They face towards the Holy City of Mecca and use a designated rug or mat for this purpose. In addition to ritual washing beforehand, Muslims incorporate an almost gymnastic set of movements into their prayers, including kneeling with the forehead placed on the ground as an act of humility before Allah.

3 - ZAKAH is the giving of alms. Muslims are supposed to give a fixed proportion of their wealth to the poor.

4 - SAWM is fasting. This means refraining from food and drink in daylight hours during the Holy Month of Ramadan.

5 - HAJ is making the pilgrimage to Mecca, at least once in life, if financially able to do so.

The level of devotion runs the gamut from the left-leaning intellectuals who have no interest in religion in any form; to the middle classes who accept it as a part of the life and culture; to the dedicated practitioners, often older people who have made The Haj; to the most extreme fundamentalists who are as much in the minority as the intellectuals. As in most societies, the majority are moderates. If asked to classify them, this is where I would place the Beyler family. Like me, Hakan has trouble with organized religion, seeing it as the cause of more problems than ever it has solved. However, his roots are deep in the religion, and he respects the practices even if he doesn't observe most of them.

This brings us to the thorny matter of conversion. Everyone here has always called me by my Turkish name, Zeynep. I have been fine with this. It has enabled us all to pretend that I'm more Turkish than any scrutiny of the evidence would support, but perhaps that has not been a bad thing... a small comfort where needed. What I had not counted on is that the family thinks this indicates that I will convert to Islam before Hakan and I marry. In spite of the fact that I have tried to tell them that I have no such intention, the Beylers seem to be hoping against hope. Maybe I should not have shown such interest in their religion, nor allowed them to give me a new name; but I feel that the expectation is there, and I'm unsure how to explain, without offending, that this is not going to happen. Hakan and I are going to have to put our heads together over this one.

I know Bill had been hoping to get to Australia for his R&R in June, but apparently there has been some foul up, and he's going in July now. You probably heard. I see that Peter is home from college and has already started his summer job. He must need the money. If they were that anxious to get him back, they must have liked his work last year. You said he is interested in studying law. I suspect that he likes the idea of courtroom dramatics, rather than the piles of paper that I think are the reality for most in the legal profession. That was an aspect of the work that Hakan didn't like… that and the prospect of spending most of his time with criminals.

The Edirne trip is coming up yet again and once more Hakan is going to tie that in with some army business. We hope to leave on Monday and will be gone four or five days.

13 June 1971

As anticipated, we left for Edirne last Monday. What that actually meant was that I left here and stopped in Bursa to pick up Hakan, after which we continued to Edirne by way of Bandırma and the southern route around the Marmara. We've generally been so hard-pressed for time that we've never managed the slight detours needed to travel from the port at Çanakkale, north along the Dardanelles to Gelibolu (Gallipoli); or in the other direction, south towards the mouth of the Dardanelles to ancient Troy. Although we were on official army business, we felt we could take the couple of extra days needed for a quick glimpse of these famous places.

At Gelibolu, we visited the memorials now in place to commemorate the terrible battles that took place at the end of the First World War. It was here that the Allies attacked the weakened Ottoman army in an effort to wrest their territory, here that Atatürk became the military hero who saved Turkey for the Turks. The disastrous battle nearly ended the military career of Winston Churchill, but that's another story. It was a bloody struggle with heavy loss of life on both sides, but the Turks triumphed and were able to build on this turning point.

Like the Bosphorus, the Dardanelles (formerly known as The Hellespont) is a strait that separates Europe from Asia. It also separates the Aegean Sea from the Marmara Sea and, as such, has always been of strategic importance. Today, it is a scenic region with little indication of the historic struggles that have taken place over the centuries. Apart from being the major city in the area, Çanakkale itself doesn't have a great deal to recommend it. It is the primary place to get a ferry going to the European side of the strait and is the closest city to archaeological Troy. This is the legendary city as described in Homer's epic poem "The Iliad", dating from the ninth-century BC.

In the 1870s, the German archaeologist, Heinrich Schliemann excavated the area, uncovering what he claimed to be Homer's ancient metropolis. While this continues to be disputed, later excavations revealed that there had been many cities at this location, built layer upon layer. When we were there, the site was in abandoned disarray with little above ground to give any indication of past civilizations, let alone past glories. It doesn't look to me as if much has been done since Schliemann left, but with so many important archaeological sites, Turkey could not possibly fund work on them all.

From the European side, it's an easy drive to Edirne where we spent the night, ready to make an early start the next day. That Hakan was there on behalf of the army played a decisive role in facilitating our own business, and we were shortly on our way to Istanbul. When I think of all I went through on that first trip and the ease with which we accomplished things this time, it's like comparing an abacus to an adding machine. Let there be no doubt that I shall not miss these trips in any form.

There is something about Istanbul as a destination that always makes my heart beat faster; Hakan feels the same. The city is shabby and overcrowded, its streets shiny with grime, its traffic a motorist's nightmare; but it has nuggets of magic that will always entice us, and I shall never tire of visiting. My greatest fear is that because the Turks value their Old Things so little, the precious Ottoman houses and buildings will disappear in some misguided attempt to catch up with the modern world. And I'm not just talking about the grand old *konaks* and mansions. There are narrow cobblestone lanes still packed with traditional wooden houses, their intricate fretwork windows and latticed balconies deteriorating, the houses themselves falling apart with neglect. When they are no longer habitable, I'm sure they'll be pulled down and replaced with the ubiquitous concrete and stucco apartment blocks. It's already happening. It makes me wish I had the money to finance extensive restorations.

After checking into our usual little hotel, we headed for the Grand Bazaar to buy our wedding rings. With a whole street of nothing but fabulous gold shops, we didn't expect the purchase to take long, and indeed, it did not. I knew that I wanted a brushed gold band, wider than the standard wedding ring. I found exactly what I wanted, while Hakan chose a more traditional version in plain gold. After the obligatory haggling, we came in under budget and left with the rings secured in my handbag.

We had a few other items on our list but nothing that presented any problems. After that, we had the evening to indulge in what felt like the need to celebrate. For Hakan there was only one place to go, and we made our way to Paradise Gardens on the Bosphorus at Emirgan. With panoramic views over the waterway, it was the perfect place to spend an evening drinking *çay* and eating *simit*, while we finalized our thoughts on the wedding and talked about the return to England.

From Istanbul and the pleasures of the city, we headed back to Bursa the next day. I dropped Hakan off at the base and was home by mid-afternoon when I found your two fat envelopes full of news. I'm going to settle down with *çay* and catch up.

22 June 1971

Sadly, but perhaps unsurprisingly, we have lost Nina. She died peacefully in her sleep last Wednesday night; we had the news Thursday morning. After sending Levent with a message for Baba, the three of us left immediately for Teyze's. On a day filled with hard light and sticky heat, the house smelled faintly of rose water and too many people as, once again, friends and relatives rallied to support the family and grieve with them. As is the custom, Teyze and Şevkiye Abla had prepared the body and wrapped it in a burial shroud. Muslims treat the dead with gentleness and respect and avoid disturbing the deceased as much as possible. The body is washed, scented and wrapped in a clean white cloth, ready for internment at the earliest opportunity. There is no embalming, no "viewing". There are no such things as funeral homes and no cremations.

An atmosphere of serenity enveloped the house. The *Hafiz* I had seen previously had returned to her place and was quietly reciting the Koran. Women were working their prayer beads; although some were crying, there were no hysterics, no dramas. The men were assembling in the garden, and for the first time ever, I saw Dayı at Teyze's house. Like Ana, he had severed relations with his older sister, but Nina was his mother, too. We waited just over an hour for the plain pine box to be delivered and the body settled into it. When the chief mourners were ready, and the *Hoca* had arrived to lead the rituals, the coffin was moved out into the garden where everyone joined in the funeral prayers before this simplest of caskets was placed on a horse-drawn funeral cart and taken to the cemetery. Only the men accompanied the body to the graveside.

Because everything happens so quickly, I now understand the importance of having a plot in readiness. Most burial sites have modest markers rather than elaborate tombstones. There is no custom for placing flowers on the grave, though I badly wanted to do this as I knew of no other way to express my feelings of sadness and loss.

Relatives observe an intense three-day mourning period marked in Islam by increasing devotional activities; receiving visitors and condolences; eschewing decorative clothing and jewellery. Spouses and close family members observe an extended mourning period. Muslims believe that the whole of this life constitutes a test to determine our place in the afterlife. Death is the return of the soul to Allah, and this inevitability permeates the consciousness of devout Muslims everywhere. While this awareness helps to keep the events of everyday life in perspective, it is also a constant reminder of the end that awaits us all.

The Prophet Muhammad said there are three things that may benefit a person after death: charity given during life that continues to help others, knowledge from which people continue to profit, and a righteous child who prays for the deceased. He also said, "Work as if you will live forever; pray as if you will die tomorrow." I think that is a neat summary of the Turkish/Islamic outlook on life and death.

We marked our increased devotion by attending a *mevlüt* in honour of Nina at Teyze's house, two days after the funeral. We shall have our own *mevlüt* for her here at our house at the forty-day mark, another milestone in the journey of bereavement.

And speaking of journeys, this recent talk of death has focused attention on the afterlife, and Ana announced the other evening that she is taking me to Heaven with her. I was dumbstruck, not at all sure what she meant. She maintains that she obviously will be going to Heaven, and it is her right to take someone with her when the time comes. She has chosen me. I have decided to take this as a compliment. Undoubtedly, she feels that this is the only means I have of getting there, but she has forsaken all others to have me as her guaranteed companion for eternity. I could be forgiven for thinking that she might have seen this as a golden opportunity to be rid of me forever, but no.

I'm not convinced of her theology in this matter, but it seemed churlish to argue, so I have graciously accepted her kind offer. End of discussion. The other members of the family appeared as nonplussed as I was but have acquiesced with good grace. Perhaps they feel as she does, that mine is the greatest need.

The Izmir court case now feels like ages ago but took place only the day before Nina died. Abla and I accompanied Baba once again. We went by coach so that we could get an early start (a very early start) and return that evening. We had no reason to stay on, but the roads are such that I don't think I could have driven there and back in the same day. We wanted to lend Baba moral support, as we had no idea what awaited.

As a result of his discussions with Hakan, Baba had scraped together a lump sum of money (I think he managed to get a contribution from Sami during his last trip to Istanbul) and had gone to Izmir the previous week to discuss settlement of the debt with the foremost plaintiff. This man represented the three businesses which were owed money by Sami, all also long-term associates of Baba's from his own business days.

Sami had obviously traded on his father's good name to an abusive extent. Baba said that Mustafa Bey seemed embarrassed to have taken his old friend to court but explained that the debt was a substantial one, and he could ill afford to lose the money. Baba, in turn, was embarrassed to be dealing with debts the like of which he himself had never incurred, but for which he now found himself responsible. He spelled out his situation to Mustafa Bey, finally persuading him to take the sum on offer in full and final settlement of the total debt.

His agreement was an extremely generous and compassionate gesture, coming about only because Mustafa Bey knew and respected Baba. Certainly, there was no inclination to let Sami off the hook. Mustafa Bey said that although he could not answer for the others, he would speak to them on Baba's behalf. The sums involved there were not nearly so big, and they might be willing to write them off.

This had all happened about two weeks before the last court session, so we had to go along to see what developments there were. On the day, the news was the best we could have hoped for. The court had had Mustafa Bey's letter saying that his debt was now satisfied, and that the others were willing to write off the lesser amounts. All this had to be legalized, but apart from the formalities, that is the end of it. Phew!

The judge, however, was inclined to go after Sami for his failure, yet again, to turn up in court. I was hoping he would, but it would have been a vindictive act to little purpose. The judge had to satisfy himself with a stern lecture on the perils of debt and the irresponsible activities of spoiled sons, and leave it at that. I was tempted to shout "Amen!" when he had finished, but as the intended audience for this sermon wasn't present, it would have felt as hollow as a forced religious conversion.

In the midst of all this, we have managed to book the ceremony (confirmed for 3 August), to order wedding invitations and to begin thinking about the wedding favours. These too, can be ordered but are expensive. Instead, we are thinking to make our own, using traditional fabric to sew little bags for sweets and sugared almonds. Additionally, Baba has been helping me handle the red tape surrounding our marriage. Among other things, we need TB and blood tests. Hakan can easily take care of these for himself in Bursa, but I need to have mine done here in town.

Most exciting of all, though, is the news that Abla has started my bridal gown. I had brought a pattern with me from London as I didn't then have any appreciation for how talented she is. Abla has never before used a ready-made pattern, so it has been something of a revelation to her and greatly simplifies her task. This way, she knows exactly what I want, and she doesn't have to rely on my inadequate descriptions or sketches. Because the pale pink brocade and trims are so rich, the dress itself is simple with a fitted bodice (the round neck and short sleeves fulfil the modesty requirements here) flowing into an A-line floor-length skirt. Abla is doing a mock-up in lightweight silk, which when perfected, will be the master pattern for the dress itself; the mock-up will then become the lining of the dress. As a seamstress yourself, Mother, I'm sure you can appreciate how skilled she is.

You most likely recall that a few weeks ago, Dayı's daughter Zehra was asking for a divorce, but that they reconciled. We have heard now that she has left her husband once again, saying this time it is final. We heard that he beat her last week, and the next day she asked Dayı to come and get her.

I'm under the impression that beatings have been an ongoing feature of the marriage and have become worse over the months. Not unreasonably, Zehra has had enough. In his defence, her husband says that she acts like a "whore and a prostitute" by hanging out of the window, hair uncovered, chatting to men as they pass by on the street. I have no idea if what he says has any merit, but people here are quick to condemn any nonconformist behaviour, and violence against women is often justified on this basis.

However, it's more complicated than that. Zehra has left her little girl behind. Unbelievable as it seems, she fled the household on her daughter's first birthday and says she doesn't want her because the child will be an impediment if she decides to re-marry. These are her words, which do make it sound rather as if she has something else in mind, as if there may be some truth to her husband's allegations. Not that this excuses any violence on his part. Not in any way.

In the meantime, because of Rukiye Yenge's unforgivable behaviour in all of this, both Baba and Ana are refusing to have anything to do with her, and the two families are not speaking. This is sad and sorry enough, but there are implications for our nuptials because Dayı is the one planning our wedding feast. Even if he goes ahead with that, his family probably won't attend because of the current frictions. Precisely where all this leaves us is not apparent.

Selfishly, I had quietly worried that the mourning period for Nina might affect our plans, but that will not be the case. In fact, apart from the ones already mentioned, there are far bigger problems that could overtake us. The general strike situation throughout the country threatens every conceivable aspect of our wedding. If the civil service follows the example of factory and other workers, we might not even be able to marry at all.

It's hard to see how things could get any worse.

29 June 1971

In the early days of my stay, I believed that the time would come when I would have told you everything, that I would have explained all that needed to be explained. I thought that my letters would get shorter as life became more humdrum. How wrong I was. I could never have predicted just how "interesting" life here could be, how little chance there would be for the days to become routine. I recall that I concluded my last letter by saying that I didn't see how things could get much worse. I was wrong about that, too.

Hakan has been in hospital, and no one has any real idea what is wrong with him. He's been suffering from severe stomach pains, the source of which is as clear as a pot of porridge. I only found out about this after they released him, and he wrote to tell me. He didn't want to worry me. Ha! Of course, I'm bloody worried! He has had these episodes off and on for a couple of weeks but was admitted to hospital only when he was in so much pain that he couldn't walk.

Investigations and tests have so far revealed nothing conclusive, but the consensus seems to be that Hakan has a grumbling appendix and may have to be scheduled for surgery. I hope he doesn't have to have an emergency operation, but if it comes to this, then so be it. At present, he appears to have stabilized and is continuing to work. If the pain comes back, I think they'll whisk him straight into hospital. For many reasons, this is something we would both like to avoid. I have had enough experience of hospitals here to be unimpressed with the state of them or to have any confidence in the facilities available. Anyone with any means to do so goes abroad for major surgery, and while an appendectomy is hardly major, I would opt for it only if absolutely necessary. We'll simply have to see what develops.

There are so many matters up in the air just now that I can't possibly begin to deal with the consequences if the worst happens (and I'm not even sure now what that is), so I have decided to carry on as if everything is on track for our wedding, 3 August. I feel utterly determined that come what may, we ARE going to get married. I won't even contemplate leaving Turkey until that has happened, and I'm going to be ready, regardless.

With that in mind, I have collected the invitations from the printers and have insisted that the family starts working on them. They have to go out at least two weeks before the day, and we don't yet have a final list of names and addresses. But none of this is up to me. You are taking care of sending out announcements to everyone I know, and I can help only to a limited extent on the task here. But I want them done. We can't send them if they aren't ready. They need to be completed ASAP so that we can get on with making up the bags for the favours. I'm past conciliatory and am making the decisions I now need to make to get this show on the road.

My fabulous wedding dress is finished and hanging in splendour in the back bedroom. Abla has done a magnificent job. It fits perfectly as long as I don't lose any more weight. Hakan is in the same boat. Because of his stomach problems, he has not been eating properly, and he says he has lost a few pounds. The hot weather doesn't help, either. Now that the dress is finished, Baba is working on my matching shoes. My whole outfit is being custom-made... as is Hakan's!

Ruth turned up here yesterday. She wanted to see my gown, which we ooohed and aaahed over together. She thinks it's divine. I also showed her my Turkey albums, finished only recently. She admired these too, and took two hours going over them, talking about the contents and taking notes for the book she is planning.

Hakan and I need two witnesses at the civil ceremony. I had wanted Abla to be mine, but she is reluctant, saying that it would not be an appropriate role for a female relative. I wasn't clear which aspect of "female relative" she deemed inappropriate, but I didn't press her obvious reluctance. During Ruth's visit, I asked her to stand with me, and she said she'd be honoured to do so. Since his good friend, Metin, is now doing his own military service, I think Hakan is planning to ask Dayı to be his witness, but with the uncertainty that stalks us, that too, is doubtful.

Levent has had his exam results for the teachers college. Unfortunately, he failed the mathematics portion, something of a blow since this is usually his best subject. Although he passed everything else, his other marks were only average, and I'm not sure, even if he passes math on the retake in September, that this will be good enough to get him into the course. It's not clear. Like everything else. Naturally, a re-take means that he cannot start in the autumn, but I gather if successful, he could join in April. I suspect he is more upset than he is showing; it's a big disappointment for all the Beylers.

The situation with Zehra and her family is in utter turmoil. Ana, Abla, and I have paid a conciliatory visit to their house to see if we can make peace. Baba is still refusing to have anything to do with the women in the family, but he sees Dayı regularly at the office where uncle has been pouring out his heart and crying over this terrible turn of events. The evening after we women paid our visit to Dayı's house, they all came here, so everyone is making an effort.

Once again, it looks as if Zehra is reconsidering her decision, but Dayı is beyond discussing it. He says they are going ahead with the divorce, and that's final. I wonder if Zehra's change of heart has more to do with her little daughter than with her husband. I cannot imagine a mother abandoning her child under anything but the most extreme circumstances. Dayı insists he wants nothing to do with the girl and will not have her in his house.

It might seem odd that Zehra's father gets to make all the decisions regarding her affairs, but I suppose, culturally speaking, he was responsible for picking her husband, and he is responsible for her welfare through the divorce and after. She involved him by asking him to take her away from her husband's house, back to her old home. If she wanted to escape a violent man, what choice did she have? None, really. But I think the reality of life beyond divorce is suddenly beginning to figure in Zehra's thinking.

There have been many impulsive actions, the consequences of which are only now being realized. As things stand, Zehra is going to have to live under her father's roof and his control and be his dependent child once again. Even though he will not beat her, it is a high price to pay to be safe. No wonder she is having second thoughts. Apparently, Mehmet too, is reconsidering, and representations of his relatives keep turning up on the doorstep, trying to persuade Zehra to return. It sounds to me like everyone needs to grow up.

Now that my enrolment in the family is about to become official, Baba decided it was time I was shown an important family possession. Full of grave ceremony, he returned from their bedroom with a mysterious little case that had evidently been designed to hold a scroll. The cylindrical container appeared at first to be made of hand-painted wood. Its rich rust colour had been handsomely decorated with gold and pastel motifs, and fine calligraphy inscriptions. On closer inspection, it might have been made of *papier-mache*, but I wasn't sure. What was not in question was the fact that this was something very old and very precious. However, it was not the case, but its contents that were significant.

I knew this was a special moment when they all gathered around to witness Baba's careful removal of the silk-backed parchment. As he unrolled the ancient document, yet more intricate calligraphy was revealed. Set out in artistic style, the script turned out to be Koranic, a form of Arabic that in Ottoman times was used only by aristocrats and nobles. Its formal, flowery language was that of the sultan's court. The manuscript is verification of an earlier family tree that had probably fallen apart. Copied and authenticated by sixteenth-century Caliphs, it confirms that the Beylers trace their ancestry back to the aristocracy of the sixth-century Fatimed Caliphate, the first great Islamic Empire. The copy had been signed by the court and stamped with the sultan's seal. I'm certain I detected a whiff of antiquity in the room.

There is no question that I am every bit as impressed as they hoped I would be. I genuinely admired both the age and the workmanship of the fine old case and its scroll, as well as the stunning lineage of the family itself. The Beylers are justifiably proud of their breathtaking heritage, which could be construed as both a blessing and an immense responsibility. I think I have been permitted to see the document so that I will be aware not only of the noble bloodline into which I'm marrying, but also to better understand my duties in that regard. I was beginning to feel a heavy obligation to convert to Islam, not to mention the need to procreate. There was much on which to reflect.

Shortly after the manuscript had been returned to its hiding place, Ana and Levent went off to bed, while Baba, Abla, and I sat up talking. I decided to take charge of the conversation and broached the subject of religion. I tried to impress on them the sense of privilege I felt in getting to know them all and learning about their lives. I talked about my own upbringing, the role of the church in my childhood, and my long-standing interest in the world's religions. I knew I had their full attention, and I wanted to tread carefully.

Nevertheless, the "but" had to come, and I made it plain that I would not be converting to Islam. I tried to explain that Hakan and I share almost identical values. We want the same things from our life together: a mutually loving and supportive relationship, a comfortable home, a successful business and, we hope, children. Organized religion - neither his nor mine - was likely to play much part in that. They didn't say much at any point. But they listened, and I think, finally understood what I was saying. They too, had much on which to reflect.

It's been weeks since I have had any news from Bill, but he came through with a long letter, which arrived yesterday. His outfit has been moved out of the Demilitarized Zone to another location near Saigon in readiness to stand down and undergo processing for return to the USA. He says his departure is not quite as imminent as it sounds; but with any luck, he could be home a month early, at the end of August. He's leaving for Sydney on the 9th of July for ten days and is ready to go! Isn't it strange that he and Hakan have both been in the army over roughly the same period? They have had completely different experiences, but I suspect there are some parallels, too. They'll have a lot of stories to swap once they get together.

Chapter 22

6 July 1971

Thank you for all the lovely birthday cards, good wishes and little indulgences that arrived right on schedule. Hakan came home about noon on Saturday, but we had a million things to do, so my birthday was not at the top of our priority list. However, we did have a nice meal together with the family on Sunday evening, and my 28th birthday has been suitably celebrated.

Perhaps the very best thing of all - and I don't think this counts as an actual birthday present - was Dad's proposal that as the noble father of a most excellent daughter, he should receive a bride price of forty Cadillacs, rather than the traditional forty camels. The Beylers understand that he doesn't have much use for camels and are light-heartedly exploring the means by which they can get his cars for him. The joke has tickled the Turkish sense of humour, and the family is telling everyone about it to enormous comic effect throughout the neighbourhood and beyond. Honestly, it was just what we needed to lift the atmosphere here. You would have thought the wedding itself might do that, but circumstances being what they are, the mood of late has been strangely tense and subdued.

It was great to see Hakan and to have him home again. It's been nearly a month since the Edirne trip, but he didn't actually get to Kavaklı on that occasion. He looked a little paler and a little thinner than when I last saw him, but he has had no more bouts of stomach pain, and we are hoping that the need for surgery has passed.

We still don't know his discharge date. The base is in limbo as the present commander is about to leave, and the new man is not yet in place. We lurch from dilemma to crisis. If his health is okay, will he be discharged from the army in time for the wedding? If he is out of the army in time, will there be a strike which affects the ceremony? If there is no strike, will Dayı still be willing to prepare the feast for us? If he prepares the feast, will his family attend?... Will ours?... Will anyone? If that all goes well, will we be able to have our honeymoon? Will we be able to leave in September? If we are able to leave, will we able to get back into England? Will the business still be there? Will Ken? Are you still with me? Please try to keep up!

The only way I can contemplate any of this is to take everything step-by-step, and just now, we are working on the little bags to be used as wedding favours. We need to make four hundred. The bag has to be made with enough of a hem on the two top edges so that the little gold rings, used to gather up the fabric, can be looped through. Once we have filled the bags with sweets, the two sides will be tied together with a red ribbon. We'll get everything ready, and then have a family assembly line to fill and tie them at the last minute. I want to add a decorative "gold" coin to the ribbon as a final touch.

The situation with Zehra is much the same. She is resigned to the divorce, though whether this is because it's what she truly wants, or because Dayı won't hear of anything else, is not apparent. There is no doubt she's been through some difficult days and is understandably downhearted. I think she has considered trying to get her daughter back, but again, Dayı absolutely won't contemplate it.

While we women are all nearly on speaking terms once more, Baba still is having nothing to do with either Zehra or her mother. They have made wounding comments to him, and he is not inclined to forgive. In fact, he told me the other evening that he thought we should cancel our plans for the wedding dinner as he didn't think he could face having to eat at the same table with Dayı's wife and daughter. To say that this came as something of bombshell would be an understatement. Frankly, it's a little late in the day to be throwing yet another spanner in the works. Although I'm beginning to feel more than a little peeved that everyone else's feelings seem to be more important than ours, I kept my cool and showed him the seating plan for the meal. When he saw that he had been placed at the opposite end of the table from the two detestable women, he relaxed a bit but didn't say much. I told him we would think about it and that he could discuss it with Hakan when he comes home. As far as I'm aware, nothing more has been said.

This brings us to the honeymoon. The heads of the major trade unions here in Turkey are calling for a general strike by all workers during the first week of August. Yes - that's right - the first week of August. The whole damn week. When Hakan rang the Çelik Palas Oteli to make a reservation for our honeymoon, they told him that they couldn't take any bookings since they expect to be closed during the strike. Now, we're not at all sure what we want to do.

At this point, we simply can't discover if hotels everywhere will be on strike, and whether there would be any point in trying to find something else. It doesn't look as if the civil service will be affected, but I take nothing for granted. Despite everything, Dayı is going ahead with plans for the wedding feast and has been around several times to discuss the menu. We are leaving almost everything to his discretion. We know he wants to do a good job for us and has excellent judgment in these matters.

Abla has informed me that she wants to have a *kına gecesi* for me on the Saturday night before the wedding. This is the Turkish equivalent of a bridal shower but is actually nothing like one. We'll have thirty to forty close women friends, neighbours and female relatives here at the house and hire a woman to play her instruments and lead us in folk dancing. Naturally, there will be food and drink as well.

The highpoint, if we can call it that, is the application of *kına,* or henna as it is called in the West. This is a kind of natural dye that is often used to give reddish highlights to dark hair. In this case, it is applied, sometimes in intricate designs, to the hands of the prospective bride. I'm not sure why, purely decorative I think, but it's a tradition throughout this part of the world and apparently goes back centuries. After the dye has dried (it is applied as a sticky green paste), it turns a dirty orange colour and is most unattractive - and permanent. It does not wash off; it wears off.

Abla was not offended when I told her I would only have my little finger done. She agreed, saying that in my place, she would do the same. The party is a wonderful gesture on her part. She is footing the bill for everything, and there is certainly no expectation that she should do so. We'll have a great time deciding on the guest list and planning the food. In the meantime, she is overwhelmed with sewing. My things have long been completed, but she is making dresses for herself and Ana for the wedding. Something always demands her attention. And we hear that there are several families who want to call on behalf of their sons. It's the season when the Turks who work in Germany - and throughout Europe - come home for their summer holidays, many with the intention or that of their families, to return to work with a new wife. Abla is once again a candidate. And in the news in other, far less agreeable ways.

You have not heard much recently about the despicable Cemile who has made herself the centre of attention once again. I have never known anyone - well, no one apart from Sami - who is such a liar. She ought to come with a "Beware" sign around her neck. No one trusts a word she says; she just makes everything up as she goes along, hot, steamy lies leeching out of her without any kind of restraint. We have all tolerated her ignorant behaviour and turned a blind eye to much that she says and does, silently hoping that the family would decide to leave. Given the amount of time she spends complaining about everything to do with the house, we could be forgiven for assuming that she is only too eager to move.

This past week, she has been telling the neighbours that she's thinking of leaving because Neriman, of all people, has been flirting with her husband. If she was going to tell a lie, it should have been a plausible one as no one, but no one, believes this. It was the blast that brought down a house of cards as now, even Baba has had enough of her poisonous tongue.

Two days ago, her husband, Ferhat, came by to say that they had changed their minds and were not planning to move after all. Baba said that was fine; they should stay as long as they liked, but the rent was doubling in August. Ferhat gulped and started house hunting again. Then Cemile herself told Ana that she couldn't bear to move - they love the house - and would we please not raise the rent. Ana asserted herself in marvellous fashion and told Cemile, in language as clear as an Alpine morning, that they should be out by the first of August. Finally, they have been told to leave in such a manner that even Cemile understood the Beylers are in no mood to negotiate.

No one will be sorry to see them go.

13 July 1971

You will never guess what I have been doing this week. Here I am - less than three weeks away from my wedding - and what preoccupations do you think engage me? Decisions about food, flowers, guests? Worries about my dress? Dreams of future happiness? Heck, no. I'm up to my elbows in paint. This unlikely disclosure comes with the announcement that Cemile and family have moved out of the house. Cue celebrations and rejoicing throughout the neighbourhood! The whole kafuffle blew up right as their July rent was due. They had not paid it when it was made plain, yet again, that they HAD to leave. Baba finally told them that he would forfeit the July rent if they left within the week. With such a splendid incentive, they quickly found a place and were gone almost overnight. Good riddance!

It is important to get the house tenanted again, but the place first needs a thorough clean and fresh paint, too. Baba does not do painting (I don't ask what that means, but I suspect it's something about "women's work"), Ana and Levent are little better than useless at something like this, Abla has more sewing than she can handle, so I have been elected. Actually, I volunteered and no one objected. I said I would do it if Levent helped to fetch and carry, and he agreed, though is often absent when I need him most. It's not as big a job as it sounds because the house is empty, and I have a roller brush on a long handle which makes work on the walls and ceilings relatively easy. In fact, this has been a welcome way to fill the days. Apart from the wedding favours, which we continue to make in the evenings, there is nothing else I can do to further the arrangements. Except worry about what might happen next.

I almost hate to say it, but we think that Hakan will be home - permanently - on Friday. I hate to say it because I feel I'm tempting fate if I do, but I'm keyed up beyond words. My stomach is overloaded with butterflies. I used this expression when I first arrived and it is one that the Beylers had not heard before. Now they ask me if "butterflies are flying" in my stomach when they know I might be excited.

After a hard day of painting, tea at Aylin Abla's has been a most welcome end to the afternoon. Over the weekend, she asked us if we would come early on Monday as she had something to show us. We arrived to find that she had unpacked her dowry and had it all laid out for us to see. She said that all this talk of weddings had her reminiscing about her own. She had decided to look again at the cherished items she had not seen since her own marriage fifteen years earlier. Having come from a family of wealthy merchants, she had an impressive array. Of course, all the household goods had been put in place and used when they set up their first home, but the antique clothing and textiles that had come down to her would be passed on eventually to her own daughters (for safekeeping, rather than use). She was obviously proud of the collection and beamed when we genuinely admired the hand-woven *yağlıks*, the exquisitely embroidered linens and the feather-light silk underwear from a previous era.

Over *çay*, Aylin Abla told us that whatever happened, she would still be providing the wedding cake (their gift to us), and that Mecit Bey would make available his Chevy Impala for use as our wedding car. "Whatever happens" is a reference to the general strike. Rather than deal with all the uncertainties of that first week in August, many places are simply planning to close. At first, I had assumed that only the biggest factories would be affected, but strike fever seems to be spreading, and even small business are feeling threatened enough to cease operations until things have calmed down. What bad luck! I think Aylin Abla is ordering the cake from somewhere and has undoubtedly threatened them with her own personal brand of mayhem if they let her - and us - down.

Lest we were all becoming too complacent about evolving events, Sami came home, unannounced, last Wednesday evening. I thought that he had turned up to see about the wedding. Hakan and I have made it plain to all members of the family that we do not want Sami to attend and that he is to be told nothing about our plans. When I saw him in the salon, mere days before the ceremony, my heart sank. But I seized the first opportunity I had to corner both Ana and Levent, and threaten them with fearsome (but unspecified) retribution if either of them revealed the slightest detail of our imminent marriage, let alone tell him the date. There must have been something about the fire in my eyes and the determination in my voice that told them everything they needed to know about the sincerity with which I spoke. I knew I could trust Baba and Abla, but I worried that someone in the neighbourhood might spill the beans, inadvertently or otherwise.

Although the Beyler children all address their older brother as *Ağabey,* I have never referred to him as anything other than Sami. Nor can I tell you when Sami and I last exchanged more than two words. On this occasion, I barely acknowledged his presence. That much was mutual. We managed to ignore each other for most of the two days he was here before going off to Izmir. Would it be too awful of me to wish that he might arrive in Izmir, only to be arrested and thrown in jail? Where's a judge when we want one?

I still don't know if he knows about the wedding... or even that he's as interested as I have assumed. His main preoccupation appears to be preventing our departure. I never heard him mention the word wedding, but I heard him say, in several different ways, that he is making it a priority to keep Hakan here, and that his brother would not be allowed to leave the country until the conclusion of the court case in 1973. I have no idea if he is right about anything he says, or if he can actually do anything to stop us going, but he would not hesitate to use whatever influence he has to make things extremely difficult, if not impossible, for us. The implications of Hakan - and me - being unable to go back to London are manifestly too enormous even to contemplate.

Baba went with Sami to Izmir where he has been referred to an ear specialist because of his severe hearing loss, which is getting worse. It causes him endless frustration, and the hearing aid he has is of limited use. It picks up too much background noise, making it ineffectual in anything but the quietest of surroundings. The doctor gave him some pills, told him to quit smoking and made an appointment for a follow-up visit next month. I don't see how pills are going to help, but then I'm not an ear specialist. Baba is becoming noticeably sadder about our return to England, and I think this is making him feel low, possibly further affecting his already poor hearing. Of course, if Sami has his way, there will be nothing for Baba to feel sad about.

Abla had her typing exam today, and having passed, is feeling very pleased. And so she should. I'm as proud of her as if I had done it myself. Prouder! Obviously, we are going to celebrate this momentous event. I think tea at the Yıldız Oteli is called for. Now, all she needs is a place to use these new skills.

We just heard that Fatma is not going to Canada after all. She has had her heart set on this trip for over two years. Everything she has done in recent months has been geared to this. Finally, she received news from Beirut that embassy representatives would be in Istanbul to interview her as a preliminary to granting an entry visa. At this point, her father (grandfather) and his brothers all began to put pressure on her to reconsider. I'm not sure why. They have had all this time to discuss her plans but decided, only at the final hurdle, to raise objections. In the end, Fatma told the embassy that she would not be attending the interview and withdrew her application. She must be devastated but is putting on a brave face. Maybe she's relieved to have everyone off her back. Still, it makes me furious. Why didn't they make their views known before she got her hopes up? How does it hurt them if she goes to visit family? Do they know something they're not telling? I think this is more than likely. But after all is said and done, it's really hard to bully a young girl, isn't it!

Just when I was reasonably convinced that I had eaten everything going, Baba came home with an unexpected delicacy: a whole sheep's head. Although I have seen them being sold from little push carts in town, and an optimistic seller occasionally finds his way to our back streets, I had never given them much thought, one way or another. Because the head is cooked and ready to eat, this could be regarded as "fast food" - Turkish style.

Ana presented it, in all its glory, as the startling centrepiece of the evening meal. I was game for it. Dubious, but game. What I had not foreseen was that as the guest in whose honour this delectable fare had been purchased, I would be required to take an eyeball, one of which Baba elegantly hoicked from its socket and presented to me at the end of a fork. It's not often I get my meal staring back at me, especially at eye level!

Now to be honest, if this had happened in the early days, I probably would have risen to the bait. I was then less confident, less sure of my position and eager to do almost anything to avoid giving offence. Sadly, for Baba and the others, they had missed their chance as I now felt perfectly comfortable refusing the offer. With gentle good humour, Baba kept insisting. And just as insistently, I continued to refuse, saying that I could not possibly accept so great an accolade, that I - a mere woman - was unworthy of such tribute. Surely it would be out of place for me to accept this rare delicacy when there were men of honour and status present. Laughingly, Baba finally relented and jovially shoved the rubbery ball into his mouth.

I wouldn't have minded trying a bit of one, but there seemed no way to cut it, the resiliency of its texture defiant even to steady chewing. I swear I saw Baba's jaws bounce with the effort, but he appeared to relish the morsel and downed the second when no one was interested in that one, either. Delicacy, yes, but one that proved less than compelling to others as well. The rest of the meat was very tasty. Since the flesh on the head is relatively thin, we used our forks to pick the meat off the bones. As a way of taking our minds off our troubles, this was better than shiny buckles on new shoes.

Keep everything crossed for us that Hakan gets home as rumoured!

19 July 1971

O Joy! O Bliss! O Rapture! He's done. He's home and he's done. He came Friday the 16th as we had hoped, but I didn't believe it until I saw him. As he only had one small bag to carry, he came on the bus, saying there was nothing from his army days that he needed to take away with him. Because we had not heard that he was not coming, I had been watching from the balcony window since late morning. Finally, after lunch, I saw him come swinging up the street and ran out to meet him just to make sure that it really was all over. . . that he really had come home to stay.

I'm afraid I rather disgraced myself on the streets of Elli Evler by giving him an enormous hug in front of everyone. I doubt a soldier returning from war could have been more warmly welcomed. The situation is that although he has finished, it will take about a month for the paperwork to be completed and his discharge papers issued. Only then can he apply for the new passport that will enable him to leave the country. That's more or less what we had anticipated. If this is how it works out, that's fine. We had not thought that we would be able to leave until the end of August or early September, anyway. No more Poor Turkish Soldier; no more Poor Turkish Undercover Agent. Once again, it's Poor Turkish Boy!

When the new commander arrived at the base, Hakan had his discharge papers ready to sign. The General looked everything over and said that it was strange that Hakan had had only two *bayram* leaves during his eighteen months in the army. Hakan said nothing, letting the paperwork speak for itself.

"You must have been in a hurry to finish," said the General.

"Yes, sir. I'm getting married in two weeks."

"Ah," nodded the General, as if this comment provided all the explanation necessary. He signed the papers, and Hakan put them in the military post for immediate delivery to Ankara where they will be processed. What the General did not know was that as the former base commander's secretary, Hakan was in charge of all leave records. Quite simply, he had never bothered to record any of his time off. According to the regulations, all such instances must be added on to his total obligation and must be served before discharge. It's a huge incentive to keep leave to a minimum... unless you happen to be in a position to keep your own records.

It's been a week of good news and bad. The good news is unbeatable, but the bad news has taken the shine off things. Not unexpectedly, but against all hope, the Kaplan Yem Fabrikası is closing down during the strike. That means we cannot have our wedding feast there. There or anywhere else, it seems. Even if we could find another venue, even if money were no object, a general strike means that no place is guaranteed to be operating. It really is too late to change the date of the wedding itself as the invitations are done and ready to go out. We'll just have to continue as best we can.

At the moment, it looks as if we can go ahead with the civil ceremony, then come back here to the house for refreshments and wedding cake with those we would otherwise have been entertaining at the restaurant. Aylin Abla is insistent that there WILL be cake; there WILL be some sort of celebration afterwards. I think I would be more upset over all this if I weren't so overjoyed to have Hakan out of the army.

Baba has been to Istanbul for the court case and is back home again. He was gone overnight and didn't even see Sami. The trips have become almost routine now, and it's easy to forget how serious the results could be if Tuncer Ağabey doesn't string this out until the amnesty… always assuming there actually will be an amnesty. This is another matter it would be grand to have settled before we leave, but if resolution means prison for Baba, that is most definitely a price not worth paying. Tuncer Ağabey asked for a further period to consider this, that and the other, and the case was adjourned until the end of September. I wonder where we'll be then.

While Hakan has been at home, with no pressure to get back to the base, we have allowed life to slow to a sluggish pace. There is something in town I have been wanting to show him, but there has always been more pressing business… until now. In the early days of my stay, Ana and I established a routine of doing the weekly food shopping together. The trip is a great deal easier if we go by car, and I have been happy to make this contribution to the work effort. Gradually, I became familiar with the places she shopped, what she bought and how much she paid. If Ana didn't feel up to it, I was sometimes entrusted with the responsibility of making this trip on my own.

You may recall previous mentions of buying live chickens to bring home for slaughter at the back of the house. Not feeling at all confident about the required poultry purchase when shopping alone one day, I told Ana, before I set off, that I'd see what I could do but promised nothing. Hoping against hope that our usual vendor would not be in the market, I found him in his normal spot and reluctantly ambled over. I said that I needed a chicken, a good one, for his regular customer, Bedriye Hanım. Of course, he knew exactly who I was, everyone does. He picked out one for me and presented it for inspection, precisely as if I knew what to look for in an abundantly feathered, fully alive, loudly squawking bird. I agreed that it seemed to be a very fine specimen - but hesitated. He looked at me expectantly, waiting for confirmation that the deal had been done.

Somewhat shyly, I asked him if he would, for a fee, kill it for me. This time he looked at me as if I were speaking Martian. I don't think he had ever before had such a request, but he paused to consider the merits of the proposal. (Mother, you always said that money doesn't talk; it screams.) Chicken-seller man and I agreed a fair price for the grisly undertaking, and without further ado, the wretched bird was dispatched to a better world. I had come prepared and, while looking the other way, presented an open bag into which the judicious villager dumped the dead fowl.

Back home, I showed Ana the chicken. She was delighted. She is capable of wringing their necks if required, but she doesn't like doing it, so she was happy to have paid only a little extra for the convenience. During our next trip to the poultry market, we struck the same deal. Then it occurred to me to ask him if he could pluck it for us, too. I know this is time-consuming, tedious work, requiring pans of boiling water and great patience, but I hoped that with some advance notice, he might take an order for collection later. Poultry man stroked his bearded chin and thought. I could see the cogs falter and slow.

Apparently his brother had a butcher's shop in the town centre. If we would select the chicken and pay for it, we could collect the plucked bird from there at the end of the day. He gave us the name of the shop; we paid up and left. Sure enough, when I got to the butcher's that afternoon, I found our bird, as clean and smooth as a bridegroom's cheeks, sitting naked and alone in the cool glass cabinet. I asked the owner if I could, in future, have the same service again. Everything is possible for a price, and I returned home triumphant. Once more my mother-in-law was extremely pleased, and I earned valuable points. For the matter of a few lira, her workload had been significantly eased, and she could now look forward to serving chicken, rather than dreading it.

Hakan knew nothing about any of this. But the other day, when Ana asked us to pick up a chicken in town, I took the opportunity to show my fiancé a change I was positive would surprise him. Playing dumb, I asked him where his mother bought chickens, and he directed me to our former poultry man in the market "because we buy them live". (Where does he think I've been living the past two years?) Despite his protests that we were going the wrong way, I drove towards the main street. After parking, I took him along to the butcher's shop and positioned him in front of a chill cabinet full of ready-to-cook whole birds, as well as big trays of plucked and cleaned quarter chickens. He was stunned. "I have never before seen this in Turkey," he said in a bemused sort of way. "No, indeed, you have not. But it's become a whole new way of life here in Kavaklı," I said.

I described to him the chain of incidents that led from killing to plucking, to cleaning out the innards, to quartering the birds and finally, to selling them fully prepared for cooking, all at a very fair price. The idea had caught on, and our butcher had quickly found himself with more demand than ever he had anticipated. Certainly

Ana told everyone she knew, and Aylin Abla helped spread the word as did every other woman looking for a shortcut to her work. The news was out that Butcher Salih had ready-to-cook poultry. His butchery business suddenly took off, leaving all the others to wonder about the reason for his busy shop. Obviously, it didn't take most of them long to copy his success, but Salih was the first, and his reputation for innovative ideas in retail poultry has been firmly established.

When Hakan and I arrived, the shop was bustling, but Salih Bey saw us come in and dropped everything to serve us. I told him I was after one of his whole chickens (Ana is suspicious of the quarter portions, as if she is somehow not getting everything to which she's entitled), and he selected the plumpest one with a fine breast. He never wants me to pay, but after a reverse kind of haggling, we usually agree on a discount... or an extra portion. As a legacy of my time here, it's entirely unexpected. Hakan says I'm full of surprises and that he will have to watch me more carefully in the future!

The other legacy I'm proud to leave behind, is the one to do with women behind the wheel: several are now driving and others are learning. I'm not claiming that they might not have come to this anyway, but I think my visibility around town strengthened individual cases where the women were so inclined. Aylin Abla says she used my example to persuade her husband of the rightness of this bold step, and now, she has not only passed her test, but is about to acquire a little car of her own. I guess we never know how the things we do affect other people.

I had not quite finished painting Cemile's old haunt when Hakan came home, so he gave me a hand and we completed the job together. We scrubbed down the bathroom and the kitchen, and tidied everything up so it looks clean and inviting for anyone interested in a possible let. So far no one has come along, but I have no doubts that they soon will. There is always demand for a good rental property.

Meanwhile, we have to get ready this week for Nina's *mevlüt*, here on the 26th. This will mark the end to the official forty days of mourning. We had thought of having it in the freshly painted downstairs, but it's more trouble to haul chairs and cushions down there than to re-organize the upstairs. We have also made *lokma* in her memory. Aylin Abla wanted to do this to commemorate the anniversary of her own mother's death, five years earlier, and suggested that we combine our efforts to make twice as much with half the work. Practical as ever, she organized the outsize cauldrons and other catering equipment needed to produce the mountains of doughnuts she believed the occasion warranted. I'm sure she ordered up the fine weather, too. Who would dare to argue with her?

Cooking on such a vast scale could only be done outside, and this past Friday, the weather could not have been better... dry, but not too hot or sunny. Aylin Abla's yard was Command Central, the focus for what became a neighbourhood project with most of the women from our street working in teams to make the dough and fry it up in the immense vats. The local children were dispatched with overflowing trays to everyone in the immediate vicinity; and the *lokma*, delivered plain, could be sprinkled with powdered sugar or spread with honey or eaten with cheese - whatever they liked.

We worked all day, downing our own servings with glasses of *çay* and *ayran*. I lost track of the quantities of flour and oil used. However much we made, there were grateful recipients. When the neighbourhood had been satisfied, Abla and I set off in Dagmar to deliver yet more to the homes of the poor, as well as to friends and relatives in town. It was early evening when we had finished and collapsed, exhausted but content.

There had been a benevolent buzz to the day, everyone joining in, all the women chatting, socializing and working together. I had felt an enormous sense of community - part of something vital, part of something fundamental - which is disappearing in the West. But most significantly, it was a fitting way to remember those who are no longer with us.

27 July 1971

We are taking it easy today. *Mevlüts* are hard work for the hosts, and we had a full house yesterday. Since not many of our friends and neighbours knew Nina personally, I had thought there wouldn't be many attending, but it doesn't work that way here. Everyone comes to show their support for the family, and the Beylers are well known and well liked. I'm glad we were able to do this for Ana's mother, and that I was able to be part of the farewell rituals.

Now we are looking ahead to the *kına gecesi* on Saturday evening. As a result of having the *mevlüt*, the middle of the house is already opened up to provide one big airy space. We'll be baking like fiends over the next couple of days, and Aylin Abla is going to make her special cheese pastries for us. I have heard that Hakan is taking his father, Levent and Dayı out for the evening. Dayı is deeply disappointed not to be providing the wedding meal for us. If he is disappointed, we are devastated, but there's no point in anguishing over it. There's nothing to be done, so we'll have to make the best of it. Under the circumstances, people will understand.

In fact, there may turn out to be something of a silver lining to this cloud. The strike at Kaplan Yem Fabrikası means we have a rather tidy sum of money that now will not be spent and over which there has been ongoing discussion. It is probably the right amount we need to take us back to England. Up until now, we have not had that money and have debated the best way to handle the situation. Abla came forward several weeks ago, offering to lend us the funds we need for the return trip. She knows that as soon as we start working, we'll pay her back without delay, but we are reluctant to touch her nest-egg.

However, if we borrow money from her, we open up the possibility of having a real honeymoon. With the feast money, we could spend two weeks touring the south and whole areas of the country neither of us has seen. It's an opportunity we may never have again, certainly not in the foreseeable future. It's so very tempting. Both Hakan and I are longing to make the trip, but wonder if it would be completely self-indulgent and irresponsible to do so. Nothing has yet been decided.

Ruth called in last week. She had heard that Hakan was home for good and wanted to visit. I think I told you that she will be my witness for the ceremony, and Dayı has readily agreed to be Hakan's. Ruth had rung me earlier to make sure we would be in, as in addition to getting the latest news, she also wanted to deliver our wedding present. Her call missed Hakan who had just gone out, and as the others were also busy with various errands, we had the house to ourselves.

Unusually for her, Ruth arrived by taxi, and I saw her direct the driver regarding an item in the trunk. The next thing I knew, they were both at the front door, and the hapless fellow was instructed to deposit his heavy burden on the floor of the parlour. As wedding presents go, this looked extremely interesting. The driver had placed a small brass trunk in the middle of the floor, its shape and size offering no clues as to the contents inside. Ruth said this would all take a while, so we had better do the "tea thing" first. She accompanied me to the kitchen where I put the kettle on, after which we had our *çay* with the brownies she had brought along.

When we had more than satisfied ourselves and had caught each other up on recent events, Ruth announced that the moment had come to open the trunk, a task she was leaving to me. As I undid the clasp and lifted the lid, the first thing I saw was an exquisite set of hand-embroidered sheets, carefully folded into place on the top tray. The bedding was made of the finest snow-white cotton, its borders decorated in pastel flowers with our initials woven into the motif. It was a lovely set, too good to use... almost. But there was more, much more.

When I removed the tray, I saw a myriad of packages contained in this treasure trove. Ruth had gift-wrapped every little item, and she had been correct when she said that this was going to take some time. I started to unwrap the presents, one-by-one. Some of the items were for everyday use: a spatula, wooden spoons, vegetable peeler and toothpick holder. Some were funny: a book of Turkish jokes, a child's game, some market tat - and best of all - an ashtray from the notorious Altın Palas restaurant. Some of the items were personal: white lily cologne for me and a spicy aftershave for Hakan, slippers for us both, along with new toothbrushes in psychedelic colours. Some of the items were courtesy of the PX: American mustard, Welch's Grape Jelly, a box of Bisquick and a packet of Oreos. Some of the items were simply exceptional: the camel bells I had been haggling over for months, two amazing old *yağlıks*, a beautiful prayer shawl for me and an olivewood *tesbih* (prayer beads) for Hakan, plus a number of old Turkish items that she had found in various markets and bazaars. Ruth, more than anyone, knows my love of Old Things and values them, too.

As I opened and exclaimed over each item, we ran the gamut of emotions. We reminisced. We shared jokes. We spoke of the future. We laughed and cried together. She said that this was the only way she knew to give me a proper American-style bridal shower all by herself. To say that she had succeeded magnificently would be an understatement. I knew all too well the hard work, planning and thought - not to mention the expense - that had gone into this extraordinary effort. I was touched beyond words and was glad that no one else had been at home after all. We two old friends - for it feels as if we have been friends for far longer than mere months - spent a memorable afternoon together. I suspect it might have been a kind of farewell.

Although we are busier than ever, there really isn't much news. We are almost finished making the wedding favours, and Hakan has gone off with Baba to buy the sweets to fill them. All the invitations have been delivered, and Abla and I have arranged to have our hair done on the afternoon of the wedding.

I haven't heard anything from Bill since before his departure to Sydney. He didn't tell me that he has been awarded a Bronze Star "for achievement in running air strikes". If he can be that successful at something he doesn't like, imagine what he can do when he finds something he enjoys!

Cherry pies. Why did you have to tell me about your cherry pies? I haven't had any since the ones you made when I was last home. I can't even remember when that would have been, but it feels like a very long time ago... in another world. I don't mind telling you that at this point, I would swap all the *baklava* in Turkey for one slice of my mom's cherry pie.

Part Four

Into a New Life
August - September 1971

Chapter 23

2 August 1971

Well, there's not long to go now. I can hardly believe it. It seems as if this wedding has been coming forever and has changed its guise so often that I'm still not sure exactly what is going to happen tomorrow. I have decided (again) that I'm no longer going to worry about anything. There is too much that is not under my control and what is, is done. The best news, as far as I'm concerned, is that the civil service is not striking; and that while all other arrangements may fail, the wedding itself is now all but guaranteed.

Showing all the restraint of beggars at a banquet, we have decided to go for the grand tour honeymoon. On the face of it, there is no way we can justify the expense, but we are confident that once we are back in England, we'll have no trouble quickly repaying any money we may have to borrow. In the end, we decided that if we didn't take this opportunity, it is something we would live to regret.

The only firm plan we have is that we shall start our trip in Bursa where we have found a hotel that will be open, and where we are assured of a room for Tuesday and Wednesday nights. After that, we shall plunge south and drive along the Aegean and Mediterranean coasts as much as we can. Many of these areas are still quite remote, and we do not know if there are accessible roads into some parts. That's all part of the adventure. We'll be gone two weeks and should be back here by 17 August. We do not want to be later than that as Hakan's discharge papers should be ready by then. We need to keep things moving along.

The *kına gecesi* was a hoot. Word of our plans spread quickly, and many more women than the thirty or so we had planned, let us know that they would be mortally offended if not invited. I think we had something like sixty in all. Abla asked me if would wear the gorgeous *bindallı* she had been given as a present. I really wanted to but worried that something might damage it, and then I would feel dreadful. But she insisted, and in the end, I couldn't resist. I may not have looked very Ottoman, but I felt like royalty in the lush blue gown.

It was a warm evening, and we threw open all the windows and doors and let the music waft up and down the street. It was a big job simply welcoming and seating everyone. The village woman came with her drums and flute, plus an assistant to lead us in the dancing. Many of the women need no encouragement. They love to dance and were on the floor with the first musical notes. We had decided not to go the tea/coffee route. I wanted Abla to enjoy the evening, and I knew that if we had to go through all that palaver, she would never get out of the kitchen. So we opted for soft drinks with our cakes and pastries, and we asked Aylin Abla's daughters to help serve.

Towards the end of the evening, one of our neighbours, a woman who considers herself something of an expert in these matters, took over the *kına* ceremony. I knew she was itching to get my whole hand involved, preferably both; but I was quite firm about the fact that only my little finger, right hand, was to be done. Reluctantly she complied, wrapping the selected digit in the green paste and giving it the minimum fifteen minutes needed to set the dye. The finger was unwrapped to reveal its startling orange colouring, and everyone applauded.

After this, I made the rounds of the room to receive individual congratulations and best wishes on my forthcoming marriage. More dancing followed, after which the party began to break up. It was no later than 11:00 pm when the last guest departed. Some of the local girls had taken over the kitchen; all the washing up had been done and everything left in immaculate order. It was a wonderful evening, precisely the sort of thing an older sister would do for a younger one. Abla has made me feel very special. With her warm heart and exceptional generosity of spirit, she is a matchless sister.

Although the men had gone off earlier for *şiş kebap* in town, I gather they spent much of the evening sitting in the garden, chatting amongst themselves, listening to the giddy noise and festive music that floated down from proceedings upstairs. Some of the men from the neighbourhood came by to greet Hakan and wish him well. Eventually, everyone drifted off to bed, leaving the two of us, still full of excitement, talking into the gentle summer night. We were beginning to enjoy all the fuss around our big day.

Yesterday afternoon, Aylin Abla sent her daughter to ask Abla and me if we would come to the house. We don't normally see her on weekends because her husband is at home, and it's family time. As Mecit Bey was out on some business, we went along, expecting to chat over tea and rehash events of the previous evening. In a way, it was that, but not what we had expected.

We arrived to find Aylin Abla uncharacteristically agitated and upset as she immediately launched into an explanation of things that had taken place at the *kına gecesi*. She had been sitting next to Nimet Hanım, a teacher of some importance in Elli Evler. At least, Nimet Hanım believes she is a teacher of some importance in Elli Evler. Although she has always appeared friendly and welcoming to me, I have sensed that there might be a tinge of hypocrisy in her effusiveness, that she might actually regard me with some suspicion. And so it proved. After the application of the *kına*, when the bride makes the rounds of the guests to receive their good wishes, it is the custom for anyone who cares to do so, usually family or close friends, to offer a little gift, typically a gold coin.

I had had no expectation that any of our guests would feel so inclined. I have been here only a matter of months and saw no reason why anyone would do this on such short acquaintance. Apparently, Aylin Abla had had other ideas, and she had a gold coin ready to give me when I came to her. Nimet Hanım understood Aylin Abla's intentions and told her to put it away, saying, "You don't know how long this marriage will last." Aylin Abla, not wanting to make a scene, put the coin away. Later, she regretted it.

She told us all of this close to tears. She was angry with Nimet Hanım for interfering and with herself, for paying her any heed. Not normally a weak-willed woman, Aylin Abla couldn't figure out why she had allowed herself to be influenced in this way, but I could understand it. Nimet Hanım is a complete bulldozer. She makes pronouncements as if they have come from on high and expects that because she has said so, anyone with a grain of sense will agree with her. She's not a bad person, just a domineering and opinionated one.

I told Aylin Abla that she was making too much of the situation and that I was far from offended. I appreciated her candour, but really, there was no need to agonize over it. Aylin said she had thought of nothing else since the incident and wanted to make amends. Now embarrassed by all the fuss, I stressed that there was absolutely no need to do anything, but she was having none of it. She said that she had reconsidered the gold coin and had decided on something better. Saying this, she produced a carefully wrapped package, which she presented to me with a kiss on each cheek. Since I knew it was not the custom to open a gift in front of the giver, I asked her permission to do exactly that. Under the circumstances, I think she would have been disappointed if I had not. Inside the paper was an heirloom cushion cover from her dowry. I remembered it well, having commented at the time on how striking it was, all shocking pink and rich red embroidery on a yellow satin background.

I spluttered that I could not possibly accept such a valuable and precious gift. A token coin was one thing, but this was quite another, and I felt uncertain about taking something that belonged in the family. She would not hear my protests. She said she knew that the heirloom would be in good hands, valued far beyond anything her own daughters would assign it. Yet again, I was rendered speechless by the thoughtfulness and generosity of someone whose very existence I was unaware a scant two years ago.

This was intended to be a quick note, but once again, I have found things to say that I did not realize were going to come out until I sat down to write. I know you will be thinking of me tomorrow, as I will be thinking of you, too. I could never have imagined that I would marry under such curious circumstances, or that none of my family would be present. This is hard for us both, but the choices I have made have brought me to this point, and I do not have any regrets.

If I had not come to Turkey, I suspect Hakan and I would not be marrying at all. With too little history behind us, there would have been too much to overcome. As it is, we have learned a great deal about each other and built on the mutual commitment we made in London. We've found out that we're a team, that we can rely on each other, and that there is very little we cannot achieve together. Oh - yes - and that we love each other very much! The wedding feels like the completion of a formality, one that marks the beginning of a fresh start and our new life together.

I doubt I shall be able to write before we return from the honeymoon. We'll be travelling far and fast in rural areas, so I'll catch up with you once we get back to Kavaklı.

17 August 1971

Just call me "Mrs Beyler" from now on, thank you very much! Married life is fabulous, and we're as happy as a pair of puppies with a slipper each. It's better than discovering that your crystal ring is really a diamond! Hakan has gone with Baba this morning to apply for his new passport. We got back last night and found that his discharge papers had come in the post the day before, so without further delay, he has gone off to see to the last obstacle before we can leave.

Naturally, I need to back up and tell you about the wedding. By way of summary, I can say with conviction that it was a memorable day, parts of it wonderful and loving, parts of it bizarre and distressing. It's always been my policy to be candid in these letters which have served as a record of events, an outlet for pent-up emotions and a means of working things out. Although our wedding day certainly had many happy aspects, it also had a downside that occurred first thing in the morning and stayed with me throughout the day.

We were all up at an early hour, greeted by damp morning air and the promise of a fine day that would not be to be too unbearably hot. To my surprise, the breakfast table had been laid, used and vacated by the time I made my way to the salon. Baba, who had already eaten, was drinking *çay* on the balcony. Abla was off on some errand, and Levent was out in the garden. I didn't see any sign of either Hakan or Ana, and Baba said simply that Hakan was talking to Ana in the parlour. Uh-oh. No one ever went into the parlour unless there were guests. It could only mean they wanted privacy. This was not good news.

I went back to the salon and stared at the frosted glass doors that separated the two rooms. Just as I made out the shadowy bulk of their figures, I heard the gentle weeping that came from within. I needed no explanation about what was going on. I knew exactly, and I was furious. With nowhere to go and no one on whom to vent, I marched back to the bedroom and fumed. I paced up and down and muttered under my breath, imaginary conversations going on both in my head and aloud in the silence. I sat. I got up. I smoked. I put out the cigarette and sat down again. I paced some more. I lit up again.

I expected to see Hakan at the door at any moment, but he didn't appear. I stared hard at the emptiness, thinking I could conjure him out of thin air. Feeling permeated with helplessness, I headed back out to the salon. They were still ensconced in the parlour, and not knowing what to do with myself, I returned to the bedroom. As I entered the room again, I saw my wedding dress hanging in its see-through wrapper, ready for the day. I paused and went to the mirror, giving myself a hard look.

"Right," I said to the mirror. "This is your wedding day. What do you want to remember about it?"

Good question. Ultimately, I was asking myself about the extent to which I intended to let Ana ruin the day. If I continued in my present state, I was likely to explode.

"And the result of that would be?"

"Misery all around."

"Is that what you want?"

"No."

"So, what are you going to do about it?"

Big pause.

"Take a deep breath, calm down and ignore the conversation going on in the parlour."

"Excellent idea."

Having agreed with myself that the only way to proceed was to turn a blind eye, I returned to the salon and sat down to have my breakfast. I decided it would help take my mind off the atmosphere if I read the papers. With fierce concentration, I failed to take in the morning's news. Though I knew Hakan was coaxing and cajoling his mother, it seemed to be taking forever. I was incensed that she had chosen our wedding morning to stage this little drama. It was a scene worthy of Sami who, as it turned out, never came but who had ensured his spectre through a designated alter ego.

Eventually, Hakan and Ana emerged. Ana went straight to the kitchen where she made herself busy, and Hakan joined me at the breakfast table. I asked nothing; he volunteered nothing. I couldn't dissect the incident and expect to remain coherent, so I said only that we'd talk about it later. We both made an effort to change the subject, but the unreported conversation hung in the air like the smell of yesterday's fish.

Neriman returned from Aylin Abla's where I suspect they had been taking care of cake and car arrangements. She seemed to be unaware of either the conversation or the atmosphere, which was probably just as well. Then Levent breezed in from the garden and livened things up. Hakan and I began to relax and indulged in a further round of *çay* as we sat on the balcony, trying to enjoy a fine summer morning.

It is customary for wedding ceremonies to take place in the evening, and ours was scheduled for 5:30 pm. Although this made sense in terms of allowing the worst of the day's heat to pass and those at work to attend, it also made for a day that dragged. Abla and I made a trip to town to pick up the flowers and collect a few items for the little reception later at the house. When we got back, we made up the bouquet and placed it in the fridge to stay fresh. Between the excitement and the heat, we didn't feel much like lunch and just nibbled some bread and cheese before having quick baths and leaving to have our hair done. While Abla and I did all the running around, everyone else contented themselves on the balcony.

Back from the hairdressers, I applied a fresh coat of polish to my nails and was ready to change. It didn't take long. Abla helped glide the silk under slip over my head, followed by my elegant gown. Since the dress itself is so rich, I didn't need much jewellery and wore only simple pearl earrings and the plain gold bangle that the Beylers had given me shortly after my arrival. I stepped into the pumps that Baba had made and applied the same make-up I usually wear. Abla fastened the veil into place, and then handed me the fresh flowers now fixed into a holder on loan from Aylin Abla. That was it. I was ready.

In fact, I was ready before Hakan who was changing in another bedroom. When he emerged, my heart skipped a beat. He was so handsome that I was glad all over again to be marrying him. We had been so preoccupied with all the arrangements that seeing each other for the first time in our wedding finery quite took our breaths away. "Wow! You look beautiful!" he said, obviously in high spirits. Then with a grin that split his face, he announced, "You're not bad for a Yank." Smiling back, I replied, "You're pretty handsome yourself - not bad for a Turk." The events of the morning faded to the background.

By the time Mecit Bey brought his brightly decorated Chevy to our gate, a little crowd had gathered in the street. While Hakan and I had the wedding car to ourselves, one of the Vedat employees drove the Beylers in Dagmar (as if she could be omitted from the proceedings). According to custom, the local boys attempted to barricade the way, hoping to earn some money by agreeing to open the road for us. This annoyed Hakan, but he had been warned by Levent to have some change ready or there would be bad feeling. In any case, they were easily bought off and cheered us on our way.

Horns blaring, we processed through the back streets to the wedding *salon* in the town centre. Here, the crowd was so great that it had overflowed the hall and spilled into the street. Inside, it was wall-to-wall people; they had even run out of standing room. I don't know how many there were, but it definitely felt like more than the four hundred we had anticipated. We had to squeeze through the crowd to get to the table where the *nikah memuru* sat waiting to make us husband and wife. Dayı and Ruth were already there, seated on either side of the registrar. After our long wait and all the build up to this memorable day, the ceremony itself was perfunctory and over in a flash. We verified our names and other details, signed a hefty book and exchanged rings. Then we rose to face the audience, and Hakan lifted my veil to kiss me on the forehead.

After that, there were congratulations all around. Neighbours had taken charge of the wedding favours and were distributing them as the *salon* emptied. We had arranged for a studio photographer to record the proceedings and take shots of the various family groupings, including one of us with the witnesses. Two couples had come from Istanbul, and we were touched that they had made the effort. Along with all the others who had been included in the original reception plans, they were invited back to the house for food and drink. Someone had handed out confetti, and it rained down on us as we left the *salon* and returned to our waiting car. While everyone else made their way to Elli Evler, we resumed the obligatory parade through town, horns blaring once again.

A neighbourhood crowd had assembled to cheer us as we returned to the house. More confetti. When we arrived in our own salon, everyone applauded and gathered around to offer warm congratulations. After a brief interval, we cut the lowest tier of the lovely three-tier cake that Aylin Abla had promised and delivered. Then everyone found a place to sit down and socialize over food.

The guests were mostly the names you know plus a few you do not. Dayı's whole family turned out as did the Vedats. Ruth and her husband were there as well as Nevin and Fatma. The rest of the group comprised the couples from Istanbul and most of our immediate neighbours, including Nisa and her husband. I think we were about forty in all. Metin is in Ankara doing his own military service, and it was disappointing not to have him with us. You were also conspicuous by your absence and greatly missed... greatly!

When most of the guests had gone, one of the Istanbul couples produced a bottle of champagne, and glasses were quickly found. Apart from Aylin Abla and me, none of the other women ever touches alcohol, so there was enough for the rest of us to have a small glass each, Hakan and I sharing one in some sort of romantic gesture the guests thought the occasion demanded. After they had toasted our long and happy union, Hakan suggested we should hurl our glass off the balcony and break it for good luck. I think he has seen too many movies for this is certainly not a custom that I have ever seen in Turkey.

I hesitated as it seemed silly to waste a glass, but he was adamant. He handed me the tumbler and I threw it out the window. It missed the pavement below and hit the grass, remaining firmly in one piece. Levent, now caught up in the spirit of the moment, ran to get it and returned, insisting that I should have another go. The same thing happened on the second try and Levent was off once more, determined that we should either break the glass or risk a short-lived marriage. It was third time lucky. The glass broke into a satisfying number of pieces, and everyone heaved a sigh of relief. At this point, it occurred to me to wonder if the hiccup in the omens confirmed Ana's suspicions or fuelled her fears.

Our suitcases were ready and waiting for the trip to Bursa. After changing clothes and packing the car, we were anxious to be off, to get away on our own. Family and friends gathered to wave farewell, and we were on our way with the last of the evening light.

I'm going to stop here because I want to tell you about our incredible journey, but I will have to write it up later. I took notes as we travelled because, as well as being our honeymoon, it was the most amazing adventure I am ever likely to have. But it is a story on its own, and I need some time to get to grips with it. Nisa lent us her camera, so at least we have some pictures for show-and-tell. We weren't in many places sophisticated enough for post cards. Although we felt the effects of the general strike throughout that week, we noticed that the further away from the urban areas we travelled, the less evidence of it there was. People in the countryside thought it was all a lot of city nonsense. Since most of them work their own land, the right to strike has little meaning. I'll try to get it all on paper while I'm here because I think things will be fairly manic once we get back to London.

We arrived home to find a sizeable stack of mail waiting for us. Obviously, the discharge papers were the most important item, and Hakan is dealing with those. There was also a letter from Ken, sending us good wishes for the wedding and telling us the business news. Apparently, the lease on the WML premises is coming to an end (we knew that but had forgotten it in the run up to the wedding). He wasn't happy with the proposed rent, so he has moved everything to a new location, details of which he gave us. He is okay; the business appears to be ticking over, and at least, he wasn't complaining.

There was also a letter from Bill with wedding congratulations. He told me all about his remarkable Australian trip, but I know you have heard from him about this, so I need not say more. Now he is simply looking forward to the conclusion of his service, which could come by the end of this month. There is absolutely nothing for him to do, and he is going out of his mind with boredom.

And of course, there were all your fat envelopes and wonderful cards. Thank you so much for the funds you have sent. I appreciate that you took a risk to send $100 through the mail, but it has arrived safely and is most welcome. We still have money left from our trip which, together with your contribution, should see us back to London. Abla insists that we take a loan from her to be sure that we have enough for any emergencies. Considering Dagmar's condition, this might not be a bad idea. She didn't give us any trouble on our travels, but we covered some very rough terrain - only camel tracks in places - and I don't think we have any suspension left. We'll see Cengiz Bey once more before we go and trust that he can perform his usual miracles. We need Dagmar to make just one last trip.

It sounds as if the wedding write-up in the local paper set the town abuzz. You must be getting all kinds of interesting responses. It makes me feel quite peculiar to learn that the little store is displaying the newspaper clipping along with one of your announcements. The shop where I bought my penny candy is now showing off my Turkish wedding memorabilia. Imagine.

As for your plans to come to London at the end of October…well, this sounds fantastic! Really, I cannot wait. It's been too long, too much has happened, and I can't bear the idea of any more time going by before I see you all again. I understand that because of college, Peter can't come, but I'm so glad you're timing the trip to bring Bill. I can't wait to get a look at him... and give him a big hug!

I must go. I haven't done anything since we got back as I wanted to write to you immediately, but laundry awaits, as do a million other things, so I'll close now and tell you more next week.

24 August 1971

Foolishly, I had assumed things would be quiet now that the wedding is over, and our life here is winding down. I had also thought that since we were on honeymoon, we would miss all the guests. Although Abla and Ana have been busy entertaining, many people knew we were away and delayed their visits until our return. The days have been filled with rounds of tea and refreshments, and I always end up feeling guilty about my impatience with the never-ending stream of guests requiring our attention. They are all so generous and sincere that I feel ashamed for resenting them, but I have never, ever adjusted to these constant social demands. I'm certain we have entertained the entire population of Kavaklı, one-by-one.

The Beylers are delighted and feel it is a mark of esteem that everyone wants to come with gifts and good wishes. It's the unrelentingness of it that gets to me. I can't get anything else done, and even now, I'm neglecting someone in order to write to you. I'm not very adept at the interdependence that most Turks would feel bereft without. My life has been about seeking independence, and I need more "alone" time than this culture allows.

My wedding dress has caused much comment. Departing as it does from the traditional white, it was remarkable by Turkish standards… by almost everyone's standards. I know you have had a lot of comments, too. I'm not sure if anyone liked it, but then, I had what I liked. Bride's prerogative.

Ana and I are tiptoeing around each other these days, co-existing in an uneasy truce. My new status has changed things between us. Before the wedding, she was comfortable and easy with me; now she is cool and distant. But I too, have changed where she's concerned. I simply don't have anything more to say to her. What is left to say?

Hakan and I have spoken about THAT conversation, and it is as I presumed. Ana could not face having a non-Turkish, non-Muslim daughter-in-law. It seems that the family had had a prospective wife picked out for Hakan. They had expected to arrange the marriage on his next trip home. Then I turned up. Frankly, they couldn't know their son very well if they were under the impression that Hakan would let anyone else choose his wife for him, but that's another story.

In addition to my numerous other drawbacks, Ana felt further compelled to advise Hakan that I'm a "two-baby woman". Apparently, this was her trump card, meant to persuade him, finally, to give me up. Whether he received this pronouncement with alarm or relief, I can but guess; the outcome we know. Ana can't help the way she feels, nor can I. Having given it my best shot, there is simply nothing more I could have done, of that I'm convinced… unless of course, I completely transformed and became someone else. Still, it is extremely frustrating to believe I have done all that I could, and it hasn't been enough. No matter how long I might stay here, it would be impossible for me to adapt beyond anything I have done already.

Hakan and I have made a last trip to Bursa. He wanted to say thank you to his former base commander and arranged that we should take him and his wife out to dinner. Sinan Paşa was charming company, though his wife looked a little bemused by us and didn't have much to say. The General is obviously a well-educated man and was able to talk widely on a number of topics. He did, however, tease Hakan about his surprisingly early departure from the army. According to his memory, Hakan had had nearly every weekend off and might have been expected to be making up leave time for months to come. As you'll recall, he had left the base before Hakan obtained his discharge. The new man is none the wiser or, if he is, has elected to overlook it.

Hakan's new passport is in the works, and he expects it to be ready a week from today. If all goes well, we'll be off shortly after that. Whatever happens, I shall write before we leave so you are current with our ever-fluctuating plans.

You have sent the most fantastic, the most welcome report, and if I failed to comment on it before, it is only because I have saved the best for last. That Peter drew such a high number in the draft lottery and will not have to serve in Vietnam is truly the most excellent possible news, surpassed only by the fact that Bill is due home a week from today! You must be ecstatic and flying high in anticipation of this long-awaited reunion. I'm desperate to hear all about his return but suspect that we will be on the road when your letter would be due to arrive. Life for all your chicks is looking bright!

Chapter 24

1 September 1971

This is it. The last letter. I can hardly believe those words as I write them. Although I'm filled with utter joy at the prospect of returning to my "real" life, I'm unexpectedly sad at the thought of leaving this one. It has caught me unprepared. At the moment, I feel that if required to do so, I could make my life here. I would need to touch base with everything at home, but then I could come back and make a go of it. I know that this is as unlikely as it sounds, but I'm caught up in the emotion of the farewells. I'm fully aware that once we return to London, we won't be coming back to stay. It's just that I'm suddenly thinking of all the people and the things I shall miss... and there are many. The aloofness of the English will sit hard beside the warmth of the community here.

Hakan collected his passport yesterday, and there is nothing now to keep us. We plan to leave early tomorrow morning. We are allowing five days to make the journey and expect to be in London late Monday the 6th. I shall drop you a line as soon as we get there, even if it's only a post card. I have written all the new WML details on the separate card enclosed so that you can put it straight into your address book. Since I have no idea where we will be living, I think it's best if you write to us care of the business. But please, please write as soon as you can and tell me everything about Bill's homecoming. We are dying to hear all about it - and him. He must be there already and pinching himself. You must be, too!

Everyone here has been subdued this week, everyone except for Hakan who is feeling the wrench of leave-taking far less than the rest of us. Enough is enough, as far as he is concerned, and the sooner we leave, the better. He is as impatient as a sprinter on starting blocks, anxious only to get going and get back. Fond as I am of Levent and even Ana, it is Abla and Baba whom I shall miss having in my daily life. We have been steadfast companions through some very dark times. I don't think even Hakan realizes how important they have become to me. For all his home leave, he has been away more than he has been here, and he has had a different focus to his life. I'm so proud of him… for having come and done his duty, and done it in such style. I'm not referring here to the notion of patriotic duty, but the duty to himself and his family to fulfil an obligation that makes it possible for him to return now, whenever he wants. It would otherwise have been an impossible situation… to want to go home and be unable to do so. I cannot imagine never seeing Istanbul and the Bosphorus again.

In the course of my journey, I have seen my culture, my country, my life and myself through another lens. There have been lessons in humility, understanding, patience and acceptance, and I have become someone I hope is a better version of an old self. You know all about the ups and downs we have had, but I wouldn't have missed any of this for all the *baklava* at a society wedding; the rewards have been too great. I feel privileged to have been allowed into the lives of these remarkable and engaging people, all strangers only a short while ago. I have had a wealth of experiences here, and I am immeasurably enriched by them all.

Having spent recent days receiving guests who had come to wish us well, we then spent the past week returning many of those visits to say our good-byes. I dislike these at the best of times, so a whole week of them has been exhausting. I couldn't possibly go into what it felt like to see Nevin and Fatma, Ruth and Aylin Abla for the last time. I'm emotionally drained, and that is before we pay our last call on Dayı this evening.

None of this has been helped by the fact that we took Aslana to her new village home. Some people who had long ago volunteered to have her were as good as their word and let us leave her with them. I had to tie her up so she wouldn't try to follow us. I felt dreadful about the whole thing. However well cared for she will be, she won't be pampered anymore, and she is never going to understand this abandonment. It is unforgivable I know, and I have vowed never again to take on a responsibility I cannot see through to the end. The Beylers (Levent, really) have agreed to continue to look after Lady, and I cannot ask them to do the same for Aslana, too. They're not dog lovers and have already done more than enough.

Baba is noticeably downhearted these days. He has returned from Izmir where he saw the hearing specialist, but I don't think there is much to be done. He really needs to have a good quality hearing aid, but that is beyond the pockets of us all at present. Hakan and I have promised him that we shall investigate hearing aids in London and try to find something suitable to send as soon as we can. Meanwhile, the court case lurches along and we must continue to trust Tuncer Ağabey to take care of it until the longed-for amnesty.

There has been no word from Sami recently. Well, none that I know of. I don't think he is aware that we are on the verge of leaving. It seems unlikely that he could stop us at the border, but until we have crossed into Bulgaria, I take nothing for granted. Hakan is totally unconcerned on this score.

Levent is making a pretence of revising mathematics for his exam retake coming up soon. If he doesn't pass this time, I'm afraid that he will be a prime candidate for his own stint of military service. Unless the Beylers try to get him a medical exemption, I don't think there will be anything to prevent him being called up. Once he has passed his eighteenth birthday, assuming he is not in further education, there really is no excuse not to go. Overall, he has been much better of late, calmer and more emotionally balanced. Maybe growing out of adolescence, with all its raging hormones, has as much to do with this as anything.

I think Abla long ago came to terms with the probability that she is unlikely to marry. I'm certain this was her reason for taking the typing course and her new interest in things outside the home. She said she is determined to find a job and will renew her efforts after we leave. We shall see how it all unfolds and perhaps think of bringing her to England. She will miss my company, and I shall miss hers... more than I can say. She has been both *avukat* and ally, and a sister in every sense of the word. Fortunately, her old friends Fatma and Nevin will still be on hand. As soon as their new apartment building is finished sometime next year, Aylin Abla and the family will be moving into town so will no longer be neighbours but will remain close by.

There has been time for one last family picnic, and it proved to be special in ways we could not have planned. It was a spur-of-the moment decision to make it a cookout and grill lamb *şiş kebaps* at the picnic grounds on the Bursa road. We bought our meat from Butcher Salih and prepared the tender lamb ready to skewer when we arrived. Naturally, we organized an abundance of other things as well - potato salad (an Abla speciality), tomatoes and cucumbers, white cheese, olives, humous, hard-boiled eggs, fresh yoghurt and vegetables to grill. We packed a kettle so we could make *çay*, and we took a jug to fill with water from the cold spring. We had warm bread from the bakery, and I bought my last box of *baklava* to take along. We all went. Baba sat up front with Hakan, and the rest of us squeezed into the back seat. Only the dogs were missing.

As it was a weekday, we had the place to ourselves, and we found the perfect spot where we made a sort of encampment with rugs, blankets and cushions. Baba even rigged up a hammock between two trees. It was a nice day, and everyone was in a good mood. We all helped get everything ready, setting out plates and cutlery and opening the many parcels. Hakan was in charge of the grill, and Levent helped with the fire, finding twigs to get it started, and then foraging for bigger pieces of wood to keep it going.

Finally, we settled with heaped plates, eager to satisfy our hunger, while waiting impatiently for the storyteller to begin. Never one to hurry, Baba allowed the anticipation to build before eventually transporting us to other times and other places. Each of us has our favourite stories, and he recounted them all. The one about *hoş geldin köfte*, the fiery raw meatballs sent to me as a "welcome", was retold at Levent's request. I can't imagine why it amuses them all so much, but I feel honoured to have passed into family folklore.

At intervals, we played ball games to stretch our legs before settling down again to tell jokes or sing songs or reminisce. A lazy, gentle interlude passed in a haze of food and affable feelings. Towards the end of the afternoon, no one felt inclined to make the move to go. So we lingered.

The only problem was that we had run out of food, and everyone was still, incredibly and unaccountably, hungry. Despite having done little but eat and drink our way through the day, everyone still had an appetite. Hakan and Baba decided to take the car to the nearest village and find a butcher's shop so we could grill more kebabs.

When they shortly returned, they certainly had meat with them. In fact, they had a whole freshly slaughtered lamb. Lest this sound a grisly business, let me say that having not found the required shop, they had stopped to think what to do next, and a friendly local asked if he could help. Our men explained that they wanted some meat for a picnic already in progress. The villager told them to follow him and led them to a little flock of sheep nearby. He instructed them to pick out the one they wanted; he would kill and butcher it immediately. So much per kilo. The deal was agreed, and the job was done. If we are a little squeamish about all this, it's only because we are not usually confronted with the way in which our meat reaches the table.

Once they had returned, it took no time at all for the men to get more kebabs on the grill (apparently the preparation of outdoor food is a manly task). I have to report that this was, without a doubt in the world, the best meat I have ever eaten. I closed my mind to the facts of the situation and thoroughly enjoyed what it meant to dine on lamb that was likely to be the freshest I shall ever eat. The men also had found a woman selling coarse village bread and bought a loaf of that to help the kebabs along. As the day ended, we brewed a last round of *çay* and finished off the *baklava*, before finally feeling we were ready to head back home.

I think Ana has made a peace offering. Do you remember me telling you about the antique pots and pans that Hakan and I discovered when rummaging around in the attic? We had both long forgotten all about them, but when we came home from town yesterday, we found that Ana had instructed Levent to bring them down. She had cleaned them up and set them out, ready for our inspection. While we looked them over, she joked that this was all that remained of her dowry and reiterated her earlier promise that I could have whatever I wanted.

The pots, in her family for generations, were so old that they had been hand hammered into their less than perfect shapes. Although they had all been made from copper, some had been covered in zinc coatings, ready for practical use. Some were black and tarnished from age and wear. All had character and their own unique features. One shallow pan has an odd elongated handle, presumably crafted for some specific purpose, now forgotten.

One of the yoghurt pots, most unusually with its original lid, had some little motifs etched into its sides. On closer examination, they turned out to be camels, crudely drawn, but camels, nevertheless. Hakan watched as I held my breath and counted. Not forty after all. Not even twenty. No, there were eighteen camels marching around the sides of the little pot. "Still," said Hakan, "that's not bad for a Yank."

I was touched that Ana had remembered my interest in these and felt able to act on it. Maybe this signals another fresh start. Life seems to be full of them just now.

Must finish packing and say more good-byes. The next news will be from London!

EPILOGUE

Autumn and winter passed, spring, too. Then in the early summer of 1972, Abla married. With the annual migration of Turkish workers back to their homeland, Nuri came to Kavaklı, marriage uppermost in his mind. Despite warnings from everyone that the Beylers would never permit their daughter to go off with a humble factory worker, Nuri was determined to meet this apparently unobtainable girl. If not love at first sight, there was certainly instant mutual attraction. Three weeks from first meeting, Abla had married her single-minded suitor and moved to Germany. They had their only child a year later, a daughter born shortly before our son. Neriman and Nuri's marriage has been a long and happy one. A bonus has been that Abla's unexpected move has enabled us to visit often and continue our close friendship.

Levent never made it to teacher training. Not long after Neriman's wedding, he embarked on his military service. In the few months since Hakan had completed his, the top brass had changed, and family influence had dwindled to nil. Levent served most of his two years on the (then) Russian border. When he returned home, he studied at the local technical college and worked until early retirement at a newly built German auto factory near Kavaklı. He and his wife and son live in Cemile's old haunt, downstairs in the family home.

Tuncer Ağabey was right in his assessment of how best to deal with the court case. Proceedings chugged along until 1973 and the 50th anniversary of the founding of the republic. As expected, a general amnesty was declared, and thankfully, that was the end of that. In the meantime, Ana and I made our peace. Time enabled us both to accept the previously unacceptable. The fact that the Beylers had had no more say in the selection of Levent's wife than they had had in that of Hakan's, undoubtedly worked in my favour as well. Grandchildren certainly helped.

Nevin never married; she continued to teach until retirement and now leads an unhurried life in an Aegean resort town. Fatma eventually went to Canada where she was reunited with her mother and settled down in her adopted country. As planned, the Vedats moved into their prestigious new apartment building in town. Widowed in middle age, Aylin Abla became the much-loved, much-respected matriarch of her family. Perhaps somewhat predictably, Ruth has remained in Kavaklı. The irony is that all of her children (she eventually had another son) now live in the USA; all struggled to learn the English that their grandmother had refused to allow them to speak at home. Despite her many grumbles about life in Turkey, Ruth is loyal to both her husband and his town. I expect her to live out her days in Kavaklı.

Happily, I can report that I kept my promise to Ana and, with Hakan's help, sent her and Baba on The Haj in 1975. Unfortunately, they both suffered strokes and passed away in the early 1990s. After a short illness, Baba died in May 1992, and Ana, nursed faithfully to the end by Levent, passed away a year later. Since then, going "home" to Turkey has never been the same.

And Sami - what of Sami? Once we left Turkey, Hakan and I never saw him again. It will come as no surprise to learn that his life continued in a downward spiral. As alcohol took its toll, his ability to conduct any sort of business declined. Estranged from the family and deserted by his expensively bought connections, he struggled on in isolation. He died in 1985 under mysterious circumstances. His body was found in a cheap hotel in Istanbul, and he was buried in an unmarked pauper's grave before the family even knew he was gone. Although the death certificate states "heart attack" as the cause of death, Hakan has often thought about the haste with which everything happened and has wondered if Sami's past work in the intelligence services had, in some way, caught up with him. We'll never know. What I do know is that though already heart broken, this final disturbing episode entirely devastated his parents in their latter years.

Back in London, Hakan's abdominal pains continued intermittently until one afternoon, he became so incapacitated with pain, he couldn't stand up. He was admitted to hospital where he was diagnosed with a kidney stone, which he eventually passed, bringing his ordeal to an end. As we had all hoped, my parents visited us shortly after our return. Bill came too, still getting his bearings after Vietnam. And in December, we travelled to Applewold for a Christmas reunion with family and friends.

London has always been home, the place where we have made our lives. We have two marvellous children (Ana was right!), a son and a daughter, both with wonderful partners, now parents themselves. They - all of them - fill up our hearts and light up our lives. Building on our early pattern of partnership in everything, Hakan and I have developed and sold several businesses and have eased into a comfortable retirement. In our personal lives, it would be impossible to wish for anything else.

There is only one more thing: Dagmar. We drove her back to London without any mishaps and parked her in front of Ken's flat. In the morning, she refused to start. Ken, a motor mechanic in his previous life, looked her over and could find nothing wrong, but that was it. Dagmar never started again. I think she was exhausted, and having completed the final journey, just slipped away.

ACKNOWLEDGMENTS

With grateful thanks to all those who supported me so generously and gave me not only their time and much-needed encouragement, but their valuable comments and suggestions: Jem & Liz, Inji & Kathy, Maryann, Annie, Carol, Margaret, Sandy, Jo, Carolyn and Mandy.

I am also deeply indebted Tim Wilson for this brilliant cover design and to Ozler Aykan for her endless patience, hard work and sound advice.

But most of all, I wish to acknowledge, with love and gratitude, the pivotal role played by my life companion, "Hakan", who has made everything possible - both then and now.